How to Behave

Southeast Asia

POLITICS, MEANING, AND MEMORY

David Chandler and Rita Smith Kipp

SERIES EDITORS

OTHER VOLUMES IN THE SERIES

HARD BARGAINING IN SUMATRA
Western Travelers and Toba Bataks in the Marketplace of Souvenirs
Andrew Causey

PRINT AND POWER
Confucianism, Communism, and Buddhism in the Making of Modern Vietnam
Shawn Frederick McHale

TOMS AND DEES
Transgender Identity and Female Same-Sex Relationships in Thailand
Megan J. Sinnott

INVESTING IN MIRACLES
El Shaddai and the Transformation of Popular Catholicism in the Philippines
Katharine L. Wiegele

IN THE NAME OF CIVIL SOCIETY
From Free Election Movements to People Power in the Philippines
Eva-Lotta E. Hedman

THE TÂY SƠN UPRISING:
Society and Rebellion in Eighteenth-Century Vietnam
George Dutton

SPREADING THE DHAMMA
Writing, Orality, and Textual Transmission in Buddhist Northern Thailand
Daniel M. Veidlinger

ART AS POLITICS
Re-Crafting Identities, Tourism, and Power in Tana Toraja, Indonesia
Kathleen M. Adams

How to Behave

Buddhism and Modernity in Colonial Cambodia, 1860–1930

ANNE RUTH HANSEN

UNIVERSITY OF HAWAIʻI PRESS *Honolulu*

Printed in the United States of America

12 11 10 09 08 07 6 5 4 3 2 1

Library of Congress Cataloging-in-Publication Data

Hansen, Anne Ruth.

How to behave : Buddhism and modernity in colonial Cambodia, 1860–1930 / Anne Ruth Hansen.

p. cm. — (Southeast Asia : politics, meaning, and memory)

Includes bibliographical references and index.

ISBN-13: 978-0-8248-3032-8 (hardcover : alk. paper)

1. Buddhist modernism—Cambodia—History—19th century. 2. Buddhist modernism—Cambodia—History—20th century. 3. Buddhist ethics—Cambodia. I. Title.

BQ464.H36 2007

294.3'9109596—dc22

2006028169

University of Hawai'i Press books are printed on acid-free paper and meet the guidelines for permanence and durability of the Council on Library Resources.

Based on a design by Richard Hendel

Printed by The Maple-Vail Book Manufacturing Group

To my parents, Jan and Mimi

Portraits (clockwise from top) of Mahā Vimaladhamm Thoṅ, Uṃ-Sūr, Huot Tath, Chuon Nath, Lvī-Em, the "five great Mahānikāy scholars," dated 1931. Photo from the National Archives of Cambodia.

CONTENTS

Acknowledgments *ix*

Introduction *1*

1. Defending the Jeweled Throne: Khmer Religious Imagination in the Nineteenth Century *18*

2. Buddhist Responses to Social Change *45*

3. *Vinaya* Illuminations: The Rise of "Modern Dhamma" *77*

4. Colonial Collusions *109*

5. How Should We Behave? Modernist Translations of Theravāda Buddhism *148*

Archives and Special Collections *185*

Notes *187*

Sources *229*

Index *245*

ACKNOWLEDGMENTS

My acquaintance with Cambodian history began with horrific accounts of the Khmer Rouge period, in refugee camps on the Thai border, and later, through deepening friendships with survivors of the Pol Pot regime in U.S. diasporic communities. My efforts to comprehend these accounts of violence and suffering led me to the study of Buddhism—through ideas and stories and explanations of the world I learned from Khmer elders and friends. Thus, for this book and for some of the ways I have learned to interpret Buddhist history, I am indebted especially to Bounthay Phath and to Sok Yi, Phin Ngim, and Duok Phith, who introduced me to the Triple Gem, Vessantar, Maddī, and Bhikkhu Sukh and helped me understand how and why these ideas and images and stories have meaning.

The subject of this book grew out of comments and suggestions from Charles Hallisey and John Strong in response to my 1999 dissertation, a textual analysis of Ukñā Suttantaprījā Ind's *Gatilok.* I am indebted to both of them for ideas about framing this historical project and to Charlie for teaching me how to read Buddhist texts. In its different incarnations, this work has also benefited from the thoughtful critiques and ideas of many different people to whom I owe enormous gratitude for their patience, support, and ideas. First and foremost among them is David Chandler, whose long-suffering encouragement, comments, corrections, and fabulous editing have guided this project from start to finish; I am truly grateful for David's generosity over many years. The book has also taken its present shape due in no small part to comments and ideas from Rita Kipp, Anne Blackburn, Douglas Howland, and Mark Bradley, all of whom read and commented on earlier drafts of the manuscript, from Pamela Kelley at the University of Hawai'i Press, and JoAnne Sandstrom, who copyedited the manuscript.

My research in Phnom Penh and writing were supported by grants and fellowships from the National Endowment for Humanities, the Graduate School at the University of Wisconsin–Milwaukee, the Center for Twenty-first Century Studies at the University of Wisconsin–Milwaukee, and the Institute for Research in the Humanities at the University of Wisconsin–Madison. Parts of the research on colonial millenarianism were carried out in conjunction with Judy Ledgerwood as part of our ongoing work on the Khmer *Buddh Daṃnāy.* I am grateful for Judy's insights on Khmer culture, apparent in many aspects of this book, and for her generosity and friendship.

My research at the National Archives of Cambodia could not have been conducted without the expertise of its staff: Chhem Neang, NAC director; Y Dari, chief administrator of the Technical Bureau; Hou Rin, chief administrator of the Repository Bureau; Chun Lim, associate chief administrator of the Repository Bureau; Mam Chean, director of administration; and Peter Arfanis. I am grateful also to Lim Yii, head librarian at the National Museum Library, for her guidance. Tauch Chhuong, Yoeum Ngin, Kaseka Phon, John Marston, Ingrid Muan, Ven. Khy Sovanratana, Ven. Chuon Bunsim, Erik Davis, Kheang Un, Ashley Thompson, and Sony Keo all helped and inspired me during several research trips in Cambodia. Christopher Goscha and Jacqueline Filliozat assisted me greatly in the course of research work in Paris.

I am grateful to a number of colleagues in Asian Studies and Buddhist Studies who have contributed ideas and direction to different articulations of this work at conferences and in other venues: Susanne Mrozick, Thongchai Winachakul, Thomas Hudak, Shawn McHale, Ann Waltner, Justin McDaniel, Charles Keyes, Susan Darlington, Niccola Tannenbaum, Prasenjit Duara, and Sophea Mouth. My thanks to Richard Jaffe for organizing the inspiring "Global Flows and the Restructuring of Asian Buddhism in an Age of Empires" conference at Duke University, for which chapter 3 was originally prepared. Finally, I have been fortunate to have wonderful colleagues in the Department of History at UWM who have responded to and encouraged this work during the past several years. I am grateful to all of them for their help and support, particularly Jeff Merrick, Aims McGuinness, Amanda Seligman, Dan Sherman, and Ellen Amster, and to Andrew Kinkaid and Sukanya Banerjee, members of the colonialisms workshop at the Center for Twenty-first Century Studies.

This book could not have been completed without love, inspiration, and copious advice from my family members Ilsa, Peter, and Mark, all of whom completed writing (and in some cases illustrating) one or more books during the time I wrote this one. I am grateful for their patient endurance and support.

A Khmer friend once observed that merit from past births is what enables one to study Buddhist scriptures in this birth and the next. Any merit attached to the translations of the words and biographies of great *bhikkhus* that appear in this volume is dedicated to Ingrid Muan, who so sadly left us before she could finish her own work on Khmer modernism in art, and to my parents, Jan and Mimi.

An earlier version of chapter 1 appeared as "The Nature of the World in Nineteenth Century Khmer Buddhist Literature" in *Pacific World,* 3rd series, no. 5 (Fall 2003). Earlier versions of portions of chapters 1 and 2 appeared as "Khmer Identity and Theravada Buddhism" in *History, Buddhism, and New Religious Movements in Cambodia,* edited by John Marston and Elizabeth Guthrie (Honolulu: University of Hawai'i Press, 2004): 40–62, and are used with permission from University of Hawai'i Press. An earlier version of a portion of chapter 5 was previously published as "The Image of an Orphan: Cambodian Narrative Sites for Buddhist Ethical Reflection" in the *Journal of Asian Studies* 62.3 (August 2003): 811–834, and is reprinted with permission of the Association for Asian Studies. Photos are used with permission from the National Archives of Cambodia.

Introduction

How should we behave if we want to make ourselves pure?
—Ind, *Gatilok*

For a layperson, making one's conduct "Buddhist" means behaving in compliance with the *Dhamma-vinay* [the Buddhist scriptures].
—Chuon Nath, *Gihivinaya Saṅkhep*

[M]erely chanting Pali is empty if one does not understand its meaning. This is so because [taking part in] rituals . . . consists of clear belief and a wisdom involving right views, for which the measure is true knowing and true and correct understanding.
—Chuon Nath, *Gihivinaya Saṅkhep*

The 1920s in Cambodia saw an exuberant burst of new printed writings by Khmer Buddhist modernists on the subject of how to behave, as good Khmer Buddhists and moral persons, and simultaneously, how to purify themselves in the context of everyday life in a modernizing world. This book examines the intertwined ethical and historical questions of what Khmer writers articulated as the Buddhist values most important and relevant to their times, how these interpretations were produced, and how they represent Southeast Asian ethical and religious responses to the modern circulation of local and translocal events, people, ideas, and anxieties. In sum, the book attempts to understand how ethical ideas are produced in a particular historical moment, in this case the "moment" of Southeast Asian colonial modernity.

The three passages above, written in the early 1920s in Phnom Penh by Ukñā Suttantaprījā Ind and Braḥ Sāsanasobhaṇa Chuon Nath, suggest the ethical preoccupations of this self-described Buddhist "modernist" movement with purification, authenticity, and rationalism. Being a Buddhist and a moral person in the modern world required a new and different kind of knowing from that required in the past. This knowledge was based on correct understanding of scripture; it was demonstrated through moral conduct in religious ritual and everyday life.

The ideas that modernists were articulating in Cambodia were resonant with forms and expressions of religious and literary modernism emerging elsewhere in Southeast Asia during this same period. Their emphasis on purification and rationalism as means for achieving "authentic" understanding of the Buddhist scriptures reflects the religious reformism adopted by Mongkut (later Rama IV) of Siam and his sons Chulalongkorn (Rama V) and Prince-Patriarch Vajirañāṇa, whose Buddhist modernization program has been described in terms of "scripturalism," the privileging of canonical texts as the definition of religious authority.[1] Vajirañāṇa recalled that when he was a young novice studying for ordination he had determined that "in order to know Dhamma firmly" he needed to learn Pali and to read the *Tipiṭaka* for himself. Equipped with up-to-date grammatical methods for reading and translating Pali, Vajirañāṇa came to believe that the *Tipiṭaka* itself advocated rational knowing. "One work which struck me," he wrote, "was the *Kālāma-sutta,* which taught one not to believe blindly and to depend on one's own thinking."[2]

Strikingly, these Khmer and Thai modernist concerns are similar to those voiced by Southeast Asian Islamic modernists. In his *Soal-Djawab* (Questions and answers), written in the Dutch East Indies in the early 1930s, Ahmad Hussan argued that the Qur'an itself contained passages that exhorted readers to "apply their minds to its revelations" so that they could accurately comprehend its meaning. These verses, he noted, "indicate clearly that the Qur'an is not to be recited without thinking about it and properly understanding its content."[3] Given the deficiencies in the "traditional manner of gaining knowledge" in Dutch colonial schools, wrote another Indies modernist, Hadji Agus Salim, in the *Fadjar Asia* (Asian dawn) in 1929, "our people simply become imitators," unable to understand "the essence of the matter." Instead of learning the Qur'an by rote, they needed to understand "each word and the meaning conveyed."[4] Authentic knowing enabled one to perform religious ritual correctly.

Viewed regionally, Buddhist and Islamic modernist expressions in Southeast Asia were in part shaped by factors joined to imperialism. These included the relatively late arrival of print in the region, the gradual demarcation of national boundaries; participation in a global market economy, and engagement with discourses of Western science, rationalism, and secularism. But imperialism alone does not explain religious modernism and the accompanying educational modernization projects, which were also a product of the interactions between colonial subjects and other non-Western and pan-Asian alliances. Cambodian and Siamese modernism was influenced by a pan-Theravādin dialogue that reached to Sri Lanka.[5] Similarly, Islamic modernists in Malaya and the Dutch East Indies were in conversation with their counterparts in the Middle East, just as Confucian and Buddhist Vietnamese reformers were part of an East Asian discourse in Japan and China as well as religious developments in mainland Southeast Asia.[6]

In this book, I argue for the central importance of Theravāda Buddhist ethics as a site for imagining and expressing modernity in Cambodia during this period. Among Southeast Asian locales, alternatives to religious education in early-twentieth-century Cambodia were particularly scarce. Buddhism remained the primary avenue for educational life as well as the dominant force shaping Khmer intellectual life until well into the 1930s.[7] Parallel to similar developments in other Southeast Asian states, though somewhat chronologically later in Cambodia, the onset of print in the 1920s was marked by the emergence of a zealous new generation of authors, of new writing styles, themes, and modernist literary movements. But in Cambodia, unlike in Vietnam and Indonesia, these earliest print expressions did not take the form of novels, autobiographies, reportage, newspapers, or secular periodicals.[8] Rather, the turn to print was focused into new styles of Buddhist writings—compendiums,[9] critical translations, and written versions of oral folklore, almost all of which were concerned with issues of morality, of *paṭipatti,* or how to behave in accordance with the Dhamma, as moral persons[10] and good Buddhists in the contemporary world.

These new print writings were the work of a group of Buddhist intellectuals in Phnom Penh whose efforts to purify current interpretations of Theravāda Buddhism began to crystallize into a modernist "movement" around 1914. Broadly summarized, their religious modernism emphasized rationalism, authenticity, and purification. They advocated new methods for Buddhist education and for the translation, production, and dissemination of new versions of Buddhist texts, which they "purified" from the grammatical and interpretive corruptions and accretions that had accumulated over time. They viewed these new textual practices as part of an effort to "modernize" Buddhist understanding itself. They believed that through a deeper, correct, authentic comprehension of the Buddhist scriptures, the *Dhamma-vinaya,* Buddhists would learn to purify or discipline the body, speech, and *citta* (heart and mind)[11] to reflect the Buddhist scriptural vision of "what is right." Cultivating *bodhi-citta* (the thought or aim of enlightenment) and purifying one's own moral conduct would consequently result in a stronger, more purified Buddhist *sāsana,* the religion practiced by the fourfold *parisāḷ,* the collective body of monastic and lay Khmer Buddhists.

The Khmer Buddhist modernism that emerged in Phnom Penh in the first few decades of the twentieth century, I argue, is best understood in ethical terms as a rationalist shift in Buddhist intellectual sensibilities about temporality and purification, a shift that gave a heightened significance to the everyday actions and relationships of ordinary individuals in the here and now of modern life. Reading through modernist ethical writings, we can see precursors to the ways in which these values prefigured the emerging notion of a *sāsana-jāti* (national religion), although delineating the growth of nationalism is not my primary aim in this book.[12] Rather, I examine the new ways in which Khmer Theravādins articulated values for living that joined their understandings of what it meant to live in the contemporary world with interpretations of what it meant to be a good Buddhist.

Studying ethical values does not mean, of course, that we are seeing all the ways in which people acted in the real world; but it does give us insight into how they made sense of the world, how they gave it order and meaning, and how they may have tried to structure their lives and relationships.

The production of these new values must also be viewed historically. In part, I examine Khmer Buddhist values as a product of reform movements in mainland Southeast Asia and the larger regional shift from manuscript to print culture. I also see them as Buddhist responses to experiences of social change and turmoil under colonialism and the interactions between colonial discourses on modernization and indigenous reforms in religious education. Within these frames, the ongoing translation of Theravādin ideas and symbols across three generations of intellectuals in the Khmer Sangha (monastic community) sought to produce vernacular idioms that had meaning and relevance for laypeople and monks in structuring their everyday lives.

I also examine the older inheritances that contributed to Khmer Buddhist modernism. These include the influence of nineteenth-century Khmer literary understandings of purification and moral development in older *jātaka* (stories of the Buddha's past lives) and other literary texts, as well as the "traditional" Buddhist purification movement that had been put in place by the Khmer king Ang Duong in the mid-nineteenth century. All of these factors led to the self-conscious effort by a group of Khmer monks and scholars in the second and third decades of the twentieth century to put forward a new articulation of Buddhist values, expressed in new print literary styles and forms.

I situate the study in the years 1860–1930 for several reasons. This *longue durée* enables us to see the complex historical, generational, and ideational underpinnings of modern Buddhist values in Cambodia. The death of King Ang Duong in 1860 marked a broad shift from more traditional notions and practices of Buddhist purification and revival to the intensification of new currents of thought among Buddhist intellectuals. The 1860s also saw the resumption of social unrest that had temporarily abated during Ang Duong's reign. The spread of millenarianism and the introduction of French administrative reforms—France declared Cambodia a protectorate in 1863—increasingly undermined Khmer social order and the monarchy. These events created a disjuncture between older Buddhist visions of social order and the lived experience that modernism was attempting to redress.

The period between 1860 and 1930 also roughly coincides with the lifetimes of two of the Buddhist intellectuals who figure prominently in this historical narrative: Braḥ Mahā Vimaladhamm Thoṅ (1862–1927) and Ukñā Suttantaprījā Ind (1859–1925). Both were highly respected Pali scholars in the Mahānikāy order in Cambodia who were educated in the established monastic traditions of the late nineteenth century.[13] They were exposed to reformist and modernist discourses through travels to Bangkok and studies with Siamese-educated teachers. Although trained in older schools of thought, they ended their scholastic careers by contributing to the construction of Khmer modernism. Both Thoṅ and Ind were closely aligned with the highly politicized "modern Dhamma" group in the Buddhist Mahānikāy order.

My study culminates in the 12 May 1930 inauguration ceremony of the Buddhist Institute, a scholarly center established in Phnom Penh for the promotion of research on Southeast Asian Buddhism. Once modernist intellectuals and ideas became firmly associated with influential Khmer Buddhist educational institutions such as the Sālā Pali, the Royal Library, and the Buddhist Institute, the transformation of their "new doctrine" into a new officially sanctioned religious orthodoxy was assured. Beginning in the mid-1930s, the Buddhist Institute became emblematic of and instrumental in the intertwining of modern Buddhist values and national identity in Cambodia, a position it held through the early 1970s until the descent into the chaos of the Khmer Rouge–led Democratic Kampuchea. Although modernists talked about their visions of social cohesion and social ethical responsibility in very different ways from Communists, the trope of "purification" of the individual and community that runs throughout the development of modern Buddhism during this entire period is one that is perhaps salient for the interpretation of Khmer Rouge ideologies as well.[14]

RELIGIOUS MODERNISM IN SOUTHEAST ASIA

Although focused on religious modernism in the Khmer context, this book situates these developments in a broader regional historical perspective. In different parts of Southeast Asia in the late nineteenth and early twentieth centuries, there was a shared perception of moral decline and the disintegration of the religiously inspired values that were understood to have given cohesion and order to previous generations. At the same time that the loss of these "traditional" values was being lamented, however, they were also being critiqued in some arenas as inappropriate or outdated in respect to contemporary culture. Southeast Asian reflexivity about this tension is lampooned in Vu Trong Phung's satirical novel *Dumb Luck,* published in Hanoi in 1936.[15] It portrays the travails of an upper-class family with the invented surname Civilization as they negotiate between modernity and traditional Confucian values. One episode in the novel highlights the tension between the family's efforts to modernize Vietnamese society through the sale of provocative Western-style lingerie at their Europeanization Tailor Shop and to protect the chastity of their own wives and daughters against rampant sexual infidelity in modern urban society. "How can one tell what is real these days?" Red-haired Xuan, the "common man" of the novel, asks sardonically as he surveys a set of rubber falsies in the Europeanization Tailor Shop. "Everything is so artificial! Love is artificial! Modernity is artificial! Even conservatism is artificial!"[16] In other less satirical Southeast Asian contexts, the tension between modern and traditional moral values played out in the form of debates about whether or not it was permissible for good Muslims to wear European clothing, whether sermons should be preached in the vernacular, and whether secular subjects such as science and geography should be taught in traditional religious schools.[17]

In Buddhist Southeast Asia, particularly in the late nineteenth century, the perception of moral decline was sometimes represented in terms of the degeneration of the power of the Buddhist Dharma or Dhamma, the truth about the nature of the world recognized by the Buddha at his enlightenment and communicated through his teachings.[18] This concern with moral decline in Southeast Asian Buddhist modernity may reflect a wider pan-Asian current as well.[19] The term "Dharma" or "Dhamma," as it is known in the Pali Theravādin literature of Southeast Asia and Sri Lanka, has also been translated simply and eloquently as "what is right."[20] The inevitable decline of the power of the Dhamma to transfigure human moral conduct is a problem of Buddhist history. Although all human beings are understood to have the capacity for perfection and enlightenment in the image of the Buddha, according to various Buddhist textual and oral accounts in circulation in the nineteenth century, the Buddha himself predicted the eventual dwindling of his Dhamma, accompanied by a degeneration among all human beings, including monks and kings, of their ability to do what is right.

Perceptions of social and religious decline, which scholars have widely associated with the changes brought about by the political, social, and economic realignments associated with imperialism, flared up in some instances in the form of religious millenarian movements. They also coincided with the rise of revivals or purification movements, evident across the Islamic world as well as in many parts of Buddhist Asia.[21]

Shawn McHale has argued that historians of Vietnamese nationalism have been too reluctant to consider the role and place of religion—particularly Buddhism—in histories of colonial nation building and modernity.[22] Part of the explanation for this omission, I think, lies in the fact that religious traditions are not inherently national. They cross national and regional borders, they manifest themselves differently at different points in history, they involve translation of texts and ideas across linguistic boundaries, and they are not secular, as modern political discourses of the nation supposedly are.[23] Understanding the development of Islamic modernism in the Dutch East Indies, for instance, necessitates studying the influence of Egyptian modernist Muhammad 'Abduh and Javanese pilgrims in Mecca;[24] studying Khmer Buddhist modernism has to be understood with respect to the regional influences of the Siamese Dhammayut *nikāya* (religious order) and French fears of Vietnamese-inspired religious movements such as Caodaism. In spite of the complex networks that the study of Southeast Asian religious modernity entails, as Dipesh Chakrabarty has argued with regard to India, the reenchantment of our understanding of the colonial world in Southeast Asia may be necessary if we are to understand the diverse ways in which people have experienced the shift to modern ways of thinking and being.[25] This book seeks to add to the investigation of these issues in the fields of Southeast Asian history and religion and, further, to argue for the analysis of such movements—in this case, a Buddhist modernist movement that emerged in colonial Cambodia—to help us understand the contours of Southeast Asian modernity.

Although scholars have only recently begun to turn their attention to the study of colonial Southeast Asian expressions of Buddhist modernism,[26] there is more extensive literature on Islamic religious modernism, and it provides a helpful comparative frame for examining Buddhist modernist expressions in the region. As in the case of Theravāda Buddhism, reform movements in and of themselves were not a new feature of Islamic history. But in the mid-nineteenth century, as Muslim reforms in various parts of the Islamic world became intertwined with attempts to understand and articulate modern experience, they spawned the religious discourses associated with Islamic modernism. Modernists were not simply responding to the experience of modernity, which they associated with European ideas, values, and customs, particularly rationality, Western science, and constitutionalism. Often, modernists advocated, to different extents and in different ways, accommodation between Islam and modern values.[27]

While scholars have pointed to the variety and sometimes conflicting perspectives of Islamic modernist discourses, several central issues emerge as shared themes, many of which also parallel modernist concerns in colonial Cambodia.[28] New interpretations of Islam sought to "purify" Islam from older corruptions and accretions and to situate the definition of what was "authentic" religious practice and doctrine in the Qur'an itself.[29] Like Buddhist modernists in Cambodia, Islamic modernists espoused rationalism and showed interest in Western science, but in other respects they took an inherently critical stance toward modern morality. Yet Islamic modernists, some of whom were influenced by social Darwinism and the civilizational discourses of the day, approached the problem of moral decline in a highly reflexive way, seeing it as an opportunity for revitalizing religion.[30] Consequently, they exhibited a similar zeal to that of Khmer monks intent on modernization and, like Khmer monks, used the imagery of "awakening" to refer to the new sense of possibility they saw in their reinterpretations of religion.[31]

The focus of Islamic modernization efforts in Southeast Asia on implementing educational reform is similar in many respects to the Khmer modernist goals for revamping Buddhist education, discussed in chapters 3 and 4 of this book. In colonial Indonesia, for example, the Islamic modernist vision for updating religious education involved the promulgation of new methods for teaching and learning Arabic grammar and translation, the introduction of secular subjects into religious school curricula, and a move toward replacing rote learning with more discursive methods of teaching.[32] Especially as they tried to introduce these new ideas into village schools, Islamic modernists in Indonesia and Malaysia came into conflict with proponents of traditional religious practices and interpretations. This conflict was asserted in disagreements that arose between *kaum muda,* the "young" or "new group" of modernists, and the *kaum tua,* the "old" or "traditionalist group."[33]

LOCAL BUDDHISMS AND "PRACTICAL CANONS"

Along with extending this translocal and regional context to understanding religious modernism in colonial Cambodia, this book also seeks to contribute to recent cross-disciplinary scholarship in the intersection of Southeast Asian studies and Buddhist studies that has begun to reappraise the importance of late vernacular Buddhist literature and the whole notion of a Buddhist "canon." This conscious opening of the field of Buddhist studies to include greater consideration of vernacular texts, particularly in Theravādin studies, is a rather recent development, signaled by work such as Gananath Obeyesekere's seminal essay "Buddhism and Conscience" and the volume *Curators of the Buddha,* which raised the question of the effects of colonial European encounters with Buddhism on the development of the field of Buddhist studies.[34] The growing interest in the construction of "local Buddhisms" reflects the influence of wider scholarly attention to local and global interactions, particularly in according a wider prominence to local, regional, and subaltern actors and forces.[35] Orientalist studies of the history and development of Buddhist literary cultures, including Cambodia, mapped a kind of core-periphery model of Buddhist history that was both temporal and linguistic, situating the core in the Indian origins of the religion and the periphery in the vernacular interpretations and practices of later Buddhists. More-recent scholarship on the processes of vernacularization and the literary regions or cultures of Buddhist history has increasingly focused on the two-way process of cosmopolitan-vernacular interactions in the production of religious imaginaries and on the ways in which these processes are often politicized.[36]

The most far-reaching study of Khmer Buddhism to date, François Bizot's extensive work on Khmer Tantric texts and practices, contests received narratives of Theravādin history in Cambodia. Bizot argues that Buddhist practice and knowledge in Cambodia before the mid-nineteenth century did not necessarily conform to the reified scholarly construction of the Theravāda in terms of the Pali canonical sources known as the *Tipiṭaka.* His scholarship calls into question the distinctive development of Theravāda, Mahāyāna, and Tantric forms of Buddhism. If the Theravāda in Cambodia had not always existed in its present-day "scripturalist" form, where did it come from? Bizot links the development of contemporary Buddhism to the importation of the Dhammayut order from Siam in the mid-nineteenth century. Although this expression of Buddhism eventually came to represent "mainstream" Buddhist thought and indeed even "Khmerness" in post-colonial Cambodia, it had simultaneous to its own rise suppressed other aspects, traditions, and lineages of Buddhism, particularly those most associated with Tantric practice and esoteric forms of teacher–student transmission.[37]

In another significant contribution to the dislodging of Orientalist paradigms, Charles Keyes argued that instead of pointing to the inconsistencies between canonical Buddhism and Buddhism as practiced by Southeast Asians, we needed to reevaluate what we assumed we meant by the contents of the Pali canon. Through a study of rituals of merit transference, Keyes observed that the texts owned and used in Thai monasteries not only vary widely but in fact do not necessarily include Pali canonical texts at all.[38] Instead, he noted, Thai villagers refer to a variety of other noncanonical texts as Dhamma, held to be sacred scriptures endowed with all of the same efficacious powers, such as the production of merit, attributed to canonical texts.[39]

Keyes' ethnographic findings influenced the development of Steven Collins' persuasive argument that the equation made by earlier scholars between the notion of a preexistent Pali canon and "original" or early Buddhism can hardly be historically supported. Rather, present-day versions of the Pali canon, he suggests, are the product of the Sinhalese Mahāvihārin sect's efforts at self-preservation and legitimation during periodic downturns of royal patronage for the sect in Sri Lanka. These efforts resulted in the introduction of the concept of the *Tipiṭaka* as a closed and authoritative body of Theravādin scriptures.[40] Sinhalese forms of Buddhism imported into Southeast Asia maintained the idea of the *Tipiṭaka* as a canon in an abstract sense only, without necessarily conflating the concepts of scriptural authority and a closed canon.[41] Collins comments that further ethnographic and historical work is needed to fully understand the actual texts that have commanded scriptural authority in particular Theravādin contexts:

> If we wish to delineate the actual "canon" or "canons" of scripture . . . in use at different times and places of the Theravāda world, we need empirical research into each individual case . . . on the actual possession and use of texts, in monastery libraries and elsewhere, and on the content of sermons and festival presentations to laity, to establish more clearly than we currently can just what role has been played by the works included in the canonical list.[42]

Collins concludes by suggesting that the importance of the Pali canon be understood as an authoritative notion rather than a closed body of texts.

Building on Collins' argument, Anne Blackburn's analysis of texts and training on monastic discipline in medieval and eighteenth-century Sri Lanka includes a carefully articulated distinction between formal and practical canons in the Theravāda. Blackburn designates Collins' notion of canon as an authoritative concept as "formal canon," while referring to the texts in a given historical contexts that are produced, used, collected, copied, read, recited, interpreted, and understood as expressions of this larger authoritative concept as the "practical canon."[43] Charles Hallisey has further nuanced this discussion by demonstrating that the scholarly construction by Orientalists of certain texts, values, and ideas as authoritative was often influenced by colonial Buddhists themselves. His theory of "intercultural mimesis" (discussed in more depth in chapter 4) grants more agency to Buddhists themselves in the representation of what constitutes Buddhist sources of canonical authority.[44]

Drawing on the work of these scholars, my discussion of local, vernacular Buddhist interpretations of the Theravāda tradition in colonial Cambodia examines not only the outlines of the practical canons current among Buddhist intellectuals in late-nineteenth- and early-twentieth-century Cambodia, but also the ways in which they drew on the idea of a formal canon as a basis of authority to transform one practical canon into another, interestingly, into one that more closely resembled the Orientalist conception of authoritative scripture.

MODERNITY AND BUDDHIST MODERNISM IN COLONIAL CAMBODIA

Modernity has been associated with certain hallmarks. Among these are changing modes of production and exchange; changing conceptions of temporality and of the physical representation of the world; mechanization and bureaucratization; rationalism, disenchantment, or demystification; the demarcation of the secular; and historicist views about progress and civilizational development. "Modernism" as it has sometimes been defined in art and literature, is understood to both express and critique these hallmarks and to exhibit reflexivity about the experience of being caught up in shifts of history. While Buddhists in many different cultural and historical contexts have been adept at representing the tensions between the "interiorized" sensations of impermanence and permanence sometimes associated with modernist expression,[45] Khmer Buddhists during the late nineteenth century faced the particular problem of how to give meaning to the experience of flux and change when older Buddhistic ways of understanding and representing the world were coming unglued.

This is the context in which I see Khmer Buddhist modernism developing. In late-nineteenth- and early-twentieth-century Cambodia, Buddhist thought acted as a cultural medium for response to and critique of the sociopolitics of modern experiences in ways that parallel David Harvey's approach to the rise of modernist art and literature. I follow Harvey's analysis of modernism in Euro-American art and literature in supposing that modernism cannot be understood without reference to the sociopolitical context in which it developed.[46] Harvey sees modernist art and literature in the late 1800s–early 1900s as part of a social movement that simultaneously interpreted, represented, critiqued, and advanced new sensations and experiences indicative of modernity. The mood, aesthetic, and politics of modernism in prewar Europe and the United States were, in Harvey's analysis, a reaction to new factors such as the experiences of mass production, mass markets, mass media, new forms of circulation and transportation, and urbanization.[47] An underlying question during this early phase of modernism, he suggests, was the tension between two perceived qualities of modern life: the sense of the world as fleeting, ephemeral, and chaotic on the one hand, and on the other hand, the belief that it contained the "eternal and the immutable." Emerging currents of modernist thought in art and literature served as a source for working out this problem, as well as for providing "ways to absorb, reflect upon, and codify these rapid changes" and to "modify or support them."[48]

In his analysis of non-European experiences of modernity, Thongchai Winichakul explores the shifts between premodern and modern Siamese notions of cartography and geography. Whereas older maps represented "an illustration of another narration, be it a religious story or the description of a travel route" and not a "spatial reality," the modern map focused on existence in the material world. The differences in the two kinds of maps reflected not only changing technologies but also "different kinds of knowledge and the conceptions behind them."[49] By comparison, Dipesh Chakrabarty has suggested that for Indians, the point of reference for understanding the modern is necessarily different from what it is for Europeans, since "being human" in India "involves the question of being with gods and spirits."[50]

I draw on both these approaches in examining Khmer Buddhist modernism in terms of the production of different kinds of knowledge and indigenous conceptions of ways of being. In colonial Cambodia, being human necessitated living in a world shaped by action, or *kamma.*[51] For modernist thinkers, this construction of reality necessitated awareness of and responsibility for one's moral conduct, choosing a road or path to follow, a way of directing the actions constantly being performed by one's mind, speech, and body. Modernist moral perception also involved a collective or communal sense of relationship. The actions of one person affected those of others, and purification thus required collective effort. This was clearly an "imagined community," not of a nation but of fellow adherents of a religion *(qanak tam sāsana),* the fourfold religious community *(parisāḷ)* comprising the assembly of all four groups of monastic and lay Buddhists, male and female: *bhikkhu-bhikkhunī-upāsak-upāsikā.*[52]

If modern expression can be said to involve an altered knowledge of reality and of human ways of being, a revision of values reflecting these changed modes of imagining oneself in the world, reflexivity about change, and a transformed experience of temporality, these new ways of knowing and being were articulated through Buddhist ideas and literature. The Khmer writer and Pali scholar Ukñā Suttantaprījā Ind wrote, "What is Dhamma in these times?"[53] He went on to consider the moral values most necessary for living *eḷūv neḥ,* "right now,"[54] contrasting the "old" with the "new,"[55] and examining the *gatilok tmī dael koet mān ḷoeṅ,* "modern morality that has arisen."[56] It is necessary "in these present times," he wrote, for "persons who are trying to be good and pure" to be able to clearly recognize "what is worldly [behavior] and what is Dhammic [behavior]."[57] This framing of moral conduct in terms of time, delineating *eḷūv neḥ,* "right now," from *'cās'* or *purāṇ,* "past or ancient times," or *mun,* "all previous time before right now," in combination with his division between the worldly (or secular) and the Dhammic (or religious) is expressive of the kind of self-consciousness of temporality that Harvey has associated with modernism.[58] Yet at the same time that Ind emphasizes the present-ness and even the newness of this time period through references to what is *tmī,* "new" or "modern," his transhistorical claims about Buddhist moral values are also made evident.

In recent decades, postcolonial studies of modernity and colonial encounter have moved from the assumption that forms of modernism were imposed as a result of European colonial influence to considering whether and how they arose from impulses within the colonial subjects' own history and culture. In the case of Sri Lankan Buddhism, these questions have been debated around the label "Protestant Buddhism." Anthropologist Gananath Obeyesekere originally coined the term to refer to a modernist expression of Buddhism that simultaneously adopted some forms and fashions of Protestant Christianity from Euro-American missionaries and at the same time rebelled against European political domination.[59] More-recent scholarship on Sri Lankan Buddhism moves away from the "one-way" examination of European modern influence. Anne Blackburn's work, for instance, explores the indigenous scholastic shifts that helped to prefigure modern Buddhism.[60] Peter van der Veer's work considers ways in which encounters between South Asians and Europeans influenced changes in each other's religious understandings.[61]

The development of Khmer Buddhist modernity, which past scholarship has hardly examined at all, requires a careful historical reading. Because of the insertion of colonial politics in the construction of Khmer modernism, it can appear, from reading French colonial sources, that Khmer Buddhist modernism was a French invention. Indeed, as will become evident in chapter 4, French accounts of the stasis and even backwardness of the Khmer religious mentality credit the *mission civilisatrice* with emerging expressions of religious revitalization in Cambodia. Historian John Tully has commented that the 1920s and 1930s have "often been cast as a politically 'dead' period for Cambodia,"[62] but in fact this characterization of the period (of which Tully is justifiably suspicious) overlooks the productivity and fertile outpouring of Buddhist ethical writings and translations. Obviously, the idioms used for understanding social and political change and the construction of meaning can vary widely, depending on the historical contexts. Novels, reportage, memoirs, and newspapers—literary forms associated with the articulation of modernity and the imagining of the communities of the city and the nation elsewhere in Southeast Asia—were scarcely in evidence in Cambodia. But perhaps this was in part because Khmer Buddhists were busily engaged in articulating modern experience in their own, heterogeneous terms. In Cambodia, where the majority of educated Khmer had been trained in Buddhist monasteries, Buddhism remained the primary medium for understanding and articulating a new self-consciousness of what it meant to be Khmer and a modern person. I think that the oversight of Buddhist literary expressions during this period as a historical source for understanding social change has arisen because the production of Buddhist translations is perceived, even by contemporary scholars of comparative colonialisms, as imitation rather than imagining. This misunderstanding could make it difficult to see how translating the Buddhist canon could serve as a site for articulating new ways of being.

OUTLINES OF BUDDHIST MODERNISM IN CAMBODIA

Like the broad body of thought referred to as Islamic modernism, Buddhist modernism, as scholars have begun to describe the accommodation between modern and Buddhist values, was not a monolithic intellectual development. Cambodia was no exception; different interpreters emphasized different ideas and were at times engaged in translating varying sorts of authoritative scriptural texts according to their own interests. In the discussion that follows, I treat the emerging body of Khmer modernist thought in terms of its general preoccupations and articulation of ethical values. I draw a distinction between the general currents of modernist interpretation and the more specific tenets outlined by the modern Dhamma group within the Mahānikāy. Modern Dhamma or Dharm-thmī was the moniker used to designate the monastic group of students and Pali scholars clustered around Braḥ Mahā Vimaladhamm Thoṅ at Vatt Uṇṇālom in the early 1900s. The term was used by the group's early adherents and detractors and was widely employed in French Sûreté and other administrative records after the mid-teens.[63]

Designating their interpretation of the Dhamma as *thmī,* "new" or "modern," the modernists' ideology opposed the traditionalism of the Dharm-cās, the "old" or "traditional" Dhamma advocated by the Sangha chief, which from their standpoint represented an impure and degenerate practice of Buddhism.[64] While the new Buddhist movement in Cambodia shared many of the characteristics of traditional Buddhist reform and purification movements,[65] modernism was not simply a reform of Buddhist ideas or a renovation of Buddhist institutions engineered by French scholars and colonial officials. Rather, what began in the nineteenth century under King Ang Duong as an example of yet another Theravāda Buddhist purification movement was transformed by these later Buddhist intellectuals into an expression of Southeast Asian religious engagement with modernity.

Modernists did not reject all aspects of older Khmer thought, and in fact several of the modernists I study here were among the most erudite products of the older Khmer Buddhist manuscript culture. In particular, the modernist emphasis on purification through conduct was already a part of the Khmer religious imagination of the nineteenth century, albeit in different forms. Commonly held perceptions of the relationship between merit and power, generated by individuals considered more pure than ordinary people, underlay political organization and social structures as well as idealized representations of order in literature. The idea of purification through moral conduct had been central to the doctrine and practice of the Vietnamese Buu Son Ky Huong tradition as it developed in the mid-nineteenth century. A similar belief was apparent in the millenarian movements that sprang up in the border regions between Cambodia and Cochinchina; the charismatic figures who led them were known as *qanak mān puṇy,* "people possessing merit," who had become purified through means such as adherence to religious precepts, forms of abstinence, meditational prowess, or the transmission of special teachings. In contrast to these older interpretations of purification, modernists were advocating a new brand of Buddhist purification that in some ways made Buddhism appear more egalitarian. Purification was available to everyone, including ordinary laypeople, though it also encumbered them with the responsibility of being more mindful about their everyday actions and relationships. Rather than kings and extraordinary figures such as Buddhas-to-be, all Buddhists had collective responsibility for purifying themselves, and by extension, for purifying the *sāsana,* the "religious doctrine."

The ability to purify one's own behavior depended on knowledge, which in turn was dependent on understanding the authentic teachings of the scriptures, not texts that had been corrupted over time through scribal errors and lack of understanding. Thus, the new Buddhist understanding necessitated innovations in pedagogical and textual practices as well that ended up hastening the transition from manuscript to print Buddhist culture in Cambodia.[66] Khmer texts were traditionally preserved either as inscribed palm-leaf manuscripts or accordion-style folded paper manuscripts inscribed with ink or chalk.[67] Since few opportunities for education existed outside the monastery, literacy and writing were closely linked to religious practice. Writing in itself was highly valued and spiritually potent. Manuscripts were produced with great care, surrounded by rituals for preparing the palm leaves and ceremonies and regulations that had to be observed by the monks who inscribed them.[68] Finished manuscripts were consecrated, and the presentation of the manuscript to a monastery required a ritual ceremony, such as the presentation of special cloth for wrapping the texts or the donation of robes to the monk-scribe in order to effect the passing of merit to the donor of the manuscript.[69] The quality and efficacy of the manuscript depended in part on the beauty of its written words, which in turn reflected the mindfulness of the monk who inscribed it, since in many cases, written syllables of the teachings were considered as microcosmic representations of the Buddha.[70] The production of a manuscript was thus an act of devotion whose quality could be judged according to its clarity, lack of writing errors, and aesthetic character. Imbued with these elements of the Buddha and the Dhamma, of merit and devotion, manuscripts were venerated as aural texts, meant to be heard, conferring merit on their listeners and on the monks who read or chanted them, and as written texts, venerated in and of themselves for their written nature. Ideologically committed to new technologies of textual translation and print dissemination, modernists rejected these traditional methods associated with manuscript production as well as other older practices, ritual conventions, and ways of transmitting knowledge connected with the manuscript culture of learning.

In spite of the modernists' opposition to traditionalism, however, Buddhist modernism was in many respects a conservative movement. It sought to identify authentic aspects of Khmer culture, most notably the history and development of Theravāda Buddhism within Cambodia and its moral values and teachings. It also sought to purify expressions of Khmer culture that had become corrupted: language, rituals, institutions, practices, and most important, everyday moral conduct and the Dhamma itself, which had been damaged by a decline in Pali knowledge and texts. At the center of this concern with purification was the *Dhamma-vinay* (Pali: Dhamma-vinaya), a "canonical" body of Buddhist texts and teachings, and particularly the *Vinaya,* the compendium of prescriptions for monastic behavior. Following from the insights developed by Mongkut's reforms in Siam, beginning in the 1830s, the early generations of Khmer monks who had been trained in Bangkok, and later, their students in Khmer monasteries, turned their attention to careful study and articulation of moral conduct based on codes of conduct outlined in the *Vinaya.* Consequently, the introduction of new educational methods including grammar, translation, and other pedagogical concerns were crucial for the modernists because they illuminated *Vinaya* and other scriptural knowledge. It was in this sense that the modernist movement most ardently began to challenge and change traditional textual understandings and practices in Cambodia. In the older Khmer manuscript culture, the clear delineation of aspects of Buddhist doctrine and *Buddhavacana,* "the words of the Buddha," was less important than the larger vision of the possibility of human perfection, represented by the figure of the Bodhisatta, over vast spans of time.[71]

This book combines historical and textual analysis to examine the development of these ideas from the mid-nineteenth century through 1930. Chapter 1 provides a literary starting point for the study, not as the repository of traditional Buddhism, but more as a perspective on the ethical perspectives and anxieties of late-nineteenth-century Buddhist scholars, who were writing about moral development in an ordered universe and about the merit and virtue with which politically powerful persons were imbued. What these late-nineteenth-century Buddhist writings omit, however, are explicit references to the destabilized political situation in colonial Cambodia at the time. In chapter 2, I suggest reading these sorts of texts as evidence of a disjuncture between ideas about how the world was supposed to be ordered and how living in it actually felt. Chapter 2 offers further evidence of this disjuncture by considering the sociopolitical changes that occurred during this period, ushered in by French "reforms," and by examining the development of other kinds of Buddhistic responses to social change, including nineteenth-century instances of millenarianism, Prince Yukanthor's short-lived venture into anticolonial agitation in 1900, and Ind's modernist work *Gatilok* (Ways of the world), composed between 1914 and 1921.[72]

Chapter 3 further charts the changing understandings of Khmer ideas of purification. It examines how the Buddhist renovation movement put in place by King Ang Duong to purify the religion was reflected in the state of Khmer manuscript collections and Buddhist learning at the beginning of the twentieth century. Although Buddhist learning had developed in significant ways since 1848, Bangkok was still the more desirable destination for Khmer monks who wanted to pursue higher learning. Drawing on funeral biographies and other sources, I examine accounts of their experiences in Siam, the influence of the ideas they carried back to Cambodia, and the initially clandestine growth of modern Dhamma among a group of young monks in Phnom Penh. Chapter 4 looks at the ways in which this modernist interpretation developed in monastic circles between 1914 and 1930, bolstered by French colonial religious policies, and the accommodations between European and Buddhist discourses of modernization.

Finally, chapter 5 returns to reading Khmer ethical writings to examine how Khmer ideas about how to behave as a moral person had shifted over the course of several decades. These new writings, as I have suggested, emphasized the themes of authenticity, rationalism, and purification of moral behavior. These themes were expressed in new literary forms and styles that reflected the new ways in which the modernists were interpreting and expressing Theravādin ideas in ways that were simultaneously expressive of the translocal and transhistorical ethical dimensions of Buddhism and geographically and temporally situated in the ordinary lives of Khmer Buddhists. I conclude by briefly considering the transformation of these ideas from modernist critique to mainstream Buddhist orthodoxy.

SOURCES

The most important sources for this study are modernist writings produced between 1914 and the early 1930s and funeral biographies of Khmer monks born before 1900, a type of text that seems to have come into being only in the late 1920s. The modernist writings include compendiums, ritual manuals, translations, sermons, and folklore compilations; these forms will be discussed in more detail in the chapters that follow, particularly chapter 5, in which some of these writings are excerpted. The latter sources contain both biographical and monastic lineage information about the deceased *bhikkhu* (or in a few cases, laypeople), often accompanied by a translation of a scriptural passage. These sources, little scrutinized by scholars of Cambodia and Theravāda Buddhism, merit even further attention than my study provides.[73]

I also draw on a range of other types of Buddhist writings from the nineteenth and early twentieth centuries, some of which have been extensively studied or translated by others, and to whom I am indebted.[74] These include *cpāp'* (didactic poetry), a varied body of translations (often in verse) of Pali textual sources, and *jātaka.* Whenever possible, I tried to use editions of the work from the period in question, although often they were compiled later, in print form, based on palm-leaf manuscripts, or reprinted without alteration. The poetry and prose of Ukñā Suttantaprījā Ind, trained as a monk in nineteenth-century Bangkok, runs through almost every chapter of the book. I have suggested that his writing represents modern Buddhist concerns at different moments in the time period I examine; his work also introduces us to one of the most eloquent and original voices of Khmer Buddhist modernism.

Some of these Buddhist sources are early printed texts; others are drawn from the first print periodicals introduced in Cambodia in 1926 and 1927, *Kambujasuriyā* and *Ganthamālā*. The former was introduced for the purpose of publishing, in Khmer, materials on Khmer culture, and at least initially was devoted almost entirely to religious topics. The latter periodical was intended as a vehicle for publishing new critically edited vernacular translations of Pali texts being produced by young monks at the Sālā Pali in Phnom Penh.

In addition to two rare individual memoirs treating the nineteenth and early twentieth centuries respectively,[75] I make use of French colonial ethnographies, travel accounts, scholarly articles, dictionaries, and documents and correspondence gained from archival research in Paris and Phnom Penh.

My focus on the scholarly and textual practices of Buddhists in Cambodia is not meant to preclude the importance of other sites for imagining modern Buddhism. Visual culture, ritual, healing practices, and ecclesiastical law are other aspects of religious life that could be examined. But the Khmer scholarly tradition or *gantha-dhura,* as it is known among Theravāda Buddhists, is one that has received little recent attention, particularly in respect to the translocal character of its development.

I Defending the Jeweled Throne

Khmer Religious Imagination in the Nineteenth Century

A Khmer vernacular poetic version of a Southeast Asian biography of the Buddha, composed at the end of the nineteenth century,[1] depicts the Bodhisatta's meditational victory over the temptations offered by Mārā, "the enemy of Lord Buddha."[2] The culminating episode in the poem is a dramatic contest between Mārā's army and Nāṅ Dharaṇī, the earth goddess, who testifies in support of the Bodhisatta over the ownership of a jeweled throne produced by the merit that the Bodhisatta generated from virtuous actions performed in countless past lifetimes. In the Bodhisatta's defense, the "lovely celestial maiden Nāṅ Dharaṇī" asserts,

"Yes, I am the Lord's woman witness
and I support that he has cut passion away;
as he gained *bodhi*-knowledge[3] bit by bit,
I knew of each action he made.

"One time, filled to the brim with perfections
he sprinkled water on the earth and solemnly [vowed]
once enlightened, to become a Teacher
and the jeweled throne clearly arose [from that vow].

"And you, have you not established something
to which any dare testify?!"
Having spoken thus, she untied her long tresses
and taking them up [with her arms upright], handful by handful, wrung
them out on Mārā's horde.

The power and force of Nāṅ Dharaṇī
flowed out magnificently [from her hair],
arising immense as an ocean,
engulfing entirely the army of Mārā.[4]

This moment of the earth's testimony is evocative, I think, of the intertwining conceptions of merit, power, Buddhist virtue, and the moral rendering of the physical universe integral to much of late-nineteenth-century Khmer Buddhist literature. The person of the Buddha received greatest literary consideration during this period as the central figure in the past and future narrative of human beings in the world. That is, the Buddha was not simply an exemplary moral figure; his cosmic biography also demonstrated and made sense of how reality worked. The moral development of individuals was determined by action or *kamma,* and the benefit or harm it created. The physical formation and temporal framework of the world itself, in this conception, was linked to the moral progress and decline of individuals living in the world and to the rise and gradual purification of the subsequent buddhas who taught the Dhamma or Truth in different eras.

Reading Buddhist literature from the late nineteenth century allows us to see both the contrast and continuities with modernist reinterpretations. I examine prevalent literary conceptions of moral development that were later challenged or reworked by modernists to reflect their own rationalized values surrounding purification, modern sensibilities about time and space, and the application of new scripturalist methods for cultivating Buddhist ethical knowledge. Their new interpretations deemphasized the ubiquity of the Bodhisatta as moral exemplar, insisting instead on the need for all Buddhists—lay and monastic, ordinary and exemplary—to bring their everyday, individual behavior in line with the *Dhamma-vinay,* the teachings of the Buddha. By contrast, the prevailing nineteenth-century literary image of morality was of sentient beings moving through the cosmic space and time of a universe ordered by moral purification. The representations of individual and collective moral development in this chapter are meant to stand in explicit contrast to the modern writings examined in chapter 5.

In the discussion that follows, I will consider several key texts that were influential in the nineteenth-century Khmer intellectual milieu, focusing on their understandings of progress and development in individuals, through time and in the cosmos. These depictions relay idealized assumptions about individual and social morality and about how reality is ordered. The coherence and orderliness of these representations in fact contrasted sharply with the far more turbulent real world in which nineteenth-century Khmer were living, a disjuncture that will be explored further in chapter 2.

Through readings of several popular texts of the period, this chapter examines three prominent themes in this literature. First, in a discussion of the linkage between the cosmos, temporality, and the history of the Dhamma in the *Trai Bhūm,* a cosmological text, I point to the prevalent imagining of a morally constructed universe, one in which the very temporal and spatial structure of the physical world has moral dimensions. This is the context in which human moral progress must take place. The second theme is the representation of moral development as individual journeys through this morally constructed cosmos. Third, I look at assertions about the relationship between power and merit, the spiritual benefit that accrues to those who live virtuously and generously support the Buddhist Sangha. While powerful persons are understood in this literature to derive their power from merit, part of their merit lies in their recognition of the limitations of worldly power, which is always subordinate to spiritual power. This last theme is the most revealing of the fissures in the viability of the late-nineteenth-century Khmer religious imagination as a means of making sense of the world. These works were popular at a time when the real political power of Khmer kings and elites was being severely curtailed by the sociopolitics of colonial control.

This discussion provides important background for understanding the changes and transformations that occurred in Khmer religious interpretations over the course of the next few decades. The contrast between Buddhist manuscript writings of the late nineteenth century and the new print works produced by modernists in the second and third decades of the twentieth century help us see shifts in Buddhist values about how to live as a moral person and how to give order and meaning to human experience.

THE MORALLY CONSTRUCTED COSMOS

Nineteenth-century literati, trained and educated for the most part in Buddhist monastic schools, studied texts that articulated a Buddhist understanding of a morally constructed universe existing in a Dhammic time frame. The cosmos, with its multiple worlds, moved through cycles of decline and regeneration that mirrored the contiguous decline and regeneration of adherence to the Dhamma among sentient beings. The identity of individuals was morally derived as well, determined by their karma as they moved through the hierarchically ordered levels of rebirth known as *gati,* depending on their accumulated stores of merit—derived from good or beneficial actions in past lives.[5] The Cambodian literary scholar Lī Dhām Teṅ[6] has commented on the number of prominent texts from the nineteenth century that depict similar events and themes concerning

> wicked, savage *yakkha* exacting retribution from humans, and humans who are righteous individuals constantly undergoing cruel and terrible torments from those who are evil. But the evil ones do not prevail, because in accordance with Buddhist theory, *adhammic* persons always fall prey to the karmic fruits of their wrongdoing, following the laws of nature that require people whose actions are good to realize benefit and find happiness.[7]

Popular religious texts of the period, some of which were best known outside monastic circles in their oral and visual forms, reinforced and duplicated a vision of time and the world as morally structured. These included versions of the *Trai Bhūm* and of *jātaka,* along with other related accounts of the Buddha and his family members such as the *Paṭhamasambodhi* and *Bimbānibbān.* After Ang Duong was placed on the Khmer throne by the Siamese in 1848, he convened a gathering of Khmer religious and literary scholars in an effort to reconstitute the

Khmer literary heritage.[8] Since the *Trai Bhūm* (along with many other Khmer literary works) had apparently been lost in the decades of warfare prior to his reign, the king reportedly sent to Siam for a copy of it.[9] According to French sources from the period, it remained a highly influential text for the remainder of the century.[10]

The *Trai Bhūm* defines human beings in respect to their place in the morally and hierarchically ordered crystalline structure of the Buddhist cosmos with its thirty-one levels of existence and *maṇḍala*-like map. Likewise, the development of human communities is described in relation to their inhabitants' observance of the Dhamma. Because of their inability to control their cravings and desires, human beings are forced to organize their societies under a king, the best of whom are known as *cakkavattin,* kings who promulgate and uphold the Buddhist teachings. Implicit in this vision is the notion that the righteousness of kings determines the prosperity of their subjects as well as the abundance of agricultural production and the regular, harmonious functioning of the seasons and other natural phenomena.[11]

Temporally, the three worlds of the text are situated in a universe characterized by continuous cycles of development, destruction, and regeneration, which are divided into temporal periods known in Khmer as *kapp,*[12] an almost immeasurably long period of time that constitutes the lifetime of the world.[13] The two major divisions are referred to in Khmer sources as the *kapp*s of decline and prosperity. The *kapp* of decline, *saṃvaṭṭa* or *kappavināś,* is the "devolving" or diminishing *kapp,* in which the human life span grows increasingly shorter as the ten kinds of bad or nonbeneficial actions *(dasa akusalakammapatha)* are introduced. These ten actions are theft, murder, lying, malicious speech, improper sexual behavior, harsh speech, frivolous speech, jealousy, malice, and wrong view.[14] At the *kapp*'s end, human life becomes desperately short and violent, all moral values are lost, and the world is destroyed by means of fire, water, and wind.[15] The *vivaṭṭakapp* or *kappacaṃroen* is the period of time in which the world regenerates, just as it was before. A long while after the destruction of the world, when the universe is still filled with water, a *brahma*-being who has escaped the destruction in the highest levels of the universe looks down into the water. If the being sees one flower, the *kapp* will have one buddha, and is called a *sārakapp* (excellent *kappa*); if the being sees two flowers, the emerging *kapp* will witness the enlightenment of two buddhas, and is called a *maṇḍakapp* (superior *kappa*), and so on.[16] Shortly after this, other luminescent *brahma*-beings converge and very gradually evolve (or devolve, as the case may be) into solid-bodied, gendered humans living in social groups, who must—as a result of cravings that lead them away from the Dhamma—develop shelters, communities, agriculture, and a system for designating rulers.

The world in which these beings develop has Mount Meru standing at its center, surrounded by a ring of mountains and four continents inhabited by different classes of humans, of which human beings inhabit the Jambu continent. The larger universe containing this realm is divided into three morally hierarchical worlds containing thirty-one realms of varying levels of experience, perception, and formlessness. The lowest realms are the experiential ones, in which beings are reborn into hells, the human and animal world, or the heavens, experiencing the combinations of pain, sorrow, and happiness that are their karmic due. At higher levels, more spiritually advanced beings, those with material remains and those without, advance toward the cessation of the cycle of birth and rebirth. The conditions, events, and places of past worlds are reduplicated, as different bodhisattas are born, perfect themselves, become enlightened, and preach the Dhamma, which other beings embrace. Again, in this regenerated world, the ten nonbeneficial actions gradually emerge, with poverty giving rise to theft, theft giving rise to a need for weapons, the possession of weapons giving rise to murder—until human life expectancy has devolved once again to an individual life span of ten immoral, violence-filled years.

Even this brief description makes clear the extent to which the corporeality of the world, its inhabitants, and its temporal cycles are tied to the moral behavior of human beings. This interplay is clearly represented, for example, in the image of the bo tree, always the site of enlightenment for buddhas, which is the first physical element of the new world to spontaneously regenerate after the frothy waters from the end of the last *kappa* gel and harden again into earth. The reemergence of the bo tree at the beginning of the new *kappa* anticipates the perfection of one or more new buddhas.[17] The interidentification between corporeality and morality is also evident in the physical evolution of the world's inhabitants from luminescent *brahma*-beings into hard-bodied humans, a progression that is clearly correlated with their development of cravings, first for food and then for sex, and that ultimately motivates them to erect shelters, build communities, and elect a king.

The movement of time is also inscribed in moral terms, with cycles of *kappa* that correspond to the establishment and loss of *dhammic* ideas and values. The temporal and spatial progress of human beings through the world, as they are born and reborn into the various realms of existence *(gati),*[18] is determined by the ripening of their *kamma,* the result of beneficial and nonbeneficial actions performed in the past. Ultimately, what identifies and differentiates individual human beings from each other and from the many other classes of sentient beings with whom they share this world—including animals, ghosts, deities, demons, and the more morally perfected beings who inhabit the other three continents of the universe—is their capacity to escape the incessant cycle of *saṃsāra* (the rounds of death and rebirth), to move beyond morally constructed, conditioned temporality to *nibbāṇa* through moral perfection, a state that only humans are able to attain.

This *Trai Bhūm* conception of individuals and the world is one that has often been termed "traditional" or "cosmological" Buddhism in Western histories of Cambodia.[19] Leaving aside the thorny question of whether or how we should use a term such as "traditional Buddhism," the broad ideas meant to be conveyed under this rubric are important to this discussion: a vision of a morally structured universe; conceptions of temporality tied to moral purification (and ritually, to agricultural cycles); an understanding of the law of *kamma* as the underlying determinant of individual identity; a linking of Buddhism and kingship, with the image of a righteous Dhammic ruler exerting a powerful influence on conceptions of community and the functioning of power. "Traditional Buddhism," however (and here the problems associated with the term cannot help but become apparent), was never a singular or static vision. An example of the way in which the Theravāda tradition has been continuously created anew in local contexts is the subject of the second part of this book, in which I trace the development of Buddhist modernism in Cambodia. Discourses connected with "traditional" Theravāda Buddhism in nineteenth-century Cambodia were simultaneously a starting point for twentieth-century modernism and an aspect of modern thought in and of themselves.[20]

MORAL JOURNEYS IN COSMIC SPACE AND TIME

The influence of the *Trai Bhūm* representation of the world is borne out in other texts of the period that follow its same broad outlines and its assumptions about cosmology, temporality, and the moral construction of the physical universe. This literature is concerned not so much with depicting the three tiers and thirty-one realms of the morally structured universe but rather with the ways in which the history of the cosmos is joined to the history of human moral progress. The cosmos serves as the setting or background for chronicling the moral development of various righteous and malevolent characters. Many popular stories from the period were concerned with the theme of individual development as characters progressed toward greater moral perfection.

Waxing impatient with what he perceived as the redundancy of this theme in literature of the period, Joseph Guesdon, a French missionary who collected and studied Khmer literature in the late nineteenth century,[21] remarked,

> Authors represent only characters in which the Bodhisattva (or future Buddha) is the hero. Moreover, the Bodhisattva and likewise the members of his entourage are always the same, whether in past or future existences. Just as historical personages have a well-known, well-defined character, authors cannot depart from these stock types; they have their hands tied. Not only are the characters the same, but the corpus of the works must be invariable. It is always a Bodhisattva who is reborn, suffers, and who triumphs over all with miraculous aid.[22]

Ignore for the moment Guesdon's implied Orientalist critiques about stasis (echoed in other colonial writings and discussed in chapter 4); his observations help to corroborate evidence offered by the texts themselves about Khmer literary preoccupations with the cosmic depiction of individual moral development in this period.[23] The canonical and noncanonical *jātaka* to which Guesdon refers—in general, the best known and most widely collected texts in monastery schools and libraries in nineteenth-century Cambodia[24]—construed morality in terms of the cosmic cycle of the Bodhisatta's rebirths. Especially ubiquitous were the stories of the last ten births, detailing his cultivation of the ten *pāramī* or perfections: generosity or giving, moral behavior, freedom from passion, wisdom, energy, patience, truth telling, self-determination, loving-kindness, and equanimity.

Jātaka took many literary forms and included recognizable versions of the birth stories from the *Khuddakanikāya* of the *Suttantapiṭaka* of the Pali canon, versions of the Khmer *Paññāsa-jātaka,* and stories only loosely connected to these collections.[25] One *Paññāsa-jātaka* story that was well-known at the end of the nineteenth century (and probably before, since it was composed at the end of the eighteenth century) was the *Pañasā Sīrasā,*[26] included in Guesdon's 1906 review of well-known contemporary Khmer literature. It relates the story of two youths (one of whom is a prince and bodhisatta) who are banished to the forest and later, after numerous travails, become the kings of two different kingdoms. As kings, they visit various realms on earth, in the heavens, and the "majestic" Mount Sumeru encircled by seven oceans and seven mountain ranges, whose slopes in all four directions are "gilded with gold, studded all over with shining and shimmering . . . precious gems" or "shining with the splendor of inlaid sapphires."[27] Outside the rings of concentric oceans and mountains, the four continents of Jambu, Āmakorīyā, Udarakaro, and Pūdsīdī are inhabited by beings of different types.

In the *Pañasā Sīrasā,* the physical appearances of landscapes, and likewise the individuals who inhabit them, reflect their moral purity. Aside from the human continent, Jambu, "Āmakorīyā, Udarakaro, the continent of Pūdsīdī, are so beautiful they resemble the realms of heaven." The uniformly lovely visages and long life spans of the beings who live in them are the attributes of communities in which all members are equally pure:

> [In Pūdsīdī] the men and women have round faces
> like full moons,
> clean and pure, without defects,
> their life spans are a hundred years.
>
> The faces of the inhabitants of Āmakorīyā,
> the continent to the west,
> are like crescent moons,
> and they live five hundred years.
>
> The people inhabiting Udarakaro
> have vividly beautiful faces
> with four equal sides,[28]
> and they live a thousand years.

Unlike human beings in Jambu, these beings are alike in their beauty and free from pain because they universally practice virtue:

All of the sentient beings in these three continents,
men and women alike,
follow the five precepts, always guarded,
never faltering, never taking the lives of other beings.

They are [all] happy,
lacking the troubles associated with farming;
they know nothing of business or trade
[but] only of gathering together for enjoyment and pleasure.

Their bodies never experience pain, illness, or injury;
there are no mosquitoes, wasps, flies, or centipedes at all;
[since] anger does not exist,
their hearts and minds are free of suffering.[29]

The text suggests that the beauty, ways of life, and life spans of the inhabitants of the other continents are more desirable than the conditions in the human world of Jambu, with its conjoined sorrows and happiness. Yet in these worlds of greater perfection and purity, the absence of suffering is tied to a lack of corresponding moral development. By contrast, human beings in the Jambu continent, like the heroes of the *Pañasā Sīrasā,* have to endure exile, countless battles with magical creatures, mistaken identities, and separations from loved ones before finding happiness or peace. Along with the entertainment value provided by these episodes, the struggles of characters such as the Bodhisatta-prince move them further along on the path toward purification. The other continents provide a Buddhist vision of felicity, as Steven Collins has termed it, but only through birth as humans do beings have the opportunity to become enlightened and escape the whole cycle of rebirth altogether.[30]

While the *Pañasā Sīrasā* draws on the horizontal spatial landscape of the *Trai Bhūm* to depict struggle and purification, the *Nemirāj,*[31] another important *jātaka* of the period, vividly depicts its vertical moral hierarchy of graded levels of heavens and hells. This text makes the karmic determination of human identity particularly clear.[32] The *Nemirāj* story is one of the last ten human rebirths of the Bodhisatta. According to Adhémard Leclère, a colonial official and ethnographer who wrote on Khmer Buddhism at the end of the nineteenth century, this story was widely known by laypeople and literate monks. Besides being read or chanted by monks, its contents were depicted on one of the gallery panels in the royal palace in Phnom Penh as well as in numerous temple murals.[33] This *jātaka* story depicts the journey of a virtuous king named Nemi through the hells and heavens, where he graphically learns the lesson that all actions bear fruit—which eventually ripens.

King Nemi is part of a long line of kings whose custom it was to abdicate their thrones to their sons and become ascetics on the day that each discovered his first gray hair. One day, when King Nemi wonders out loud which is more beneficial, generous giving of alms or world renunciation, Braḥ Indra comes to reassure him that while the latter is ultimately greater, the combination of moral behavior and generous almsgiving is both meritorious and indispensable to the well-being and further development of oneself and the Sangha. After Indra returns to heaven, the other gods long to meet this virtuous king. Indra sends his charioteer Mātali to fetch Nemi, and the driver offers to show him the hells and heavens, the route or "road" belonging to people "who have performed acts of wrongdoing,"[34] as well as that belonging to "those who have performed good actions."[35] Nemi's journey elaborates the hierarchical universe structured by merit and the imagery of the ripening of good and bad actions, particularly (in the passages below) in connection with the exercise of power and authority.

The journey begins in the hells, where Nemi witnesses the tortuous ripening of the fruits of wrong actions:

> Mātali, Charioteer of the Gods, showed the king a river named Vetaraṇī, which few beings can cross, filled with painful, boiling, churning water hot as tongues of flame.
>
> King Nemi watched people falling into the river Vetaraṇī . . . and asked, " . . . what acts of wrongdoing have they performed . . . ?"
>
> Mātali, Charioteer of the Gods . . . described [the ripening of] the fruit of wrong actions . . . saying, "They were people who possessed power but whose ways of exercising it were disgusting.[36] They oppressed, criticized, and derided beings less powerful than themselves. In worldly life, they performed these disgusting actions, accumulating demerit,[37] and now they must endure the River Vetaraṇī."[38]

After witnessing more gruesome scenes like this, King Nemi is transported to the levels of the heavens, where his sensations become markedly more pleasant. He learns of the wonderful celestial rewards experienced by people who give generously and create benefits for others:

> King Nemi [said], "This palace with the appearance of meritorious actions,[39] splendid with glittering walls made of diamonds and crystals, divided into symmetrical sections! It resounds with celestial music for dancing, with drums and tambourines, accompanied by such exquisite singing that to hear it transports one to glad-heartedness. . . . Heavenly Driver, such delight I am experiencing! . . . I ask you; what kind of beneficial acts[40] did these sons of gods perform to reach this level of heaven and dwell so happily in this palace?"
>
> Mātali . . . described [the ripening of] the fruit of meritorious actions, . . . saying, "These were all people who behaved morally.[41] During their lives in the world they were lay people *(upāsak)* who built gardens, lakes, wells, and bridges; with pure-heartedness, they supported all serene monks, they respectfully offered robes, food, beds and chairs, and the requisites of medicine to all genuine and true monks. These people all observed holy days *(uposath),* taking eight pre-

> cepts every fourteenth, fifteenth, and eighth days and at celebrations and [other] holy days as well. Concentrated in moral behavior, these were individuals who directed their comportment toward generosity and almsgiving, and as a result, they now dwell so happily in this palace.[42]

With its evocative descriptions of torture-ridden hells and glittering heavens replete with jeweled palaces and celestial handmaidens, the *Nemirāj* graphically situates the moral development of individuals within the same hierarchical retributive framework imagined in the *Trai Bhūm.*

The depictions of moral development that appear in these texts are indicative of the period. Purification is represented as a cosmic journey like King Nemi's or a quest filled with struggle against mythical antagonists and larger-than-life oppressors, as in the *Pañasā Sīrasā.* The results of good and bad actions might sometimes be opaque in ordinary life, but in these texts they ripen into rewards that are as conspicuously desirable as vivid, glittering mansions.

It is difficult to know exactly how the imagining of morality in terms of cosmic rewards and retribution was understood by end-of-the-century Khmer individuals, whether literally, symbolically, or both simultaneously. The extent to which the imagery of a multitiered, morally constructed universe and the meritorious individual pervaded everyday life, however, is suggested in ritual performances that reduplicated the *Trai Bhūm* cosmology and reenforced the notion of beings moving through a hierarchically structured moral cosmic time frame through acts of merit making. Rituals of merit transference at funerals to benefit the future life prospects of deceased parents, for example, emphasized the perception that there was fluidity and movement of beings in the moral cosmological schema, like King Nemi traveling through hells and heavens in a chariot. State funerals observed and recorded by Leclère at the end of the century conveyed this cosmological structure writ large, reproducing in ritual form the cosmological map of the world. In the case of the cremation of the queen mother in 1899, for instance, the funeral pyre was made to represent Mount Meru, and ritual ceremonies enacting the rotation of the sun and moon were performed as part of the transfer of merit to the deceased queen.[43] In 1906, Leclère witnessed the coronation ceremony of King Sisowath, which explicitly recreated the cosmology of the *Trai Bhūm* through the enactment of a meticulously orchestrated procession that depicted the king as the *cakkavattin* of the text.[44] These rituals, which mirror the imagery of the texts I have described, suggest the normative importance of these literary conceptions as a way of understanding individual moral development.

MORAL RELATIONSHIPS IN THE *VESSANTAR-JĀTAK*

A popular text that was widely recited at funerals and often used in sermons connected with merit making was the *Vessantara-jātaka.* This *jātaka* exemplifies the themes that I have suggested are characteristic of Khmer moral understanding during the late nineteenth century: the moral construction of individual identity, the equation between physical landscapes and moral development, the hierarchical nature of moral progress, and a perception of power as tied to moral virtue. The narrative of the Bodhisatta's penultimate birth as a human being, the *Vessantara-jātaka* is one of the best-known products of the Pali literary imagination and has been important throughout Theravādin Southeast Asia. Its prominence in Cambodia at the end of the nineteenth century was noted by French ethnographers, whose comments on its usages also give us some sense of how it was performed and received by Khmer audiences of the period.

Known in Khmer by the title *Vessantar-jātak,* the story relates the birth of the Bodhisatta as a prince of the Sivi kingdom named Vessantar, son of King Sañjay and Queen Phusatī. A radiant and virtuous youth dedicated to giving alms, he is married to the almost equally beautiful and virtuous Princess Maddī. Vessantar and Maddī have two children, variously known in Khmer texts as Jāli and Kaṇhājīnā or Jūli and Kresna. When the prince gives away his magical rain-making elephant to the neighboring kingdom of Kalinga, whose inhabitants are experiencing a drought, his angry subjects banish him to the forest. Because of their great devotion to Vessantar, Maddī, Jāli, and Kaṇhājīnā make the fateful decision to accompany him into exile. Meanwhile, an old Brahmin named Jūjak, who is married to a beautiful, conniving, and much younger woman, is instructed by his wife to go and obtain Vessantar's children as slaves. Jūjak travels to find the Bodhisatta and, making sure that Maddī is absent, asks Vessantar to give him the children as alms—a request to which Vessantar readily assents.

After giving the gift, Vessantar must struggle to transform his pain over the suffering of his children into equanimity. He eventually informs Maddī of the gift and guides her from inconsolable grief to acceptance. Although Vessantar also gives away Maddī (and she is subsequently returned to him), it is the painful gift of the children that substantially furthers Vessantar's moral development. As a result of the gift, Vessantar is understood to have finally perfected the *pāramī* or virtues necessary for future rebirth as a buddha, an enlightened teacher who can spread his Dhamma to others, and thus lead them to enlightenment and the cessation of future births.

Writing from the end of the nineteenth century, Guesdon reports that the *Vessantar-jātak*[45] was one of the "most highly esteemed" of all Khmer texts, and Leclère suggests it was not only the "most important" and "most beautiful" text, but also "the most popular of Cambodian books," one that was known by everyone, through recitations at temples, through murals that filled numerous temple walls, and through theatrical productions. It was "the text *(satra)* that the monks read most often to the laypeople, on certain holidays during the year, and the one that the Cambodian people like best to hear."[46] Leclère adds that the traits of individual characters from the story were so universally recognized that they were used to tease children and as shorthand descriptors: a mention of Jūjak-brahmin could silence unruly children; a devoted mother was a "Maddī," a generous person a "Vessantar"; an old man married to a young woman was a "Jūjak."[47] Leclère's ethnographic comments on recitations of the *Vessantar-jātak* provide a rare and vivid account of how contemporary audiences responded to the text:

> The assembled congregations are rarely silent in Cambodia and . . . when a monk reads a *satra* to the laity, it is not unusual to hear throat-clearing, sneezing, and even talking. . . . [But when the *Vessantar-jātak* is read] . . . the silence is profound and nothing can distract the attention of the listeners. . . .
>
> In the sad passages, the voice of the monk alters, and one can hear sighs all around him. But where one must see the behavior of the audience is when he reaches [the passages] concerning the little children, when, hidden under lotus leaves in the water, their father calls them in order to give them as alms to Jūjak . . . , when they plead with their father not to give them away, when the cruel brahmin beats them. Then, there are tears in every eye, and one hears the sobs; the monk halts to catch his breath, the women dab their eyes with the edges of their scarves, silently, and the men pass the back of their hands across their cheeks. . . . The despair of the mother who searches for her children and who cannot recover them reaches the mammas, and it is not unusual to see one of them, very emotionally, clasp her child to her bosom in defense against Jūjak-brahmin, the Cambodian bogeyman.[48]

The Vessantar story, so well-known to Khmer audiences in its various textual, visual, and theatrical versions, may have described an act that made mothers pull their children closer, but it also articulated a vision of a larger world in which this act could make sense. Vessantar was not understood as an individual father who loved his children but as a being moving through a cosmic universe and time frame toward purification and perfection in which he finally achieves perfection of his last *pāramī,* generosity, by giving away his children as slaves to Jūjak.[49] For those who knew the trajectory of the Bodhisatta's perfection of giving, as Khmer audiences of the period would have done, this moment in the text is not simply the climax of one story, but of many. Other *jātaka* stories reveal the Bodhisatta's gifts of alms, wealth, food, his eyes, other body parts, or his entire body; still others depict the Bodhisatta giving away his wife and himself as slaves. While these gifts, in various *jātaka* stories, are often given blithely, the gift of the children is by contrast portrayed as far more difficult—because "children are the very best gift."[50] In a Khmer verse version of the story,[51] the depth of Vessantar's grief is conveyed with the single line, "Then, Prince Vessantar the Ksatriya, having given his gift, went inside the leaf hut, and sad, pitiful weeping could be heard."[52]

Another vernacular manuscript of the story[53] expands on Vessantar's grief, drawing out the description of his pain and detailing the development of his emotions and thoughts before and after he gives the gift of the children. For instance, in one passage Vessantar is shown caressing his children and saying,

> Oh my precious children, you do not know your father's heart. If he gives you as alms to the brahmin, it is for nothing less than the aspiration one day to be the Lord Buddha himself. Oh my children, if your father can become a buddha, he will deliver the condemned who are in the hells and he will give them the means of taking birth in the heavens.[54]

As he finishes this speech, Vessantar takes the hands of his two children and stretches them out to place them in the hands of Jūjak, the Brahmin. Then he picks up a container of water and sprinkles some of it on the earth. At this moment, the earth quakes, trees tremble; the waters of the oceans churn, form into whirlpools, and rise up in the air; and Mount Sumeru bows down, touching its summit to the peak of nearby Mount Vongkot.[55] As he listens to the laments of his children being led away and beaten, Vessantar cries,

> "Alas! I am like a great fish, caught in a net, like a fish that cannot come or go, cannot advance or retreat. Now that I have given my children as alms, I can not take them back. I cannot. . . . The suffering in my heart is immense. I cannot aspire to become Lord Buddha now, because my suffering is too great. I will shoot an arrow at this brahmin, I will kill him, and I will retrieve my children and bring them back here."[56]

As he considers this course of action, Vessantar reflects on the giving of gifts, and then recalling the four kinds of gifts that every Buddha in every *kapp* has given—the gift of his person, the gift of his life, the gift of his children, and the gift of his wife—he is able to collect himself and calm his mind, finally becoming "beautiful like a true Lord Buddha."[57] In this version of the text, the episode ends with Jūli (Jāli) telling his younger sister Kresna (Kaṇhājīna),[58] as they are led away by the Brahmin,

> "Oh Kresna . . . the ancients have said, and this applies well to us: 'Children who have been separated from their mother are like those without a mother. Those who have a father but are separated from him are like those without a father.' By going with this brahmin, it is as though you and I have neither father nor mother."[59]

Leclère concludes from comparisons with contemporary Sri Lankan and Siamese versions of the story that this passage represents a distinctive Khmer addition to the text.[60] He notes that in the nineteenth century, monk-scribes tended to stay close to the text of the manuscript they were copying or translating, particularly if it was a Pali text, since few monks knew Pali well, but that a copyist or translator might choose to develop subjects he found particularly engaging. Guesdon's assessments of Khmer translation practices concur, although he concludes that Khmer copyists had "no scruples" about altering texts, either out of misunderstanding of the Pali or because of the "exigencies of Khmer versification," which might necessitate changes for the sake of creating harmonious rhymes and meters. As a result, he writes, it was "very difficult" to find even two identical copies of the same texts.[61] It is not far-fetched to surmise that a copyist's or translator's additions signify a moment in which, from his viewpoint, the image in the text is crucial to understanding the text but is either insufficiently emphasized in its present form or is in some sense incomprehensible to Khmer audiences. This kind of elaboration is thus suggestive of the Khmer religious imagination of the period, both through emphasis on points of great interest to Khmer audiences and through the translation of imagery to the vernacular.

Given the well-documented ritual usage of versions of the *Vessantar-jātak* in merit-making ceremonies such as funerals, where merit was traditionally transferred to the deceased, this latter vernacular rendering of the text contains a tension that adds to its already compelling literary aspects and perhaps helps to explain how and why the text acted with such force on its audience. The children's aloneness in the midst of Vessantar's merit making seems to emphasize that each individual is unprotected or alone in the fruition of his or her own karma. When we step outside the Buddhist logic of the progress of moral perfection, it appears that not even a virtuous father who loves his children can protect them from cruelty. Yet when Vessantar sprinkles water on the ground within the story to signify the merit he has earned by giving the gift of the children, this mirrors the ritual sprinkling of water by monks in Khmer rites of preaching the story to signify that merit has been made by those who have listened to the recitation. This is merit that they can transfer to help deceased loved ones who are alone and unprotected in the fruition of their karma.

Both the literary and ritual dimensions of the *Vessantar-jātak* suggest that one person's actions affect others. The effort to both depict and ritually mitigate the stark aloneness and lack of protection of the children may reflect the ethos of the times, a period of unrest and uncertainty in which few people could effectively control their own moral destinies. The way in which individuals' moral actions are intertwined in this story to form a kind of cosmic moral community contrasts with the depiction of moral relationship that is expressed in modernist writings of the 1920s. In these later texts, the interconnections between the actions of different individuals for shaping collective experience are represented in terms of intertwining causal acts and results in the everyday world. By contrast, in the *Vessantar-jātak,* the idea that one person's acts have cosmic moral reverberations is depicted quite literally, in the quaking of the earth, the churning of the waters, and the act of obeisance performed by Mount Sumeru.

For the parents holding their children, this series of climactic scenes in the *Vessantar-jātak* perhaps provided textual and ethical moments in which it was possible for those in the audience to recognize their own interdependence. When Vessantar gives away his children, all beings in the three realms and even the physical landscape of the earth itself are shown to be joined together. For the characters within the story, Vessantar's act of moral purification triggers a response of awe and astonishment that the text seems to want to project onto its audience:

> Then, the prince, with his heart glad, gave his two children, Jāli and Kaṇhājīnā, to the Brahmin, for children are the very best gift. Because of this, you should feel awestruck; your skin should be crawling and your hair standing on end because of that moment in which the prince gave his two children as a gift and the earth trembled and shook.[62]

The enormity of this moment, with its cosmic reverberations, is reiterated again in terms that extend to and include the celestial world of the *Trai Bhūm* cosmography as well, delighting the gods, as Vessantar's wife Maddī recounts,

> My Lord [Braḥ Aṅg] has caused the earth to reverberate, your fame[63] reaching all the way to the *deva*-world, unusual lightning spreading across the sky of the Hemavānt Forest, an echoing voice resounding as if from the mountains [themselves].
>
> Gods in both realms, Nārada and Pabbata, together with Braḥ Indra and Braḥ Brahm, Pajāpati and Soma, King Yāma and King Vessavāṅ, all rejoice because of you; all the gods who were born in the Tāvatiṃsa heaven, together with Braḥ Indra, rejoice.[64]

Again, in this scene, in which Vessantar's perfection of giving causes the celestial beings to rejoice and the earth itself to quake and rumble, the images employed by the text offer a glimpse of its assumptions about the underlying nature of reality: Vessantar's act has moral reverberations for all other beings because moral action gives meaning and order to the universe. Because the practice of Dhamma (the teaching that Vessantar will give once he is a Buddha) shapes the nature and passing of time, the implications of this moment extend into and influence beings in the future and the past as well.

POWER AND MERIT IN BIOGRAPHIES OF THE BODHISATTA

The depiction of the morally constructed universe and individual progression through its cosmic spatial and temporal framework in these well-known texts was joined by a third theme related to moral development: the intertwining of merit and power. To examine the importance of this theme during the late nineteenth century, I will return briefly to the *Vessantar-jātak* and then move to a reading of portions of a vernacular poem on the enlightenment of the Buddha, composed at the close of the century by Ukñā Suttantaprījā Ind. Its assertion of the moral construction of world and person at the end of the century coincides with the decline of the political structures in society that reduplicated similar hierarchical notions of power, merit, and social organization. By considering the issue of power, I begin reading the texts as sources for Cambodian political history, a reading that also allows their ethical themes to be interpreted in a more nuanced manner.

Returning to the *Vessantar-jātak*—the prince's sojourn in the forest had come about after his angry subjects had banished him for giving away an auspicious rain-making elephant to a nearby drought-stricken kingdom. After the gift of the children takes place, Vessantar continues to live in the forest with his wife Maddī. Meanwhile, his children are discovered and redeemed by their grandfather, King Sañjay, who accompanies the children and a large retinue of followers to the forest to find Vessantar and Maddī. When Vessantar is reunited with his parents and children, accompanied by the roar of the earth and a rain shower from the *devas*, his subjects become aware of his virtue and implore him to come back and take his rightful place as their king:

> When the royal family was reunited, a loud thundering sound arose, all the mountains made a noise, the entire earth trembled. At that time, the very moment when Prince Vessantar was reunited with his family, rain was compelled to fall in a shower. The reunion of the grandchildren, daughter-in-law, the prince, and the king and queen at that point in time would make your skin crawl and your hair stand up. All of the townspeople who had come together into the forest arranged their hands together [in a gesture of respect] toward Prince Vessantar, weeping, their faces awestruck, and implored the royal Vessantar and Maddī. The entire populace of the kingdom spoke all together, saying, "Braḥ Aṅg, our Lord and Lady. Please, both of you, rule over our kingdom."[65]

Here again, the earth quakes and the mountains roar (causing everyone's skin to crawl) as a testimony to the store of merit required to reunite the royal family. Realizing their past mistake—their inability to recognize Vessantar's merit—the same townspeople who caused him to be exiled beg him to become their king. The recognizable superiority of his power is clearly linked to his asceticism, purity, generosity, and merit.

Vessantar is not only filled with merit (signified by the roaring and quaking of natural phenomena) but is also indifferent to worldly kinds of power. If Vessantar can give away both his rain-making elephant and his precious children, and live serenely in the forest, he is obviously impervious to the means through which power can corrupt. His indifference, his merit, and his recognition of the higher truth of Dhamma make him an ideal ruler.

Aspects of this same logic about merit, power, and kingship pervade many other texts of the period. *Rýaṅ Jinavaṃs* (The story of Jinavaṃs)[66] and *Rýaṅ Rājakul* (The story of Rājakul),[67] for instance, provide models of the kind of highly vernacular adventure story in which a bodhisatta-prince is lost or exiled or has his identity otherwise obscured. After many travails in which he is always victorious because of his merit and virtue, he is returned to his kingdom to take his place as ruler. When his life is threatened, he always survives; he always wins the beautiful, virtuous princess; he is always dutiful, respectful, and wise, and furthers the cause of justice.

Perhaps the most highly idealized vision of the intertwining of power and merit is found in the biography of the Buddha in his last birth as Siddhattha, born into the Sākyan Gotama clan, in which he finally attains moral perfection and the knowledge of awakening. A Southeast Asian rendering of the biography is found in the *Paṭhamasambodhi,* a text composed in Bangkok by the supreme patriarch of the Thai Sangha in the mid-nineteenth century (though based on older versions of the biography).[68] The Khmer translation of this biography had appeared in various versions in Cambodia by the end of the nineteenth century. Leclère calls the *Paṭhamasambodhi* "the principal text of religious education" among the Khmer,[69] and as in the case of the *Vessantar-jātak,* notes the enraptured silence of the audience, including children, as they listened to recitations of the text that he observed.[70] He received a prose manuscript version of the *Paṭhamasambodhi* from the supreme patriarch of the Khmer Sangha, Samtec Braḥ Sangharāj Diaṅ, which he found to be in close correspondence with current versions of the text circulating in Siam and Burma during the same period; his comments indicate that this particular version of the biography was well-known in Cambodia.[71]

This prose version of the *Paṭhamasambodhi* spans the entire career of Gotama Buddha, including his moral development as a bodhisatta until the time of his death and *parinibbāṇa.* While the text reviews his bodhisatta heritage, including his life as Vessantar and the next birth in Tuṣita heaven, it also traces his noble lineage as the son of a king, eventually merging the spiritual and worldly lineages in the figure of Vessantar. Siddhattha's noble lineage begins with the founding kings of Kapilavatthu, is then traced to Vessantar and through Vessantar's children Jāli and Kaṇhājīnā (who in this text, marry), through their offspring and 82,000 successive generations to the great-grandparents of King Sudhodan and Māyā, the parents of Gotama Buddha, both of whom are understood to be the direct descendants of Jāli and Kaṇhājīnā. In this version of the text, the Bodhisatta speaks as soon as he is born, saying, "I am on the summit of the world . . . no one can be compared to me; I am in my last birth, I will return no more to the world."[72] His father, King Sudhodan, calls at once for a Brahmin, who makes calculations based on the *Trai Pheṭ* and other brahmanic texts and then prophesies, "Your holy and royal son shows all the signs of auspiciousness: if he remains a layperson he will become a king of the earth, a *cakra patrarāj;* if he leaves the world for the religious life, he will become a Lord Buddha, that is certain."[73]

The intersection of the two noble lineages of the Buddha emphasizes his possession of both spiritual and worldly forms of power, suggesting the manner in which these two aspects of power are conceptually merged in the portrait of exemplary moral development.[74] A virtuous merit-filled person is powerful; a powerful person must necessarily be meritorious.[75] The text also details the karmic construction of identity, with every aspect of the Bodhisattva's biography traceable to past events. Even the name Siddhattha was determined by moral actions performed in a former birth, in a former *kappa.* In a birth as the younger sister of the bodhisatta Dīpaṅkāra, the future Gotama Buddha offered oil to the future Dīpaṅkāra Buddha, vowing to take the name of Siddhat[76] when she some day became a buddha.[77] Just as the text makes sense of the present life of the Buddha through past moral action, other characters, too, are depicted traveling through this cosmic time frame. The Buddha travels to the celestial realms to preach a sermon for the benefit of his deceased mother, who has assumed a new identity as a deity in the Tuṣita heaven.[78] At another point in the story, the Buddha encounters the levitating figure of Ajita-kumara, a son of Ajātasattu (the patricidal disciple of Devadatta who later recants and becomes a disciple of the Buddha), and recognizes him as the future Buddha Metteya.[79]

These examples suggest a manner of thinking about individuality that moves fluidly through time, backward and forward through past, future, and present, intertwining the stories and lives of multiple characters from different points in time into an entangled, interconnected web of causation from which it becomes difficult to isolate one or another individual from the lifetimes and events of others. The conception of individuality found in the *Paṭhamasambodhi* is a web of such intersecting identities, resembling the literary form of the many Khmer oral and textual stories concerning the cosmic biography of the Buddha that intersect and elaborate on each other, appearing in many respects as one massive trunk story with thousands of branches rather than distinct stories about different, unconnected individuals.

Another venacular version of the *Paṭhamasambodhi* is an epic poem titled the *Rȳaṅ Paṭhamasambodhi* (History [or story] of the *Paṭhamasambodhi*), probably written in the 1880s or 1890s by Ukñā Suttantaprījā Ind. The text offers a distinctive Khmer verse elaboration of scenes from the life of the Buddha. As a text composed primarily for entertainment, it functioned somewhat differently from Leclère's version of the *Paṭhamasambodhi,* which was read to lay audiences assembled in monasteries. Like some of Ind's other poems, the *Rȳaṅ Paṭhamasambodhi* was composed as a literary work but seems to have circulated in oral as well as manuscript (and later printed) forms. In trying to reconstruct elements of Ind's biography in Battambang Province, where he passed much of his life and where many of his descendants remain, I met one of Ind's grand-nephews who could still recite portions of Ind's work from memory. An elderly man when I first met him in 2000, he remembered going to the monastery with other youths in his village to memorize Ind's poetry for recitation. Working from a manuscript version of the poem stored in the monastery library, the young men would copy a portion of the poem on a wooden slate made from painted kapok wood,[80] writing with a form of locally produced chalk. Once they had memorized that portion of the poem, they would repaint the slate and copy out a new section to learn.[81]

Although composed primarily for "entertainment" and circulated in this partially oral form, a poem such as the *Rȳaṅ Paṭhamasambodhi* still maintained religious authority, as did any text inscribed on palm leaf during this preprint period in Cambodia. In addition to the sacrality connected with writing itself, the poem concerned the life of the Buddha, and it was known to be translated from the Pali biography by a well-known Pali scholar and religious thinker. Thus, although the text circulated somewhat differently and might be heard in informal settings outside the monastery, its religious authority nonetheless functioned similarly to that of other texts I have discussed in this chapter.

While explicitly concerned with relaying the events leading up to the Buddha's enlightenment, the poem's presentation of the intertwining notions of merit, kingship, and moral perfection—with the imagery of the three worlds cosmography as its backdrop—makes it worth exploring as a source for understanding identity and power at the close of the nineteenth century. Further, the text depicts idealized notions of power at a time when the real power of Khmer elites in Cambodia and Siamese-controlled Khmer regions was being constrained by the introduction of administrative reforms aimed at centralizing power and effecting other profound changes in social and political organization. In this historical context, the poem can be read as a vernacular response to these sociopolitical pressures.

The text opens with a brief description of the kind of magnificent worldly *(lokiya)* power possessed by the Buddha in his life as Siddhattha, a prince of the Sākyan tribe:

> We will illuminate from the beginning
> the time in which our Lord and King of the World
> experienced the peace and wealth of a *khattiyā*
> in the great city of Kapilavatthu.
>
> His royal lineage
> conferring glorious, noble, and exalted position,
> he [conferred] glorious and delightful paternal joy
> on the *mahā purus* [king] ruling the city.
>
> Tranquilly, he slept with his concubines,
> occupied with playing music;
> his royal consort
> was a princess called Bimbā.
>
> The chief of women was a jewel of a maiden,
> her body was endowed with beauty;
> she had a flourishing son
> whose name was Prince Rāhul.
>
> Noble merit, glorious merit without end,
> splendid beyond compare in all respects;

one hundred and one in his entourage
offering tributes to the precious prince.

In ten directions there was awe of his great power,
there were none whose power could rival his;
the prince who ruled from the palace,
little more than twenty-nine years old.[82]

In the poem, Siddhattha suddenly leaves his royal palace and position behind after apprehending the inevitable suffering of human existence in the form of illness, aging, and death. The rest of the text is devoted to a depiction of the Bodhisatta's progress toward attaining "*bodhi*-knowledge"[83] or enlightenment. While the poem presents Siddhattha as one who never wavers from his goal of "seeking out the fruit of his own path, a Noble Way / to the peace of *nibbāṇa,* which is happiness,"[84] the jealous god Mārā attempts to deter him with threats, force, and reminders of the wordly pleasures, emotions, and powers he will have to renounce. Once it becomes clear that the Bodhisatta will soon become enlightened, a crowd of "large and small gods" gather to observe him. Mārā, informed of the Bodhisatta's impending achievement, vows to prevent him from attaining purification. He leaves the *deva*-realm to confront the prince in the forest and tries to cajole him to go back to his palace:

"Oh Prince Siddhattha, son of Sudhodan,
don't be stupid, leading a renouncer's life!
In seven more days, a gem-wheel[85] will appear
signifying that a wheel-turning monarch[86] will arise.

"This is why you should return to your kingdom;
don't go falling in love with the *Buddha*-wheel.[87]
It is far more fitting that you love your position and rank;
big wheels[88] are powerful in the world!"[89]

At that, Lord Glorious and Splendid Prince of Men,[90]
He who was to be Enlightened,[91]
after hearing Mārā-māyā speak,
gave this reply:

"Hail Mārā-māyā; do not come here to obstruct me;
I will not follow your advice.
I have no desire to become a big wheel
as [impure] as saliva and urine.[92]

"I have come here desiring *bodhi*-knowledge[93]
as a bridge for other beings to cross over;

Mārā, don't come here to try and tie me
with a fetter that can never be joined.

"Will you please get away from me, Mārā;
my cart of impurities[94]
has only one broken axle remaining,
I will soon open a pathway for beings to tread."[95]

Mārā's speech evokes well-known episodes of the Buddha's biography that are left out of this poetic version of the story but that the Khmer audience would surely have known from other accounts. Here, the passage alludes to the prophecy given to Sudhodan upon Siddhattha's birth that his son was destined to become either a world-renouncing Buddha or a wheel-turning world emperor. Preferring the latter destiny, Sudhodan had, as the well-known story recounts, sequestered him away behind palace walls and surrounded him with the lavish beauty and comfort that his son now sought to renounce. The gem-wheel to which Mārā refers in the poem is connected with the iconography of the *cakkavattin* king. According to the *Trai Bhūm* and the *Cakkavatti-sīhanāda-sutta* (from the *Dīgha Nikāya*), the *cakkavattin* is accompanied by seven signs, including a jewel-encrusted gem-wheel that rises into the sky glowing like a second moon.[96] In this latter text, studied and translated by Steven Collins, the *cakkavattin* is depicted in alternating terms of his greatness and righteousness. On the one hand, he is a world-conquering hero, with his armies, seven emblems of power, and one thousand virulent sons, "crushing enemy armies." On the other hand, he will rule the world "without violence," relying on the power of the Dhamma rather than that of a sword.[97]

The righteousness of a wheel-turning king is dependent on his understanding, practice, and propagation of the Dhamma or, as Collins has translated it, "what is right":[98]

> depend on what is right (Dhamma), honor and respect it, praise it, revere and venerate it, have Dhamma as your flag, Dhamma as your banner, govern by Dhamma. . . . Let no wrongdoing take place in your territory; if there are poor people in your territory, give them money.[99]

The *sutta* goes on to admonish the king to seek out teachings on what is right from Brahmins and ascetics, and follow their teachings, and then concludes, "[A]void what is bad. . . . You should take up what is good and do that. That is the noble turning of a Wheel-turning king."[100]

As Collins has pointed out in his analysis of Buddhist felicities, different interrelated texts evoking the *cakkavattin* imagery make somewhat different claims about the relationship between *cakkavattin* kings and the appearance of buddhas.[101] In the *Trai Bhūm,* for instance, a *cakkavattin* is said to arise only in *kappa*s in which there are no buddhas.[102] According to the *Cakkavatti-sīhanāda-sutta,* however, the Buddha Metteya will arise during the reign of the *cakkavattin* king Saṅkha, who, under the influence of the Buddha's teaching, will give up his throne and become a world renouncer himself.[103] While kings in Buddhist literature are often depicted as possessors of almost unlimited power, righteous kings such as the future Saṅkha and King Nemi of the *Nemi-jātak* recognize the intrinsic limitations of worldly power and the superiority of the path of world renunciation. Righteous kings, in this idealized conception, always defer to buddhas.

It is this moral contrast between kings and buddhas that the poet of the *Rýaṅ Paṭhamasambodhi* wants to convey; kings are powerful because they are meritorious, but ultimately, what makes them just is their recognition that there is a greater power that gives meaning and coherence to the world. The struggle between Siddhattha and Mārā that forms the poem's dramatic action is a contest for possession of the jeweled throne spontaneously generated in one of the Bodhisatta's past lives when, already "filled to the brim with perfections,"[104] he made a vow to teach others a path toward *nibbāṇa*. Yet while the poem takes pains to accentuate the majesty of kingship, even the immense splendor and power of a great king who is destined to become a *cakkavattin* appears as repulsive as "saliva and urine" when compared to the power generated by a buddha through the cultivation of moral purity.

The full contrast between these two forms of power is strikingly rendered in the dramatic last stanzas of the poem, which evoke the inexorable connections among human action, merit, and the landscape of the world itself. In this poem, the imagery of the three-tiered cosmos is deployed to indicate significant moral revelations in the texts. When the earth shakes and quakes, the mountains roar, the earth wrings out ritual water from her hair, or the unseen heavens, hells, or other continents are on view, the text is working to reveal the underlying nature of the world: it is morally constructed, shaped by human moral action; its cosmic temporality is connected with the gradual cultivation of perfection by buddhas; individuals are reborn in it according to their accumulation of merit. In this case, Mārā appears as a king at the head of his forces, but as a deity, his power as a king is hyperbolized even beyond that of a human king. His soldiers are not mere soldiers, but *yakkha*[105] who have the ability to transform themselves into monkeys, *nāga*,[106] *garuḍā*,[107] snakes, and savage tigers in order to "display the power of all the three worlds";[108] their mounts are not mere horses and elephants, but the offspring of mythical beasts and wild animals.[109] As they surround Siddhattha, Mārā begins his campaign to unseat Siddhattha from his jeweled throne:

> Thinking, "Siddhattha possesses merit.
> Seeing an enemy with merit is very strange indeed;
> that being the case, the only course for me is to distort the truth,
> to accuse him of seizing my throne."
>
> Thinking thus, Prince Mārā readied his speech,
> and advanced to the royal prince named Siddhattha;

"You there, sitting upon the jeweled throne;
it is not at all suitable for you to be seated there.

"The jeweled throne is mine
and exists to elevate me in the world;
why have you come to take as yours a throne
unsuitable to the level of merit you possess?"[110]

At that time, all during that time,
the Lord Buddha endowed with Royal Rank[111]
listened to his enemy Mārā-māyā accuse him
and lay claim to the Throne reserved for One who Possesses the Qualities of a Teacher.

Then a smile lit his lovely royal face
and in a friendly manner toward the *yakkha,* not at all perturbed:
"Greetings, Mārā; why are you negotiating,
falsely claiming 'this jeweled throne is mine'?

"This throne arose by means of the merit
I firmly established in previous lives.
Why, Mārā, have you appeared to reprimand me?
I have only to call forth a witness."[112]

Menacingly, Mārā draws his forces closer and challenges Siddhatta to produce a witness. The text continues:

At that time, that very time,
the Lord Prince of Men Supreme in Wisdom[113]
answered Mārā so as to bar him from seizing the throne,
"I call upon Dharaṇī as my lovely witness.[114]

"When I established holy perfections
I took the earth as my authority,
pouring water to commemorate celestial knowledge,
I then received this very throne."[115]

When Mārā realizes whom the Buddha has called as his witness, he switches tactics and begins to make rude insinuations:

Prince Mārā spoke derisively,
mocking and leering at the Lord Supreme Master of the Three,[116]
"Hey Siddhattha endowed with moral behavior;[117]
why are you taking a woman as your witness?

"Aren't you One who has Established Progress?
And you have a woman as such a very close friend
that you're willing to depend on her as your witness,
to set up a woman as your representative?!"

At that moment, that very moment,
the lovely celestial maiden Nāṅ Dharaṇī,
hearing Mārā's lewd mockery,
to Mārā quickly directed her reply. . . .

"Yes, I am the Lord's woman witness
and I support that he has cut passion away;
as he gained *bodhi*-knowledge bit by bit,
I knew of each action he made.

"One time, filled to the brim with perfections
he sprinkled water on the earth and solemnly [vowed]
once enlightened, to become a Teacher
and the jeweled throne clearly arose [from that vow].

"And you, have you not established something
to which any dare testify?!"
Having spoken thus, she untied her long tresses
and taking them up [with her arms upright], handful by handful, wrung
them out on Mārā's horde.

The power and force of Nāṅ Dharaṇī
flowed out magnificently [from her hair],
arising immense as an ocean
engulfing entirely the army of Mārā.

Pity the forces of Mārā drowning in the River Ganga;
such suffering and misery is beyond compare.
Some die by drowning, others' bodies slashed apart by swordfish,
some, contorted and dismembered by the force of the water, simply
disappear.

Others are trampled by horses and elephants,
legs and arms broken off, stomachs pierced through;
some become victims of *nýak,*[118] *nāga*s and sharks,
their blood flowing across the surface of Lady Water and Lady Earth.

Flood water reaching up to the level of the atmosphere,
the dead soldiers of Mārā spread across the earth's globe,

only the king of the *asuras* himself remained
with Father Mountain and Mother Sea.

During the time these events unfolded
Mārā king of the *asuras*
understood his forces were utterly spent
as he watched the horrible suffering of his army 200,000-strong.

Fearful he grew that the Lady of Water
would unleash the flood against his life [too];
the *asura* became softhearted toward the Bodhi,
his powerful aggression toward the Teacher all gone.

"Please younger brother I press my hands together in earnest
in front of [Father] Mountain and Mother Sea;
I will write a *sūtra* enumerating the qualities
of the Jewel-Lord, the Fully-Enlightened Arahant."

Thus, Prince Mārā, defeated by merit,
established respect for the Buddha-*guṇa,*[119]
accepted going-for-refuge[120] as [the means] for bringing an end to existence,
and returned to the dwelling place of the gods.[121]

This scene in the poem, visually well-known from its many artistic representations in Southeast Asia,[122] presents the final test of the Bodhisatta's single-minded concentration on his goal of purification. Having already tried and failed to tempt the Bodhisatta with seductions by his three lovely daughters, Mārā, who is jealous, has turned to the use of force and deception to unseat the Buddha from the jeweled throne, even though, as the poet has him note, "seeing an enemy with merit is very strange indeed." The last portion of the poem, I have suggested, exemplifies conceptions of the two-tiered structure of power, the intertwining of power and merit, and the nature of the world as shaped by human moral action.

The linking of religious and royal authority in these passages is quite clearly articulated, first with the dual possibility of world domination or world renunciation, joined in the figure of Siddhattha, and second, with the contest for power between the two princes. Like a real, not idealized, worldly king—but again to a hyperbolized extent—Mārā is a morally ambivalent figure who is powerful, potentially malevolent, duplicitous, and selfishly jealous. In Khmer vernacular usage, he is understood as an "obstacle to progress or movement" or as death itself; he is also referred to as "the enemy of the Lord Buddha" and one who actively prevents others from "allowing merit and benefit to arise."[123] Yet Mārā is also clear-sighted enough to recognize the superior merit of the Bodhisatta, and he is intelligent and merit filled enough to concede defeat and take refuge in the spiritual power of the Buddha. The Bodhisatta rejects Mārā's offer to become a *cakkavattin* because "it is impure, like urine and saliva." A buddha's power, derived entirely from merit and purification, is far more potent than a king's power, overwhelming the kind of violent force (even in its hyperbolized form) that kings are able to generate. But in spite of the clear hierarchy in this two-tiered conception of power, the interlinking also ends up affirming the meritorious identity of kings, as scholars of the Theravāda have long noted. Kings may have to undertake some nasty actions in order to fulfill their duties as kings, but they must still be regarded as meritorious beings or they would not have taken rebirth as kings.

The poem's depiction of the comparative rankings of worldly and spiritual power asserts the traditional mores of Theravādin ideas concerning kingship, authority, and merit. Worldly power was supposed to be exercised, albeit reluctantly, by a virtuous prince who ruled according to Dhammic principles. His rule was just, and created harmony and prosperity for his kingdom's inhabitants. Dhammic power, greater than any form of worldly power, was the ultimate authority, giving order and meaning to existence. The harmony and prosperity of individuals in the world thus depended on the Dhammic linking of merit and power to create justice.

And yet in light of the sociopolitics of power and authority in a context of colonial control, it is difficult not to also read the poem's assertion of this idealized conception of power partly as a response to the tensions of the times, an expression of modern self-reflexivity about being caught up in history and in periods of transition. The poem affirms the image of a world that makes sense according to all the Buddhist theories of how reality functioned, with the present, past, and future determined by moral actions that ripen and bear fruit, like the spontaneous generation of the jeweled throne formed by the Buddha's enormous accumulation of merit. But the image in the poem of the ephemeral jeweled throne produced by merit and under siege by strange and violent forces may, like the larger preoccupation with order, merit, and power as literary themes in this period, in fact represent its fragility in the face of tumultuous change rather than its solid mooring as a model of and for social reality.

Khmer Buddhist nineteenth-century literary discourse represented individuals, the physical world, and time itself as interconnected, morally charged, and created by moral action. The texts that I have examined in this chapter were those that appear to have been among the most widely known texts in late-nineteenth-century Cambodia. Until the latter part of the nineteenth century, they also functioned as valid mental conceptions of the arrangement of space and power in Khmer society. But these conceptions of the arrangement and identity of social communities and individual selves were moored in a political world in upheaval, in which the moral and hierarchical arrangements of space and power described in the texts were coming unhinged.

The literary representations of intersecting notions of power, merit, and moral purity contrast with their historical political context, to which we now turn, in which French-initiated administrative reforms were severely curtailing the real power of Khmer elites. This contrast suggests a conceptual disjuncture between religious imagining at the end of the nineteenth century and real experiences and perceptions of power and uncertainty. This sense of disjuncture may have opened up a space for the development of modernist thought in the early twentieth century. With its critique of old traditions and its sense of urgency about finding new forms and frameworks for writing about moral purification, modernism could take hold because the explanatory power of these older conceptions was in some respects unsatisfactory.

2 Buddhist Responses to Social Change

The nineteenth century was a difficult and turbulent time in Cambodia. One Khmer official recounted in his memoir that by 1848, after decades of warfare,

> [t]he country was shattered. In every village, [people] struggled to find sources of income but could not. None of the rice farms or garden crops had been planted because everyone had been too afraid of Vietnamese and Siamese soldiers coming into the rice fields. . . . Entire villages were devastated, abandoned, deathly quiet. It was sorrowful and heart wrenching beyond description seeing the misery of widows with tiny children, their heads resting in their laps, whom they were powerless to feed.[1]

The literary preoccupation with depicting meritorious persons, righteous kings, and the immutability of karmic law in the latter part of this volatile century, I have suggested, might be read as a reaction to the instability of chaotic times and a growing uneasiness about the viability of these conceptions as descriptions of the world. The previous chapter considered Buddhist representations of human moral development within the spatial and temporal framework of a morally ordered, coherent cosmos. But this was not the world in which Khmer Buddhists found themselves living.

This chapter tries to chart a path through the nineteenth- and early-twentieth-century Khmer sociopolitical experience of warfare, slavery, colonial occupation, and political, religious, and social reform. It also examines several modes of Khmer Buddhist response to those events, particularly to historical events that caused significant change in Khmer society such as warfare, new systems of taxation, social reform, and colonial occupation. The responses to these events reflect the contours of a wider Buddhist discourse of social critique that was incorporated into Buddhist modernism. I argue in this chapter that the nineteenth and early twentieth centuries saw a progression of self-reflexive expressions of social change and criticism articulated in terms that were simultaneously Buddhist and modern. Thus although modernism rejected or substantially reconfigured many nineteenth-century Khmer Buddhist values, especially in respect to millenarianism and cosmicized notions of moral purification, in other important ways, the experiences of change in the nineteenth century and the critical discourses about them were part of its underpinning.

My discussion of Buddhist discourses of sociopolitical critique maps the shift from millenarian rebellions in the early and mid-nineteenth century to turn-of-the-century and later writings by Prince Yukanthor and Ukñā Suttantaprījā Ind on social and moral decay. As a widespread unifying feature of Buddhist modern experience throughout Southeast Asia, the extent to which millenarianism of this period can be seen as traditional is debatable. Although the complex of ideas connected with millenarianism such as the arrival of the fifth Buddha of the *kappa* and the associations between unrighteous rulers and natural calamities were clearly premodern Buddhist ideas, they came to be employed in historically particular ways in the nineteenth and early twentieth centuries.[2] Within Cambodia and along its borders, millenarian ideas fueled and shaped religious movements and rebellions that responded to historical currents of uncertainty and change, and protested against the shifting structures of power and new patterns of administrative centralization that marked this period.[3] As French colonial social and political control deepened at the end of the century, Buddhist intellectuals and elites in Cambodia also began to write critically about a degeneration of morality they perceived in modern Cambodia. Although in some cases they rejected millenarian ideas as ridiculous, their work implicitly drew on millenarianism's central ethical premise that social decay was caused by the movement of human communities away from practicing the Dhamma and toward un-Dhammic values and actions.

The uneasiness about rapid social change that finds expression in nineteenth-century Khmer sources in some respects resembles the sensations of anxiety and "fragmentation" identified in studies of modernity elsewhere that David Harvey (and others) associate with new modes of production and exchange, an altered experience of temporality, and new social mores and arrangements.[4] In broad terms, these factors were emerging in nineteenth-century Cambodia. Along with the expansion of global markets linked to colonialism, forms of bureaucratic reorganization in respect to religious and governmental institutions as well as efforts to centralize political administration were introduced at different points in the nineteenth century by the various Siamese, Vietnamese, Khmer, and French powers controlling Cambodia. These reforms challenged the underlying conceptions of the nature of reality, temporality, moral development, and power considered in chapter 1.[5] But the turmoil and change of the period was also the product of Cambodia's political vulnerability, which had led to decade after decade of war and violence. To situate the Cambodian experience in relation to other studies of modernity, then, it is necessary to look not only for the presence of the kinds of conditions, values, and aesthetics widely ascribed to modernity, but also to the particularity of the Khmer context: how Khmer modernity was shaped by the distinctive sociopolitics of the Khmer situation and how it drew on Buddhist ideas as a medium for fashioning new social values.

One significant component of the nineteenth-century experience of modernity was the geographical, ethnic, and political delineation of states. The century opened with violence and warfare precipitated by Siamese and Vietnamese efforts to keep Cambodia as a vassal state, in the traditional mode of political patronage. From 1848 to 1860, a relatively effective Khmer kingship was reinstated by a monarch who, with Siamese support, exerted authority in part through the classic Theravādin mode of renovating and purifying Buddhism. French protectorate rule commenced in 1863, and for the rest of the century, imperial efforts to rule via reformed central administrative authority met with continuous unrest in Cambodia. The social turbulence of much of the century contributed to the increasing fragility of the Khmer monarchy, a condition that intensified in the last quarter of the nineteenth century.

In Mās' description, it was not just landscapes and villages that were shattered by violence and social turmoil but also families and individuals; "my heart was broken," he wrote, recalling his emotional state in 1848.[6] Preoccupied with survival, the majority of the populace must have begun to feel the changes brought about by altered political organization only gradually. By the end of the century, however, reforms in state, regional, and local governance were making themselves evident in daily life at all levels of society through changes in tax collection and corvée labor requirements, the legal prohibition of slavery, and unprecedented social problems such as a steady rise in the level of opium addiction in the protectorate. The extent to which these changes were perceived as modern problems by the wider populace is debatable, but they seem to have contributed to an ethos of political and intellectual disquiet.

SOCIAL ORDER

Graphically referred to by one British diplomat of the time as the "dismembering of Kamboja," much of the precariousness of Khmer life in the early nineteenth century was the legacy of its geographical situation between the two rival powers of Siam and Vietnam.[7] Political power during this period in Southeast Asia was centered in the courts of kings and their vassals, while royally appointed governors and ministers levied taxes and corvée labor at the local level. The wars of the period, fought with armies raised by the provincial ministers and officials, caused massive destruction in many regions of Cambodia. Entire populations fled into the forest or were captured as prisoners of war and forcibly relocated with the conquering armies, the survivors destined for slavery.

A Khmer verse chronicle translated by David Chandler describes a Siamese attack on Phnom Penh in 1833:

> They took everything away, and burned what had been people's houses, until not one of them remained; they took off everyone's possessions, masters' and slaves' alike, and they carried off all the people until not a man was left.[8]

The poem continues with an account of a Vietnamese attack several years later. Khmer families, including the patroness whose experience the poem chronicles, were forced to flee into the forest to escape Vietnamese troops:

> Their misery was great. There was no food at all, no fish, no rice, nothing normal to stave off their hunger; instead, they dug for lizards, without pausing to think. . . . They hunted *saom* roots in the depths of the forest, and other roots as well to make into a kind of soup. . . . They ate like this until their hunger went away, but it was hard to swallow the food; they sat silently beside the road, intensely poor, and miserable.[9]

French and British sources, corroborated by Thai sources as well, indicate the high toll in human suffering that the relocations of such large populations engendered.[10] In his 1821–1822 journal of diplomatic visits to Siam and Cochinchina, John Crawfurd writes of the Siamese,

> [T]heir wars are conducted with odious ferocity. Prisoners of rank are decapitated, and those of the lower orders condemned to perpetual slavery, and labour in chains. The peasantry of an invaded country armed or unarmed, men, women, and children, are indiscriminately carried off into captivity, and the seizure of these unfortunate persons appears to be the principal object of the periodical incursions which are made into an enemy's territory.[11]

In 1834, a French priest named Father Régereau described the capture of Khmer prisoners by Siamese troops:

> The manner in which the Siamese make war is to seize all of the property that they encounter, to destroy and set fire to all of the places through which they pass, to take prisoners and slaves, ordinarily killing the men and seizing the women and children. . . . If during the journey, they cannot march further, they strike them, they maltreat them, they kill them, insensitive to their weeping and moaning, without pity they massacre the little children in sight of their mothers.[12]

The French civil servant and mapper August Pavie recorded an account of a forced march from Khmer captives he encountered in a Siamese village later in the century:

> Taken away from our fields under the pretext of war, we have lost everything by forced abandonment, by pillage: harvests, elephants, horses, cattle, all our belongings. Carried away here, marching for long weeks, all day, all night, receiving blows, without rice, we have left the majority of our elders, and likewise our children, dying or dead on the forest paths, without power to ease their dying misery, or to honor their remains.[13]

These accounts from different parts of the century bear enough similarity to convey something of the long-enduring anxieties of the period; warfare engendered loss and suffering for its victims and contributed to the "atmosphere of threat, physical danger, and random violence" Chandler perceives in his extensive reading of sources from the period.[14]

At the beginning of the nineteenth century, Cambodia's position relative to both its neighbors was extremely weak. During the first decades of the century, both Siam and Vietnam regarded Cambodia as a vassal kingdom and expected tribute from Cambodia's rulers.[15] Chronicles indicate that the Siamese and Vietnamese monarchs perceived the Khmer in remarkably similar terms, as an inferior civilization lacking in "laws and order" and liable to "constantly forget" those they do hold, "savages whose nature is evil and vicious, [who] as often as they submit, so often do they revolt."[16]

In the late eighteenth century, the Siamese, after repeated military incursions, had incorporated the northwestern Khmer provinces of Battambang and Siem Reap into their administrative control.[17] By the early 1800s, the Vietnamese had also begun to exert a quasi-colonial control in the southern and eastern regions of Cambodia, attempting to introduce Vietnamese administrative models, agricultural methods, and cultural forms to the Khmer.[18] Khmer resistance to these reforms led to uprisings beginning in 1836, as well as larger anti-Vietnamese rebellions in 1837–1839 and 1840–1841. At the same time, the Thai military presence in the northwest was increasing. Throughout the 1840s, warfare continued between Siamese and Vietnamese forces, with neither army able to take decisive control of the Khmer capital in Phnom Penh.[19] Finally, treaty negotiations between the Siamese and Vietnamese resulted in an agreement that the Khmer king would send annual tribute to both kingdoms.[20] The Vietnamese withdrew, and a Khmer prince named Ang Duong was placed on the throne in Udong in 1848. With a new emperor coming to power in Hue, Vietnamese interest and influence in Cambodia diminished, while on the Thai side, "relations between Siam and Cambodia have continued in a satisfactory manner," we learn from an 1864 Thai chronicle, making reference to the fact that Ang Duong had spent many years living among members of the Thai court.[21]

When King Ang Duong finally came to the throne, Tā Mās recalls that in his natal region,

> in [Langvaek] Province . . . where there had once been 150 houses, there were now only 60 or 50 or 25 left, and the population was much smaller than before. Novices and priests also suffered because the *vihāra*s had been plundered. Gold and silver buddhas had been removed, and soldiers had set fire to many *vihāra*s. In many places, the remaining *vatt* lacked roofs. Their roofs were sunken down and broken apart, allowing rain to come in on the monks. The monks had been unable to find anyone willing to repair the roofs because one war after another for fifty years had prevented it. . . . I myself was very poor, without any family.

> . . . I knew only suffering and misery. . . . I wanted to ordain in the discipleship of the Lord Buddha in a *vatt* in the town of Udong in order to have *magga-phala* [fruit from attainments on the Path] for my next life and to avoid having *akusala* [demerit] in this life, and to learn the purity of the Pali scriptures[22] and also to rid myself of *akusala*. But in Vatt Sotakorok there were no scriptures left. Fire and theft had destroyed some. The Siamese took some and the Vietnamese took some, and in the *vatt* where I was ordained as a *bhikkhu,* there remained only ignorant and backward monks. They had no interest at all in finding the *Vinaya-sātra* or *Abhidhamma* or *Tipiṭaka* texts.[23]

As a child growing up in the midst of warfare, Tā Mās, the son of a local official, had lost his grandfather, parents, brothers, and uncles to wars against the Vietnamese. His grandmother was abducted as a prisoner of war by the Siamese. Once peace was achieved in 1848, his response to the violence of his early life was to ordain as a *bhikkhu* and study scripture in an effort to purify himself. But as he describes it, his effort to turn to the Triple Gem of the Buddha, Dhamma, and Sangha for solace was complicated by the destruction of Buddhist material culture during the decades of warfare that preceded the reign of Ang Duong. The installation of the Siamese-oriented Ang Duong on the Cambodian throne brought the measure of peace to Cambodia suggested by Tā Mās' memoir, but the problems engendered by decades of warfare—such as poverty, loss, and the disrepair and disruption of social institutions and cultural traditions—left the monarchy weak and the kingdom vulnerable to further unrest.

Khmer historical sources suggest that Ang Duong regarded the renovation of Cambodian Buddhism as one of the most important dimensions of revitalizing and pacifying his kingdom.[24] Religious practice and ideology were harnessed at both individual and state levels as a means of restoring order and creating harmony. After more than a century of turbulence, the resumption of religious practices signaled a return to the rhythms of normal daily life. For individuals, as Tā Mās' memoir suggests, ordination was a means of purifying themselves and reorienting their lives after the suffering they had experienced. On a larger cultural scale, the revitalization of religious life was in part a political process, explicitly enacted to legitimize a new reign and confer charisma on its ruler. But it had a more practical and spiritual dimension as well. Activities such as the rebuilding of temples, the reestablishment of temple schools, the recollection and recopying of texts lost or destroyed during war, and, presumably, merit making for family members whose deaths could not be commemorated during wartime because of a lack of monks, ritual materials, and safe circumstances under which to perform religious ceremonies were part of the reconstitution of social order and meaning after the turmoil of warfare.[25]

Mās' memoir describes Ang Duong as a king "the inhabitants put their hope in," an exemplar of a Dhamma-king, "who keeps the Dhamma, lives a pure and clean life, and exhibits kindness and modesty."[26] Another chronicles emphasizes

Ang Duong's piety and benevolence as a patron of Buddhism in material, spiritual, and educational terms, describing the king as a man who had "a mania for construction," personally supervising the erection and renovation of the temples built under his patronage.[27] In 1859, the French naturalist Henri Mouhot writes of the extensive construction of temples and palaces in Udong, then the capital of the kingdom.[28] Other Khmer and European sources indicate that the interest in temple repair and construction begun by Ang Duong continued to flourish after his death. Records of the Garnier expedition (1866–1868) make mention of a recently constructed *vatt* in a town outside of Udong where "modern Cambodian art has unfurled all of its magnificence" (which was, however, in Garnier's eyes, still just "a pale reflection of what is displayed on the Siamese temples in Bangkok").[29] In 1861, at French insistence, Ang Duong's son and heir Norodom moved the capital to Phnom Penh, where new royal buildings, including Vatt Bodum Vadday, the central Dhammayut monastery of the kingdom, were established under his patronage. In the northwestern province of Battambang, inhabited by ethnic Khmer but remaining under Siamese political control until 1907, temple and stupa construction also flourished beginning in the mid-nineteenth century with the patronage of the Siamese-installed governor and Khmer aristocratic families.[30]

By the time of Ang Duong's death in 1860, the peace he had brokered had come undone. Ang Duong's son Norodom assumed the throne after his father's death, having made himself a vassal to the Siamese court with whom he had close ties. In the meantime, the French military presence in Cambodia had increased until finally, in 1863, the French, fearful of Thai expansionism and already installed in Vietnam, made political inroads in Cambodia through a protectorate treaty with Norodom. Throughout the rest of the century and especially after 1886, the monarch's real power diminished gradually as he was increasingly forced to rely on the French military to protect his interests against civil unrest. In spite of this arrangement, as far as the majority of Khmer were concerned, French interference in their daily lives was minimal since for the most part, the Khmer monarchy maintained its administration of the kingdom through the 1880s. This perception began to crumble in the mid-1880s with the introduction of French-initiated governmental reforms that sought to diminish the power of Khmer elites to administer and raise revenue from villages under their jurisdiction in the countryside.

The upheavals of the nineteenth century, moving from the decades of war with Siam and Vietnam into a series of rebellions later, were chaotic not only because of the uncertainty and violence that warfare entailed but also because of the toll inflicted on the hierarchical sociopolitical order. Although scholars of Southeast Asia have perhaps overstated the extent to which the *Trai Bhūm* conception of cosmography alone has dominated the spatial imagination of Southeast Asians,[31] Khmer social and political relationships during this period were nonetheless hierarchical and expressive of a map of the moral cosmos with a righteous king at its center.[32] Before the creation of the modern Southeast Asian states around the beginning of the twentieth century, it has been suggested, kingdoms were largely unbounded, with vacillating borders and fluid spheres of influence. Termed "mandalas" or "galactic polities" by some scholars, these kingdoms were patterned on the reduplication of the ordered cosmic hierarchies discussed in chapter 1. The most powerful kingdoms (in terms of military, economic, agricultural, and cultural dominance) served as the centers. Power radiated out and away from the centers to weaker surrounding principalities that signaled their vassal status by paying annual tribute in the form of gifts such as trees crafted from gold and silver, local products such as cardamom and lacquer, and corvée labor.[33]

As late-nineteenth-century literary representations asserted, organization in society was hierarchically arranged, based on the ideal that one's social standing and circumstances in life were linked to one's moral virtue and religious practice. Although the legitimacy of this notion was perhaps becoming strained, throughout the nineteenth century Cambodia was a highly stratified "vertical" society in which a few people wielded power over most of the rest of the population. But the Buddhist ideal of the *cakkavattin* necessitated that the king act as the moral fulcrum of the kingdom as well as its political center. To be king involved the promulgation of benefit—of merit—for the whole kingdom, largely through acts that promoted religion such as building temples and collecting Buddhist texts, acts that were moral imperatives besides being politically wise.

With the king occupying the position of greatest authority, the Khmer court was divided into departments or houses, in which the highest-ranking members of the court—the king, the *mahā obhayārāj* or "second king,"[34] the *mahā oparāj* or "heir apparent," and the first queen—each had control over a certain number of high officials and the provinces that fell under their respective jurisdictions. The provinces were divided into subunits known as *sruk* (districts), consisting of several *bhūmi* (villages). Each province was administered by a royally appointed governor with lesser officials under him at the district and village levels. These officials were joined by other ministers with higher and lower grades of rank such as *ukñā,* who owed allegiance to various members of the royal family and had duties ranging from tax collection to writing poetry. Each of the titles that might be conferred on nobility carried with it a certain insignia or degree of honor, *huban,* that in combination with the royal house from which the title was issued, rendered one official clearly "above" or "below" another.[35] There were lower-ranking officials as well, such as judges, who were appointed locally by the governor or one of his underlings. Technically, anyone could be appointed to offices, but in reality, officials were selected largely according to the functioning of what has been termed a "patron-client system": as a reward for services rendered or favors done, or in response to gifts presented to a higher-ranking patron or the king. Although heredity was not always a factor in the transmission of titles, in many cases sons tended to inherit the offices of their fathers or were able to gain access to other favorable positions because they came from well-placed families with court or regional connections.[36]

The system held together, observed one contemporary French official, as tenuously as all governments on earth, based on a ritual known as *bhik-dik-sampath,* "drinking the water of the oath."[37] Twice each year, members of the court and regional officials gathered in the capital to swear allegiance to the king by reciting an oath in which they promised loyalty in thought, deed, and military support and by drinking water that had been sacralized by the king's brahmanic priests who soaked weapons in the water to be administered. Just as the behavior of the king was linked to the well-being of both the state and the Dhamma, the nobles' duties went beyond supplying armies and corvée labor. They were expected to behave as moral exemplars, upholders of the Dhamma and Sangha as well as the king. The politico-moral dimensions of taking the oath, and its reverberations at all levels of society, are evident in the oath itself:

> If enemies make attempts against the kingdom, and if I do not rush to its defense; if, in the same case, I hide myself, and if by my example, I give birth to sentiments of fear, of terror among the people, I will no longer be worthy of being your servant.[38]

The overlapping of politics with the *kammic* hierarchy of the three-tiered universe was further evidenced in the oath by the punishment invoked for those who failed in their duties to the king:[39]

> I invite the angels of the villages, those of the trees, the good and evil spirits, the genies of the air and of the wind, the lords of the four cardinal points, the goddess of the earth, all of the devils and demons, . . . to take away my life if I am ever unfaithful. If I break my oath, may I be reborn in a miserable condition and may I, in this world, be struck with lightning from the sky, bitten by caimans and other voracious animals . . . may I die wretchedly and without a funeral, or finally, may I be killed by your weapons, Sire, and may I then plunge into the hells and stay there for one hundred thousand centuries.[40]

The notion that wealth and rank were a *kammic* inheritance tied to moral and religious responsibility was also reenforced widely in the *cpāp'*, Khmer didactic poetry that formed part of the basic learning of primary education.[41] For instance, the *Cpāp' Tūnmān Khluan* explains,

> The wealth you have is commensurate
> to your generosity in previous lives;
> now having taken birth in this life,
> your wealth is determined by past cause.
>
> If you have a high position,
> possessing wealth and slaves,[42]
> keep your thoughts aimed at what is upright
> and in futures lives, you will obtain them again.[43]

This conception of rulers was at once an ideal of social harmony and a source of sociopolitical instability and uncertainty in the period. Although the *cau-hvay sruk* (provincial leaders) held enormous moral and political authority over the people in their jurisdictions, including the ability to levy taxes and labor and to commute or inflict capital punishment, their hold on power was fragile in the sense that they could be stripped of their rank and privileges at the will of their own higher-ranking patrons.[44] When an official fell from power, his many retainers also lost their positions, thus potentially triggering the realignment of social networks within an entire locality.[45] Historians conclude that a certain degree of overtaxing and abuses of justice were endemic to the system, but the fact that Khmer life was so often disrupted by war and unrest probably contributed to the perception in sources of the period that the corruption and taxation perpetrated by Cambodian officials was greater than in the past.[46]

Since social order was dependent on the smooth flow of the reciprocal benefits conferred by patron and clients on each other, it suffered when either or both sides could not fulfill their obligations. Warfare and unrest placed demands upon local leaders to levy armies and laborers, and under these conditions, raising revenues from agricultural and other sectors became more difficult. This situation caused tension in the relations between elites and peasants, evidenced in the mood of spiritual and material dissatisfaction that led to several tax revolts and millenarian movements in the second half of the century. The strain that these forms of turbulence placed on society added to the weakening of a hierarchically ordered social structure that was undergoing challenges from the reform-minded administrations coming to power in both Siam and French-controlled Cambodia. In both kingdoms, these reforms—which will be considered in greater detail later in this chapter and the next—were intended to modernize political administration (with the intertwined aim of bringing local elites under tighter central control), centralize Sangha administration, and abolish slavery. The second half of the nineteenth century saw increasing fragility and corruption in the Khmer administrative system, which in turn gave French colonial officials greater opportunities and justification for accelerating their intervention in the kingdom.

At the same time, the disruption of sociopolitical hierarchies during the latter half of the nineteenth century had wider ramifications for Khmer society than simply wresting political and economic control from certain elite families. The conception of a morally charged, hierarchical arrangement of space and time had given shape to notions of identity and power, in both idealized and real contexts, that were harmonious and made sense. The strains on this vision of reality widened the sense of disjuncture between the ways in which meaning and order were represented in the Buddhist literature discussed previously and the sociopolitical turbulence of everyday life. This disjuncture opened up the possibility for alternative Buddhist visions of order and disorder to be asserted.

MILLENARIANISM

The extent of the destruction and poverty described in Mās' memoir helps set the stage for understanding the years of social unrest that followed the cessation of warfare with Siam and Vietnam. Although social reconstruction was begun under Ang Duong and continued into the reign of Norodom (r. 1864–1904), the circumstances of life for most Cambodians remained harsh. Unrest throughout the remainder of the century both contributed to the slowness of the recovery process and signaled the population's continuing uneasiness. This dissatisfaction was in turn exacerbated by the transformations in the social arrangement of power in the kingdom brought about by French political control. As a tributary king, Ang Duong had nonetheless managed to imbue the monarchy with some real power. Norodom, politically weak even before he aligned himself with the French in 1863, was forced to rely on the French military to protect his interests against civil unrest because the power attached to his monarchy was largely symbolic.

The French presence brought a greater degree of peace to the countryside in the regions the French controlled, but besides the piracy and banditry that was a constant problem at the time, revolts and rebellions continued to erupt in both Thai- and French-controlled Khmer areas. Motivated in part by political considerations such as taxation, the rebellions also reflected millenarian religious ideas.[47] While not exactly an expression of early anticolonial nationalism (as it was later rendered by Khmer intellectuals),[48] neither was millenarianism merely religious thought on the "fringes."[49] Millenarian movements did tend to surface on the borders of emerging central authorities in Siam and French Indochina, but they drew heavily on current normative interpretations of Buddhist ideas about the moral ordering of the world, merit, kingship, and power. Nineteenth-century millenarian discourses differed from these more mainstream expressions of Buddhism to a certain extent in that they focused on dissatisfaction in the present rather than moral development in a cosmic time frame. But even as a form of social criticism and a medium for expressing the experience of social change and disquiet, millenarianism was a way of making sense of these experiences from a solidly Buddhist perspective. Nor was it particularly radical; at the same time that millenarianism critiqued the moral conduct of particular kings as corrupt and ineffective at creating prosperity and well-being for the realm, its ideological map of power and social organization retained the monarch as the moral center of the cosmos.

Generally, the millenarian rebellions were led by charismatic religious leaders termed *qanak mān puṇy*[50] in Khmer, "those possessing merit," whose religious authority was linked to prophecies and Buddhist texts predicting the birth of the epoch of the next Buddha, Metteya, and to the ideal of the *cakkavattin,* or wheel-turning Dhamma-king seen as the forerunner of Metteya's epoch. The Metteya prophecy, whose Indian Buddhist origins are obscure, has emerged in a number of Mahāyāna and Theravāda Buddhist historical contexts.[51] In various versions, it predicts cycles of decline of the Dhamma, connected with an unrighteous ruler whose errors of judgment engender the proliferation of poverty, violence, and immoral behavior and diminish the average span of a human life to a few years. Following the decline, in which only a few people remain, the Dhamma is renewed and gradually regenerates. The human population increases and develops under the guidance of a righteous ruler until the epoch of the next Buddha, Metteya, when the people are ready to benefit from the preaching of another buddha. In the late-nineteenth-century Khmer versions of these movements, their "millenarian" nature[52] involved the belief that in the midst of social turmoil producing calamitous death and destruction, the arising of a righteous ruler termed a *dhammik*—a vernacularization of the Pali *dhammika dhammarāja* (righteous king)—was imminent; the *dhammik* would usher in a new golden age of justice and Dhamma, preparing the way (at some unknown point in the future) for the coming of the next Buddha.

The rise of Khmer millenarian thinking during the latter half of the nineteenth century is evidenced by political revolts and by the popularity and circulation of prophetic texts known as *daṃnāy,* "prophetic sayings," usually attributed to a past or future buddha (Gotama or Metteya) or the god Indra.[53] In Cambodia, as in northern Thailand and Burma, bloody confrontations resulted when millenarian followers armed primarily with protective tattoos, amulets, and mantras that they believed would render them invulnerable to harm were slaughtered by conventionally armed government troops. Millenarian leaders, presenting themselves as figures (or incarnations) of the past and connecting themselves with the *dhammik* and the eventual arrival of Metteya at some point in the future, in many ways personified and gave expression to a mood of dissatisfaction with contemporary conditions as well as the effort to make sense of these conditions through current religious and ethical ideas.

Millenarianism in Cambodia apparently gained its first nineteenth-century expression in connection with anti-Vietnamese revolts in southeastern Cambodia during the 1820s and 1830s, probably in response to oppressive treatment of Khmer workers forced to excavate a canal near Chaudoc.[54] In 1820–1821, the Khmer revolted against Vietnamese military officials under the leadership of a charismatic monk named Kai who was understood to be endowed with predictive powers. The Vatt Prek Kuy chronicular account of the event, translated by Chandler, tells of the eventual defeat of the rebels after Kai broke the Buddhist precept against killing in a clash with Vietnamese troops. Kai was killed because "his amulets and charms had lost their power" after he broke the Buddhist precept.[55] Others of the rebels (including Buddhist monks) were arrested and executed in Saigon, while incessant rain fell for seven days. With "nature out of balance" because of the killing of monks, floods and epidemics raged.[56] There was no clear day or night, and the entire Khmer kingdom "was unhappy."[57]

Unrest in this border region with Vietnam, populated by both Khmer and Vietnamese, continued to flare up. The Hue court attempted to subdue the turmoil by forcing Vietnamese settlers into the region (drawn from convicts and others who could not refuse) and by trying to assimilate the region's ethnic Khmer to Vietnamese customs.[58] These policies only worsened the mood of insurrection. In 1840, a widespread guerilla-style rebellion erupted, led by Siamese-supported Khmer nobility against the Vietnamese emperor.[59] This rebellion in turn triggered an 1842 revolt within Vietnam, led by a Khmer or Chinese monk named Lam Sam. Lam Sam, who was attributed with special powers of invulnerability, attracted a formidable seven to eight thousand followers. In spite of the Vietnamese emperor's efforts to quell the revolt, the rebels were able to defend themselves in the mountainous region of Chaudoc until imperial troops finally forced them out.[60]

In this difficult-to-control border region between Vietnamese- and Khmer-dominated areas, two further expressions of nineteenth-century millenarianism arose in the next decades that particularly merit examination in connection with understanding the links between Khmer millenarianism and later modernist thought. While Khmer modernists later rejected the mythic dimensions of millenarianism, they shared its perception that the well-being or turmoil of human communities was linked to their knowledge of and conformity to the Dhamma and its emphasis on purification through everyday moral conduct.

Buu Son Ky Huong developed as a primarily Mahāyāna and Vietnamese religious doctrine; the later Pou Kombo rebellion was directed against the Khmer court in Phnom Penh. These two transregional movements drew on established Buddhist discourses as a medium for expressing dissent—in other words, as the source of ideas, symbols, and images that animated and gave shape to political expression and social critique. The broad mood or ethos of these movements was a sense of uneasiness, disorder, and disharmony—a description that evokes the Buddhist conception of something being "out of joint" (like a dislocated shoulder), the commonly employed Buddhist metaphor for explaining *dukkha,* "suffering," one of the three "marks of existence."[61] In Buddhist understanding, *dukkha,* although experienced in many different forms, is generated to a large extent by the human inability to accept the inevitability of change. *Dukkha* is integrally connected with temporality; all ordinary human experience of time is characterized by it, and it ceases only with the attainment of nibbāṇa, which is apart from temporality.

Millenarian movements asserted the image of what things should be—but were not: the feeling that the moral ordering of the realm itself was out of joint and that the king was not fulfilling his role as moral fulcrum of the kingdom. Like texts on idealized figures of merit and power, millenarianism articulated a traditional Buddhist form of social criticism in the sense that it drew on premodern Buddhist concepts and symbols to respond to the current sociopolitical context. The prominence of millenarian ideas in this period suggests further the perception of disjuncture between the expectations and experience of social order considered earlier, of disorder and disharmony.

The origins of the Buu Son Ky Huong religion have been examined and documented as part of Hue-Tam Ho Tai's study of the Hoa Hao sect in southern Vietnam. Tai details the manner in which millenarianism became further entrenched in the Vietnamese-Khmer border region following the 1849 cholera epidemic in southern Vietnam. During the cholera epidemic, a millenarian healer called the Buddha Master of Western Peace began to attract adherents, who followed him to the mountainous region of Chaudoc to establish new communities. From 1849 to 1856, the Buddha Master of Western Peace disseminated his Buu Son Ky Huong doctrine among Vietnamese and Khmer settlers. Basing his teachings on sixteenth-century Vietnamese predictive texts, the Buddha Master preached the imminent arrival of the next buddha, Maitreya (Metteya). According to these teachings, the degeneration of the Dhamma had nearly reached the point of apocalypse, an event foreshadowed, in Tai's analysis, by the cholera epidemic and harsh conditions of frontier life. Only those who purified themselves through proper moral action and self-purification would escape the coming violence and be reborn at the time of Metteya.[62] Drawing on Vietnamese Zen ideas concerning the Buddha-nature inherent in all individuals who pursued self-purification, Buu Son Ky Huong advocated that "the Way of the Buddha is not far from the Self: If one does good, one will become a Buddha; if one does evil, one will become a demon."[63]

It is significant, as Tai points out, that the Buddha Master never viewed his teachings as heretical or contradictory to mainstream Mahāyāna Buddhism nor as in any way critical of court-sponsored Confucianism.[64] Rather, he saw himself as a purifier and reformer of the Dhamma who was also concerned with spreading his doctrine to laypeople. He deemphasized monastic withdrawal, suggesting instead that purification of the mind should be achieved through the development of ethical action in one's everyday behavior.[65] The Buddha Master's doctrine probably combined elements drawn from Zen, Confucianism, and the Theravāda Buddhism practiced by the Khmer inhabitants of the frontier region. His emphasis on purification through everyday moral comportment rather than monastic withdrawal and his strong concern with applying Buddhist doctrine to lay life is certainly echoed in the thought of the later Khmer Buddhist modernists. This is not to say that Buu Son Ky Huong directly influenced Khmer modernism, but rather that elements of this doctrine, some of which contributed to the formation of modern expressions of Khmer Buddhism, were absorbed in Khmer millenarianism.

Although the Buddha Master died in 1856, his Buu Son Ky Huong doctrine continued to be influential among the scattered settlements of the Chaudoc region, promulgated in part by figures who claimed to be his reincarnation. In 1868, for instance, a Khmer peasant who had a miraculous recovery from cholera reported himself to be the Buddha Master's reincarnation. He attracted a following as a healer until he was arrested and detained by French officials in 1870 for seditious activities. During the 1870s, another claimant named Nam Thiep became renowned as a healer, hypnotist, and producer of amulets—and also as an anti-French agitator until his arrest by French authorities. A third claimant emerged briefly after writing treatises on Buu Son Ky Huong doctrine around 1900 but was almost immediately silenced by colonial officials.[66] Although continued French persecution forced Buu Son Ky Huong followers to envelop their religion in the outward trappings of mainstream Mahāyāna Buddhism, the doctrine remained important in the region, intertwined with anti-French resistance in southern Vietnam in the form of the Dao Lanh sect (in the 1870s and 1880s)[67] and later reinterpreted and incorporated into Hoa Hao–ism.[68]

A direct outgrowth of the Buu Son Ky Huong teachings of the Buddha Master of Western Peace, the Dao Lanh (Religion of Good) sect helped to set in motion the most significant instance of Khmer millenarian unrest within Cambodia during the 1860s. On the Vietnamese-controlled side of the border, after the French had taken control of Saigon in the early 1860s, a disaffected Vietnamese officer from the imperial army named Tran Van Thanh joined forces with other military rebels and retreated into the geographically treacherous border region. There he formed Dao Lanh, a resistance movement based on Buu Son Ky Huong ideologies, practiced healing, and distributed protective amulets to his followers. Nam Thiep, the reincarnation claimant, became associated with the movement by the mid-1860s.[69] At the same time in the contiguous Khmer-controlled side of the border between Caudoc and Tay-ninh, particularly in Ba Phnom Province, a Khmer monk or former monk calling himself Pou Kombo[70] had begun to rally peasant support to revolt against oppressive taxation policies originating under Norodom in Phnom Penh. With the French now in power in Saigon and providing the military might for Norodom's tenuous reign in Phnom Penh, Pou Kombo joined forces with Tran Van Thanh in a series of raids and revolts against French military outposts that intertwined Pou Kombo's millenarian claims to the throne with unrest over taxation.[71] Pou Kombo's forces also attacked Catholic settlements, killing a French priest,[72] and ransacked villages that failed to join the rebellion.[73]

The Pou Kombo movement seems to have grown out of the larger millenarian milieu already firmly established in the western frontier of Cochinchina and southeastern region of Cambodia, with both Vietnamese and Khmer antecedents and influences. Both Buu Son Ky Huong and Khmer millenarianism drew heavily on Buddhist cosmological ideas concerning the decline and regeneration of the Dhamma in conjunction with *kappa*s of decline and prosperity. Both predicted the arrival of Metteya after a period of catastrophic social turbulence in which a few people would be saved because of their good actions, but many more would be lost because of their immorality. Consequently, both millenarian movements drew on religious teachings that heavily emphasized individual purification and the necessity of exemplary moral conduct in present and previous lives. Both religious movements also took on significant political connotations, although in the Vietnamese case, where colonial rule was more direct, the orientation of the rebellions was more explicitly anti-French than on the Khmer side.

But the differences in the two movements also reflects somewhat different Confucian-influenced Mahāyāna and Theravāda interpretations of eschatology and enlightenment. While the Buddha Master of Western Peace was understood to be an enlightened being or "living buddha" who had been sent to make predictions concerning the arrival of Metteya, Pou Kombo instead claimed royal blood and drew more heavily on Theravādin imagery of the just king who would usher in a righteous reign and thus create suitable conditions for the birth of the future buddha. Followers of the Buddha Master of Western Peace such as Tran Van Thanh were not claimants to the Vietnamese throne but rather proponents of the Buddha Master's articulation of the Four Debts, which involved the recognition of responsibility and piety toward parents and ancestors; the emperor; the Triple Gem of Buddha, Dhamma, and Sangha; and compatriots and humankind.[74] By contrast, all historical accounts indicate that Pou Kombo presented himself as the *qanak mān puṇy* who was the righteous ruler or *dhammik* of Buddhist prophecy.

It was thus important for Pou Kombo's legitimacy to claim royal as well as religious lineage. While one chronicle source indicates that Pou Kombo was perhaps of highland ethnic minority origins,[75] Pou Kombo himself appears to have either claimed or implied that he was a Khmer prince who had spent several decades in Laos.[76] The name Pou Kombo itself, according to Leclère, was that of a son of a previous Khmer king, Ang Chan (r. 1806–1835), who apparently died a few hours after birth; Leclère reports that this Pou Kombo was the third "imposter" to have assumed this identity.[77] Although Pou Kombo's precise motives for using the name are not known, royal lineage would clearly have bolstered the legitimacy of his claim to be a *dhammik* or righteous ruler. Since many men of the period spent time in robes, his status as a monk or former monk would not be unusual in itself, but the strong emphasis on his Buddhist associations from sources of the period suggest instead a perception of him in terms of particular religious prowess, a *qanak mān puṇy* or individual possessing such a high degree of meritorious power that he was understood to possess *iddhi,* "extraordinary supernatural abilities."

In contrast to the Buu Son Ky Huong writings produced by the Buddha Master's followers, the Pou Kombo movement does not seem to have spawned any doctrinal writings. His movement coincided, however, with the rise and circulation during the mid- to late nineteenth century of *daṃnāy.*[78] This genre includes the *Buddh Daṃnāy* and the *Soḷas Daṃnāy,* which contain prophecies spoken by the Buddha to figures such as his disciple Ānanda or to King Pasenadi of Kosala, whose disturbing dreams prompted him to seek out the Buddha for interpretation. French sources indicate the wide circulation of these texts in Cambodia throughout the latter half of the nineteenth century, and Keyes has documented the circulation of four similar texts at least by the late nineteenth century in northeastern Siam. In the Lao region of northeastern Siam, Keyes' research suggests, the most important means of spreading millenarian ideas and news concerning individual leaders or *phū mī bun* (in Thai, persons possessing merit) was through the performances of traveling troubadors.[79]

The prophetic texts depict the *dhammik* as a savior-ruler figure who will arrive to save the good and pure from the social chaos wrought in large part by the corruption and moral excesses of those in power who have declined to preserve the Dhamma and thus triggered social ruin.[80] Just kings were those who preserved the Dhamma by upholding the "tenfold rules of kingship," lists of virtues attached to kingship that are elaborated in Pali and vernacular versions of *jātaka* and in the *Trai Bhūm* and *Paṭhamasambodhi.*[81] The lists stress liberality and generosity, as well as the fairness and compassion that kings must demonstrate toward their subjects, slaves, and retainers. The *Trai Bhūm* states that kings who adhere to these rules will ensure peace, happiness, and prosperity, as well as "stability and balance":

> Rice and water, plus fish and other food . . . will be available in abundance. The rain from the sky, which is regulated by the *devatā,* will fall appropriately in accordance with the season, not too little and not too much. The rice in the fields and the fish in the water will never be ruined by drought or damaged by rain. . . . [T]he days, nights, years, and months will never be irregular.[82]

By contrast, kings who disregarded the rules would wreak havoc on their kingdoms and subjects by distorting the natural rhythms and functioning of the rains, winds, and seasons. Droughts and floods would occur, causing widespread famine.[83] In one Khmer *daṃnāy* version, as corruption and immorality mount,

> [t]he celestial deity of rain does not permit rain to fall anywhere, causing drought, causing the grass to wither and the rice to die on the stalks. Because the people of the earthly realm were inclined away from the Dhamma,[84] the deity of the wind[85] did not permit the fruits of food to ripen.[86]

Social disorder worsens until hierarchical roles in society become confused. Not only does the king disregard the rules of kingship, but family relationships disintegrate to the point that children no longer show respect for their parents, wives lose respect for their husbands, and the people lose all recognition of appropriate social ties and bonds. As the entire society—including kings, monks, nuns, novices, and laypeople—forget to observe the precepts, the sky turns dark, and day and night cease to be apparent. Violence increases as a war breaks out in all directions, and when so many people have been killed that the blood flows as high as "the belly of an elephant,"[87] the *dhammik* finally makes his appearance to usher in a new era of peace and prosperity.[88]

The circulation and importance of such millenarian representations of the just savior-*dhammik* in oral poetry, prose texts, and popular performances in border regions of the country already influenced by Vietnamese millenarianism help to explain Pou Kombo's appeal and power, as well as the threat he represented to French authorities. Pou Kombo, who in Moura's explanation was regarded by his followers as "a sort of god,"[89] was harnessing this powerful religious imagery. In political terms, the Pou Kombo rebellion developed during a period of intense unpopularity for Norodom as he restructured the tax system to increase revenues—a restructuring that Pou Kombo apparently promised to rescind.[90] He and his followers managed to oppose French and Khmer troops for two years, spreading the rebellion and attacking French military strongholds, until Pou

Kombo was finally captured and executed. Even when his troops were defeated, Pou Kombo at first eluded capture by disappearing into a swamp with some of his supporters.[91] He was finally apprehended, and at French insistence, his severed head was sent to Phnom Penh for display in order to persuade the populace that the rebellion had been crushed through French military power.[92]

Although never as effective or widespread as Pou Kombo's movement, the millenarian impetus proved compelling in Cambodia through the end of the century, spawning figures and revolts that if not explicitly "millenarian" shared some of the features of Pou Kombo's movement.[93] In the 1860s, a former slave named Sva laid claim to the Khmer throne and caused unrest in southwestern Cambodia and along the Vietnamese border.[94] His efforts were abetted by various Vietnamese mandarins, until his capture in 1866.[95] In 1887, in the midst of an insurrection led by Sivotha, a brother of King Norodom,[96] a novice and charismatic figure called Nong claimed to be the incarnation of the protector-spirit of Cambodia. He incited the population to rebel against authorities in Kompong Svay, an area that had long been at odds with the throne.[97] Another millenarian-type figure claiming royal blood surfaced in Kampot Province at roughly the same time and joined the tax revolt in progress there. Promising his followers that the lustral water he sprinkled on them "makes those it touches invincible, and they cannot be hurt by the bullets of the French," he conducted several protective rituals for rebel soldiers near the French garrison and declared himself the true king.[98]

Revolts were also occurring in Thai-controlled areas. Ukñā Suttantaprījā Ind wrote a poetic account of a revolt in Battambang in 1898, when Khmer cardamom pickers rose up against an oppressive tax collector. The leader of the revolt, a peasant named Ta Kae, is described in the poem as a man whose "mind was strong, stubborn, without fear . . . a kind man such as he one can rarely find." Ta Kae was guided—or, as the poem implies, misled—by a Vietnamese monk named Sav who conferred protective amulets on the rebels. The Thai general who was dispatched to put down the revolt beat the monk to death with a large pestle, accusing him as "the main enemy, imagining yourself a great man," the culprit who had incited the peasants to revolt.[99] Another revolt directed against Siamese authorities occurred between 1899 and 1902, when ethnic Lao villagers in northeast Siam began to circulate prophetic texts about an imminent catastrophe and the arrival of the Lord Thammikarāt, the righteous ruler. The predictions crystallized into a movement around several different leaders claiming to be *phū mī bun,* who attracted thousands of followers. In 1902, they attacked and ransacked provincial posts of the Siamese government.[100] Keyes, drawing on Thai historical sources, reports that the peasant army, armed with old muskets, farm tools, and protective amulets, warned the Thai troops, "'Don't anybody shoot or do anything at all. Sit in meditation and our side will shoot but a single shot.'"[101] Unfortunately for the rebels, the Thai soldiers began to fire, and the rebellion was quickly disbanded.

This discussion provides evidence of the extent to which millenarian discourse was a part of the religio-political imagination of the period.[102] It tended to have its most powerful expression on the peripheries: on frontiers, among peasants such as the cardamom pickers, among ethnic minority groups. But even this limited historical survey has made evident that millenarianism was not a uniform Khmer response to social change. While millenarian ideas surfaced in different regions of Cambodia and on the Siamese borders during the nineteenth century, the rebellions themselves remained localized; they never attracted enough adherents to ignite the entire population. Nor were the claims and social ideals put forward by millenarian adherents uncontested; while members of the royal family lent support to a millenarian figure during the Kampot uprising, Ind, who was obviously sympathetic to the aims of the 1898 revolt in Battambang, derided the monk Sav's claims to possess the supernatural powers of a meritorious person. In his later writing, he characterized all the nineteenth-century *dhammik* claimants "[who] pretend to be *qanak mān puṇy*" as "wicked persons."[103] Yet even if millenarianism was sometimes acted out on the margins, instrumentally adopted by some and ridiculed by others, the widespread circulation and political assimilation of ideas, texts, and images concerning the decline of morality and the Dhamma, the imminent arrival of catastrophe, and the hope for a righteous *dhammik* savior-ruler should be regarded as a significant measure of the religious ethos of the time.

Millenarianism, I have suggested, expressed a mood of dissatisfaction, self-reflexivity, and an awareness of change among Khmer. Along with the immediate political concerns that gave rise to millenarianism, it seems likely that it expressed a moral crisis, a way of responding to social unrest that conveyed a longing for the restoration of idealized conceptions of meaning and order. These idealized conceptions asserted a normative Buddhist understanding of the *kammic* ordering of existence, identity, and power. Millenarianism afforded a way of interpreting factors such as drought or oppression caused by overtaxation in terms of the degeneration of the Dhamma, which in turn could be linked to past or present moral causes, such as the unrighteous behavior of a king or the wielding of power by illegitimate or morally suspect individuals. But the utopian nature of the vision seems to have worked in an even more nuanced way. As literary and cultural historian Ashley Thompson has suggested, Buddhistic assumptions about history went beyond the conception that the past represented the remembrance of a better, more righteous world; the past was in fact a definitive template for what the future would become as sentient beings cycled from Buddha era to Buddha era.[104] Besides the political effects of millenarianism, its religious dimension gave individuals a way to address problems of the present in ethical terms: to correct problems in society, one could purify one's own moral conduct and try to bring it in line with the Dhamma. This important current of millenarian thought was later rearticulated in the ethical writings of Buddhist modernists.

While millenarianism during this period was prominent as a Khmer discourse for making sense of the world and the experiences of war and violence, oppression, poverty, and other aspects of sociopolitical change, it could not halt the transformations taking place in French Indochina and Siam. The encounters of

French colonial administrators with millenarian-inspired figures such as Tran Van Thanh, Nam Thiep, and Pou Kombo during this period colored French perceptions of Buddhist movements and people and had a decided impact on the policy decisions that emerged later. At the end of the century, at least for the next several decades, the effectiveness of millenarianism as a form of social dissent seems to have diminished, probably because even minor claims of predictive or protective powers, whether connected with a larger rubric of millenarianism or not, brought their claimants under the immediate scrutiny of colonial officials. It may also be that as the violence and unrest of the nineteenth century subsided, the perception of social turmoil that had fueled the apocalyptic visions of the millenarian prophecies receded.

FRENCH REFORMS AND SOCIETAL CHANGE

By the latter part of the century, the Siamese and French governments, the two political powers that controlled Khmer-inhabited areas, were aggressively engaged in reforming traditional social structures. These reforms affected Khmer life in ways that further contributed to the corrosion of the traditional hierarchies that defined and ordered social identity.

Reformism itself was part of a larger intellectual and political impulse in Southeast Asia during this period that had both indigenous and foreign sources. Stanley Tambiah and Craig Reynolds have argued that in Siam, the classic Theravādin-style religious reform that culminated in the mid-nineteenth-century formation of a new religious sect by Mongkut had its origins in the establishment of the Chakri dynasty seventy years earlier.[105] But as European powers entered into the contest for leadership in the region, the force of political realignments and positioning, as well as cultural influences resulting from extended encounters with colonial Europeans, also contributed to the reformulation of traditional political administrative styles and structures. In Cambodia, where French control accelerated throughout the 1880s and 1890s, sociopolitical reform was imposed by French colonial rule, which gained momentum as a result of the civil unrest and institutional fragility in the Khmer government after Norodom took the throne.

In both Siam and Cambodia, new administrative policies sought to shift the traditional hierarchical and "galactic" arrangement of power in the kingdoms to one in which the central government had tighter control over all parts of its territory and over all levels of government. The pace of these reforms intensified in both countries in the 1880s. In Siam, King Chulalongkorn (Rama V) achieved the political authority necessary for accelerating his governmental modernization efforts during this period.[106] In Cambodia, previous French efforts at administrative reform had met with resistance from the monarchy and hierarchy of elites, and French authorities had seen little utility in trying to usurp their control. While in a regional sense Khmer kingship had been weakened throughout the nineteenth century by the helplessness of its monarchs in the face of the Thai, the Vietnamese, and the French, the prestige of the kingship as a political and moral force remained intact much longer. Throughout the first twenty-five years of his reign, Norodom, even when he lacked the political and military strength to control the peripheries of his kingdom, retained his symbolic authority. When the French were finally able to force more and more administrative compromises on him in the 1890s, they were careful to protect the status of his position as a means of ensuring order in the kingdom. With a certainty that Norodom could be coerced into cooperation, the greater problem for the French lay in taking control of the Khmer administrative system in which power flowed from top to bottom—and revenue from bottom to top. Convinced that Cambodia was a potentially rich region that could be made to pay for the costs of maintaining the protectorate as well as generate revenue for France, French administrators began in the mid-1870s to turn their attention to understanding and reforming the Khmer political administration.

In December 1876, with Norodom's brother Sivotha beginning to agitate in the countryside, French officials introduced a series of far-reaching reforms that highlighted the aspects of Cambodian rule they found most frustrating and backward. They demanded the abolition of what they viewed as superfluous high-level ranks at the palace, such as the "second king" and the other positions that functioned to divide the kingdom into different revenue-producing compartments for members of the royal family. They also diminished the number of provinces and their corresponding functionaries, designating a fixed number of titles that could be awarded in each province, and demanded that the government pay salaries to all civil servants. These reforms were designed to combat the problems of graft and corruption, which they perceived as a fundamental flaw in all political structures in Cambodia, "a country," wrote one French official, "where the exploitation of the weakest by the strongest is absolutely consecrated by long practice and supported with angelic patience by those same who bear it."[107]

Along with these reforms, the French abolished life-long slavery, restructured the institution of debt slavery prevalent in the kingdom, and reduced the monarchy's tax monopolies on goods other than opium, liquor, and gambling. In reality, the reforms introduced at this point by the colonial administration were largely ignored and had little of their intended effect on Khmer life at this time. During the next decade, however, using the rhetoric of the oppressiveness of corruption and the inhumanity of slavery as their official justification, French colonial officials renewed their efforts to further enfeeble Norodom.[108]

In 1884, the newly installed governor-general of Cochin China, Charles Thomson, believing that Norodom was sufficiently weakened by unpopularity and internal unrest to be forced to make real concessions, confronted Norodom with a choice between abdication or acceptance of the Convention of 17 June 1884, which effectively instituted the administrative reforms that the French intended this time to enforce. The convention put Khmer officials under the jurisdiction of

French civil servants at all levels of government. Khmer courts and judges, for instance, were placed under the direct supervision of French judicial administrators; responsibility for most court cases was taken out of the hands of the Khmer. The convention also introduced land ownership, abolished both hereditary and indentured slavery, and gave French officials ultimate responsibility for collecting taxes. These last two features of the convention, the abolition of slavery and the restructuring of the taxation system, were specifically designed to dismantle the traditional power of regional elites by greatly diminishing their access to sources of labor and revenue. Not surprisingly, the reforms attached to the convention were viewed with hostility by Khmer officials and were factors prompting the 1885–1887 rebellion led by Prince Sivotha. Unlike the previous millenarian-style rebellions in Cambodia, the 1885–1887 rebellion was explicitly political and anti-French, with rebels reacting against the administrative reforms forced on the king by the French.[109] Lasting eighteen months, this war caused many villagers to flee into the forest to escape fighting and pillaging, and reportedly took the lives of about ten thousand Khmer and one thousand French.[110]

The French reforms that dismantled slavery and promoted opium use in the protectorate altered Khmer social and economic relationships. Before the enforcement of slavery reform, the social stratification in Khmer society consisted, at the bottom levels, of free and enslaved classes. The difficulties of agricultural life in this period, comments historian Khin Sok, meant that well-placed slaves of aristocrats were often better nourished than free people, termed *qanak jā.* Despite this reality, he argues, the class of free persons "took a great deal of pride in claiming the title *{qanak jā},*" viewing their own status favorably in relation to the "socially discredited" classes of slaves.[111] The enslaved classes were divided into several categories. *Qanak khñuṃ* (debt slaves), were individuals who voluntarily sold themselves into slavery. Although regulations regarding the interest on the debts incurred by this category of slaves changed over time, the laws tended to favor the masters, and the debts were often nearly impossible for the *khñuṃ* to repay. The *khñuṃ* were considered to have a somewhat higher social ranking than *qanak ṅār* (nonindentured hereditary slaves). *Qanak ṅār* divided into several subclassifications: people who entered into slavery as prisoners of war, as a result of having been sentenced to slavery for treason or other grave crimes, or the lowest class of *qanak ṅār,* members of hill-tribe ethnic minority groups captured by slave traders and sold in lowland markets. All of these types of lifelong slaves were considered hereditary slaves in the sense that their descendants were also slaves. In the case of criminal or political prisoners sentenced to slavery, their entire extended family shared the sentence, along with all of their descendants. *Qanak ṅār* were further subdivided into types, each category of whom bore different titles according to the duties they performed, such as taking care of military horses or picking cardamom.[112]

The French began their reform of slavery in 1876 by gradually abolishing hereditary slavery and restricting the interest on the loans given to debt slaves in exchange for their servitude, making the possibility of eventual liberation more feasible for the *khñuṃ*.[113] The 1884 convention abolished slavery outright, although it continued to exist in Cambodia until the end of the century,[114] and the practice of debt slavery continued at least into the 1920s.[115] Similar reforms were simultaneously being implemented in Siamese-controlled Khmer areas; even before slavery had become a politicized issue in Cambodia, Chulalongkorn in Siam had been making gradual attempts to abolish the practice, beginning with a law that phased out inherited slavery.[116] These reforms were undermining the traditionally elevated positions of elites by diminishing their access to human resources, power, and privileges. For people at the bottom of the social ladder, debt slavery also had profound implications, since it had long been their only recourse for ensuring the survival of their families in difficult times.[117]

Like slavery reform, tax restructuring affected all levels of Khmer society in a manner that demonstrates the intertwined nature of economics, politics, and morality. Following the convention of 1884, taxation became an issue of mounting political tension. As millenarian discourses of the period suggest, an oppressive or unfair tax burden implied disorder and injustice in the kingdom, which in the eyes of the people, reflected immorality on the part of their rulers. Thus, the enfeeblement of the monarch and Khmer elites through new taxation policies helped fuel a perception of moral degeneration and added to the mood of social unease that lingered as a result of the turmoil of the nineteenth century.

One important dimension of tax restructuring was the opium policy introduced as part of the convention of 1884. Designed to give the French more control over Khmer elites, it became a major aspect of the colonial strategy for increasing tax revenue in Cambodia. The policy featured a concerted effort to increase the colony's import and consumption of opium,[118] which before European colonization had been confined largely to pharmaceutical use in Cambodia.[119] In Cambodia, a limited opium franchise was first created by King Ang Duong, apparently in response to the introduction of the opium trade by European merchants, thereby enabling the crown to rent out the right to sell opium.[120] Beginning in the 1860s, when Norodom wanted to raise revenue for construction of a new capital in Phnom Penh, he undertook substantial tax restructuring, including an expansion of the opium franchise that enabled him to increase his profits from its import and sale. In 1877, French officials dissolved other monopolies owned by the crown, leaving the monarch little source of tax revenue beyond the franchises they granted for liquor, opium, and gambling. The 1884 convention removed control of the liquor and opium monopoly from the king and gave it to the French. This action generated anger among many Khmer since it constituted a significant seizure of power and revenue from the Khmer king and ranks of nobility. As a result, opium dens became targets of particular destruction during the rebellion led by Prince Sivotha following the 1884 convention.[121]

Following the lead of the British in China, French colonial administrators began to actively promote opium use in Indochina.[122] For the next four decades, opium revenue was a cornerstone of the colonial fiscal policy, providing as much as

25 percent of the Indochinese colonial budget between the years 1899 and 1922.[123] Imported from India or Yunan and refined in Saigon, opium was bought and resold in Cambodia by Chinese merchants, selected by the customs division of the administration, who ran government-licensed opium dens. Norodom and his successor Sisowath (r. 1904–1927) received allotments of opium for private consumption, provided free of charge by the French officials who oversaw their civil allowances.[124] But opium was consumed by members of all social classes, particularly after 1897, when the new governor-general of Indochina, Paul Doumer,[125] reorganized opium importation and production to make it even more efficient. Among other initiatives, new, lower grades of less expensive opium were introduced so that workers could afford the drug; these policies increased opium consumption 50 percent between 1897 and 1900,[126] and it continued to grow for the next several decades.[127]

MODERN SOCIAL CRITICISM

With the reforms of the 1880s, Khmer socioeconomic life had begun to be altered in noticeable ways. The dimensions of these policies that affected Khmer at many levels of society—the abolition of slavery and new policies on opium franchises that led to a visibly increased opium use in Indochina—are considered in two early examples of Khmer modern social critique, one written by Prince Yukanthor in 1900 and the other by Ukñā Suttantaprījā Ind in 1914–1921. Published in newspapers in France, Yukanthor's critical memorandum, which challenged French colonial rule explicitly, ultimately had little effect as a "line of action" for further social change.[128] Ind's more nuanced social critique, embedded in his lengthy modern work *Gatilok,* was part of the modernist reinterpretation of Buddhism in the second, third, and fourth decades of the twentieth century (explored in the next three chapters) that eventually contributed to the formulation of Khmer nationalism.

Although different in tone and intent, both critiques are illustrative for understanding the highly religious and moral terms in which social criticism was refracted in this early prenationalist and precommunist period. As in millenarian discourse, problems such as corruption, oppressive government control, and overtaxation were represented as moral issues; opium addiction was emblematic of the degeneration of moral values in colonial society. This tendency to reflect on and pose solutions to the problems of contemporary life through the medium of Buddhist ethical reflection is indicative of the writings of the modernist faction of the Khmer Sangha, whose work will be examined in the next chapters.

The social critiques offered by Yukanthor and Ind suggest the ways in which the new French policies were understood to conflict with Buddhist moral values. In regard to slavery, efforts by French colonials and modern-minded Siamese reformists to abolish slavery challenged implicit Buddhistic assumptions on which society rested, including the idea that social life was structured by a *kammic* ordering of people based on their moral histories in the cosmos. The French policies promoting opium use were similarly complex in both political and social terms. On the one hand, in seizing the opium franchise, the administration deprived Khmer elites of a lucrative source of income. On the other hand, the policy of promoting opium use was problematic from a moral and religious standpoint; opium, like alcohol, countered the prescription of the fifth precept—to abstain from the use of intoxicants. For Buddhists, then as now, breaking the fifth precept was seen as dangerous because intoxication is seen to exacerbate other degenerate qualities in human beings and lead to an overall loss of control.

In 1900, Prince Yukanthor, one of Norodom's sons traveled to Paris and submitted a memorandum to the French government condemning the colonial reforms. The rhetoric of social order and disorder employed by Prince Yukanthor reveals the Buddhistic premises of his analysis; he argued that the proper hierarchical arrangement of society was morally sanctioned (through the law of karma) and harmonious.[129] From a Dhammic perspective, it was clear that French policies were undermining the preexisting patterns of order, harmony, and compassion that structured society. In an article for *Le Figaro,*[130] he responded to the French abolition of slavery by arguing for its greater humanity in the Cambodian context than the options of starvation and poverty provided by French policies:

> We have slaves. I have them. But I have never understood the horror that you place on this word, before having come to see the reality it designates. Among the liberties in which you take glory, it seems to me that many among you still have the one of starving to death. This is one that we are displeased you have given to our people. For this is the only one that you have been able to give.[131]

Yukanthor countered a French characterization of the Khmer as infantile and barbarous, insisting that the facts of history and climate suggested the opposite. On the contrary, the antiquity of Cambodia's social world was quite evident, and the country's physical situation, with a tropical climate and abundant resources, meant that the Khmer had not had to develop the fierce instincts of war evident in European cultures. He harshly criticized the French government for undermining Buddhist law, a law based on justice and love, which was the basis of a harmonious social order in traditional society:

> The King is the absolute master, it is true. But when a mendicant monk passes near the sovereign, the King will descend from his elephant, from his horse, from his vehicle, to bow before the trifling monk. . . . He must for there to be order.
>
> In the celestial system, the movements of the heavenly bodies are regulated, and that gives harmony. It is the same in our traditional society that you seek to destroy. Order gives happiness to all. Disorder cannot but give misfortune to all.

> Disorder permits neither justice or love. And [in disorder] the Buddhist law does not exist.[132]

His characterization of colonial society as riddled with moral excess, injustices, and follies perpetrated by the resident superiors "under the influence of alcohol, of opium and of the advice given by their indigenous mistresses and secretaries"[133] contrasted with the image he conveyed of a virtuous, balanced Cambodian society of the past, prior to French rule. Buddhist society was just not because of abstract principles of liberty but because the individuals who governed it behaved in accordance with Dhammic values such as loving-kindness and compassion.

The "Yukanthor affair" as well as the earlier rebellion led by Sivotha represents a rejection by at least some Khmer elites of the administrative system ushered in by the French.[134] Sivotha had motivated enough social unrest to militarily and politically seize portions of the country (even to the extent of levying his own customs service in some areas)[135] and to exploit general dissatisfaction concerning the moral legitimacy of his brother the king. Yukanthor employed a more modern mode of response. He produced a written memorandum that fully captured the ironies of colonial conceptions of liberty, rights, and justice to criticize colonial policies, and circulated it in print form in the metropole. In the end, his protest had even less clear political effect than Sivotha's, except to further compromise his father's authority and to consign Yukanthor to lifelong exile in Bangkok.

It is difficult to gauge whether or not Yukanthor's memorandum was a representative viewpoint in this period. Certainly, some elites, such as those Yukanthor criticized in his memorandum as French collaborators, must not have shared all of his views of the deleterious effects of French policies.[136] Cut off from political influence, he continued to meet with Khmer monks and students in Bangkok, a situation that so alarmed colonial officials that he was put under surveillance; fears about his continuing influence on monks helped to prompt later restrictions on their travels, discussed in chapter 4. In spite of its ultimate ineffectiveness, his memorandum helps to further demonstrate the ways in which Buddhist ideas could be harnessed to respond to social change, simultaneously advancing and critiquing modern values, and in this sense anticipating later modernist writing.

Among Buddhist writers, Ukñā Suttantaprījā Ind offered a more guarded version of social critique in his ethical manual *Gatilok.* An advocate of the modern Buddhist interpretations that will be examined in subsequent chapters, Ind employed new rational textual and discursive methods and ideas while simultaneously pointing to an alarming departure in contemporary colonial society from the practice of authentic Buddhist values. Formerly an official under the Siamese governor in Battambang, Ind had been brought to Phnom Penh from the provinces and installed in government service to work on Khmer orthographic reform during the period in which he wrote the *Gatilok.* In Phnom Penh, his work brought him into daily contact with other literati, members of the royal court, the

Sangha, and French colonial administrators. He also had the opportunity to absorb the larger impact of sociopolitical changes brought about by colonial policies, as well as to observe the 1915–1916 demonstrations.

From the end of 1915 into the first months of 1916, a spontaneous peasant demonstration arose, with more than thirty thousand villagers from provinces around the country streaming into Phnom Penh to air their grievances to King Sisowath about taxation and particularly about French corvée labor policies.[137] The demonstration grew more violent in the countryside, as peasants began to threaten local leaders who were responsible for enforcing the new policies. In Milton Osborne's analysis, the affair was not simply an economic matter exacerbated by the corruption and graft extracted by local officials, as colonial French analysts —who continued to perceive the peasantry as "timeless" and "changeless"— insisted, but rather a reaction to the social changes introduced by French policies. Taxation and corvée service had, under Khmer administration, been a looser matter. As the French took more direct control of tax collection, the efficiency and stringency of the new system, along with the abolition of debt slavery, contributed to a growing feeling of resentment and of loss of traditional means of manipulating the system. Added to this, a major disparity in income and taxation was becoming apparent. While a French official earning 12,000 piastres a year might pay 30 piastres in tax, a Khmer farmer earning perhaps 40 to 90 piastres a year paid about 12 piastres in taxes, along with the taxes required to pay his way out of corvée labor requirements, taxes on slaughtering livestock, and high prices for government franchised salt, opium, and alcohol.[138]

These events form the backdrop for Ind's work written during this period; its primary focus, however, was on the decay of moral values and the question of how a "modern" Buddhist is meant to behave. Along with Yukanthor's memorandum, it supplies one of the few written social critiques from the period predating the rise of print culture. Ind's lengthy manual comments on many issues in contemporary Khmer society, including taxation, opium and alcohol use, and slavery.

Ind uses images and stories involving taxation, corruption, and addiction to represent the degeneration of morality. In one narrative, the "Story of the Minister Who Was Addicted to Opium," an addicted official uses his power and rank to inflict harm on others, extorting revenue from villagers to finance his growing opium use. In other instances, opium and alcohol use, to which Ind makes repeated reference in the text, are used both literally and metaphorically to depict the character of modern society. He describes opium smokers as unrefined, lacking in "shyness and modesty,"[139] and physically and mentally decrepit:

> Nowadays, as you have certainly realized already, among those who smoke opium, there are people who have attractive bodies, people who have pleasing looks, people who are prosperous. Yet opium, *gañja,* and other such substances are things that invariably cause people to become altered and decrepit, leading them to delusionary states of mind that cause them to perform all types of disreputable behaviors.[140]

Opium and liquor consumption caused intoxication or "drunkenness," which aggravated other forms of moral misconduct and was thus prohibited by Buddhists in the fifth precept:

> [P]eople nowadays are already filled with drunkenness. This drunkenness is *lobho,* which means longing to be associated with or wanting something, which is one kind of drunkenness. *Doso* means rage and anger, which is one kind of drunkenness. *Moho* means ignorant confusion and not knowing right from wrong, which is one kind of drunkenness. *Mānadiṭṭhi* means stubborn conceit and boasting; this is one kind of drunkenness. All of these kinds of drunkenness may already exist in a body, and if you add drunkenness from drinking liquor as well, this new drunkenness increases the power and influence of the previous kinds of drunkenness. If one is greedy, it will lead one to become even greedier; if one is angry or deluded or arrogant, it will lead one to even greater anger, delusion or arrogance.[141]

Like Yukanthor, Ind implies that degenerating moral values are particularly problematic "nowadays." Ind's representation of the drunkenness of contemporary society contrasts with and updates Buddhist prohibitions against intoxication of the past, which depict the punishments for drunkenness in future rebirths. In the older didactic poem *Cpāp' Tūnmān Khluan,* which Ind references in his work, the dangers of intoxication are explained by a father to his son:

> One further word of counsel from your father;
> I entreat you to remember—do not drink alcohol.
> It leads your heart and mind to wrongdoing,[142]
> to grievous ignominy. . . .
>
> In worldly terms,[143]
> drinkers are rebuked and scorned.
> But when they meet with death,
> an [even worse] suffering awaits.
>
> There, they experience the consequences [of their actions],[144]
> their bodies scorched with hot irons,
> [even] their livers and spleens within
> their stomachs, in a state of agonizing pain.
>
> Flames from the hot irons engulf them,
> hissing smoke rises all around,
> *Yāma*-guards moreover force them to drink
> glittering red-hot molten copper.[145]

In a demythologizing vein characteristic of his modernist approach, Ind takes up the present life ethical ramifications of intoxication, while leaving aside its more hellish future karmic consequences. He joins the Buddhist logic prohibiting intoxication due to loss of moral control with ideas that reflect the international debate over opium: opium use fostered corruption and crime; it led to mental and physical decline; it signaled depravity and a breakdown of moral values.

Slavery also holds a prominent metaphorical place in Ind's work, primarily as a condition of human ignorance.[146] Debt slaves are generally represented as unscrupulous, deluded, and unrefined people whose lack of moral clarity has led them to sell themselves into servitude. One debt slave sells himself to multiple masters and ends up being apprehended and confined to the house with a chain around his neck, a deplorable state but one he has brought upon himself.[147] Another debt slave kills his master's rooster under the mistaken impression that he will be able to get more sleep and ends up working even longer hours as a result.[148] Like debt slaves who keep finding new masters to redeem them from the old, "individuals who try to exchange places to find happiness [only] arrive at *dukkha,* anger and regret."[149]

It might be possible to read these ambivalent depictions of debt slavery in the same vein as Yukanthor's suggestion that slavery represented a better option than starvation for the Khmer. I think it is more likely, however, that Ind, writing a decade and a half later and at a greater remove from the initial abolition of slavery, instead reflects a metaphorical ambivalence about the larger implications of freedom and subservience in colonial society, comparable to Michael Salman's analysis of the rhetoric of slavery in the Philippines during the same period.[150] This reading would tend to be confirmed in another passage of the *Gatilok.* In it, Ind, like Yukanthor, draws on French ideologies concerning liberty, but in combination with a more derogatory portrait of debt slavery:

> This story originates in a French volume.
>
> There was a domestic dog who ran out to play in a forest, where he saw a wild forest dog with a thin body standing in one place. They went to give each other a friendly reception according to their own language, and came to be friends. The domestic dog asked, "Friend, how do you find food? Every day, is there enough or is it insufficient?" The wild dog answered, "I look for food with all my energy. Sometimes it's plentiful and sometimes I can't find anything." The domestic dog replied, "My friend, in the forest you don't have enough nourishment. It's too hard to live in this place. But friend, if you want to come live with my master in the countryside, and live with me there, my master is very kind. He gives me rice with different kinds of fish to eat as my usual fare." The wild dog asked, "What is your master's work? What kind of things do you do?" The domestic dog answered, "My master doesn't have any heavy work for me to do. They use me to guard the house when they sleep, and whenever they go play in the forest we must go with them to help catch wild animals by tracking them. Hey friend, our master's work consists of only those two things. Then we can eat delicious food and go to sleep."

"Oh! Your master's work sounds like plenty enough. And that thing tied around your neck, what do you call it?" "Oh! Do you mean this thing they call a collar, friend?" "Why do they want to put that collar on your neck?" "Hey friend, this collar serves as a sign that says I belong to them." "Yes, but if you have a master over you and he wants you [to wear] this collar to demonstrate you belong to him, then friend, is it not common for animals who have a master, in cases when he is dissatisfied with them, to hit them with a big stick on the head?

"Forget it, friend. I am a wild dog. I don't have any boss over me. I look for food happily, according to my own wishes, not to gain favor or to please or out of fear of someone. I look for food according to my own wishes and strength. I can eat a lot or a little; it's not the business of any boss but depends on my own pleasure. If I want to sleep, I sleep, and I come and go when and where I want. It's not necessary for me to go to the trouble of informing anyone when I leave. No, friend—usually animals who have someone feeding them are really comfortable physically because their masters protect them from calamities that happen once in a while. But their food depends on them. They cannot eat whenever they are hungry. They can't eat when they want to—only in the morning and evening. I think that that collar of yours is way too tight. As for me, I want my neck to be free. From my perspective, as a member of the race of wild dogs, I don't want a collar around my neck."

The wild dog spoke thus and the domestic dog returned home to his residence.[151]

Rather than viewing the protection offered by the master as security against poverty and starvation, the wild dog looks "for food happily, according to my own wishes, not to gain favor or to please or out of fear of someone." It is better to face starvation than to be someone's slave, the story suggests. But the commentary that follows the story points beyond this literal interpretation to the more subversive possibility that Ind's appropriation of a French fable about liberty is intended as an understated critique of the colonial condition:

> What [contemporary] parallels do you see in this story? . . . I cannot provide comparison in all the detail that is possible, but the story parallels the condition of a person who has a master and a person who does not have a master, like the wild dog whose speech we have heard and the dog with the collar. It also relates to all the forms of high status that individuals display, such as symbols or *"medailles"* and so forth. A person with glory, authority, and rank has them hung on his clothes to boast and flatter himself in this world—but the decorations are like the collar. They are things that cause one to tremble with excitement, that make one intoxicated with glory. Anyone with wisdom should reflect on the lessons of the Dhamma[152] instead.[153]

It seems from this passage that the story's condemnation of slavery has a larger purpose in mind. The "domestic dogs" are not mere debt slaves but officials and elites who are "deluded" because they are "intoxicated" with the ranks, insignia, and *"medailles"* offered by the colonial government.[154] Only intoxication can explain the muddled perception of officials who fail to recognize that the *medailles* and collars do not represent actual freedom; this should be as obvious to discern as the dog's master wielding a large stick. In an earlier piece by Ind, a poem composed after a 1909 trip to Angkor with members of the Khmer court and translated by Penny Edwards, Ind painfully observed Khmer coolies laboring to carry out the French vision of the renovation of Angkor:

> Sir Monsieur Commaille, from France,
> Takes cement and paints it on like paper as reinforcement.
> Wherever moss grows thick enough to block your view
> Sir has it swept out clean.
> Coolies are hired as labor
> Chopping wood and hauling stone slabs to and fro
> Or sweeping the paths spotlessly clean;
> People come and go but there's no dust to be seen.
> I walk up to the path which Sir [is having] swept
> And, seeing our Khmer race as coolies,
> Am overcome with pity for the Khmer race, dirt poor,
> Working as coolies for somebody else's money.[155]

The mood of the poet's emotional state watching the restoration of Angkor by a French "Sir" and Khmer coolies as the king of Cambodia tours Angkor following the retrocession of Siem Reap Province to Cambodia is more nuanced than the "Buddhist" fable of the dog with a collar. But both passages share a decisively negative imagery of servitude. In Phnom Penh, Ind was observing other Khmer officials like himself, not coolies, in the service of the colonial government. Still, his ironic use of a French fable lauding the value of liberty to critique the French restriction of Khmer liberty is carefully indirect, as is his telling of another French fable about tyranny. The mice who plot endlessly to place a bell around the neck of their oppressor always fail to achieve their objective. Likewise, Ind advises, "If you meet together but only discuss, you are like the group of mice. Meet together and take the bell and tie it around the cat's neck. People with wisdom *(paññā)* will analyze and understand this."[156]

These words coincided with a new antitaxation mood among the wider populace. Throughout the second and into the third decade of the century, tensions concerning taxes mounted as the colonial administration cut roads through the jungles and undertook projects such as the construction of a resort complex on the Gulf of Siam. These projects were paid for by Khmer taxes and built by corvée workers, numbers of whom lost their lives under the difficult working conditions imposed on them. In 1924, a new tax on uncultivated land further increased the tax burden on farmers. Finally, in 1925, peasant resentment toward the taxation system erupted briefly: villagers in one province beat to death the French resident, Felix Bardez, whose administrative zealousness led him to try to circumvent traditional local practices by collecting taxes himself.[157]

These events in the early decades of the twentieth century followed a long period in which Cambodians had experienced profound social change marked by warfare, colonial occupation, and subsequent political and social transformations. Buddhist thought was an important site for responding to and representing these experiences. In millenarian movements, in popular vernacular texts and performances connected with Buddhist prophecies, and later in Buddhist intellectual writing such as Yukanthor's memorandum and Ind's ethical manual, we see different expressions of modern social criticism formulated in Buddhist terms.

The new social and intellectual milieu in which these critiques were formulated saw the rise of a self-consciously modernist Buddhist faction in the Khmer Sangha by 1914. For a population experiencing profound social flux, millenarianism had perhaps provided a more localized and compelling way of interpreting reality than the orderly and optimistic cosmic depictions of individual moral progress discussed in chapter 1. But as in the thought-worlds of the *Trai Bhūm* and the *jātaka,* millenarianism gave emphasis to the moral agency of bodhisattas, kings, and other exemplary, meritorious figures over that of ordinary persons. All of these Buddhist conceptions were rooted in a narrative of history, time, and social order that was coming under increasing strain as the real power of Southeast Asian kings and officials was being diminished, and as some intellectuals were adopting rationalized, demythologized forms of knowledge.

In the next chapter, I turn to examining the "modern Dhamma," as Buddhist intellectuals of the period referred to their new interpretation of Buddhism. This new religious expression reinterpreted or rejected dimensions of nineteenth-century Buddhist thought and practice, especially those aspects that conflicted with its rationalist perspectives. But it also maintained the general nineteenth-century privileging of moral perception as well as the millenarian emphasis on purification of moral conduct. This movement was in many respects an outgrowth of the wider social and political events described in this chapter, especially with respect to the social change and uneasiness that necessitated new visions of social order. It also developed within the context of the continuing renovation of Cambodian Buddhism begun under Ang Duong, and the religious reforms that were being introduced in Siam during this same period.

3 *Vinaya* Illuminations

The Rise of "Modern Dhamma"

By 1914, a new articulation of Buddhism concerned with the question of how to live in the modern world had come to life in Cambodia. It was shaped by the experiences of social and political change in the nineteenth century and by the traditions of Buddhist social criticism discussed in the previous chapter. It was also the outgrowth of a long-standing Theravādin impetus toward purification and reform at times of crisis or dynastic transition.[1] To a great extent, it reflected and drew on the more general project of modernization and reform under way during this period in Siam and colonial Cambodia with respect to political administration and social and educational restructuring.

This new current of religious thought in Cambodia was known in its first few decades as "Dharm-thmī" or "modern Dhamma." In spite of the modern self-consciousness this name suggests, modern Dhamma proponents were highly concerned with purification and with establishing the authenticity of their interpretations by connecting them with the time of the Buddha. Modern Dhamma thus shares many characteristics of a classic Theravādin purification movement, in the terms suggested by Stanley Tambiah in his historical study of Buddhist reforms.[2] But it also contained modernist dimensions, which included an explicit rejection of traditional methods and approaches, an embrace of new pedagogies and technologies, a sense of urgency about articulating new ways of being appropriate to the present time, and at the same time, an inherent critique of aspects of modern life particularly with respect to individual and social moral values. From the standpoint of modern Dhamma modernism, a purified reinterpretation of Buddhism would enable individuals to find the right path in the modern world; as individuals purified their own conduct, they simultaneously purified the religion and the religious community as a whole.

Huot Tath, one of the architects of modern Khmer Buddhism, suggested that the origins of the modern Dhamma movement could be traced to the power of understanding the *Vinaya,* the Buddhist texts outlining monastic codes of conduct. Once a group of young monks at Vatt Uṇṇālom in Phnom Penh had begun to study and translate the *Vinaya,* he wrote, they simply could not stop discussing "right and wrong ways of behaving."[3] In Huot Tath's terms, the *Vinaya,* with its commentary, was like a seed, and "having once begun to read it . . . , it took root in our hearts and minds *(citt)* and continued to grow."[4] His analysis evokes the historical question of how it was possible that between 1848—when the Khmer kingdom apparently lacked a copy of the *Dhamma-vinay*—and 1914, when this incident took place, the *Vinaya* and its delineations of moral conduct that so preoccupied Huot Tath and other young monks became the central concerns of a new Khmer Buddhist modernism.[5] And further, how and why did the particular Buddhist values associated with the modern Dhamma movement come to serve as a contested modernizing terrain, one that was vociferously opposed by the old order in the Khmer Sangha?

This chapter examines the ways in which Buddhist reforms under way in both Cambodia and Siam during the nineteenth century contributed to the rise of the modern Dhamma movement. To begin to understand how traditional Theravādin reform movements were reconfigured by Khmer monks into a form of Buddhist modernism requires that we first turn to surveying the state of the reconstituted manuscript culture in Cambodia at the end of the century, a result of the renovation put in place by Ang Duong beginning in 1848. Second, we must consider the effect of Khmer monks' experiences and perceptions of Siamese Buddhist reformism, particularly their encounters with new approaches to Pali scriptural study in late-nineteenth-century Bangkok. As Khmer monks recounted in their later writings and oral recollections to students, these experiences led to illuminations that prompted them to challenge conventional Khmer Buddhist modes of translation and textual production. These developments culminated in the events of 1914 described by Huot Tath, in which new scrutiny of the *Vinaya* served as the catalyst for the promulgation of a reinterpretation of Buddhist values.

My examination of this period focuses less on the *Vinaya* itself than on its influence and reinterpretation, via Mongkut, through various monastic practices, vernacular texts, translations, and other modernist discourses, and the changes in pedagogical methods it inspired. The idea of the *Vinaya* as a potent text that privileged a notion of purification through moral conduct was a powerful authenticating force at the center of this religious movement. In the historical context of colonial Cambodia, the conditions in which the *Vinaya* could captivate the hearts and minds of some Buddhist intellectuals and its subsequent interpretation as a source for Buddhist modernism grew out of the confluence of the intellectual, political, and religious discourses and events of the late nineteenth and early twentieth centuries, religious purification movements in Siam and Cambodia, and the social reforms and critiques examined in the previous chapter.

As Dominick LaCapra has observed, significant texts possess not only a "documentary" historical aspect that we can examine but also a "worklike" ability to transform lives in different historical moments, both in their contemporary period and dialogically, through interactions with readers of later periods, "bringing into the world something that did not exist before in that significant variation, alteration, or transformation."[6] Interpreting the history of Khmer monks' interpretations of Mongkut's interpretations of the *Vinaya* and his search for authentic and transformative truths in the *Vinaya* is perhaps a case of an amplified or third-order application of LaCapra's notion of the documentary and worklike aspects of "'great' texts."[7] Yet his characterization is useful in terms of highlighting the complex historical situatedness of the *Vinaya* as an ancient great text whose very antiquity made it capable of giving voice to modern Khmer thought and practice, in Huot Tath's words, "like a seed . . . taking root."

PURIFYING RELIGION IN A MANUSCRIPT CULTURE

One vital aspect of the Buddhist renovation begun by Ang Duong to mark the start of his reign was the recollection of texts lost or destroyed during wars with the Siamese and Vietnamese.[8] The restoration of libraries was a symbolic act that generated merit for the king and for his kingdom, as well as demonstrating the king's moral integrity and commitment to upholding and purifying the *sāsana,* "religion." It was part of the king's duty to safeguard the Dhamma through his own exemplary behavior, his patronage of the Sangha, and his concern with Dhamma texts. Texts placed in temple libraries and schools supported the education and moral purity of monks, but not all texts were intended to be read or studied. Manuscripts in the royal collection were apparently maintained more for symbolic and ritual purposes than for scholarly use, although the sacred dimensions of these texts during the nineteenth century remain obscure, as French commentators on manuscript culture had limited access to or understanding of them. Jean Moura, for instance, writes in the early 1880s of the difficulties involved in viewing the royal *baṅsāvadār* (historical chronicles),[9] and in 1899, Antoine Cabaton, who was commissioned to inventory the library of King Norodom, also comments that his inventory was incomplete as he was not permitted to view many of the manuscripts contained there, "in spite of my best efforts."[10]

In 1854, Ang Duong is said to have written to Rama IV requesting a copy of the *Tipiṭaka,* "having established that in Cambodia the doctrine of the Buddha was obscure and feeble because there was neither a *Trapiṭak* nor a *Sūtr* for study."[11] The absence of Pali canonical texts in Cambodia at this point in time may not have been simply the legacy of long warfare. In his pioneering work on Khmer Buddhism, François Bizot has argued that before this mid-nineteenth-century request by Ang Duong, the *Tipiṭaka* was probably not used or known in Cambodia as an entire corpus. Although Pali became prevalent in the thirteenth century as a religious language, and epigraphical references to "Vinaya," "Abhidhamma," and "Sūtta" exist in Cambodia, Bizot suggests that Pali scholarship in Cambodia was "mediocre" at best, and that inscriptions with the titles of the "Three Baskets" bear other interpretations. He believes it likely that these terms referred to manuals for monks containing formulas and summaries extracted from the Pali, which were intended to be memorized by monks, not necessarily studied and understood. Buddhist rules and prescriptions for living, such as the *Vinaya* precepts for monastic life, based on either canonical or perhaps even extracanonical sources, he suggests, were written as vernacular language texts.[12]

While scholarly investigation has not yet made clear exactly how far back to extend Bizot's characterizations of Pali scholarship in Cambodia, the situation he describes applies aptly to the nineteenth century. Since Buddhist literary collections at the time of Ang Duong's reign were apparently extremely limited, monks who were trying to reestablish Buddhist learning and practices were forced to travel to Siam to collect religious texts and advance their knowledge of Pali. There are relatively few sources that supply detailed descriptions of text-collecting trips in Siam prior to 1900, but the tradition seems to have extended from Ang Duong's reign into the early twentieth century. In the 1870s, for instance, a monk named Duong, who was the abbot of Vatt Braḥ Buddh Nibbāṇ in Kong-Pissey went to Siam and returned with twenty *gambhīr,* which included the *Maṅgaladīpanī* (a medieval Thai commentary on the *Maṅgalasutta*), *Sāratthasaṅgaha, Parīvāravatth, Braḥ Abhīdhamm, Mūlakaccāyana, Trai Bhūm, Buddhaguṇ,* several *jātaka* (including the *Vessantara-jātaka*), several commentaries, and a manual on *vipassanā* (meditation) practice. The texts were presented to Braḥ Buddh Nibbāṇ monastery and entrusted to the care of a man named Āchāry Pol, in order "to permit [Abbot Duong] to undertake the teaching of Pali, of which he had a fairly extensive knowledge."[13] A monastic biography of Braḥ Mahā Vimaladhamm Thoṅ, a prominent monk born in Phnom Penh in 1862 who later became the first director of the newly created Sālā Pali in 1914 and an important mentor of the modernist faction,[14] recounts that he too left for Siam in 1903, at the age of forty-one,

> as he desired to have sacred manuscripts for Cambodia, manuscripts that only Siam possessed, he asked authorization from the Supreme Head of the Sangha to go to Siam by way of land in spite of the dangers and difficulties. . . . After a stay of one year in Siam, he returned to Cambodia, bearing with him a number of manuscripts.[15]

Even for monks who could not undertake the journey to Siam, the work of textual collection was an important preoccupation, evidenced in the significance attached to this religious activity in funeral biographies. One biography recounts that the monk Jha-Lan, born in 1875, felt compelled to leave Kompong Cham (northeast of Phnom Penh) to find *Dhamma-vinay* texts. As a young *bhikkhu,* he "went off in search of *gambhīr* in order to study *Dhamma-vinay.* He went away for training in correct understanding of Dhamma recitation to the *saṃṇāk* [monastery; monastery school][16] of Samtec Braḥ Diaṅ (then supreme patriarch of the Sangha) in Phnom Penh."[17] The lists of meritorious activities for monks and others in the biographies suggest that after religious building, contributions of texts were perceived as the most significant means of making merit in the early part of the twentieth century. For example, the funeral biography of the abbot of Vatt Baṅbas' in Prey Vang, Braḥ Candavinay Gaṅ-O (1880–1953) records among his accomplishments that he "donated texts of the *Braḥ Traipiṭak* in Pali, and *saṃrāy* of the *Vinaya* in Khmer."[18] The biography of the abbot of Vatt Krabuṃbejr in Koh Dac Province, Braḥ Suvaṇṇakesaro Hū-ṛāy (1889–1954), lists donations of texts among his meritorious activities. Along with the religious buildings and Buddha images he erected, he "provided . . . many texts, including a palm-leaf *saṃrāy* of the *Maṅgalatthadīpanī* . . . , seven volumes of the *Abhidhamma,* and a text of the *Paṭhamasambodhi.*"[19] Another abbot, Braḥ Nillajoti Prāk Ū (1890–1958) of Bodhisat Province, "inscribed palm-leaf manuscripts in order to offer them, and purchased various texts for observing the *sāsana* of Lord Buddha."[20] In a rare funeral biography of a housewife and laywoman in Siem Reap named So-Suan (1880–1960), who became a Buddhist nun, the woman is commended not only for her many generous gifts to the Sangha, but also for her purchase of a *Braḥ Traipiṭak* for a local monastery.[21]

By the end of the century, the success of these text-collection efforts is confirmed in French inventories that document the existence of at least several notable collections. In 1899, Norodom's royal library contained numerous palm-leaf manuscripts, including law texts, chronicles, biographies of the Buddha in Pali and Khmer, *cpāp',* medical texts, vernacular *saṃrāy* versions of *Tipiṭaka* texts, the *Rāmakerti,* and manuals of Sanskrit mantras used for recitation by *bakou*s (Khmer Brahmanic priests), as well as texts from Bangkok that the inventorist describes as the "libretti" of dramatic Indian poetic theatrical works, written in Siamese. The role of the Siamese language during this period was, in his words, "comparable to that of Italian in Europe in opera of the past."[22] But either the library still lacked Pali canonical texts altogether (in line with Bizot's argument), or the inventorist was not allowed to see them, which seems equally possible, since the manuscript culture that imbued them with preciosity as sacred objects was still largely intact.

Georges Groslier, a scholar of Khmer arts writing in the early part of the twentieth century, notes the long tradition, prior to the mid-nineteenth century, of protecting sacred manuscripts in edifices surrounded by water. This practice shifted between 1870 and 1913, when royal copies of texts were moved to a small building behind the throne room; though not as dramatically separated, the texts were still being housed in a distinct sacred space.[23] The protective maintenance of sacred texts is similarly evident in a 1903 incident involving École française d'Extrême-Orient (hereafter EFEO) director Louis Finot, who wrote that he was frustrated by a lack of access to Khmer manuscripts. He had requested help from provincial administrators in procuring texts from local elites but had failed, for instance, to obtain a full text of the Khmer *Rāmakerti,* the Khmer version of the *Rāmayāna,* of whose existence he was assured. Although he knew that Khmer mandarins possessed manuscripts of local, family, and monastic chronicles and law texts, they refused to grant him access to any of these texts, which, he argued, were essential for the colonial administration's efforts to understand indigenous Cambodian legal codes.[24] Similar episodes concerning texts are apparent in other colonial correspondence.[25]

The reluctance shown by turn-of-the-century Khmer mandarins and monks to allow their manuscripts to be used for certain kinds of administrative and scholarly purposes demonstrates the enduring hold of manuscript culture at that time. A decade later, tensions over the meaning and value of texts as sacred objects ignited the controversies surrounding the modern Dhamma movement and developed into a significant fissure between traditional Theravādins and modernists within the Mahānikāy order (described later in this chapter). Although this conflict over texts had hermeneutic, pedagogical, and orthographic dimensions, at its heart it involved the perception of texts as physical objects. As in other colonial contexts where indigenous religion and other aspects of traditional culture were catalogued and exhibited by colonial officials, scholars, and their native counterparts,[26] colonial scholars such as Finot regarded Buddhist texts as objects to be inventoried, collected, curated, and used above all for scientific study of history and religion. In contrast, the Khmer families, individuals, and monks who owned texts viewed them primarily as sacred objects to be used and maintained for ritual and religious purposes rather than for conveying or documenting historical and legal information. Most important was that, in their minds, texts presented to temples were meant to generate merit; to remove texts donated for this purpose was unthinkable.[27]

By 1912, EFEO scholar George Coedés had succeeded in gaining enough access to temple libraries to conduct a more comprehensive inventory of Khmer monastic collections, commenting that, "the inventory of pagodas that I have made during my recent visit to Cambodia has convinced me that this country possesses as much richness as its neighbors and it would require only a minor effort to constitute a library capable of rivaling the Bernard Free Library of Rangoon or the Vajirañāṇa [Library] of Bangkok."[28] His report includes details of particularly well endowed libraries in Phnom Penh and Battambang. At Vatt Braḥ Kaev in Phnom Penh, for instance, he inventoried the private collection of 150 manuscripts possessed by one of its monks, which "contains all of the essential works of Pali literature."[29] The oldest collections of manuscripts he observed, dating from the end of the eighteenth and the early nineteenth centuries, were in monasteries in Battambang at Vatt Bodhivāl and Vatt Ṭaṃrī Sa; the former had apparently been assembled at the beginning of the nineteenth century from Siamese sources and the latter donated by the Siamese governor Phya Kathathan while Battambang was still a Siamese province.[30] The manuscript collection at Vatt Bodhivāl in Battambang may well have been the most comprehensive collection in Cambodia before the 1920s. Its Pali collection included three copies of the *Maṅgaladīpanī*, eighteen *jātaka* manuscripts, and other *Tipiṭaka* and commentarial titles.[31]

Most other collections were of later date, Coedès found, and "the vast majority of the Pali manuscripts have their origin in Siam, where they were copied from Siamese originals."[32] Among Pali texts, Coedès noted that the most prevalent texts, "of which few pagodas in Cambodia do not possess several chapters," were the *Maṅgaladīpanī* and the *Paṭhamasambodhi*, the Siamese version of the life of the

Buddha (discussed in chapter 1).[33] Other French sources from the period indicate that monastic collections also contained Khmer vernacular literature, particularly Khmer versions of the *Vessantar-jātak,* other *jātaka* of local composition, and *cpāp'.* Monastery collections also contained secular literature, including songs, *nirās* (travel poetry), and technical manuals (*tamrā* or *kpuan*) on subjects such as medicine or astronomy.[34]

The reconstitution of text collections in this period represented a classic Theravādin form of religious reform, which was synonymous with a notion of purifying Buddhism. A monastery, like the kingdom, was better off—stronger and purer—if it possessed texts. A prevailing view of texts was of physically potent objects that affected the spiritual well-being of the individuals who handled them; their exact contents were of lesser importance. Texts were understood to be sacred in much the same way as relics, which embodied physical elements of the Buddha. Being in physical contact or proximity with texts, touching them, seeing them, or hearing them, connected one with the Buddha and his teachings devotionally. These acts generated merit first, and led to greater intellectualized forms of understanding only as a secondary aim, if at all; rather, devotional acts generated a different kind of insight, more akin to meditational understanding. Until the modern Dhamma movement emerged, little distinction was drawn between different types of texts, among nonscholarly monks and laypeople at least, nor was an effort made to attach greater authority to some types of texts than others.

The sacred physical and devotional aspects of textuality were in many respects diminished and altered with the transition to print culture that occurred during the 1920s. The nineteenth-century preoccupation with purifying and strengthening the Buddhist *sāsana* in Cambodia through text collecting was not simply lost, however. Rather, Khmer monks began to reinterpret and redirect the notion of purification itself. This altered understanding arose in large part through the influence of monks who went to Bangkok to retrieve texts and Pali knowledge. Ideas about purification that had been connected to copying, collecting, and maintaining Buddhist texts in general became increasingly intertwined with the interpretation and study of a particular part of the *Tipiṭaka,* the rules and discussions of conduct, and monastic discipline found in the *Vinaya* and its commentaries. As these monks returned home, their notions of purification became the basis for the articulation of a modern Buddhism that sought to separate the idea of the authenticity of texts from the materials on which they were written and, through the veracity and potency of authoritative interpretations of texts, to reorient the conduct of every Khmer Buddhist.

These new currents of thought developed around a multilayered notion of purification, including purification of Buddhist interpretations and practices, purified recensions of texts, and purified self-conduct. Stanley Tambiah has described the textual and interpretive aspects of this conception as "scripturalism," a term he employs to describe Mongkut's "concern with finding the true canon, of understanding the truth correctly and discarding false beliefs and magical practices."[35] Along with the tenets of scripturalism, Khmer monks who studied in Bangkok imported a sense of the value of education in general and of new, reformed Buddhist educational methods in particular. For some Khmer intellectuals, the exposure to new representations of the modern geographical and physical world current in Siam under Mongkut and Chulalongkorn, and the more cosmopolitan culture they encountered there, seems also to have fostered a heightened awareness of the distinctiveness of Khmer culture and identity. Finally, as a result of their studies in Bangkok, the returning scholars had—as their biographies tend to describe it—experienced an "awakening" or "illumination," a transformation in vision and understanding that took hold in their "hearts and minds."[36]

BUDDHIST LEARNING IN SIAM AND CAMBODIA

Braḥ Mās-Kuṅ, born in Kompong Cham in 1872, traveled to Siam in 1892 shortly after his ordination as a *bhikkhu* in Kompong Cham "to study the *Braḥ Traipiṭak*."[37] His biographer stresses the difficulty of this journey at the time. He traveled to Phnom Penh and after some days there found a fishing boat to take him up the Tonle Sap to the Sangker district of Battambang. Within Battambang, he traveled from Sangker to Mongkolburi and then Sisophon, walking from village to village and staying overnight in local monasteries. In Sisophon he was invited to join the traveling party of a district chief headed for Bangkok. They journeyed by foot through wilderness and mountainous areas—arduous days of travel that lasted from early morning until late at night—through Sisophon and the Siamese provinces of Sa Kaeo and Pradumthani. From Pradumthani, a ship's *kappiten* (captain) who had accompanied them from Sisophon arranged for a steamer passage for Braḥ Mās-Kuṅ to Bangkok, where from a pier on the Chao Phraya River, the captain led the monk to Vatt Jetabhan.[38] The entire journey from Phnom Penh had taken more than a month.

To understand why Braḥ Mās-Kuṅ felt compelled to undertake this grueling journey requires a regional perspective on Buddhist reforms and Sangha networks in the nineteenth century. Khmer efforts to renovate Buddhism during this period were strongly influenced by Siamese reformist ideologies from the Dhammayut sect introduced by King Mongkut in the mid-nineteenth century, which drew on a Sinhalese Mahāvihārin recension of the Pali canon and Mon monastic practices. Siamese reformist ideas were circulated to Cambodia by traveling Khmer monk-scholars drawn to the vibrant Buddhist literary culture of Bangkok created by Mongkut, his son Chulalongkorn, and their officials. The forces that ushered in these new currents of thought, it has been argued, were not primarily the result of knowledge of Western technology and science brought to Siam during this period, but rather the influence of the modernizing, rationalistic climate of Bangkok intellectualism under Mongkut and Chulalongkorn, a culmination of the reforms initially put in motion in Siam by Rama I toward the end of the eighteenth century.[39]

Mongkut's religious innovations resulted in the formation of a new order called the Dhammayut and ushered in a new ethos of demythologizing rationalism among some Buddhists in Bangkok.[40] Mongkut and other Dhammayut teachers and leaders sought to intellectualize monastic education and to spread this purified religion to laypeople—to the exclusion of magical ritual practices and the centrality of narrative texts, such as *jātaka,* for teaching and interpreting the tradition.[41] Even as they worked to introduce religious and administrative reforms and innovations in the kingdom, Mongkut and members of his court were also interested in Western science. In 1867, one of Mongkut's officials published a book (the first Siamese-printed book) called *Kitchanukit,* which argued for the reinterpretation of Buddhism away from the erroneous cosmological views of the world promulgated by the *Trai Bhūm* and toward an understanding of Buddhism that emphasized moral conduct in the context of an individual's present life.[42] Reflecting the "spirit of Mongkut's movement," as Thongchai Winichakul has described it, it also argued for a separation between "worldly matters" and "religious matters."[43] The publication of *Kitchanukit* marked the onset of a widening trend among many Siamese intellectuals to view some aspects of Buddhism with a demythologizing eye, emphasizing the social ethical aspects of Buddhist texts and teachings to the exclusion of its cosmologically oriented ways of envisioning the structure and workings of the world.[44]

When Mongkut's son Chulalongkorn came to the throne in 1868 (r. 1868–1910), he further extended many of his father's ideas with the development and introduction of policies designed to bring about modernization in religion, education, and political administration. Chulalongkorn's reign has been viewed by historians as the culmination of a movement toward centralization, bureaucratization, and modernization. Craig Reynolds has suggested that this movement had begun at the beginning of the Chakri dynasty with Rama I's efforts to regain control of tributary states, consolidate political control, and purify the Sangha following a chaotic period that had seen the fall of the Thai kingdom Ayutthaya to the Burmese in 1767 and the troubled reign of King Taksin (1767–1782).[45] By the beginning of the twentieth century, Chulalongkorn, with the help of a new generation of Siamese administrators including his brothers Princes Vajirañāṇa-varorasa and Damrong, had begun to extend his new policies and institutions into the provinces in a successful effort to apply uniform religious and educational standards throughout the kingdom.[46] These policies also significantly furthered the transformation of the regional "galactic polities" of which Siam was composed into a politically, culturally, and linguistically unified modern nation-state.

Bangkok consequently became an important center of monastic training for Khmer monks and novices during the nineteenth century. In Bangkok, Khmer monks pursued opportunities for obtaining higher education in Pali and finding and copying texts that were currently unavailable in Cambodia. When they returned to Cambodia, they took back not only the texts Khmer monasteries lacked, but also the reform ideas current in Bangkok.

The extent of Siamese influence is made evident by the biographies of both of the leading Khmer monks of the nineteenth century, Samtec Braḥ Sangharāj Diaṅ (1823–1913) and Sugandhādhipatī Pān (c. 1824 –1894), who received their ordinations in Bangkok.[47] Samtec Braḥ Sangharāj Diaṅ, the Sangha chief who oversaw most of the Buddhist renovation in Cambodia, was captured as a prisoner of war by the Siamese army as a young boy and sent as a slave to Bangkok, where he became connected to the entourage of Prince Ang Duong. He was ordained as a novice at the age of eleven, and by the time he ordained as a monk in 1844, he had already won notice from Rama III for his brilliance. According to his funeral biography, his reputation as a scholar and monk-scribe was well established in monastic circles in Bangkok by the time he was twenty-five. Probably at the request of Ang Duong, he translated a Khmer version of the *Trai Bhūm* from the Siamese,[48] as well as the *Pāṭimokkha,* a section of the *Vinaya* regularly recited by monks.[49] He apparently also composed a number of poetic works during his life, including a version of the Khmer *sātrā lpaeṅ* (verse-novel) *Jinavaṅs* (popular in Cambodia at the turn of the century) on a past life of the Buddha.[50]

In 1849, after Ang Duong returned to Cambodia and was installed on the Khmer throne by the Siamese, he requested that Diaṅ be sent to him in Udong to head up the restoration of Buddhism in the kingdom. Working under the authority of the king, Diaṅ began undertaking the first of several reorganizations of Sangha administration that would occur during the next half-century.[51] Appointed to the high monastic rank of *braḥ mahāvimaladhamm* in 1853 at the age of thirty, within a year he had moved up to a rank of *braḥ mahābrahmamunī;*[52] in 1857, he was appointed *samtec braḥ sangharāj* (supreme patriarch). One of his early acts as supreme patriarch appears to have been the institutionalization of monastic exams in Pali, three-month-long exams offered first in 1858. Diaṅ retained his close connections with the Khmer throne during Norodom's reign and was venerated by the general populace until his death in 1913.[53]

Another high-ranking monk educated in Bangkok was Samtec Braḥ Sugandhādhipatī Pān. Although his social origins are not clear from biographical sources, Pān's parents had been relocated from Kompong Thom to Battambang as prisoners of war by the Siamese during a period of "turmoil,"[54] which suggests they may have been captured slaves; Pān was later uncertain of his parents' names.[55] Born in Battambang, Pān was ordained as a novice in 1836 at Vatt Bodhivāl in Battambang; in 1837 he went to Bangkok to study Pali, "in light of the deplorable state of Buddhist education in his [natal] pagoda."[56] He began his studies at a Mahānikāy monastery, Vatt Saket, where he "studied the *Braḥ Traipiṭak,*" and was ordained as a *bhikkhu* at the age of twenty-one. In 1848, according to one biography, a lay supporter arranged for him "to study *sikkhāvinay*" (*Vinaya* training or discipline) at Vatt Paramanivās[57] under its abbot, Chauv Ghun Braḥ Ñāṇarakkhit Sukh. Another biographical source suggests that he also studied Pali "translation" under the direction of Mongkut, who was still in the monkhood at this time.[58] He reordained as a Dhammayut *bhikkhu* in 1849 with Mongkut, Sukh, and Chauv Ghun Braḥ Amarābhirakkhit Koet (a respected *Vinaya* scholar and later abbot of Vatt Paramanivās in Bangkok) presiding at the ceremony.[59] He continued his monastic duties and studies at Vatt Braḥ Kaiv Luoṅ, and after sitting for Pali examinations, began to climb the Thai Sangha hierarchy.

The date of his return to Cambodia and founding of the Dhammayut sect in Cambodia has been attributed to the reigns of both Ang Duong and Norodom, either in 1854 or 1864.[60] While the exact date is uncertain, it is clear that in symbolic and political terms, the erudite monk Pān—and with him, the establishment of the Dhammayut sect—emanated from the highest court circles in Bangkok. Pān was accompanied on his return to Cambodia by a number of Siamese monks, including Koet, by then a high-ranking Sangha official, who presented the kingdom with a collection of eighty Siamese texts (presumably the *Tipiṭaka* requested by Ang Duong).[61]

Under Norodom, Pān constructed the seat of the Dhammayut order in an ancient monastery in Phnom Penh that was renamed as Vatt Bodum Vaddey and dedicated to the new order.[62] In the mid-1880s, he sent a delegation of Khmer monks to Ceylon to obtain relics and a bo tree seedling, which was planted in front of the newly reconstructed monastery in 1887.[63] He died in 1894, with the title *samtec braḥ sugandhādhipatī,* the chief of the Dhammayut order and the second-highest monastic rank in the kingdom.[64] Leclère describes him as "certainly the most highly educated, most respected and most consulted man in the kingdom," adding that he "appears to have raised the teaching of ethics" to higher levels.[65] He was apparently literate in Pali, Sanskrit, Thai, Lao, Burmese, and Mon and could also read ancient Khmer inscriptions.[66] Dhammayut sources suggest that he was an important compiler of *Vinaya* commentaries, monastic training manuals, and manuals on merit-making rituals.[67]

Samtec Braḥ Sangharāj Diaṅ and Samtec Braḥ Sugandhādhipatī Pān were both widely respected and well-educated monastic leaders. From the 1850s onward, they were able to foster the renovation of Buddhism envisioned by Ang Duong and to introduce reforms in Pali studies and Sangha administration. But in spite of their work, the number of educated monks in Cambodia with a high degree of Pali knowledge appears to have remained fairly modest throughout the nineteenth century, necessitating the continued flow of Khmer students to Bangkok. In addition, their own close ties to Bangkok perhaps contributed to its continuing attraction and prestige as a site for higher education. Khmer monks educated in Bangkok carried back texts and curricular traditions from their own studies. At better-equipped monasteries such as Vatt Uṇṇālom in Phnom Penh, where Diaṅ taught until his death, and at Vatt Bodum Vaddey, the Dhammayut center, monastic learning reduplicated current Bangkok curricula. After the 1890s, when monastic curricular reforms were being introduced in Bangkok, Khmer Buddhist learning continued to follow the nineteenth-century curricula until the advent of Khmer modernist reforms in the 1920s, discussed in chapter 4.

In spite of the introduction of some Sangha administrative reforms by Samtec

Braḥ Sangharāj Diaṅ, Khmer monasteries remained highly decentralized until about 1910.[68] It is nonetheless possible to draw some conclusions about the general education received in monasteries in the late nineteenth and early twentieth centuries. At the primary level, most young boys became literate in Khmer, learning to read, write, and compute;[69] they were also given instruction in vernacular religious literature such as didactic poetry and verse narrative versions of *jātaka*[70] and in manuals or technical treatises[71] on astrology, medicine, and ritual procedures.[72] Some funeral biographies report young boys studying *sātrā,* and certainly, students were exposed to the preaching or recitations of various texts by their monk-teachers. These texts varied from monastery to monastery depending on the skills of the particular monks who lived there and the contents of the monastery's text collection. An abbot in Kompong Speu, for example, who was born in 1883, had a repertoire of texts that included both secular and Dhammic genres *(phlūv lok, phlūv dharm),* which included meditation texts, a commentary on the *Abhidhamma,* and in particular, the *Dasa-jātaka,* which "he preached in a strong, clear voice."[73] This source explicitly differentiates between the texts the abbot "knew" *(ceḥ),* "preached," or "recited" *(desanā, sūtr)* and the texts he was "able to speak and explain."[74] The significance of this distinction will emerge more clearly in the discussion following, since the manner of "knowing" texts became one of the central issues involved in modernist reforms—and monastic tension in the decades following this period.

Young men who were able to continue their education often ordained as novices between ages thirteen and fifteen. Funeral biographies suggest that few of these young *sāmaṇer* could remain in their village monasteries; more often, they were forced to move to seek out qualified teachers.[75] Novices generally spent six to seven years studying religious literature and Pali, with some biographies also referring to meditation practice.[76] Some funeral biographies suggest merely that novices spent their seven years studying the *Braḥ Traipiṭak* or *Buddhavacana,* "words of the Buddha";[77] others offer more detail on the texts they studied. For instance, Braḥ Mahābrahmamunī Deb-Ū, who was born in 1891 and later became the abbot of Vatt Svāy Babae in Phnom Penh, spent seven years (1905–1912) as a novice in Cambodia's leading Dhammayut monastery of the day, Vatt Bodum Vaddey. His stay there took place before its renovation as a "model" *vatt* school, but it still must have contained among the best educational resources available at the time, including Samtec Braḥ Sugandhādhipatī Pān's library from Siam.[78] Following Pān's death, his successor as head of the Dhammayut order and abbot of Vatt Bodum Vaddy, Samtec Braḥ Maṅgaladebācāry Iam (1829–1870) also donated a substantial collection of palm-leaf manuscripts to the monastery.[79] Iam had had the scholarly Pān as his preceptor, and Iam himself was Deb-Ū's preceptor —although it is not clear from the biography how closely he was involved in teaching Pali.[80]

The records of Deb-Ū's monastic curriculum at Vatt Bodum Vaddey suggest the influence of Pan's training in Siam. By the time Deb-Ū had finished his novitiate at Vatt Bodum Vaddey, he had learned to "recite and *translate*" (emphasis mine) six Pali texts.[81] These included *Mūlakaccāyana, Aṭṭhikathādhammapada, Maṅgaladīpanī, Sāratthasaṅgaha, Visuddhimagga,* and *Pathamasāmant.*[82] In the traditional form of monastic training at this level in Khmer monasteries, monks were normally trained merely in recitation of Pali through rote memorization—which did not guarantee that a monk understood the meaning of the text or words he was reciting. The titles in this list reflect the curricula being used for *samāṇera* education in most Siamese monasteries up until the 1890s.[83] Thus Deb-Ū's education was probably among the most advanced and rigorous levels of training a monk could receive in Cambodia at this time.

Yet in spite of this, his biography continues, at the conclusion of his seven years of study Deb-Ū found that

> he could not quell the yearning in his heart and mind for more; he was not yet satiated and could not compel himself to feel satisfied with this end [to his studies]—for he was certain that he did not yet understand the essence [of Buddhist teachings]. The method of teaching the words of the Buddha *(Buddhavacana)* in the Pali texts was to consider everything, in a precise and exhaustive manner. But most [Khmer] teachers at that time were unable to provide their students with explanations that would allow them to gain clear or deep comprehension, or to illuminate all subjects. Most often, their teaching consisted merely of having students repeat after them as they recited the scriptures *(gambhīr).*[84]

KHMER MONKS IN SIAM

Like other Khmer monks who wanted to pursue further Pali study, Deb-Ū decided to go to Bangkok. He applied to Samtec Braḥ Maṅgaladebācāry Iam for a travel permit, and left Cambodia. By 1913, colonial improvements in roads and seaports (undertaken with Khmer corvée labor), had made the trip to Bangkok considerably easier than in the past.[85] He spent his first year in Bangkok at Vatt Buṇṇasiriāmātyārām learning Thai, and then began his Pali studies at Vatt Pavaranives under Vajirañāṇa (1860–1921), Mongkut's son and by then supreme patriarch of the Thai Sangha.[86] He spent nine years in Bangkok, returning to Cambodia in 1921 where he taught *Dhamma-vinay*[87] and Pali grammar at Vatt Bodum Vaddey for several years, before being invited to assume the abbotship of Vatt Svāy Babae.[88]

In addition to the details of his monastic exams and teachers in Bangkok, Deb-Ū's biography relays an account of the most striking intellectual and spiritual experience of his studies in Bangkok:

> During the time that he was a student in Bangkok, he experienced a brilliant illumination in respect to the *Braḥ Dhamma-vinay.* This occurred because the

monks who were his teachers supplied their students with thorough and detailed explanations.[89]

If the biography is read in the context of other monastic sources from the period, Deb-Ū's "brilliant illumination" might be understood to concern the interpretation and understanding of the *Vinaya* in both a narrow and broad sense. The phrase *"Dhamma-vinay"* (or *"Dharm-vinay"*) is used in Khmer sources from the period to refer to the *Tipiṭaka,* as opposed to Buddhist texts and teachings as a whole.[90] But the term is also employed more broadly in period sources to delineate "ways of behaving according to what is right and wrong"[91] and ways of living that lead to the "happiness of freedom and purity."[92] While in this broader sense the phrase might be translated more succinctly as "morality" or "ethics," this translation fails to convey the sense in which, for monks, it was simultaneously tied to knowledge of specific *Vinaya-piṭaka* teachings such as the *sikkhāpada-sīla* (precepts). The phrase *"Dhamma-vinay"* invoked notions of authenticity, legitimacy, and purification tied to new ways of interpreting Buddhist teachings.

A Khmer biography of Mongkut helps to demonstrate how Khmer monks experienced and represented their new illuminations about the *Dhamma-vinay.* Their emphasis on *Dhamma-vinay* had its origins in Mongkut's own early monastic experience. As a young man, he observed troubling behaviors among his fellow monks that directly contradicted the *sikkhapāda* (precepts for monks), such as those regarding celibacy, and prohibitions against handling money, taking part in entertainment, or eating after noon. In his confusion, he turned to the *Dhamma-vinay:*

> [He] made an effort to learn *Braḥ Dhamma-vinay* from the *Braḥ Tipiṭaka* [in order] to know and understand correct and incorrect behaviors. He had observed *bhikkhus* and novices in his monastery perform actions that were in many respects contrary to the *Dhamma-vinay.* Some monks preached the *Mahā-jātak* as verse-*lakhon* with musical accompaniment. Other monks rented themselves out to chant the *Mālai* [sutta]. Still others came dancing in and shrieking out theatrical performance *(yiker)* lyrics. Some of them worked as goldsmiths, artists, or cement layers, accepting payment. Others were imposters who "ordained" every morning and "disrobed" every evening [in order to] go out for women; they ate food after noon and handled money, buying expensive goods in the market from the merchants, consuming food or medicines that had not been offered to them as alms, working as physicians.[93]

This disillusionment led to a crisis of faith for Mongkut. But as he turned to the *Tipiṭaka* for confirmation of the inappropriateness of what he observed, he made a vow "in front of the Buddha who is the Master and all of the *devadā*" that when he had ordained, his "heart and mind were free of impurities toward the Triple Gem. I did not ordain with a desire for any kind of gain in profit or prestige or any kind of fame or praise at all."[94] On the basis of this purity, he vowed that if he could not find clarification to the questions of monastic behavior and the authenticity of the Theravādin lineages in Siam within the next few days, he would leave the monkhood and live instead as a devout layperson. Mongkut feared not only that the behavior of individual monks violated *Vinaya* precepts but also that monastic ordination procedures themselves were illegitimate. Soon after his vow, the biography continues, he encountered a teacher named Braḥ Sumedhācāry, who had come to Bangkok from the Mon country "to illuminate and propagate *Braḥ Dhamma-vinay* in Siam."[95]

> When Samtec Braḥ Paramakhau [Mongkut] observed his comportment[96] and heard his Dhamma-preaching concerning the paths of monastic conduct, a pure, unblemished faith arose in him giving him the clear perception that here was a teacher whose lineage was authentic.[97] He undertook to practice [this form] of monastic conduct[98] and began to study *Vinay Braḥ Traipiṭak* under the tutelage of Braḥ Sumedhācāry.[99]

For Mongkut, the issues of proper monastic conduct and authentic lineage became clarified within the Mon tradition. Along with his concern about ordination procedures, he had questioned the authenticity of the most basic daily monastic behaviors: the wearing of the robes and the carrying of the alms bowl, or *bat.* Mon monks did not wear their robes in the same manner as Siamese and Khmer monks. The robes for all Buddhist monks consisted of three separate robes *(ticīvaraṃ):* one covered the lower part of the body, the second, the upper; an additional robe was placed around the shoulders when the monk went out in public. The difference in style concerned the question of how to properly fasten the two upper robes around one's body.[100] Since the *Vinaya* passages on this topic were difficult to understand, different interpretations had emerged; two were current in Siam at the time—the mainstream style and the Mon style. As the Thai supreme patriarch Vajirañāṇa has described it, the different styles of wearing the robes centered on the question of how *bhikkhus* could manage to accept alms while remaining appropriately covered:[101]

> *[B]hikkhus* had to roll the robe like a loofah-gourd and then pull it up, putting the edge over the shoulder and holding the loofah-roll with the left hand as Mahānikāya *bhikkhus* wear it. Later, *bhikkhus* put the loofah-roll over the shoulder without pinching it, thus loosening and opening the loofah-roll to bring the right hand out as Mon *bhikkhus* do.[102]

Mon monks also observed regulations concerning the attire of *sāmaṇer* (novices) that made them more equivalent to those followed by *bhikkhus*; rather than keeping one shoulder bare in public, Mon novices were expected to cover both shoulders with their robes. They also carried their alms bowls in their hands rather than suspended from a strap or bag slung around their shoulders. And finally, they pronounced Pali differently, with respect to the pronunciation of nasal consonants and by adding a final "a" to words such as "*Vinay*" and "*sāmaṇer*," sounds that were normally dropped in the pronunciation of Pali adopted by most Thai and Khmer monks of the day.[103] By the time Mongkut established his new order in 1836, he had adopted Mon interpretations concerning monastic practices such as the manner of wearing robes, the carrying of the *bat*, and the pronunciation of Pali. He had also imported twenty-seven monks from Sri Lanka whose lineage he considered pure and authentic for a reordination ceremony in Bangkok, to ensure the legitimacy of his own ordination line.[104]

While all of his reforms focused on ascertaining the authenticity and purity of monastic conduct, the most far-reaching of his innovations were in the area of monastic education. Mongkut's own experiences had taught him that many of his compatriots in the Sangha had only a limited understanding of the authentic teachings of the Buddha. With the establishment of his new order, he began to introduce new, more vigorous standards for Pali education in the Sangha to make certain that monks not only understood the Pali they were chanting, but also that texts were accurately copied, edited, and translated and that laypeople be introduced to the authentic meaning of the Pali words and texts they heard. He sought to downplay the influence of texts such as the *jātaka* and instead increase the centrality of *Tipiṭaka* texts such as the *Vinaya*.[105]

Even though Mongkut left the monkhood in 1851 to become king, his elevation to the throne ensured that his influence on the future direction of Siamese Buddhism was profound. With the succession of his son Chulalongkorn as king and the appointment of another son, Vajirañāṇa, as supreme patriarch of the Thai Sangha, Mongkut's monastic educational reforms were promoted and deepened. By the time Khmer monks of Deb-Ū's generation arrived in Bangkok, the reformed educational agenda introduced by Mongkut had become established in Mahānikāy as well as Dhammayut centers of learning in Bangkok.[106] From the perspective of Khmer monastic experience, they were startling innovations. Deb-Ū's biography describes the pedagogical methods he encountered at Vatt Pavaranives in some detail:

> [The Thai teachers] had developed a grammar method that was conjoined to the teaching of the Pali commentaries. This replaced the [older] *Mūlakaccāyana* grammar, which was too long and took forever to learn, and in addition, was difficult to understand. By contrast, the new method of grammar was organized in a manner that made it possible to learn quickly, and it was easy for students to grasp its broad concepts. The method that was most frequently used for explaining and teaching textual translation was grammatical. As far as the method of translation went, once a section was close to translated, they taught [students to use a combination of] the grammatical method of parsing a sentence along with the "blotter" [or absorption] method[107] in order to give the structure and meaning and not to alter the grammatical style.

> The system of parsing a sentence, they derived from the commentaries.[108] For example, in the commentary to the *Dhammapada,* which scholars have previously translated, there are long and short passages of grammatical parsing in order for students to understand what is already clearly known and which words are supposed to be connected with other words. This style of teaching by using explanations of this sort is one that students appreciate. They understand more clearly how to translate Pali, in a more thorough manner.[109]

Although Deb-Ū's biography is more detailed than most, the terms in which his experience in Bangkok is presented, from his "brilliant illumination" in respect to *Dhamma-vinay* to the epiphanies caused by grammatical parsing, are echoed in other biographies as well, including those of monks who studied in Mahānikāy monasteries. The biography of Braḥ Mās-Kaṅ (1872–1960), who arrived in Bangkok even earlier than Deb-Ū, recounts similar experiences. As a young monk who was studying at a provincial monastery in Kompong Cham, Mās-Kaṅ—like Deb-Ū—realized that he was not going to be able to progress any further in his knowledge of scripture if he remained in Cambodia. In 1892, a year after his ordination as a *bhikkhu,* he left for Siam.[110] Mās-Kaṅ's studies at Vatt Jetabhan, a Mahānikāy monastery in Bangkok, also involved grammatical and translation training.[111] Although his studies were interrupted for several years by illness, he spent ten years altogether as a monastic student in Siam, returning to Kompong Cham in 1901 to serve as a teacher.

His biography recounts the insights he had gained as a result of his education in Bangkok in this way:

> His heart was filled with joy toward the *Dhamma-vinay* that he had learned and studied in Siam, and that he had come back to train other monks, novices, and young boys to understand. He wanted to teach them to recite and translate from the Three Refuges, the five, eight, and ten precepts *(sikkhāpada-sīla),* to translate Pali homages *(namassakār)* on the qualities of the Buddha, Dhamma, and Sangha for morning and evening worship at the *vatt.*
>
> At this point in time, the Sālā Pali in Phnom Penh had not yet begun educating people about the *Dhamma-vinay* in this manner. Thus, the laypeople on the whole had yet to achieve freedom and purity because they lacked opportunities for hearing and truly understanding the *{Dhamma-vinay}.* Since the practice of translating Pali into Khmer was not yet widespread, they had never been able to achieve the happiness that came from the freedom and purity of understanding [the *Dhamma-vinay*]. Monks and laypeople of the time merely transmitted the same traditions that they had themselves been taught, such as asking for blessings and protection *(vatt jayanādī),* and so on.[112]

In addition to the training in Pali grammar, textual translation, and monastic conduct that these young Khmer monks received, Bangkok introduced them to an active literary world in which print was being popularized and, simultaneously, disseminating new views of Buddhism. Even before the publication of *Kitchanukit* in 1867, Mongkut had introduced a press for printing and circulating Pali works favored by the Dhammayut *nikāy*, including the *Pāṭimokkha* and other works used in Dhammayut education.[113] Under Chulalongkorn, the new print culture continued to flourish, with seventeen different newspapers and forty-two periodicals appearing in print during his reign, including one introduced in the 1880s by the staff of the newly constituted Vajirañāṇa Library.[114] A full printed version of the *Tipiṭaka* appeared in Bangkok in 1888, while a new Siamese translation was completed in 1893 and available in print by 1896.[115] In the 1890s, Sā, a Dhammayut monk who was supreme patriarch at the time, wrote a new "rationalized" version of the *Paṭhamasambodhi*, which was serialized in a periodical called *Dhammachaksu* and later reedited and printed as a single volume by Vajirañāṇa in 1905.[116] Chulalongkorn himself wrote and published an influential essay on the necessity of reinterpreting the *jātaka* from a demythologizing perspective in 1904.[117] Although the *jātaka* may have been discredited among Siamese Buddhist intellectuals as literal representations of Buddhist history, a popular series of periodicals, gazettes, and newspapers that incorporated translations from the *jātaka* and *hitopadeśa* in translated prose versions circulated in the latter decades of the nineteenth century in Bangkok; these translations led to the growth of modern fiction genres in Siam.[118]

These influences are particularly evident in the work of Ukñā Suttantaprījā Ind, who spent the years 1881 to 1888 studying in Bangkok, probably in a Mahānikāy monastery, and then returned to Thai-controlled Battambang. His earlier monastic training in Phnom Penh at Vatt Uṇṇālom perhaps also contributed to his appreciation for Siamese Buddhist intellectualism. Literate in Thai, French, and Pali in addition to Khmer, by the years 1914 to 1921, when he was collecting and compiling Khmer, Thai, and French folklore into his highly original modernist work *Gatilok*, he wrote, extolling literary life, that "literacy is equivalent to possessing a celestial eye and a celestial mouth."[119] The "celestial eye" was an image used in the *jātaka* for depicting the Buddha's ability to see his own and others' past lives; Ind gave it a highly rationalized interpretation:

> All types of texts—geographical texts, historical texts, and so forth—are things that go way back in time. Those of us who are literate can read them, understand their contents, and discuss them together. In this sense, it is as though we possess a celestial eye.[120]

The course of Ind's written work from his late-nineteenth-century *Ṙýaṅ Paṭhamasambodhi* to his turn-of-the-century "Battle of Ta Kae" and *Nirās Nagar Vatt* to his 1921 *Gatilok* shows an increasing attention to the history, acts, and conduct of his own countrymen and countrywomen, whom he terms *"yoeṅ Khmaer"* (we Khmer) or *"jāti Khmaer." "Jāti,"* a Khmer word of Pali origin meaning "birth, race, kind, or category," was later inscribed with the meaning "national," but in Ind's 1921 writing, it assumed the connotation of something akin to the current European usage of "civilization" or "culture," which tended to incorporate racial overtones, a comparative outlook on religion, and a sense of civilizational progress or development.[121]

In the *Gatilok,* he articulates the linkages among culture, language, religion, authenticity, and purification that seem to characterize the new ethos of emerging modernism. For example, he admonishes Khmer Buddhists not to take part in the worship of Braḥ Go (Lord Ox or Cow), a legendary black bull venerated in northwest Cambodia. After dissecting the elements of the Braḥ Go legend as too preposterous to be taken seriously, he attacks cults of this sort on the further basis of their inappropriateness to *"jāti khluan"* (our kind).[122] "By contrast," he asserts,

> [T]here are cultural groups *(jāti)* of people who do hold cows as sacred . . . [such as various] religious groups *(jāti)* . . . in India. . . . But what about [those of] us Khmer who venerate the fully enlightened Buddha Gotama as the Foremost Teacher? Why should we venerate a cow? Why should we take the name "cow" *(go)* as holy . . . ? We Khmer have never venerated the cow as the vehicle *(yāna)* of Lord Śiva as Hindus do. When we feel an attachment to "Braḥ Go" or uphold the [sound of the] word *"go,"* it should be for the name of Lord "Gotama," because the Lord Buddha is our master from the lineage of *"gotama-gotra,"* and this is what we should rightfully associate with this sound *"go."* . . . Khmer use cows as domestic animals. They *are* "vehicles"—but only for pulling carts and plowing rice fields. And we also allow them to be killed and eaten. It seems evident nowadays that one cow is pretty much like another.[123]

Of another spirit cult surrounding the figure of Yāy (grandmother) Daeb that he likewise views as inauthentically Khmer and Buddhist, he comments,

> People who worship Yāy Daeb know nothing about her history. . . . When she was alive, did she possess some manner of merit and virtue enabling her to help free Khmer from suffering, or to defeat the enemies of the Khmer, or to protect against disease? Did she perform good deeds associated with our land in some manner? Is Yāy Daeb's history found in chronicles or in any Pali religious scriptures that tell us why we should believe in and worship her and make the claim that she has special powers? For example, we can take the figure of Joan of Arc in French history, whom the French respect and venerate because when she was alive, she helped save her king. She became a general who raised an army and went to war against the enemy, capturing back territory belonging to her people. Later, when she had exhausted her merit, she fell into the hands of her enemies, who burned her alive. All of the people in her kingdom remember the good deeds of this girl who helped save their land. They erected a statue of her

> as an extraordinary woman so those of her same *jāti* could honor and venerate her as one of their own, right up to the present time.
>
> Returning to Yāy Daeb, when she was alive, in what manner did she free our Khmer *jāti* from suffering, causing ancient people to want to build a statue for all Khmer to worship and venerate her . . . ?
>
> . . . Did you know that the word *"daeb"* is a translation of the Sanskrit *"daitya,"* meaning "demon" . . . ? How did people come to believe that they should worship her or that the word *"daeb"* isn't really the word *"daeb"* at all, but is a transformation of the sound *"deb,"* referring to Nāṅ Debdhīta, which alludes to Nāṅ Umābhagavatī, the consort of Lord Śiva? . . . Out of respect for Nāṅ Umābhagavatī as the wife of Lord Śiva, [ancient followers of Śiva] erected a statue . . . and called her "Yāy Deb" . . . which over a long period of time, came to be pronounced as "Yāy Daeb." . . .
>
> But even if we recognize the statue as Nāṅ Umābhagavatī, it is not right that we who are followers of the Buddhist *sāsana* worship and venerate a statue of Yāy Daeb. Doing so causes us to become troubled, to lose the Going to the Three Refuges that is our heritage, to be bankrupt and naked.[124]

This passage suggests the welding of new perspectives on Khmer religious practice with ideas of purification and authenticity current in Dhammayut-influenced Siam. This new approach derived its authority from education in Pali and new scriptural translation practices, including knowledge of linguistic etymology or philology. From a modernist viewpoint, existing religious practices, even those that appeared to be rooted in ancient tradition, had to be reevaluated for their textually based doctrinal authenticity.

The influence of a Siamese education on individual monks must have of course varied, but the overall effect was that of producing an elite coterie of monastic teachers and scholars who returned to Cambodia not only with new ideas about monastic conduct, pedagogy, and practice, but also with the more-subtle acquisitions that are represented in the monastic biographies and other writings excerpted here: an inspired sort of zeal to transform their countrymen and countrywomen, a deep interest in matters of authenticity and purification, a self-consciousness about the value of education, and a new self-consciousness about Khmer language, ethnicity, and "culture." As Ind's example suggests, these values were central to the rise of the modern Dhamma movement in Phnom Penh of 1914, whose history we can now consider.

THE KHMER SANGHA AND THE MODERN DHAMMA GROUP

Outwardly, the Dhammayut influence in Cambodia seemed to French observers at the end of the nineteenth century to be primarily a matter of monastic practice. Writing in 1899, Adhémard Leclère (a colonial official and ethnographer) observed the differences between the Mahānikāy and Dhammayut in terms of procedural matters:

> The doctrine is the same, the costume is absolutely the same, the discipline is identical and the interpretation of texts has never divided nor troubled Cambodian monks. . . . [The new sect] does not differ from the old church except for the manner of carrying the *bat* or wooden bowl, the receptacle for alms. In the great congregation [the Mahānikāy], there is a manner of carrying the *bat* suspended from the shoulder by a cord; in the Dhammayut, the *bat* cannot be suspended, it must be carried in the hand.
>
> The original cause of this reform, I am told, is that the custom of carrying the *bat* suspended from the shoulder is brahmanic, and the custom of carrying it in the hands is of Buddhist origin. One monk told me that the Buddha, before becoming Buddha, carried it suspended from the shoulder like the other ascetics of his time, but he ceased to carry it thus after he had discovered the Four Truths. I do not know where this monk has found this detail, but I observe that it is known by a great number of religious Cambodians and given as the cause for the reform introduced in the Buddhist church in Cambodia by Louk Préas Saukonn [Sugandhādhipatī Pān].[125]

While it is possible that Leclère did not understand the deeper ideological perspectives tied to the interpretation of monastic procedural matters, it also seems possible that the divisive debates that emerged in the early twentieth century around Dhammayut interpretations of *Vinaya* rules had not yet developed. The perceived differences between the two sects might well have centered primarily on the *bat* issue alone.[126]

By the early decades of the twentieth century, however, the issues of robe style, the rules for novices, and the issue of Pali pronunciation appear to have become more widely perceived as the crucial differences between the two sects than the manner of collecting alms.[127] In addition, perceptions about the strictness of the two orders were being voiced. For instance, a 1916 French surveillance report suggests that while Khmer monks in general were "peaceable, hospitable but very formal, haughty, little educated" and generally possessing a "vagabond humor," monks of the two orders could be distinguished by the "stricter observance of religious regulations" among the Dhammayut.[128] By the 1930s, this perception seems to have been cemented; a 1937 administrative report on the history of the two sects in Cambodia, apparently drafted by the Khmer minister of the interior, Chea, suggested that the major difference between the two sects was that of strict adherence to the *Vinaya:* the Dhammayut sect "observes the Buddhist codes of conduct strictly" while the Mahānikāy "is not very rigorous in its observance of the codes."[129] It may be that the shift from Leclère's observations about the carrying of the *bat* to these later perceptions of difference reflects the stormy controversies that emerged concerning modernist interpretations of the *Dhamma-vinay* during the intervening decades.

There is also little indication in French sources of problematic disputes between the Mahānikāy and Dhammayut orders in Cambodia during the late nineteenth century, particularly while the widely respected Samtec Sugandhādhipatī Pān was still alive. By 1880, a second reorganization of the Sangha hierarchy had been enacted by the king and the supreme patriarch along the lines of the French-initiated reform of the civil administration.[130] The reform of the religious hierarchy was evidently intended to introduce a more centralized control of the Sangha, just as the civil reforms assured closer control of Khmer mandarins. The abbots of individual monasteries were under the control of a *megaṇ* (head of a *gaṇ* or "diocese"),[131] who in turn reported to a higher official placed at the level of the *apanage* (a subprovincial unit), who reported to the highest-ranking Sangha officials, including the heads of each order, in the capital.[132] In the nineteenth-century reorganization, some *gaṇ* were given over to Mahānikāy control while others were put under Dhammayut control, reflecting the older Khmer pattern of administration still partially in place, in which authority was linked to patronage.[133] This system of control tended to create conflicts, since Mahānikāy monks resented being placed under the jurisdiction of Dhammayut officials, especially given the disparity in the numbers of monks and monasteries.[134] These problematic features of religious administration were finally wholly abolished with the later 1919 reorganization of the Sangha. The *apanage* system was eliminated, and the Dhammayut and Mahānikāy orders were each given their own channels of higher authority, with their own officials installed at the level of *megaṇ*.[135]

In spite of the appearance of a formalized central hierarchy, French sources indicate that before 1900–1910, monastic authority remained largely decentralized.[136] Like the civil reforms, these administrative reforms seemed to take hold slowly, but by 1910, the new channels of Sangha authority appear to have finally crystallized. Following this period, significant rulings on procedural matters, disciplinary actions, and disputes were also reviewed by the minister of religion and the Council of Ministers, as well as the king and the résident supérieur. As this tighter system of control became more entrenched, resentments between adherents of the two sects—which may have existed even before—seem to have surfaced more visibly.

In addition to the differences previously noted in Dhammayut styles of wearing the robe and carrying the *bat,* Dhammayut monks followed a somewhat different almanac of holy days from that used by the Mahānikāy, thereby irritating some Mahānikāy followers since it seemed to them to devalue the sanctity of their own calendar.[137] The Dhammayut manner of pronouncing Pali was also offensive to some laypeople and monks, who regarded it as foreign and "Burmese,"[138] or as Ind satirized it, arrogant and affected, causing people to have an urge to "punch [the speakers] in the mouth":[139]

> [S]ome groups of students . . . have learned Pali and memorized it by heart, and argue for only one kind of [pronunciation] . . . putting in all eight of the final

> vowel sounds, so it sounds like "*sukha, mukha, . . . pada . . . , jāti, dhātu* . . . and so on, and no longer resembles the pronunciation of our Khmer language. . . . Speaking in this manner follows the correct [pronunciation] of Pali, but it sounds wrong to people in the kingdom. Whenever they hear it, it offends their ears. . . . Those with wisdom ought to reflect on this further.[140]

These problems, however, were not the most urgent of the tensions dividing the Khmer Sangha. Imported by the court, the Dhammayut order had remained relatively small, elite-oriented, and urban. As one Khmer court official observed in his report on the internal politics of the Sangha, perhaps because of its smaller size and the value it placed on discipline and austerity, the Dhammayut rarely exhibited signs of internal feuding.[141] By contrast, the Mahānikāy order became increasingly caught up in a state of internal strife as a result of the reformist ideas brought back from Siam.

As monks of both orders returned from Bangkok, I have suggested, they brought with them not only new ideas and forms of education, but also something of a reformist zeal, firm ideas about the value of a new kind of education in Pali and translation, a heightened sense of cultural difference, and a deep interest in matters of authenticity and purification. Some Mahānikāy monks returning to Cambodia from Siam insisted on wearing their robes in the Dhammayut manner, and also tried to enforce Dhammayut-style regulations concerning the attire for novices.[142] The controversy that developed around this practice became one of the primary means of circulating new Buddhist viewpoints. For Mahānikāy monks wearing robes in the new Dhammayut style, the vociferousness of the resistance they encountered forced them to articulate and justify their reformist agendas. Although the majority of Mahānikāy monks did not join them in this practice, the effect was to introduce new attention to the *Vinaya* in order to clarify the debates. This turn to scripture crystallized into an antitraditionalist movement.

Mās-Kaṅ's biography provides an illustration of a Mahānikāy monk involved in the robe controversy. By the time of his return to Kompong Cham in 1901, his awakening to the *Vinaya* had prompted him to adopt the Dhammyut regulations concerning robes. He recognized that Khmer Buddhists were entrenched in tradition, but his early success with monastic building and renovation projects convinced him that "if one's heart and mind is dedicated to a purpose with great effort, there is nothing one cannot accomplish."[143] "At this time," his biography recounts,

> his main focus in regard to [promoting] conduct according to the *Vinaya* was teaching both novices and monks how to arrange and fold the robe correctly, according to the Buddhist precepts, and on the part of novices, to arrange the outer robe to conceal the body, to discontinue pleating the outer robe over the shoulder and wrapping the cloth around from the outside, as they were accustomed to doing in the past.[144]

He "dedicated himself to trying to help *bhikkhus*, novices, and laypeople achieve right conduct," his biography continues, because

> he recognized that the country was not yet modern. *Vatts*, too, needed to modernize —and the *Dhamma-vinay* that was inscribed in the texts, and learned and recited at that time, was not yet very pure. This is why he made such a strong effort to exhort them directly, from his own lips, on every possible opportunity.[145]

Like other Mahānikāy monks who advocated the Dhammayut style of wearing robes, however, Mās-Kañ eventually found himself in the midst of growing controversy.[146] According to Huot Tath, turmoil within the Mahānikāy began to mount steadily after 1914, but individual cases could not be brought to religious courts until after October 1918, when a new royal ordinance went into effect that legally prohibited monks in the Mahānikāy order from observing Dhammayut practices.[147] Within a few months of the issuing of the October 1918 ordinance, seventeen Mahānikāy monks in Kompong Siem had been tried and charged with violating the ordinance; they were ordered to either change their robe style or leave the monastery.[148] By 1937, an administrative report on religious affairs gives a list of over forty "robes" cases, spread through nearly every province in the country, that had reached the level of the Ministry of Cults for adjudication.[149]

The disparate Mahānikāy viewpoints on the robes debate were clearly passionately felt by both monks and laypeople, but in a sense, these controversies were only the outward manifestations of a deeper ideological split within the Mahānikāy concerning the interpretation and translation of the *Vinaya.* Related to this issue was also the emergence of differing perspectives about texts as sacred objects and receptacles of sacred ideas. One effect of these debates was to give rise to a modern Dhamma faction within the Mahānikāy. The group that resisted reformist innovations came to be known as the "traditionalists" or "old Dhamma group" (Dharm-cās'). A second effect of these debates was the rapid demise of the traditional Buddhist manuscript culture in Cambodia.

By the time of the death of Samtec Braḥ Sangharāj Diañ in 1913, even monks who had not traveled to Bangkok for study were being exposed to the new currents of thought concerning the *Vinaya.* For instance, the funeral biography of Braḥ Cin-Jā (1883–1958), an abbot of a monastery in Kompong Speu, states that soon after his appointment as abbot around 1913, he was "among the first to wake up to the *Dhamma-vinay.* He then introduced his students to this text as well, and stirred them into action to study it."[150] In addition, French efforts to bolster Buddhist education in the protectorate (considered in chapter 4) began around 1909. By 1912, the Sālā Pali in Phnom Penh began—very gradually—to promote an approach to Buddhist education crafted largely by monks and scholars associated with the modern Dhamma movement. Monks who studied there were engaged in more-extensive studies of Pali grammar and translation of *Tipiṭaka* texts than had been available in the past, and the list of texts that they encountered was significantly expanded beyond (although still including) the *Mūlakaccāyana,* the *Maṅgalatthadīpanī,* and the commentary on the *Dhammapada* that had been the standard texts for the previous generation of monks trained in Cambodia.[151]

Two of the primary actors in the modern Dhamma movement were Chuon Nath and Huot Tath, two young monks who had been trained in Phnom Penh rather than Bangkok. As their new Buddhist interpretations developed, Chuon Nath and Huot Tath came to champion the understanding and practice of a rationalistic, scripturalist, demythologized religion, similar in many respects to the reformed Buddhism of Mongkut. Their approach emphasized the importance of Pali study, and particularly of the *Vinaya.* Their rationalized interpretations, like Mongkut's, also deemphasized the role of cosmological texts and particularly of the narrative accounts of the Buddha's past lives depicted in the *jātaka.* They reacted against the pedagogical tradition of rote memorization and recitation of texts, instead emphasizing the translation and interpretation of texts and sermons between Pali and the vernacular, so that both monks and laypersons not only took part in a performance of texts, but more important, understood the content of what was being read, preached, or recited.

Born in Kompong Speu and ordained as a *bhikkhu* at Vatt Bodhi Priks in the Kandal Stung district of Kandal in 1904, Chuon Nath (1883–1969) was educated as a novice first at Vatt Bodhi Priks and later at Vatt Uṇṇālom. He returned to Vatt Uṇṇālom after his ordination as a *bhikkhu,* where he continued his Pali studies.[152] Influenced by the currents of Siamese reformism that were part of the intellectual climate of Cambodia around the beginning of the twentieth century, Chuon Nath was drawn to scriptural language study, and lacking any formal resources for studying Sanskrit in the monastic educational context of Phnom Penh, initiated his own Sanskrit studies with an Indian peanut vendor who came to his monastery, inviting Huot Tath (1891–1975?), who had also been born in Kompong Speu, to join them. Although in these early years Chuon Nath and Huot Tath developed their ideas independent of French influences, they pursued French language study as well, an unusual undertaking for young monks.[153]

In his biography of Chuon Nath, written decades after these events in the early part of the century, Huot Tath recalls that soon after his ordination at Vatt Uṇṇālom in 1912, a royal official commissioned the preaching of *Vinaya* texts throughout the period of *vassa,* the annual retreat. As young instructors at the École Supérieure de Pali, Huot Tath, Chuon Nath, and Uṃ-Sūr (1881–1939) were recruited by the supreme patriarch to carry out the lengthy sermons:

> The sermons did not last the entire *vassa,* however, because the preaching of the *Vinaya* and its explication led the *bhikkhus* and novices at the *vatt* to develop understanding and to become awakened; for days, they could not stop talking about right and wrong ways of behaving.[154]

These discussions about the *Vinaya* worried and ultimately infuriated Supreme Patriarch Samtec Braḥ Dhammalikhit Tae Uk, who had been appointed in 1914 as Diaṅ's successor, according to French reports, largely because of his seniority in the Sangha rather than his merits as a scholar.[155] Dissension among Uk's faction grew to such an extent, Huot Tath recounts, that the older, high-ranking monks began to mock them by "observing that those young monks are speaking of ways of behaving that are different from tradition *(cās')* and from previous times *(mun).*"[156] The *Vinaya* sermons were halted, but a faction of monks emerged that began to seriously study *Vinaya* texts and commentaries. "Even though few dared to express it openly in light of the opposition of the monks with high monastic ranks *(mahā-thera),*" Huot Tath wrote, "there were many monks during this time who loved the *Dhamma-vinay.*"[157]

The modernist movement emerged out of the clandestine *Vinaya* study groups that formed in response to this incident. As in Mongkut's Dhammayut nikāya in Siam, Chuon Nath, Huot Tath, and the other young monks favored a more demythologized presentation of Buddhism. They worked urgently during this period to edit and translate versions of *Vinaya* texts drawn from palm-leaf manuscripts, and secretly circulated them. Of this period, Huot Tath recounted,

> The three of us [Chuon Nath, Huot Tath, and Uṃ-Sūr] united together to lead all the other *bhikkhu*s, urging them to try to make the effort to read the Buddhist scriptures, commentaries, and manuals on conduct *(gambhīr-ṭīkā-kpuon-cpāp')* and to extract the exact meanings, which before this time, monks often did not understand, or if they did, only in a superficial or faltering way. . . . The work of organizing the true conduct according to the teaching of the *Vinay* was extremely time consuming. . . . Braḥ Grū Saṅghasatthā Chuon Nath read through some of the chapters *(khandhaka)* of the *Vinay,* along with their commentaries. I did this also, reading different *khandhaka* with their commentaries. When we were finished reading, we made extracts that we composed as books. . . . The task of reading texts and commentaries during that period was extremely difficult, not at all easy, for all of them were inscribed on palm leaf, and all of them were in Pali.
>
> We read not only the *Vinay* in this manner, but also various other scriptural texts and commentaries . . . [including] texts concerning ordination ceremonies. We carried out this work at night, from 8:00 to midnight, in Braḥ Grū Saṅghasatthā Chuon Nath's room, along with Braḥ Grū Rimalapaññā Uṃ-Sūr, who met with us to help with this work. . . .
>
> At that time, nearly all of the monks and novices at Vatt Uṇṇālom had experienced awakening. They wanted to know right and wrong, and we could not remain quiet and unresponsive any longer. Even some monks and novices associated with monasteries where all of the [other] monks belonged to the faction that remained hard-hearted toward the *Dhamma-vinay* studied secretly, to gain competence in *Dharm-vinay* in order to gain knowledge along with all the rest of us.[158]

Huot Tath's description of this work illustrates the self-conscious process of modern scripturalist methods as they developed in Cambodia. In contrast to the older scribal practices that had predominated among Khmer Buddhists, Chuon Nath, Huot Tath, and Uṃ-Sūr were approaching the texts in an entirely new manner. Their methods were akin to those described by Deb-Ū, who later joined their efforts to produce a new print recension of the Khmer *Tipiṭaka.* They used commentaries and subcommentaries to grammatically analyze and extract "exact meanings," which monks of the past, with their "superficial or faltering" knowledge of Pali could not successfully negotiate. In addition, whereas monk-scribes of the past had not been concerned with producing complete volumes of a particular text, the young modernist monks were collecting various palm-leaf texts, consulting related works, and compiling systematic treatments on particular topics such as ordination procedures. Furthermore, at least as far as Huot Tath's memoir makes evident, they were copying and disseminating texts without observing the same kind of ritualistic treatments of textual materials that were observed in the past. While the production and financing of the printed translations and compilations produced by the modernist monks did become closely associated with merit-making ceremonies, particularly cremations, and were distributed as means of making merit, the devotional and ceremonial aspects of manuscript preparation were clearly diminished. By the mid-1920s, with the introduction of the Buddhist periodicals *Kambujasuriyā* (1926) and *Ganthamālā* (1927), the ritualistic dimensions of textual production were even further dispensed with, as edited versions of Buddhist texts were printed and serialized.

In their work of producing *Vinaya* editions and extracts, the only available sources for the monks to use, Huot Tath's memoir tells us, were older recensions of Pali texts inscribed on palm leaf. These *saṃrāy* texts were not strictly "canonical" in the formal sense of the term,[159] and took different forms: Pali versions of texts rendered in verse, Pali *gāthā* or verses interspersed with translation and commentary from various sources, and vernacular renditions loosely based on Pali texts. The problem with these texts from the modernist perspective was that they did not differentiate between *Buddhabhāsita* (words spoken by the Buddha) and other kinds of words. Added to this difficulty was the habit of the Khmer public of viewing anything at all inscribed on palm leaf as efficaciously sacred. Thus, in his preface to an early version of the *Sigālovāda-sutta,* Huot Tath writes that "in order to correct the comprehension by the populace" he had edited and translated the text in a form that would make evident "which verses are actual *Buddhabhāsita.*"[160] That way, whether the reader knew Pali or not, he or she would be sure to know which words were authentic *Dhamma-vinay.*

In the traditional manuscript culture that modernists were seeking to supplant, merit would have been produced simply through the physical acts of pronouncing or hearing Pali verses or *gāthā.* By contrast, in Huot Tath's understanding, it was first necessary that this Pali text be *understood* in order to be meaningful and authoritative, and second, that it be disseminated to a "wider populace," who, through new print formats, would be able to determine which parts were more authoritative than others. In Cambodia, this position represented a transformed notion of sacred authority, different from the vast and undifferentiated designation of nearly all texts as scripture or sacred texts apparent from late-nineteenth-century sources.

In spite of its clandestine nature, the movement had begun to spread, splitting the Mahānikāy. References to the two factions by the names *buak-Dharm-thmī* (modern [new] Dhamma group) and *buak-Dharm-cās'* (traditional [old] Dhamma group) began to appear more widely.[161] But as the modern Dhamma movement spread from Phnom Penh to the provinces, the traditionalist faction sought royal support to have it censored. Huot Tath's memoir continues,

> At this same time, all of the monks in the capital and in the provinces who had awakened were exerting themselves to study scriptures *(sūtra)* to gain knowledge of the *Vinay* precepts *(Vinay-sikkhā),* the Buddhist codes of conduct *(cpāp'),* and ethical ideas *(Dharm-vinay),* which they had not been accustomed to understanding in the past. They tried hard to explain and disseminate [what they learned] so that all Buddhists could be exposed to this knowledge, so they could hear and understand, and spread it from one to another, all over the kingdom of Cambodia. For Buddhists who were serious in their convictions, [this knowledge] delighted their hearts and minds,[162] for it caused their hearts and minds to be cleansed, purified, and oriented even more firmly toward the ethical principles of the *Dhamma [-vinay],* which are so clearly elucidated in the sacred texts and commentaries.
>
> For Buddhists whose religious orientation was superficial, and who held obstinate, narrow-minded convictions, [this knowledge] hardened their hearts and minds, making them hostile and angry. As far as they were concerned, they were accustomed to one manner of behaving, and now they were being asked to turn to another instead. They would not agree to accept these beliefs, and furthermore, they felt hatred and bitterness toward those who taught the *Dhamma,* calling anyone who introduced modern Dhamma "dissenters," [accusing] them of corrupting the conduct inherited from the past. Not only were these monks enraged individually, but they also gathered together others with the same attitudes and met to draw up formal complaints against those teaching the *Dhamma-vinay,* joining Samtec Braḥ Dhammalikhit Uk, the Sangha chief at Vatt Uṇṇālom, who was displeased, and who was mounting [a campaign of] insults and criticism toward those monks engaged in reforming ways of behaving.[163]

These passages represent a succinct distillation of the modern Dhamma viewpoints that most infuriated the traditionalists and that from their perspective were undermining the notions of sanctity associated with the older manuscript culture. The emphasis on ethical behavior advocated by the modernists was not in itself new, but it had been articulated before in a different manner, in the form of teachings about the exemplary figure of the Bodhisatta and his behavior and perfection of virtues as he progressed through different births. The new, modern zeal to produce understanding through the promotion of *Vinaya* texts and to disseminate it "all over the kingdom of Cambodia" necessitated changes in patterns of monastic education and practice, as well as a transformation of vision with regard to what was important and meaningful from a Buddhist perspective.

Further, the modernist claim that some monks were being "awakened" by the new doctrine and methods of study is not one that can be made lightly in the context of Buddhist soteriology. While the modernists framed their realizations in terms of having become "awakened"—as opposed to the sense in which the Buddha's *nibbāṇa* or enlightenment was understood to be an "awakening"—the claim still carried with it the suggestion that there were different levels of knowledge and experience one could possess. In the traditionalist framework, special status was associated primarily with meditation prowess, which was understood to endow monk-adepts with extraordinary powers or *iddhi.* Supreme Patriarch Uk's own status in the Sangha hierarchy and the high regard in which he was held by many traditionalists may well have been linked to his meditational attainments rather than his scholarly background.[164] Instead of privileging the vocation or *dhura* of meditation, the modernists maintained that correct understanding depended on modern scholarly practices. While traditionalist practices were labeled as corruptions or distortions, the new practices would bring monks to correct knowledge of the *Dhamma-vinay,* which in Huot Tath's words led to "delight" and "awakening" through the cleansing or purification of the "heart and mind," which in turn led monks to adjust their conduct to reflect the authentic (and implicitly, older, truer) ways of being Buddhist.

In 1918, Huot Tath recounts, the conflict between the modernists and traditionalists came to a head.[165] Chuon Nath and several other modernist monks were summoned to a meeting with an angry supreme patriarch and other officials by King Sisowath himself, to confront the issue of *jātaka* interpretation that was causing an uproar in provincial monasteries.[166] Petitions sent in from provincial Sangha officials alleged that the modernists "preach that the *sāstrā-Mahājātak* [the *Vessantara-jātaka*] is false. This *sāstrā* is one that has been upheld by our ancestors as correct and true."[167] Chuon Nath and Huot Tath were called into a meeting with the king, Council of Ministers, and Sangha officials. Chuon Nath's response (recalled in Huot Tath's memoir) illustrates the demythologized interpretations characteristic of the Khmer modernists:

> The monks are not preaching that the entire [text] is false. When they preach about "falsity," they are referring to segments of the text that were added later, such as the part describing how Tā Jujāk resorted to eating an entire pot of rice and curry leading his stomach to burst open with such a deafening noise that it caused all the elephants in the pavilion to stampede. The monks are not saying that these words are false, but rather that they were added in later for the amusement of listeners. They are not really the holy words of the Lord Buddha. Those who listen to the *Dhamma* must learn how to examine it closely.[168]

The reason for the urgency of their translations lies in this last statement. For Chuon Nath, Huot Tath, and the members of their faction, the possibility of purification was based on the ability to understand definitively and authoritatively what the scriptures said and then transform one's behavior based on this authentic understanding. *Vinaya* texts were central to the revitalization of Khmer Buddhism because they revealed true and correct ways of behaving, or *paṭipatti.* The problem faced by Khmer Buddhists of this period, in Huot Tath's account of Chuon Nath's beliefs, was that too much *Vinaya* knowledge had been lost by the Khmer in previous periods of war and destruction, thus resulting in a weakened Buddhism. With the current modernist focus on the *Vinaya,* it was only now being rebuilt.[169]

In spite of the favorable impression Chuon Nath's speech made on the king—Sisowath awarded Chuon Nath a prize of 20 riel for his brilliance[170]—Uk's faction was still too powerful for the court and colonial administration to disregard. Shortly later, Royal Ordinance 71 of 2 October 1918 was promulgated. It ordered all monks and laypeople connected with the Mahānikāy to respect the precepts and rituals "continuing from the past" that represented the "methods established and put into place by the deceased Samtec Braḥ Mahā Sangharāj Diaṅ";[171] monks connected with the Dhammayut were likewise to observe the traditions associated with the past, as established by Samtec Braḥ Sugandhādhipatī Pān.[172] Monks or lay followers who disregarded the ordinance were subject to prosecution by the religious court (composed of high-ranking Sangha officials). Of special reference, article 1 singled out the manner of wearing robes as confined to the traditions of each order; article 2 ruled out the teaching or dissemination of any reforms of these traditions; article 3 required all texts used in Buddhist education to be submitted for approval to the minister of interior, the Council of Ministers, and the king.[173]

By the time Ordinance 71 was introduced, Chuon Nath had completed a new edited version of the *Pāṭimokkha* and Huot Tath had written *Kaṭhinakkhandhaka.* According to Huot Tath's memoir, they dutifully applied to the minister of the interior for permission to use their new compilations for teaching purposes. To their disbelief, they received a letter denying permission to circulate their books. As Huot Tath recalls, it read,

> Permission will be granted only for study of *Vinay* written on palm-leaf; *Vinay* written on paper in the manner of a book is considered to be "new *Vinay,*" which is not in accord with the traditions established during the time of Samtec Braḥ Mahā Diaṅ.[174]

The phrase "new *Vinay*" was a clear reference to the modern Dhamma movement. The matter of textual writing material, which to Huot Tath's later memory at least had never struck them as a problem, demonstrates how far they had moved away from the traditional manner of viewing textual production as a sacred and devotional act. Stunned and disappointed as they were, Huot Tath recalls, the letter merely caused them to redouble their clandestine work. Copies of the banned books began to circulate widely, causing modernist-leaning monks to give consideration to the difference between the content of scripture and the materials on which it was inscribed or written.[175]

In the meantime, Huot Tath finished a book he considered to be of vital importance for clarifying *Vinaya* interpretation, a volume on monastic regulations for novices titled *Sāmaṇera-vinaya.* Conscious that the book would infuriate the supreme patriarch, Chuon Nath and Uṃ-Sūr added their names to Huot Tath's as coauthors of the volume. A lay supporter with connections to the throne named Ukñā Adhipatīsenā Keth interceded to convince the résident supérieur to print the book, thus circumventing the normal channels of authority. When Uk tried to prosecute the three modern Dhamma monks under Ordinance 71, Prince Monivong intervened with his father on their behalf, and the book (and its authors) survived any further efforts to halt its circulation. After 1922, when Chuon Nath and Huot Tath became closely associated with Louis Finot, then director of EFEO in Hanoi who undertook supervision of their further training in Sanskrit, philology, Buddhist history, and other subjects, he helped to clear the way for the further publication of Buddhist texts in Cambodia, particularly through the institution of the Royal Library and later, the Buddhist Institute.[176]

The other translations produced during this period by the modernists were nearly all concerned with conduct or behavior. Chuon Nath, Huot Tath, Uṃ-Sūr, and another modern Dhamma advocate named Lvī-Em translated numerous abbreviated versions of *Vinaya* texts—all considerations of monastic regulations—including the *Pāṭimokkha* (Disciplinary code)[177] and the *Kaṭhinakkhandhaka* (Chapter concerning the making of robes), as well as texts intended to serve as "*Vinaya*" for laypeople, such as *Gihipaṭipatti* (Conduct for laypeople) and *Gihivinaya* (Vinaya for laypeople), compendiums of regulations for lay conduct, and the *Sigālovāda-sutta* (Advice to Sigāl) on ethical guidelines for the householder. These texts (considered in chapter 5), Huot Tath wrote, "were brought into being one after another, for the purification of ordained and laypeople who wanted to become free from impurity, so that they could study scripture and practice accordingly."[178] In Huot Tath's recollection of the events, the modernist concern with understanding and disseminating texts on "ways of behaving" during this period emerged as a result of the power of the texts themselves; once they had begun to study *Vinaya* "we could not stop ourselves," and thus the modern Dhamma project stemming from the *Vinaya* "took root in our hearts and minds *(citt).*"[179] For Huot Tath and the other modernists, being able to encounter and truly understand authentic Dhamma was enough to transform one's bearing in the world.

The controversies within the Mahānikāy regarding modernist reforms continued for another two decades, and monks continued to be disciplined for infractions of Ordinance 71.[180] The publication of Huot Tath's *Sāmaṇera-vinaya* marked the beginning of the traditionalists' gradual slide from power and the end of an orthodoxy defined by practices associated with Samtec Sangharāj Diaṅ. A compromise (and perhaps revisionist) position began to emerge that Diaṅ had deliberately refused to rule on the interpretation of the *Vinaya,* accepting both the modernist and traditional Mahānikāy interpretations as valid.[181] By 1937, internal documents indicate that the minister of the interior and the Council of Ministers had acknowledged that the ordinance prohibiting deviation from nineteenth-century Sangha conventions was a problem, for the most educated monks in the protectorate were most solidly behind the innovations. While the traditionalist faction was still "numerous enough that it is impossible to eliminate them," Khmer and French authorities sought a means of bringing together the two sides and abolishing Ordinance 71 without igniting the population.[182] The method proposed was to produce a definitive "commission for the verification of the *Tipiṭaka*" composed of members drawn from all factions (Dhammayut, modernist, and traditionalist Mahānikāy) to examine the *Vinaya* and produce an abbreviated and definitive compendium of monastic rules drawn from the *Vinaya.* The methods to be used by the commission involved the techniques of scholarly translation and study of the Pali texts—borrowed from the reforms introduced by Mongkut in Siam a century earlier.[183]

Before we look more closely at modernist ethical writings, it is necessary to consider how the modern Dhamma was promoted during the 1920s through the establishment of new Buddhist institutions. As I have suggested in this chapter, the modernist zeal for purifying Khmer Buddhism was persuasive, energetic, and ultimately appealing and powerful. But the modernist project was also aided by its resonance with French colonial plans for Cambodia. The next chapter examines how colonial administrators and scholars contributed to the rise of modern Buddhism, particularly its demythologizing and scripturalist tenets, to further their own political and ideological agendas.

4 Colonial Collusions

Cambodia is "a country of profound faith . . . , [its religion] natural and spontaneous like our parishes of the Middle Ages," observed a French administrative report from the mid-1930s. It was thus regrettable that "in a domain where the calm of meditation, the serenity of philosophical discussions are the normal ways of religious conviction and thought," a "discipline rather different from traditional conceptions" had recently arisen. Bolstered by its ties to the administration itself, the report asserted, this "new doctrine" was spreading widely among the population, producing both "enthusiastic converts" and "others resolutely hostile in the name of teachings received in the time of their youth." The report's author feared that the tensions surrounding the "new doctrine" might "one day degenerate into political difficulties," for "all proselytization and all propaganda engenders violent discussion and gives human passions occasion to penetrate a domain they should not."[1]

The various claims about change, stasis, and tradition embedded in this report serve as a useful starting point for considering the influence of French policies and colonial discourses on modern Buddhism in Cambodia. As the report suggests, by the mid-1930s, the new doctrine promulgated by the modern Dhamma movement was already becoming established as a religious and intellectual force. Its primary mouthpiece was the Buddhist Institute, which, along with the Sālā Pali and the Royal Library, had been created with administration support. The report thus pushes several questions that I have not yet considered to the forefront of this study. In what sense did the colonial context of Khmer modernism matter? How did French colonial discourses enter into the production of Buddhist modernist values?

Although Chuon Nath and Huot Tath were among the most brilliant and well-educated men of their generation, it is doubtful that their ambitious agenda could have taken hold as rapidly as it did without French patronage. Chuon Nath's and Huot Tath's attempts to find the true path of *Vinaya* interpretation resulted in such severe dissension and acrimony within the Mahānikāy that at various points, they became targets of both verbal and physical attacks, with bricks lobbed into their *kuṭi* (monastic cells).[2] But in spite of the turmoil they helped to fuel within the Mahānikāy, the tone and direction of their innovations coincided with visions of Buddhist modernization held by some French colonial scholars. Although French influences were less crucial ideologically to the intellectual directions of modern Khmer Buddhism than Siamese ideas, the French regime in both intended and unintended ways provided a political context conducive to the development of a modernist movement in Cambodia.

The idea of fashioning a more modern (from a European perspective) scientific and historical outlook among Buddhists served to allay the apprehensions held by some members of the colonial administration about the powerful and potentially disruptive hold of other competing currents of Buddhist thought: millenarianism in its Vietnamese-influenced, anticolonial incarnations, and Dhammayutism, which came to be perceived by the French administration as an extension of Siamese cultural and political influence. As a result, the ascendancy of the new doctrine became connected to efforts by some French officials to modernize Buddhism, while it also benefited from the French effort to control the potentially disruptive powers of native religion. Both Khmer and colonial modernizers became convinced that they could achieve their different but often complementary aims through the transformation of indigenous religio-cultural bodies and forms into modern institutions for Buddhist education.

In this chapter, I turn to examining the development of modern Buddhism in Cambodia through the lens of colonial policy. As much as French policy makers might have wished otherwise, this was never a one-sided encounter in which "Khmer Buddhism" was reshaped to reflect colonial aims. The relationship between colonial policies and ideologies and the emergence of modern Buddhism was part symbiosis, part subversion, part a war of wills and deep ideological commitments, and part collaboration. Colonial administrators such as François-Marius Baudoin, the long-time résident supérieur of Cambodge; scholars from the École française d'Extrême-Orient Louis Finot, George Coedès, and Susanne Karpelès; and modernist monks and scholars including Braḥ Mahā Vimaladhamm Thoṅ, Samtec Braḥ Dhammalikhit Lvī-Em, and Ukñā Suttantaprījā Ind, along with the younger coterie of monks around Chuon Nath and Huot Tath, contributed to the production of a new articulation of Buddhism that, for a variety of reasons, suited their different purposes.

To understand this collusion requires charting the prolonged interaction between French colonial fears of subversion; discourses on science, religion, and education; declining Khmer traditionalism; and emerging Khmer Buddhist modernism. The interactions between French ideologies, administrative strategies, and shifts in Khmer religious thought and pedagogical practices served as the impetus for the development of several new Buddhist institutions in Cambodia in the relatively short span of three decades, between 1900 and 1930: two new Pali schools, the Royal Library, and the Buddhist Institute. These institutions in turn fostered the circulation and growth of the new discipline.

The relationship between emerging modernism and the formulation of French colonial religious policy is a version of what cultural historian of religion

Charles Hallisey has termed "intercultural mimesis." In an influential essay on the construction of Buddhist studies, colonial scholarship, and Orientalism, Hallisey defines "intercultural mimesis" as "occasions where it seems that aspects of a culture of a subjectified people influenced the investigator to represent that culture in a certain manner."[3] His study suggests how indigenous ideas shaped scholarly representations of Buddhism created by "curators" of Buddhism such as T. W. Rhys Davids, Adhémard Leclère, and other colonial-era scholars and "amateur" Buddhologists.[4] The Khmer case I examine illustrates the complexity and significance of the process that Hallisey has identified. It involved regional flows of ideas and influences as well as the translation of scholarly representations into policies and practices. The growth of local, modern Buddhist values in Cambodia in the early twentieth century, I argue in this chapter, developed out of a sometimes ironic and sometimes unintentional intercultural mimesis between a translocal circulation of ideas drawn from the Buddhist modernization project taking place in Siam, French imperial ideologies and policies in Indochina, and Khmer religious intellectual absorption with the problem of how to live as a modern Buddhist in authentic Theravādin terms.

THE SANGHA AND COLONIAL RELIGIOUS POLICY

Much of French policy toward Buddhism in Cambodia was baldly political. Most colonial administrators involved in orchestrating cultural policy in the protectorate seem to have recognized the political efficacy of patronizing the Khmer Sangha, and certainly, there never appears to have been a concerted effort on the part of the French administration to convert Cambodians to Catholicism.[5] To make indirect rule feasible in the eyes of the Khmer public, it was necessary for the administration to back the king in his role as Dhamma protector. In addition, colonial religious policy was marked by two other prominent concerns. First, the religiously inspired millenarian nature of the revolts of the nineteenth century in various parts of Indochina, including Cambodia, had given colonial officials reason to fear traditional cosmologically oriented Buddhism. From an administrative standpoint, highly educated, respected monks and scholars who advocated a demythologized Buddhism and were trained in a modern scientific worldview and pedagogical methods were more reliable religious leaders than the powerful *dhammik* of the nineteenth century.

Second, French fears of both Vietnamese and Siamese influence in Cambodia became pronounced after the turn of the century—considerably diminishing the desirability of allowing the free circulation of monks within Indochina or of sending young colonial subjects to Bangkok for higher education. Although from an administrative standpoint this fear was justified by the unrest in Cambodia and Cochinchina particularly after 1916, other aspects of the motivation to tighten control over circulations in and out of the protectorate may have had more intangible sources. The gradual restriction of monk freedoms after the turn of the century supports historian John Tully's analysis that François-Marius Baudoin, résident supérieur in Cambodia from 1914 to 1922 and again from 1924 to 1927, "was determined to seal the country off from overseas subversion, which was viewed as contagion."[6]

The Buddhism that the French first encountered in nineteenth-century Cambodia was a complex and diverse tradition that featured not only the kinds of textual and monastic practices singled out in these chapters for consideration and designated by Theravāda Buddhists as the *gantha-dhura* (scholarly "burden" or "vocation"),[7] but also deeply entrenched traditions of spirit and meditation practices.[8] Some colonial-era sources that provide accounts of spirit rites at village, provincial, and court levels give a sense of French official attitudes toward these practices. For instance, a 1903 letter describes a *qanak tā* (spirit) ceremony to be conducted in Kompong Cham in honor of the appointment of a new governor. The elaborate ceremony, which included food, music, temple flags, and a procession of specially clad persons transporting the *qanak tā,* was to center on the sacrifice of a male buffalo in his prime to the local tutelary spirit. Were local Khmer officials to ignore any aspects of this ceremony, they feared the resulting discord and dissatisfaction among the populace, and also the likelihood that the spirit would wreak havoc. Problematically, the letter continues, the French résident had so far provided only enough funds to purchase a sickly female buffalo for the ceremony. The résident's office promptly agreed to provide more funding, on the grounds that "local custom must be respected."[9]

As French administrators tried to respect some local customs, early-twentieth-century records also give clear evidence of the extent to which they feared others. After the experience of the nineteenth-century rebellions (discussed in chapter 2), French apprehensions centered in particular on the kind of religiously potent figures connected with these movements and on any local practices associated with the creation of power and invulnerability. These fears on the part of colonial administrators mirror developments in Siam, where Chulalongkorn's efforts to spread Sangha education reforms to the provinces were intended in part to combat the spread of similar movements, especially on the Lao border.[10]

In Cambodia, early-twentieth-century French administrative reports demonstrate a growing wariness of the potentially disruptive nature of millenarian beliefs and practices.[11] By 1914, Khmer monks demonstrating even minor displays of religious power were placed under surveillance. The more careful scrutiny of monks seems to have had several causes: first, the resumption of explicitly anti-French magical and millenarian-related unrest in Cochinchina and more general unrest in Cambodia, and second, growing suspicion about the activities of Khmer monks in Bangkok. After 1914 a reported increase of "anti-European sentiment" among Indochinese exiles in Siam magnified the administration's anxiety about monks' political activities.[12] This sentiment coincided with a new perception of French vulnerability among Thais and Indochinese subjects after the onset of

World War I.[13] A confidential report from Battambang in 1914, for example, reveals that surveillance was being carried out to determine provincial inhabitants' views of the war. The author of the report noted that most peasants seemed "indifferent to the [current] affairs of the Occident" and that all the various monastery chiefs professed their absolute cooperation with and allegiance to the administration. He had been alerted, however, to a sudden resurgence in the region of "ritual ceremonies of invulnerability" that involved "sprinkling water specially consecrated with magical prayers all over the bodies of rebels" to render them invulnerable to bullets.[14] When he confronted the abbot at one of the monasteries where the rituals had been performed, he was reassured of the "loyalty of the population and the devotion of all monks." The abbot commented that "starting from this very day, he planned to say daily prayers in his pagoda for the success of the French army" because "of all the Occidentals, the French were certainly the best, the mildest, and the most humane."[15]

The years 1913–1916 in southern Vietnam marked a reemergence of the kind of religio-political activity that had been associated with Buu Son Ky Huong in the nineteenth century, discussed earlier, which the French administration thought they had suppressed. Hue-Tam Ho Tai understands these developments as both a continuation of older apocalyptic thought and a prelude and transition to the rise of Caodaism and the secular political movements of the mid-1920s.[16] In 1913, for the first time since the millenarian preaching of the Potato-selling Monk at the turn of the century, a young Vietnamese man who took the name Phan Xich Long (Red Dragon) harnessed millenarian religious ideas to lead an anti-French revolt in Saigon. Although it was quickly suppressed, it spawned other more overtly political disturbances––in part reflecting the tense economic conditions for peasants in Cochinchina and, as Tai suggests, the lack of other channels for protest.[17]

Phan Xich Long's revolt followed the general pattern and even the geography of the nineteenth-century movements discussed in chapter 2. Wearing Buddhist robes, Phan Xich Long sought out magical and religious training in the Seven Mountains region between Cochinchina and Cambodia and made his way to the southwestern Cambodian port city of Kampot and later to Battambang. He established his first temple in Battambang where he began to recruit followers before returning to Cochinchina to found an anti-French religious movement. An elderly "living Buddha" associated with his movement prophesied Phan Xich Long's right to the throne, and after being crowned as emperor, he called for a strike against the French. Two revolts followed, in 1913 and 1916. Although the unrest was short-lived, it severely panicked the administration, prompting investigations and purges of secret societies and other organizations, and resulted in the arrests of more than fifteen hundred colonial subjects suspected of subversion.[18] In fact, secret societies were just beginning to organize networks of anti-French resistance during this period in various parts of Vietnam, sometimes using Buddhist monasteries as covers for fund-raising and other seditious activities.[19]

Reading through French surveillance records of monks in Cambodia during the period between 1913 and 1917, the fear that the same sort of subversive religious discord could ignite Khmer areas is palpable. Protests, riots, and general unrest on a much larger scale than in Hanoi, and of an economic and political nature, had occurred in Cambodia at the beginning of 1916. These outbreaks were part of a larger pattern of rural discontent and violence among peasants in Cambodia—which became particularly fierce around 1913.[20] In 1916, demonstrations drew hundreds of thousands of peasants to seek out the king in Phnom Penh to protest corvée labor laws, taxation, and general economic distress. The administration began to allege that monks were organizing the peasants, which, Tully argues, was probably true.[21] Although relations between members of the administration and the Sangha were not uniformly tense, a warier French attitude toward monks began to develop. A new law regulating monk cross-border travel was promulgated scarcely a month after the February 1916 riot of Phan Xich Long's followers in Saigon, and following closely on the arrest of two monks in Sithor Kandal charged with producing seditious amulets.[22] An April surveillance report indicates that about the same time, "several very localized movements of unrest" had been discovered in Vietnamese monasteries in Cambodia, and meetings of Vietnamese secret societies had been observed as well. Several "suspects" had also been caught on the Cochinchinese border, trying to cross into Cambodia.[23]

The exhaustively documented 1916 case of the two monks from Sithor Kandal suggests the seriousness and severity with which the possibility of monk involvement in the 1916 affair and the general disquietude around the region was being viewed. In the panicked aftermath of the 1916 demonstrations, these two monks were among the suspected agitators. They were arrested and initially sentenced to corporal punishment for producing tattoos that conferred invulnerability, thereby "pushing the inhabitants to revolt."[24] Although they were eventually exonerated of most of the charges (after it was revealed they had been violently coerced into performing the invulnerability rituals), the amount of scrutiny devoted to their case signaled the further intensification of surveillance on monastic activities.

In a letter to provincial Sangha officials and abbots, Samtec Braḥ Maṅgaladebācāry Iam, the head of the Dhammayut order, explained new restrictions on monks' travel and residency, asking that provincial officials aid the administration in preventing the production of lustral water and tattoos for rendering invulnerability, along with all other "seditious" activities.[25] In another, more candid letter to the minister of the interior, however, Iam commented that although he would comply with the order to restrict monk activities, he was dubious about its success:

> I have received from his Majesty the order . . . to instruct all monks in provincial monasteries to observe the Buddhist precepts, to refrain from involvement with malevolent forces who show themselves to be hostile toward the administration, and not to give them cabalistic signs and charms allegedly possessing the property of rendering one invulnerable. . . . I can well send the agreed-upon message

> . . . but I fear the possibility of obtaining the results with anything like the urgency the administration would want.[26]

Besides the tendency toward magical and millenarian activity that the administration wanted to bring under control, another local custom contributed to Iam's fears that the Sangha would not submit quickly or easily to the articles outlined in the new ordinances: the traditional fluidity of Khmer monastic life in respect to ordination, monastic identity, and travel.[27] Unlike monks in some Buddhist cultures, Cambodian boys and men moved in and out of monasteries and the monkhood at different points in their lives. The length of time they spent at pagoda schools and in the monkhood in general depended on factors such as family resources (for supporting education and ordination) and personal inclination. Most boys did ordain at several points before adulthood, as novices and at least briefly as *bhikkhu*s. A 1916 surveillance report notes that "Cambodian society does not have any regard for those who have not lived in a monastery. . . . [W]ith very few exceptions, all Cambodian [men] spend some greater or lesser amount of time in pagodas." Ordination was also, the report continues, a necessary precursor to marriage, since "parents . . . refuse the hands of their daughters to any suitors who have not given evidence of their recognition of the Buddha . . . by taking robes."[28]

During the nineteenth century, the only formal documentation of monk identity was bestowed at ordination, in the form of a *chāyā,* the record of the monastic name given to a *bhikkhu* at ordination, along with the date and time of his ordination ceremony.[29] The information was recorded by an elderly monk on a monastic registry. It was then copied onto a strip of palm leaf that was wound up into a roll the size of a thumb, tied with thread, rolled up in a protective cover, and threaded on a string.[30] The resulting *chāyā,* as one administrative report notes, was "of the sort that can never be opened,"[31] and was obviously intended for ritual rather than administrative and identification purposes. Monks traveled freely between monasteries, where they could break their journeys for long or short periods of time, crossing regional and ethnic borders as they pleased.

Under the protectorate, even as early as the late nineteenth century, Khmer monks were supposed to obtain passports for travel, but they often did not comply with this regulation.[32] After the turn of the century, French officials became increasingly convinced that the mobility granted to monks had to be curtailed. Besides its fears of millenarian agitators on the Cochinchinese border, the administration was becoming anxious about the possibility of Siamese influence. Concerns about Khmer monks in Siam were connected in part with Prince Yukanthor, whose venture into anticolonial journalism (discussed in chapter 2) had earned him exile to Bangkok at the beginning of the century. Surveillance reports clearly indicated that some monks in Bangkok were in regular contact with Yukanthor, who was suspected of continuing anti-French machinations.[33] But the dangers posed by monks traveling to Bangkok also reflected a more generalized anxiety about the political and cultural influence of independent Siam in the wake of the Russo-Japanese War of 1904–1905. Siam did serve as a safe haven for some other Indochinese dissidents. Inspired by the idea of an Asian state defeating a European power, Phan Boi Chau (1867–1940) had gone to study in Japan. Phan authored a highly influential anticolonial manifesto, *Viet-Nam Vong Quoc Su* (History of the loss of Vietnam), which circulated widely back in northern and central Vietnam. By 1909, disillusioned with Japan's collusion with Western powers, Phan was expelled from Japan and gradually made his way to Siam, where from 1911 to 1912 he continued his anticolonial activities among Vietnamese exiles who had established themselves in a rural community near Bangkok.[34]

This political context inflected a new, more threatening cast onto the older tradition of Khmer Pali studies in Siam. In particular, French feared Siamese political and intellectual influences taking hold in Cambodia through the organ of Dhammayutism, the sect originated by Mongkut and still closely associated with the Thai royal family. Intelligence reports from the period tend to represent the "exodus of Khmer monks to Siam" as though it were a deluge rather than a steady trickle. This exaggerated perception probably reflects the fact that monks returning from Siam often achieved greater prominence and influence in the Sangha than their counterparts of the same generation who had been educated within the country.[35] As these Siamese-educated monks become *upajjhāy* (monks in robes for at least ten years who could serve as preceptors in ordination ceremonies), their monastic networks afforded their own students a greater possibility for undertaking the journey to Siam.[36] Sangha connections had been forged between the elder generation of Khmer and Siamese monks, and travel routes were increasingly easier. It seems probable that the number of Khmer monks going to Bangkok after 1900 did grow, though there is no obvious means of determining the numbers of individuals involved before 1908.

Restrictions imposed on monk travel to Siam intensified between 1907 and 1916. In 1907, an ordinance requiring all monks to carry identity cards was instituted, mirroring regulations already put in force by Chulalongkorn in Siam.[37] Monks traveling outside the protectorate were required to carry passports as well,[38] and by 1908, in Phnom Penh at least, monks had begun to comply.[39] In the provinces, however, these tighter restrictions seem to have been ignored by many monks and were not uniformly enforced by Sangha officials and the colonial administration until 1916, with the introduction of another new law.[40] This ordinance required monks to carry a *chāyā* of a new sort: a *certificate de bonne vie* signed by their preceptors, ascertaining the legitimacy of their ordination.[41] All monks were required to obtain and carry passports across borders, even within Indochina, and the *āchāry* (chief lay teacher) at each monastery was made responsible for checking monk documentation and reporting visiting foreign monks to local authorities within three days of their arrival.[42]

The motivations for the new law are made abundantly clear in administrative reports from the period 1915–1916, which are filled with allegations against monks. The "great respect traditionally accorded to the clergy" afforded them protections and freedoms well-known to the population, which "miscreants put to their own profit" by adopting the saffron robes without ordination and using the monasteries to escape detection from the police.[43] "A considerable number of Cambodian monks go to Bangkok under the pretext of Pali studies, where they stay in pagodas in the capital of Siam,"[44] another report alleged. The issuing of passports for Pali education had to be brought to a halt, another urged, "to let the monks know that the Administration is not a dupe to the pretence of studies or the objects of study [texts] that they invoke in order to obtain this authorization."[45]

In official correspondence, the heads of the two orders justified the new ordinance by insisting that it was introduced as a means of protecting Buddhism. In a letter to provincial Sangha officials they warned that an escaped prisoner had "disguised himself as a monk and the public celebrated ceremonies with him," and that in another instance, a criminal disguised in robes had cheated individuals out of 400 piastres, maintaining that the money was to be used for religious purposes.[46] Whatever private views of the new law the Sangha leaders' letter fails to reveal, it does reflect the religious preoccupations of the period with authenticity and purification, discussed previously. For Khmer recipients of the letter, the injury of these acts would be obvious; the merit accrued in religious ceremonies, which were often expensive or even required a subscription fund in a particular village to which all inhabitants would contribute, was rendered invalid because the celebrants were not authentic monks able to act as "merit-fields."[47] All told, the letter continued, "a large number of individuals disguised as monks, guilty of misdeeds, have been found in pagodas by the Administration." This disheartening state of affairs, which led to "the dishonoring . . . of true monks," also created the necessity of identity papers "for establishing the authenticity of monks."[48]

From an administrative viewpoint, these new colonial policies in combination with the administration's program of renovating Buddhist education in Cambodia (discussed below) were fairly successful in stemming the movement of Khmer monks to Bangkok. By 1922, in an inspection report to the résident supérieur evaluating the Pali school policy in Cambodia, George Coedès and his colleague Sylvain Levi commented that École Supérieure de Pali was filling a crucial need, since "for a long time, there had been a custom [among monks] of going to Bangkok in order to find the knowledge they were missing here. They returned with a foreign imprint, which for obvious reasons, was not very desirable."[49]

On the Vietnamese border of the protectorate, however, the French attempt to control the movements of monks and to hamper their ability to foment millenarian-type activities was not entirely halted.[50] By the mid-1920s, a Vietnamese millenarian-type sect known as Cao Dai (Supreme Being) or Dai Dao Tam Ky Pho Do (Great Way of the Third Era of Salvation) began to attract hundreds and then thousands of Khmer adherents during a bleak economic period for Khmer farmers that preceded the worldwide depression.[51] Caodaism, which sought to synthesize doctrinal aspects of Buddhism, Taoism, and Confucianism as well as spiritist practices, predicted the arrival of thc Buddha Metteya in the Tay Ninh Seven Mountains region. As in nineteenth-century versions of Buddhist millenarianism, the imminent appearance of a *dhammik* in the Khmer-Vietnamese border area would usher in a new age of prosperity. For the French, the associations between millenarianism and anticolonialism as well as the fear that Vietnamese and Khmer rebels might join forces prompted the use of increasingly brutal tactics of arrest, fines, and imprisonment to discourage the spread of Caodaism.[52] French efforts were aided by condemnations from Sangha leaders and from the new Khmer monarch, King Monivong (r. 1927–1941), who, in his role as defender of the Buddhist *sāsana,* issued a 1927 decree prohibiting Khmer from participation in the cult.[53] Added to the administration's policies, these responses furthered the decline of Cao Dai potency within Cambodia.[54]

French policies restricting the cross-border and domestic travel of monks, as well as attempts to clamp down on the production of what the Dhammayut chief had referred to as the "cabalistic signs and charms allegedly possessing the property of rendering one invulnerable,"[55] coincided with the rise of the modern Dhamma movement and its notions of moral, textual, and ritual purification. In some instances, the aims of the movement and the French administration's religious policy reflected each other closely, although they were not always motivated by the same concerns. Purification, the broadest trope of modernist thought, was echoed in Résident Supérieur François Baudoin's defensive efforts to close Cambodia off from outside magico-political influences.[56] John Tully's reading of Baudoin's security policies in Cambodia as motivated by a fear of "contagion"[57] is redolent of late-nineteenth-century social debates about hygiene, "contagion," and immigration in France. Andrew Aisenberg has demonstrated how, throughout the nineteenth century and particularly after Louis Pasteur's pathbreaking 1878 introduction of germ theory as the basis of contagious disease, "contagion" became a central cultural metaphor for French thinking about the tensions between individual liberty and social control. Some contagious diseases such as infectious *"cholera asiatique"* were perceived to have originated in the East, and by the end of the century, homeless immigrants within France were being viewed as potential sources of disease-spreading germs.[58]

From the administration's standpoint, then, in addition to the political efficacies involved in keeping monks from traveling, the view that merely one or two mobile and "homeless" politically "infectious" individuals could contaminate large populations was not without its metaphorical bases in French social policy.[59] Likewise, the *certificate de bonne vie* and other identity papers required by monks established their connections to particular monasteries, mitigating their status as free agents, who, like living microbes, lived off one host body and then moved to "infect" another, transmitting subversive ideas such as millenarianism or overt anticolonialism and conferring the power to perform protective spells and amulets. Modernist monks and scholars, on the other hand, were in general dismissive of the same sorts of magically oriented Buddhist practices that the colonial administration feared most. But while the administration was involved in authenticating legitimate ordination and issuing new forms of *chāyā* for security reasons, modernists' interest in ascertaining the authenticity and legitimacy of ordination and ordination procedures stemmed from a quite different set of preoccupations, related to correct *Vinaya* interpretation.

These similarities suggest the broad strokes of a Franco-Khmer intercultural mimesis that contributed to the construction of modern Khmer Buddhism. This mimesis was never, as I suggested earlier, an entirely bilateral process; both the Khmer modernists and the French administration were borrowing ideas from religious reforms in Siam, where King Chulalongkorn had been simultaneously trying to effect a religious purification and extend his government's authority to the outlying provinces of his kingdom. Perhaps because the French administration in Cambodia was trying to control Buddhism rather than replace it, they found it easiest to work within the existing framework of ideas. Issuing a new kind of *chāyā,* for instance, was an example of an attempt to slightly revise Sangha traditions for their own purposes, drawing on the model of the Thai Sangha Act of 1902 that had already been implemented in Siam. The administration's larger effort to defuse the magical, cosmological, and millenarian elements of Khmer Buddhism, however, probably could not have succeeded to the extent it did if demythologization and concern with the authenticity of Buddhist rituals were not already powerful currents of thought associated with modernism. Thus, while administrative officials were intentionally and perhaps also unintentionally appropriating contemporary Buddhist discourses regarding legitimation and authenticity for controlling the Sangha, it is important to underscore that their motivations for the reforms were entirely different from those of modernists.

French efforts to control the Sangha served to bolster the modern Dhamma movement, though it was not until the mid to late 1930s that this became fully evident. From 1915 on, administration officials were aware that the dissenting modernist faction within the Mahānikāy was making it difficult for the newly appointed traditionalist Supreme Patriarch Tae Uk (discussed in chapter 3) to control his own order.[60] This had consequences for colonial security, for if the Mahānikāy was in disarray, individual monks were less likely to respect the authority of the supreme patriarch whom the administration regarded as crucial to its efforts to thwart potential subversion within the Sangha. Initially, the administration tried to bolster the supreme patriarch by censuring modernists such as Chuon Nath and Huot Tath with the 1918 ordinance that had so disheartened them in their early attempts to modernize by editing and printing *Vinaya* compilations. In 1929, when another similar edict was issued forbidding innovation in regard to Sangha practices, it was too late to have any real effect and was probably intended merely as a gesture to placate the traditionalist faction. By 1929, injunctions against print had largely dissipated, and members of the modern Dhamma faction were gradually moving into positions of prominence. Over the next decade, it seemed apparent that the traditionalist faction was losing its hold on the religious imaginations of Khmer monks and intellectuals.

Thus, after 1900, growing security fears on the part of the colonial administration served as one of the motivations for developing Buddhist education in the protectorate. The institutions designed to advance Pali studies—funded by the administration to help counteract millenarianism on the Cochinchinese border, to stem the "exodus" of Khmer monks to Siam, and to promote a modernized, demythologized education for monks—inadvertently lent support to what some administrative officials later characterized as the "regrettable" spread of the "new discipline."[61]

MODERNIZATION AND BUDDHIST EDUCATION

While French discourses about modernization and Buddhist education were not as integral a source for the intellectual and religious directions of Khmer Buddhism modernism as Siamese Buddhist reforms, they represented an important aspect of current ideas about modernity on which Buddhist intellectuals could draw. Further, these perceptions were an extension of the larger colonial ideologies that informed French policy decisions connected with France's understanding of its *mission civilisatrice* in the colonial world, as well as with European scholarly discourses about religion.[62] As French administrators became persuaded that they had to turn attention to the renovation of Khmer Buddhist education, both for political security reasons and out of the ideological motivation of improving and developing the "Khmer mind," one of the most pressing problems was that of introducing a modern scientific worldview into Buddhist learning. While the modern Buddhism that developed in Cambodia shared some common characteristics with what contemporary scholars have dubbed "Protestant Buddhism"—a Buddhist modernism that emerged in colonial Sri Lanka, aspects of which explicitly mimicked Christian missionary practices (such as catechisms, Sunday schools, and missionary schools)—French administrators did not draw widely on Christian forms as models for Buddhist renovation.[63] Rather, the French approach to modernizing Buddhism grew out of contemporary European scientific and historicist approaches to religion as well as ideas and practical programs of educational reform and innovation introduced under Mongkut, Chulalongkorn, and Vajirañāṇavarorasa in Siam, where French scholars connected with the EFEO had close ties. These ideas worked in tandem with the Khmer modernist thought taking shape in Cambodia.

By the beginning of the twentieth century, educated Khmer were coming into contact with French colonial perceptions and characterizations of Khmer civilization that emphasized its glorious past, decline, and current stagnation and its urgent need for modernization. Henri Mouhot's "discovery" of the Angkorian temples in 1859 had led to a profound French fascination with the ruins of the ancient civilization that in many ways also colored French colonial attitudes toward the Khmer.[64] Late-nineteenth- and early-twentieth-century colonial writers expressed incredulity that the contemporary Khmer were the descendants of the great Angkorian civilization.[65] Indicative of this attitude, one colonial official wrote,

> Heredity has developed the sentiment of his [the Khmer] powerlessness and weakness to such a degree that in the presence of the work of his ancestors he sincerely doubted it was their [creation]. What a lot of times we have heard Cambodians imputing the construction of the Angkorian monuments to genies![66]

Colonial writers also lamented Khmer "backwardness," particularly in respect to scientific knowledge, which had been "frozen in place,"[67] and complained that "even the most erudite Khmer are completely ignorant in this regard."[68] Scientific knowledge, such as knowledge of physical phenomena, was subsumed under religion, and, from a French perspective, was represented in religious teachings in frustratingly archaic and mythical terms. Despite the range of religious writing including *jātaka,* doctrinal writings, and scriptural compilations and commentaries that were being steadily produced in Cambodia throughout the nineteenth and early twentieth centuries, it did not appear to colonial observers to represent original thought, capable of serving as a vehicle for modern development. The Indochinese languages, wrote the governor-general of Indochina in 1918, "had not given birth to any modern literature worth retaining; and it is known besides that they are imperfect, lacking technical vocabulary, for the exposition of scientific knowledge coming from the West."[69]

Such perceptions undergird Leclère's 1899 *Le Bouddhisme au Cambodge,* in which Leclère relayed his conversations and correspondence with leading monks of the day, including Braḥ Samtec Sangharāj Dian̊ and Sugandhādhipatī Pān. Leclère's respect for the moral doctrines of Khmer Buddhism was complicated by his distress over the scientific views it contained. In regard to Buddhist representations of conception and the development of the fetus in the womb, for example, he commented apologetically,[70] "You would think I could dispense here with explaining a doctrine that is more physiological than religious, but as it is included in what is taught to monks at the two great monasteries in Phnom Penh, I guess that I can hardly fail to mention it in a work on Buddhism."[71] The problem with the classical version of conception[72] taught in monasteries, Leclère argued, was that from a modern scientific perspective, it suggested that "the masculine seed is unnecessary, human reincarnation is the work, not of the carnal act between a man and a woman, but of a woman and a principle of life (the *préas ling*) come from the outside."[73] While this view of conception was in fact rejected by many Khmer monks, who viewed conception as the result of sexual union though guided by the natural forces of karma, Leclère reported, they did debate about the extent to which karma shaped the attributes of the fetus in the womb. While aspects of the classical theory were rejected, Leclère commented, there was a widely believed "superstition," for instance, that "one can know if the infant that the mother carries in her womb comes from hell or from heaven" depending on the suffering experienced by the mother in the course of her pregnancy.[74] Leclère, trying to present Buddhist scientific views in the most sympathetic light possible, explained:

> Whereas occidental science teaches that we are always the product of the human series to which we are born, more or less advantageously developed by the social milieu in which we have been raised, in which we live, Buddhist metaphysics teaches that the being is his own product alone, and that the new being has received nothing from his father and mother, aside from their care, and that their nature, their character has no influence on either his physical or moral organization.[75]

Viewpoints such as these were troubling to Leclère in that they threatened the continuing viability of Buddhism in the modern context. The archaic scientific understandings embedded in Buddhist teachings and texts that continued to be taught in Khmer texts and monasteries represented the "dangerous" success of Buddhism's "domain of sacred errors," "dangerous" in that it could "ultimately destroy Buddhism."[76] Like all religions, Leclère philosophized, Buddhism contained a tension between its moral doctrine and the views of the world it had absorbed from the ancient culture in which it had developed. While the Buddhist views of the world that had developed in India 2,440 years ago were in Leclère's assessment more scientifically advanced than those that developed in early Judeo-Christian contexts, later Buddhism had not been subjected to the same kind of scientific scrutiny as Christianity. The scientific misconceptions apparent in contemporary Khmer Buddhism turned out, in Leclère's analysis, to have a racial cause. While Buddhist doctrine was morally and philosophically "elevated," the "poverty" of its archaic notions of the universe were perpetuated by

> the intellectual weakness of the masses it [Buddhism] has morally governed. . . . [T]hey are excessively contemplative, slack, without initiative, very imaginative; they seem always to have had for their sacred domain absolute respect for their ancestors, even the most barbaric.[77]

These comments are representative of French perceptions of the Khmer rooted in European intellectual concerns during this period with social Darwinism and racialized eugenic theories.[78] From this perspective, the difficulties involved in introducing modern ideas and projects into Cambodia, according to colonial writings, had as their source the Khmer lack of civilizational development, which was in turn pegged to the racial characteristics of the Khmer. They were, in short, "not innovators but imitators."[79]

The broader colonial ideologies concerning educational reform in Indochina, intended to address the problem of Khmer backwardness, also reflected these racialized perspectives. A report on Khmer education from the 1880s, for instance, suggested that "the situation of schools, from an intellectual point of view . . .

clamored for a number of modest but urgent modifications."[80] The problems were caused in part by a "deplorable" lack of resources but they were, again, rooted in indigenous traits and qualities. Khmer traditional education was taught by rote methods, through which "native instructors . . . attempt to transmit their vague knowledge to their students, without methods, without principles." This seemed to compound the deeper characteristic observed by the administrator-author, that "[t]he Cambodian is, it seems to me, rather indifferent by nature." One of the most urgently needed modifications in schools was thus to urge native instructors

> to call the attention of their students to the phenomena that take place around them, of arousing their curiosity, of developing in them the habit of observation, in short, of adorning their minds with practical and helpful knowledge.[81]

Beginning in 1905, a Council on the Improvement of Native Education,[82] consisting of French civil servants along with several French-educated Khmer members of the Council of Ministers,[83] was convened to consider problems and policies relating to the improvement of native education. During their initial meetings in 1905 and 1906, the council agreed that the insufficiencies of traditional education provided in monastery schools were disquieting. But as French official Charles Bellan pointed out, pagoda schools were somewhat beyond the jurisdiction of the administration:

> In Cambodia, all children must pass through the pagoda. They learn to read and write there and that is the extent of it. . . . But will the monks accept following and dispensing a new [form of] education? The monks remain completely outside of the influence of the administration. On this independent body our influence must be as discreet as possible so as not to awaken sensitivities.[84]

At this point, the council recommended interjecting some "discreet" materials for teaching local geography and other beginning scientific perspectives into pagoda schools. By 1907, however, the council had begun to advocate reforms drawn from the Siamese model. Echoing the Siamese government's deployment of religious and educational inspectors into the provinces to report on conditions and compliance to new regulations, the council recommended bringing monk-teachers under tighter supervision by introducing French and French-educated native educational inspectors.[85] "In Siam," Bellan noted, "the clergy teach reading, basic sciences, arithmetic, geometry, geography, etc."[86] The Siamese model was invoked again in a 1910 meeting, when one official commented almost wistfully that even though pagoda schools remained the most financially expedient means of raising levels of indigenous education in Cambodia and that change would inevitably occur slowly, "without wanting to hold out hope for an influence on the monks analogous to that existing in Siam," he thought it might be possible to hasten change somewhat by providing "modern educational manuals" to the pagoda schools.[87] These modern manuals, written in French and Khmer, were to introduce basic scientific perspectives, as well as new methods for teaching morality, ostensibly to counteract the traditional dominance of the *cpāp'* in primary education.[88]

By 1910, the council had concluded that although "the education of monks is absolutely insufficient," there were some grounds for optimism:

> The Cambodian wants to improve himself; he comes to us slowly, but surely. It behooves us to not discourage him and to facilitate for him the means of receiving our education by creating schools in the pagodas, where all classes of society congregate, drawn by traditional religious and secular sentiments, and where their frequent attendance is assured.[89]

A new kind of education in the old setting of the monastery would "replace the one that the people recognize as insufficient, and which was one of the principal causes of the degeneration of the Kingdom of the Khmers."[90]

In 1913, a renewed effort was being made to study the situation in pagoda schools. A report by Henri Russier, who had been appointed head of educational services, urged that in order to continue to "utilize monks" as teachers in the pagoda schools, it was important "to supplement their traditional religious educations with more modern forms of knowledge."[91] The council concluded that "with diplomacy, with patience, with perseverance, the monks will be led to professing certain scientific truths themselves that are not arrived at through the teachings of the Buddhist religion." By providing simple examples of the usefulness of "modern science" ("for example, the Supreme Patriarch is ill and is cured through French medicine"), the monks could be persuaded to accept more modern and scientific educational principles.[92]

The language of the council's policy report suggests the need to more closely consider what "modern" signified, from French administrative and scholarly viewpoints, in relation to Buddhist education. In a broader sense, two interconnected historicist perspectives dominated the European scholarly approach to the study of Buddhism: first, a trend toward demythologizing, and second, an effort to identify and translate the authentic Buddhist canon—as opposed to the hodgepodge collection of late-vernacular myths and stories that Buddhists themselves understood to be sacred. Both of these aims were crucial to the scholarly construction of Buddhism as a rational religion that reflected Victorian sensibilities. Influenced by social Darwinism and also by the theoretical work of scientifically minded scholars of religion such as Friedrich Max Müller, who sought to identify the "origin" or "essence" of religion, Victorian translators of Buddhism were trying to reconstruct "original Buddhism"— a Buddhism based on those texts considered to be the authentic words of the Buddha, interpreted through a filter of post-Enlightenment rationalism. The translators, an amalgamation of scholars and colonial civil servants, many of whom had lived for years in Buddhist cultures, found contemporary Buddhist practice to be at odds with the canonical doctrines they were translating and thus labeled these practices as degenerations of the original.[93]

In late-nineteenth-century Cambodia, as in the Buddhist cultures of Sri Lanka, Burma, and Laos, European scholars seeking a systematic textual and doctrinal account of the religion encountered local Buddhisms represented and dominated by fragments of narrative texts such as the *jātaka.* These texts seemed to Europeans to reflect the unscientific, mythological perspectives of a corrupted Buddhism. Colonial-era writings tended to characterize them as "crude" and "childish," full of "inconsistencies . . . [and] many distortions in ideals,"[94] written for the purpose of rendering subtle philosophical writings "palatable" to the uneducated masses.[95] While the prominent scholar T. W. Rhys Davids' first translated work was a volume of *jātaka,* he understood its importance primarily as an unspoiled record of a primitive stage in human history.[96] Responding in 1878 to the work of evolutionists such as Herbert Spencer and E. B. Tyler, Rhys Davids suggested that while "the accounts of modern travelers among the so-called savage tribes are often at best very secondary evidence" based on the possibly misleading cultural interpretations of native informants and passing through the "more or less able" medium of a European mind,

> in the *Jātaka* we have a nearly complete picture, and quite uncorrupted and unadulterated by European intercourse, of the social life and customs and popular beliefs of the common people of Aryan tribes closely related to ourselves, just as they were passing through the first stages of civilization.
>
> The popularity of the *Jātaka* as amusing stories may pass away. How can it stand against the rival claims of the fairytales of science, and the entrancing, man-sided story of man's gradual rise and progress? But though these less fabulous and more attractive stories will increasingly engage the attention of ourselves and of our children, we may still turn with appreciation to the ancient *Book of the Buddhist Jātaka Tales* as a priceless record of the childhood of our race.[97]

In this European formulation of Buddhist studies, then, the *jātaka* and other related narrative texts were to be viewed as sources for sociological research. The *Tipiṭaka* was the true sacred canon of Buddhists, and could be viewed as a source for authoritatively understanding what Buddhist doctrine was meant to be.

These general perspectives were dominant in Buddhist studies during the same early-twentieth-century period during which the three EFEO scholars who most influenced the development of French-patronized Buddhist education in Cambodia began their Indochinese careers. All three—Louis Finot (1864–1935), George Coedès (1886–1969), and Suzanne Karpelès (c. 1890–1969)—were brilliant, accomplished Indologists with an impressive knowledge of Southeast Asian cultures, languages, and history.[98]

Louis Finot, already an established Indologist when he came to Indochina in

1898 to direct an archeological institute, founded EFEO, shifting its mission from the conservation of ancient monuments to a more wide-ranging scholarly institute dedicated to the study of Indochinese civilization, past and present, and its connections to the cultures and histories of other regions of Asia, such as India and the rest of the Far East.[99] He was instrumental in helping to shape EFEO's philosophies and to orchestrate its influence on the colonial administration's policies on indigenous culture and religion.[100] Described as a calm, reserved, quiet, and scholarly man, "devoid of any egotism," and preferring meditative surroundings, he also possessed "the talents of an organizer."[101] He served as director of EFEO from its beginnings to 1904 and during much of the period between 1914 and 1929.[102] During these years, he helped to establish and later to reorganize the Pali School in Phnom Penh, including the training of Chuon Nath and Huot Tath in Sanskrit and European scholarly methods—through which he developed a strong bond with both men.[103] As Huot Tath related later, these studies had a profound influence on their intellectual development at the time and gave rise to a twelve-year correspondence between the two, until Finot's death in 1935.[104]

George Coedès also influenced the development of Khmer Buddhist institutions, particularly the day-to-day work of planning and implementing ideas. His training in France was as a classicist, but his early comparative textual work on Greek, Roman, and Oriental cultures led him to Indochina, and much of his career was spent in Southeast Asia. Between 1900 and 1918, he was associated in different capacities with EFEO in Hanoi, but much of that time was spent either in Cambodia or preoccupied with Cambodian studies and cultural policies. From 1918 to 1929, although retaining his role as an adviser to reforms in Buddhist education in Cambodia, he became the director of the national Vajirañāṇa Library in Bangkok at the request of Prince Damrong, who had been a close friend of his in France.[105] With many of the Chulalongkorn-era innovations already well established in Bangkok, the reign of Chulalongkorn's successor, King Vajiravudh (r. 1910–1925), was a period associated with the linking of Buddhism and national identity in Siam. Coedès' close associations with the Vajirañāṇa Library, one of the intellectual centers of modernized Buddhism in Bangkok, and his extensive knowledge of Siamese Buddhism help to explain why and how many French religious policies concerning Sangha reform, Buddhist education, and textual production appear to be modeled on Siamese precedents.[106]

Coedès' influence in Cambodia continued during the years 1929 to 1946, which he spent in Hanoi as director of EFEO. It is difficult to determine how Coedès' long marriage to a Khmer woman and his six children with her might have affected his perspectives on the colonial project; to colleagues, he appeared devoted to his wife, and she was thought to have exerted a strong influence on him.[107] He also wrote fondly and respectfully about "my Khmer friends," particularly in respect to his involvement with a small group of Khmer scholars with whom he worked closely on the production of a Khmer dictionary, from August 1915 to early 1917.[108] One of these men was Braḥ Mahā Vimaladhamm Thoṅ, whose key role in shaping modern Buddhist institutions in Cambodia will be considered shortly. Coedès wrote that he admired Thoṅ for his "science and his competence," describing him as a "handsome and intelligent figure of a *bhikkhu* whom I am honored to count among my teachers."[109]

The effect on Khmer Buddhism and Buddhist institutions of a third EFEO colleague of Finot and Coedès was particularly enduring. Suzanne Karpelès had trained as an Indologist under Louis Finot and two other scholars who spent part of their careers in Indochina, Albert Foucher and Sylvain Lévi. She was recruited into EFEO in Hanoi, where she arrived in 1923, apparently to take up the work of editing and translating critical editions of Buddhist texts. After a few months in Hanoi, her research took her to Bangkok, where she learned Thai and worked on editing and translating a portion of the *Dhammapadaṭṭhakathā.* Like Coedès, her scholarly work brought her in contact with leading Thai religious reformers. During a stint at Angkor in 1924, for instance, she and Henri Marchal, the archeologist who led the EFEO monument conservation effort, met with Prince Damrong, Mongkut's son and Chulalongkorn's half brother, who was a key adviser and policy architect during Chulalongkorn's and Vajiravudh's reigns.[110]

Administrative records indicate that Karpelès was subsequently brought to Phnom Penh explicitly because of her knowledge of the Vajirañāṇa Library in Bangkok.[111] She went on to become the first librarian at the Royal Library in Cambodia after its founding in 1925. Her rapid absorption into the work and politics of textual production in Cambodia led her, in 1929, to propose the establishment of the Buddhist Institute, which was founded in 1930. She helped to found the first Buddhist periodicals in Cambodia and oversaw the work of the Commission for the Production of the *Tipiṭaka,* which commenced in 1929. As historians David Chandler and Penny Edwards have observed, Karpelès' recruitment and encouragement of such men as Pach Chhoeun and Son Ngoc Thanh into the activities of the Buddhist Institute not only contributed to their development as prominent Khmer nationalists, but probably also contributed to the associations that emerged between nationalists and Khmer religious leaders such as Chuon Nath and Huot Tath.[112] Penny Edwards has argued that Karpelès' work at the Buddhist Institute significantly aided the "crystallization" of the "ethnically discrete rubric of nation" in Cambodia.[113] In spite of the novelty she presented to Khmer Buddhists as an unmarried woman educated in Buddhist languages and literature, she was both highly regarded and beloved by many members of the Sangha.[114]

I include these biographical sketches because the process of intercultural mimesis, as Hallisey employs it, is in part personal, and depends on individual perceptions and relationships. If we are to understand the roles of these EFEO scholars vis-à-vis the creation of new Buddhist institutions in Cambodia, we need to recognize that they all found Buddhist texts and learning intrinsically meaningful. Trained in Sanskrit and Buddhist textuality in Europe, all three received their on-the-ground knowledge of Buddhism in Southeast Asia. Finot, Coedès, and Karpelès patronized and supported various monks including Chuon Nath and Huot

Tath, but it is not clear that their personal relationships with Khmer monks were limited to patronage. Coedès' reference to Thoṅ as one of his "teachers" suggests, rather, that influences and ideas about modernizing Khmer Buddhist education ran both ways. Of the three, Finot was perhaps at the greatest distance from native influences; both Coedès and Karpelès, through their own textual research and work as librarians, were immersed in the Siamese and Khmer Buddhist intellectual and literary cultures of the day and had regular daily involvement with Buddhist colleagues. The idea of Pali education was inherently compatible with their own scholastic experiences, and the educational system they promoted to members of the administration was drawn from Khmer and Siamese design. Their correspondence indicates that their interest in promoting Pali education in Cambodia probably had as much to do with their own personal perceptions of its importance as with their arguments concerning the use of Pali education as an instrument for stemming Dhammayut influence and assuring colonial security. Their letters over the years, particularly between and by Coedès and Karpelès, including some of the hand-scrawled drafts of royal ordinances they wrote on behalf of King Sisowath, show that their own perspectives did not always coincide with the rhetoric they presented to the résident supérieur. They had devoted their entire lives to studying the Buddhist production of meaning, and it hardly seemed necessary to explain why it was important—except that they had to find ways to elicit support and funding from an administration with competing claims for its resources.

Finot's own scholarship on Buddhism provides an illustrative model for what he and other European scholars of the day understood as a modern approach to the study of Buddhism. His work is also instructive for viewing the effect of the colonial context of Buddhist studies on European understandings—Khmer influences on Finot are apparent. The historicist impulses that shaped his own scholarship on Buddhism were deeply resonant with Siamese and Khmer modernist aims of purification and practices connected with authentication, translation, and scripturalism. During the same years in which he was busy advising the administration on Buddhist educational policies in Cambodia, Finot also authored two works that became intertwined with the development of modern Khmer Buddhism.

In 1914 he began research on the Southeast Asian *Paññāsa-jātaka* (Fifty *jātaka*), collecting Lao-Siamese, Burmese, and Khmer versions of the text, which were all quite different.[115] He systematically compared the versions of the texts, charting their literary variations and examining the interconnections in the Buddhist literary cultures of Southeast Asia. Finot's study followed on the voguish circulation and reinterpretation of texts such as the *jātaka* and the Indian *hitopadeśa* as cultural works rather than sermons and sacred texts in Bangkok at the turn of the century.[116] When Thoṅ proposed the addition of Khmer vernacular literature in the Sālā Pali curriculum in the early 1920s, Finot wrote back, affirming that "an educated man should know his national literature," referring to works such as the *Paññāsa-jātaka.*[117] According to Lvī-Em, who later edited the first print version of the Khmer *Paññāsa-jātaka,* Finot's comparative study spurred the publication of new printed Siamese and Burmese versions of the text in 1924 and 1925, as well as a new Khmer palm-leaf manuscript version in 1926.[118] In 1926, the newly introduced *Kambujasuriyā* began to serialize *jātaka,* which Karpelès classed as literature "belonging to the domain of the profane" or as "national folklore" and sought to publish because of their high popularity with the populace. These works, she believed, would help to widen the reach of the press as well as bolster its funding.[119] Finot's "scientific" literary analysis of the *Paññāsa-jātaka* contributed to the shift in its reappraisal and reappropriation as "national literature."

Finot's other influential work in Cambodia, *Le Bouddhisme, son origine, son evolution,*[120] exemplified his approach to Buddhist studies even more dramatically than the *Paññāsa-jātaka* study. The book, which contained a map of India and photos of Buddhist Indian art, presented Buddhism in terms that were scientific, historical, and academic, emphasizing the origins of Buddhism in Indian culture and history and tracing its development and eventual disappearance there. Much of the book centered on the reign of King Aśoka—not in the form of the legendary stories known in Cambodia and Siam through such texts as the *Trai Bhūm,* the *Lokapaññatti,*[121] and "many other narratives in which it is at times difficult to distinguish the truth from fabrications," Finot wrote, but through the "very certain historical record *(baṅsāvatār)*" left by the Aśokan inscriptions that had been deciphered by a nineteenth-century Scottish archeologist.[122] Finot's history also included a biography of the Buddha depicting him solely in terms of his lifetime as Gotama Buddha—in contrast to the more usual Southeast Asian biographical rendering of the Bodhisatta that emphasized his rebirths, the prophecy at his birth, and his victory over Mārā, as depicted in nineteenth-century narrative poetry such as Ind's *Rýaṅ Paṭhamasambodhi,* discussed in chapter 1. Finot divided Siddhattha Gotama's life into four stages: his departure from the palace, his enlightenment and the truths he realized, his subsequent preaching, and his death. The work as a whole drew extensively on archeological and epigraphical evidence.[123]

As a Buddhist history, *Le Bouddhisme, son origine, son evolution* was markedly different from the Buddhist chronicles, *jātaka,* and commentarial texts known to Khmer monks; rather, it exemplified the kind of historical approaches that Finot taught to Chuon Nath and Huot Tath in Hanoi in the early 1920s. The work was translated at the request of Suzanne Karpelès by a librarian at the Royal Library, Juṃ M"au,[124] with the assistance of Braḥ Grū Vimalapaññā Uṃ-Sūr, the modernist colleague of Chuon Nath and Huot Tath, who was then working at the Royal Library.[125] In his introduction to the Khmer version of *Le Bouddhisme,* titled *Qaṃbībraḥbuddhsāsana* (Concerning Buddhism), Juṃ underscored the novelty of Finot's history from a Khmer scholarly perspective. He confessed that the translation, which he undertook in 1925, was a task of "exceedingly difficult and burdensome proportions" because of its foreign vocabulary—French, Pali, and Sanskrit—and because it used an academic vocabulary for which there was sometimes no Khmer counterpart. The work was serialized in *Kambujasuriyā* in twelve parts, beginning in 1926. Juṃ claimed that it was of "wide interest" to "all who were followers of the Buddha's teaching."[126] While it is difficult to know how wide a segment of Khmer Buddhists it actually reached, *Le Bouddhisme* was clearly influential among educated Buddhists. After its initial serialized publication, it was reissued as a book in 1928, with eight thousand copies printed in its first run.[127]

As their own writings suggest, the European scholarly methods and approaches exemplified by Finot's work were well-known to Khmer modernist monks and were to varying degrees integrated into their own modernization agenda for Buddhist education. Individual modernist monks must have had their own differing perspectives on the extent to which European science should be incorporated into Pali education. What they shared, however, was a perception that the study of the *Vinaya* and its teachings on moral conduct were the heart of an authentic expression of Theravāda Buddhism. It is important to emphasize that modernism constituted a "movement" only in this respect, not as a unified political front advocating modernization in all respects. This new interpretation of Buddhism was a form of modernism in the sense that it came to represent a Khmer Buddhist articulation and simultaneous critique of modern experience. Designating their interpretation of the Dhamma as *thmī,* "new" or "modern," modernist ideology opposed traditionalism but was in many respects conservative, reflecting a tendency to valorize ancient knowledge and practice as purified and authentic, and thus modern. For modernists, new educational methods including grammar, translation, and other pedagogical innovations carried to Cambodia from Siam were crucial for the extent to which they illuminated *Vinaya* and other scriptural knowledge, not simply because they became conflated with modern scientific methods in the European sense.

On their side, EFEO scholars preferred to supplant traditional Khmer methods of study with current European pedagogy and a curriculum that included geography, Buddhist and Indochinese history, Sanskrit grammar, and French.[128] Initial French attempts to use Buddhist education for modernizing Khmer intellectual culture, in 1909 and 1914, met with limited success. By 1922, the newly revised curriculum that was put into place in the Sālā Pali in Phnom Penh reflected many Khmer traditional sensibilities regarding monastic education, but it was increasingly dominated by a modernist agenda focused on *Dhamma-vinay* study that also promoted some European scientific methods of study.

DEBATES ON THE CURRICULUM OF THE *SĀLĀ PALI*

The curricular plans for Buddhist education between 1909 and 1930 reveal the extent to which colonial religious policies represented a negotiation between French views of modernization and differing Khmer perspectives about how to conduct monastic learning. French conceptions of "modern" scholarship privileged historicism and rationalism, with a resulting emphasis on reconstructing "original Buddhism" through scientific method. While Khmer traditionalists upheld the methods attached to manuscript culture, including the rote recitation method of learning Pali, they based the authority of this tradition on venerated nineteenth-century Khmer monastic figures such as Pān and Diaṅ. Khmer modernists advocated a break with older textual traditions, yet like European scholars, they were highly interested in the period of early Buddhism as a source of authenticity and purity. Their view of history was somewhat different, however, in that it was connected with the vitality of the Dhamma. In the modern age, the Dhamma was marked both by moral degeneration and by the inherent possibility for improvement and progress. As a result, modernists wanted to purify religious understanding in order to reconstitute Buddhism correctly and authentically as a way to live in the present world. The French and Khmer modernizing aims were deeply complementary but different. Put simply, the French wanted (for themselves and their Khmer colleagues) to be modern in their understanding of Buddhism; the Khmer wanted to be Buddhist in a modern world.

The early debates over modernization at the Sālā Pali shaped prominent Buddhist institutions that to a large extent retained their characters through the early 1970s. The new pedagogical ideas that were introduced at the Sālā Pali, together with the advent of print, led to the establishment of the Royal Library, the Buddhist Institute, and the Commission for the Production of the *Tipiṭaka.* I conclude by considering how new reading and writing practices centered at the Royal Library brought an end—in a vital sense—to Khmer manuscript culture. This discussion simultaneously charts the further progress, during the 1920s, of the modernist faction of the Mahānikāy over their traditionalist detractors, whose loss of significant political influence was signaled by the end of manuscript culture and the establishment of the Buddhist Institute in 1930.

The first French effort to renovate Buddhist education in Cambodia followed closely on the retrocession of the ethnic Khmer provinces of Battambang, Sisophon, and Siem Reap (also known as Angkor) to the colonial administration in 1907.[129] Important to the Khmer monarchy and to the colonial administration for symbolic and political reasons, the retrocession of the region containing Angkor Vatt back to Cambodian control after a century and a half of Siamese domination was also immensely exciting to French scholars and others in Indochina. Even before the retrocession, French scholars had been highly engaged in studying the history and archeology of Angkor, and travelogues and other accounts of the ruins had excited a wide popular interest in France.[130] After the retrocession and for the rest of the French colonial regime in Cambodia, the French lavished attention and resources on the restoration of Angkor Vatt and the surrounding temple complexes.

In the euphoria attached to the retrocession of Battambang and Siem Reap, the first (and ultimately unsuccessful) Pali school, the École Supérieur de Pali d'Angkor Vatt, was established in August 1909.[131] Intended in part to stem the influence of the Siamese over monks, it also represented an initial French effort to take traditional Buddhist learning in hand. In a letter to the résident supérieur,

Paul Luce, the inspector of civil services proposed that the school should be established at Angkor, the site that represented "the greatest manifestation of the Khmer genius at the time of its dominance." The loss of the provinces to Siam had constituted "a terrible misfortune for the Cambodian people" and a "continual sorrow" to its kings. As King Ang Duong had extracted a "sacred promise . . . from his sons on his deathbed, that they would recover the lost provinces," the establishment of a center for Buddhism—the "roots" of Khmer culture—in this place would be a highly symbolic commemoration of the return of the provinces. "This is why we should plunge the roots of the Cambodian tree in the soil of Angkor," Luce waxed passionately.[132]

The ordinance establishing the school decreed that "in consideration of the honorable antiquity of the Pali language in Cambodia," the school (and its counterpart to be opened later in Phnom Penh) must be established in order to further the learning of this "indispensable" language and to "elevate the intellectual and moral level of our subjects."[133] Since the Pali scriptures would be reproduced "on palm-leaf and with printing" and "these texts will be more refined than those of Bangkok," Khmer monks were henceforth forbidden "to go to study in Siam."[134]

Except for the promise to provide palm-leaf and print scriptural texts for monastic study—a provision that failed to materialize—the school's curriculum, designed at least in part by members of EFEO, offered little innovation from the traditional monastic education current in Cambodia.[135] But the plan for the school had the effect of standardizing higher monastic education in a more systematic manner than in the past, mirroring the earlier overhaul of monastic curricula that Vajirañāṇa had initiated in Bangkok in the 1890s. Students were to study the traditional *Kaccāyana* grammar, *Dhammapadaṭṭhakathā, Maṅgaladīpanī,* and *Sāratthasaṅgaha,* texts that formed the monastic curriculum imported from Siam during the nineteenth century.[136] Regularized, yearly examinations, which did entail a number of pedagogical innovations, were also introduced. The exams were largely written rather than oral, and they involved not only the recitation of designated *sutta* but also the translation and explication of selected passages. Included as well were the requirements of an essay on the history of the life of the Buddha for first-level students and a sermon on a topic chosen by the examination commission for the second-level group.[137] A commission to oversee the exams was to include a "French functionary," designated by the résident supérieur, as well as a Khmer member to be chosen by the Council of Ministers. Reports on all of the proceedings would be presented to the résident supérieur.

More significant than any changes in the curriculum, however, was that the exams were intended to carry new administrative implications. As in Siam, an incentive for monks to pursue higher education and sit for the exams was incorporated: monks who elected to leave robes would be allowed to transfer their ranks to commensurate civil service posts.[138] In addition, the ordinance decreed that henceforth, only monks who had taken part in the examinations could be appointed to higher monastic ranks, including the posts of *megaṇ* (heads of dioceses) and *mevatt* (heads of monasteries).[139] Although these rules were not uniformly enforced, the general effect was to introduce a movement toward knowledge of Pali as a criterion for administrative posts, a criterion that obviously favored the gradual upward movement into the Sangha hierarchy of educated monks and those engaged in textual study. Although not all scholarly monks were members of the modernist faction, most modernist monks were scholars. Thus, under these new regulations for Sangha promotion, well-educated modernist monks gained an advantage in contests for Sangha promotion.

In its first year, 1909, the Angkor school initially enrolled forty-seven students. Within six months, however, it was clear that in spite of being the "roots of the Cambodian tree," Buddhist education was having serious difficulties sustaining itself in the "soil of Angkor." The king and provincial officials had provided some initial funds for the school, but the administration had anticipated that donations and offerings from local inhabitants would otherwise support it. By February 1910, however, it was clear that the monk-students at the school were starving and ill. The school's director, Braḥ Buddhavaṅs Mī,[140] wrote pleadingly of the "urgency" of the situation: "the inhabitants of Angkor are not very generous, the cause of which is their poverty."[141] Because of the "difficulty of material life" at the school, half the students left within the first year, and several others died from illness.[142] Equally problematic for the school's enrollment was that ambitious young monks, as well as prominent teachers, were reluctant to isolate themselves in the provinces, away from the advantages of the capital. Further recruitment proved impossible, and the school was closed in June 1911.[143]

Perhaps because the administration's dramatic vision for the Angkor school had proved so misguided, officials were willing to cede more control over plans for the second school to EFEO scholars and Phnom Penh–based Buddhist intellectuals. In December 1912, EFEO's director in Hanoi forwarded a report to the governor-general of Indochina that contained George Coedès' arguments for establishing a second Pali school in Phnom Penh. Besides the importance of developing the intellectual culture of Cambodia, for which "I do not know studies more proper for developing the germs of a very real intelligence in them, impotent for want of an object, than the study of Pali and of the literature for which it is the key," Coedès suggested,

> [f]rom a political point of view, the existence in Cambodia of a Pali school will present the advantage of stemming the annual exodus of young monks who go to Siam, in search of an education which they would certainly prefer to receive in their native land.[144]

The establishment of a new Khmer Pali school, Coedès argued, would help to counterbalance the growing influence of the Dhammayut, "who are reserved, if not outright hostile" to the colonial administration.[145] In spite of Coedès' warnings about the urgency of this situation, it took two more years (and escalating security concerns) for him to orchestrate the founding of the new École de Pali.[146] Both the résident supérieur and governor-general were finally persuaded by these arguments, but objected that the EFEO plan to place the school "under the control of its personnel, who were to be purely native," be augmented by installing Coedès in Phnom Penh. He knew Pali, the résident supérieur commented, and would be "good at controlling the school."[147]

The original plan for the new Pali school curriculum was similar in many respects to the curricular reforms that had recently been introduced in Siam several decades earlier.[148] It made canonical *Tipiṭaka* texts—including the *Vinaya* —central, while relegating the two prominent, noncanonical commentarial texts, *Dhammapadaṭṭhakathā* and *Maṅgaladīpanī* to a more secondary status. It included elementary grammar and translation in the first two years; *Vinaya* and *Suttantapiṭaka* studies, along with key commentaries, in the middle years; *Abhidhamma* studies and "modern" (in the European historical sense) Buddhist biography and history in the final years.[149] The program admittedly represented "a tenuous thread tying the École de Pali to occidental science," but it was prudent to let such transitions occur slowly, and there was no doubt that "the education offered here [would] become increasingly open . . . to the methods and results of French Indology."[150] If this curriculum plan seemed conservative from a European point of view because it was still devoid of sciences such as archeology, it was seemingly as modern—in terms of its emphasis on grammatical methods of Pali learning, *Tipiṭaka* study, and historical biography—as the monastic climate of Phnom Penh could bear, especially in view of the exacerbation of antagonisms between the modernist and traditionalist factions in the Mahānikāy. In the end, it took nearly another decade before even this modestly modernized curriculum could in fact be introduced.

Although the hopes of EFEO scholars that the new Pali school could rapidly introduce modernizing influences into traditional Buddhist education could not be realized in 1914, the appointment of Braḥ Mahā Vimaladhamm Thoṅ (1862–1927) as director remained a clear indication of the direction that the school was meant to take. Described in his 1927 obituary by Finot as a man whose "liberal and enlightened thought was manifested in the establishment of a program that permitted the first glimmers of European science to penetrate the Cambodian clergy,"[151] Thoṅ was a brilliant linguist and highly venerated Mahānikāy monk. He was educated primarily at Vatt Uṇṇālom by Samtec Braḥ Sangharāj Diaṅ but had the opportunity to travel to Bangkok to collect texts at the beginning of the century. Along with his mastery of Pali, Thoṅ was apparently one of the few Khmer scholars of the day who perceived Sanskrit study to be integral to the understanding of Khmer Theravādin texts and ideas. He was an instigator of the orthographic reform project that coincided with the opening of the Pali school, and as a scholar, had devoted himself to studying the *Vinaya.* He composed eight texts on the *Vinaya,* including works reviewing the *Vinaya* regulations for monks and a *Vinaya* for laypeople; a text titled *Pabbajjākhandhaka-saṅkhepa,* on entrance into the Sangha;

and the *Uposathakatha,* on regulations for laypeople on *thṅai sīl* (holy days).[152] A more established and less controversial figure than his younger colleagues Chuon Nath and Huot Tath, he nonetheless lent his reputation to the promotion of their modernist aims and strategies and provided the corrections for all of their early translations of *Vinaya* texts and commentaries.[153] In the anxious, carefully worded introduction to the print edition of his controversial 1918 work *Sāmaṇera-vinaya,* Huot Tath invokes Thoṅ in nearly every sentence. The work was composed,

> at the invitation of the Venerable Braḥ Mahā Vimaladhamm Thoṅ, director of the Sālā Pali of Phnom Penh, who requested that the *Sāmaṇeravinaya* be compiled, edited, and made ready for printing. [The work] was carried out according to his [Thoṅ's] wishes in order to benefit all students. It was he who invited Braḥ Grū Saṃsatthā Nath, Braḥ Grū Vimalapaññā [Uṃ-] Sūr and me to be the compilers of this work, and it was brought to completion in accordance with his request.[154]

Although Thoṅ had achieved a high monastic rank, his modernist orientation may have cost him promotion to head of the Sangha following the death of Samtec Braḥ Sangharāj Diaṅ in 1914. During the highly contested selection of a new supreme patriarch that year, King Sisowath helped to engineer the elevation of Samtec Braḥ Dhammalikhit Sanghanāyak Uk to the post over Thoṅ.[155]

Plans for the school were being developed during this same year, also the year that Huot Tath's and Chuon Nath's *Vinaya* sermons ignited passionate debate at Vatt Uṇṇālom. In spite of the earlier plan to introduce the modernized curriculum described above, the atmosphere of internal controversy in the Sangha made this impossible to achieve. In its initial term, students were following the monastic curriculum of the late nineteenth century: beginning students were studying the *Kaccāyana* grammar, while middle- and upper-level students were devoting themselves to the *Dhammapadaṭṭhakathā* and the *Maṅgaladīpanī.*[156]

In a published EFEO report written for European scholars, Coedès was candid about the slow pace of modernizing Buddhist education:

> These two texts [the *Dhammapadaṭṭhakathā* and the *Maṅgaladīpanī*] constitute the foundation of traditional education in Cambodia and Siam. It is important, for the establishment of the school, to respect this tradition. Premature innovation would certainly be poorly welcomed by the monks, for whom all reform is *a priori* suspected, and who could unfortunately compromise the success of this institution.[157]

At the school's highly public inaugural ceremony, however, Coedès was intent on allaying possible misperceptions about the school on the part of the administration. In his address, he stressed that the potential for modernization at the school was masked by its traditional program of study. Speaking to the high-ranking French officials present, including Résident Supérieur Baudoin and the governor-general of

Indochina attending from Hanoi, Coedès explained Pali as "that Indian dialect that is the close parent of our European languages . . . often compared to Latin." "In Cambodia," he suggested, "where Pali studies thus properly constitute classical studies . . . this school is destined to become an intellectual center like those already possessed by Siam and Burma."[158] He elaborated the modernizing vision behind it:

> Do not believe, in seeing this large assembly of monks, that it is merely a matter of a theology school, where a purely religious education must be given. In this country, where the [monastic] vows are not eternal, it is also the custom that for young men desirous of undertaking the study of Pali, they must take up the robe that assures their material subsistence for a time and seek it out in the calm meditation of the pagoda. [D]uring its initial years, this education will be obliged to take recourse to traditional methods. But it will be our constant concern to disengage, little by little, this education from the theological and scholastic apparatus that shackles and hinders it from developing into all that it can be: a marvelous instrument of intellectual culture.[159]

By 1922, curricular revisions, crafted largely by Thoṅ,[160] Coedès, and Finot, were presented to the administration as the outline of a new Buddhist curriculum that would promote a "rational education" in religious languages, as well as all other sciences "indispensable to the understanding and explication of religious texts."[161] The administration was sensitive to the ongoing problems between the traditionalists and modernists, problems they did not want to further enflame. Yet once the proposed revisions were codified by royal ordinance, they had the effect of placing the school's curriculum almost completely under modernist control. Traditionalist monks, trained in old-school pedagogical methods, would have little possibility of participating in the school's new program. Administratively, the school was also placed under the supervision of the École française d'Extrême-Orient, which meant that Finot was able to intervene in all curricular issues and personnel decisions at the new school.[162] He used this power to promote young monks such as Chuon Nath, Huot Tath, and Lvī-Em to teaching and administrative posts within the school.

Finot's view of the problems attached to traditional Khmer translation practices echoed those of young modernists such as Chuon Nath and Huot Tath, discussed in the previous chapter. While Finot's desire for introducing new pedagogical methods seemed to stem more from a perception of Khmer limitations rather than (like Chuon Nath's and Huot Tath's) a zeal for illuminating the *Vinaya,* he had nonetheless arrived at the same conclusion as they: students at the Sālā Pali should be made to learn to translate and analyze rather than memorize and recite. In a 1918 report on the Phnom Penh school, Finot observed,

> If you ask a student at the École de Pali how Buddhism envisages the origin of the universe and of life, the nature of mental operations, transmigration, the sacred,

> salvation, et cetera . . . [his] response will be furnished by the Canon that he has been made to study, but without giving him any comprehensive idea of what it contains. It is essential to liberate the students from this perpetual recitation of texts that only encourages memorization, at the cost of thinking, and thus aggravates the original tendency of the native mentality.[163]

Thus on the one hand, Finot defended the pace of modernizing reforms at the Sālā Pali to the résident supérieur, arguing that "in some countries, the religious conscience is easily frightened" and that in order not to "compromise the success of the new school," it had to be allowed to "utilize its original, traditional physiognomy to reassure all these susceptibilities."[164] Simultaneously, however, he looked for ways to speed up the introduction of scientific methodologies at the school. In 1922, when Thoṅ proposed the addition of improved Sanskrit instruction as well as a course to instruct Khmer monks on their "national literature and the origins of their language,"[165] Finot seized the opportunity to push the administration for funds for scientific training. After traveling to Phnom Penh to seek out an appropriate new teacher for these subjects, he wrote excitedly to Baudoin that on a recent trip to Phnom Penh, he had met an extraordinary young monk named Chuon Nath, who was "remarkably intelligent, . . . strongly intuitive and full of desire for learning. . . . It would be a great service to Cambodian studies," he continued, "to constitute a small group of elites . . . possessing a good traditional culture as well as a familiarity with the uses and methods of European science." He proposed to educate him in archeology, inscriptions, and editing critical editions of texts and suggested that he would henceforth "occupy myself with Nath's education."[166] Thoṅ agreed, and decided to dispatch Huot Tath for instruction as well.[167] Baudoin, who had already received Coedès' reports about advances in Pali education in Siam, agreed that in order to "liberate [Khmer] institutions" from the influence of methods being introduced in "the neighboring country," Chuon Nath and Huot Tath should be allowed to travel to Hanoi.[168] In June of 1922, they commenced their study of Sanskrit and European scientific methods with Louis Finot in Hanoi. They returned in late 1923 and took up their new teaching posts under Thoṅ in 1924.

As director of the Sālā Pali during its first decade, Braḥ Mahā Vimaladhamm Thoṅ had begun the welding of monastic learning to new modernist interpretations and methods. Thoṅ's vision for the Sālā Pali is laid out most clearly in a 1918 annual report in which he suggested to Baudoin that the existing curriculum needed to be supplemented with other kinds of texts and approaches. The existing curriculum was effective in that it led students to "know how to write in Pali, how to read and explicate the *Braḥ Sutt, Vinay,* and *Braḥ Abhidhamm. . . .* In short, they know perfectly how to distinguish right from wrong."[169] But in addition to what they were learning already, Thoṅ suggested, the students should be exposed to more Buddhist history and Sanskrit studies, and he asked that instruction in French be added to the curriculum (a request enthusiastically forwarded by Baudoin to the governor-general for approval).

Thoṅ saved the most ardent part of his letter, however, for advocating a much greater role for *Vinaya* studies in the Sālā Pali curriculum. "In my opinion and to ensure that Pali education progresses," he suggested that the *Vinaya* be taught "more than the other *piṭaka*s, because the *Vinay* is the fundamental basis of the Buddhist religion."[170] His letter went on to explain why the moral conduct clarified in the *Vinaya* was essential knowledge for Khmer monks and for the Khmer kingdom:

> The *Braḥ Vinaya* defends against doing wrong and ordains the doing of good. Until recently, because of a lack of adequate instruction, monks and novices have not competently learned the Buddhist regulations. They ignored these regulations because they have had too much freedom. They performed wrong actions, according to their inclinations, and this caused disorder in the religion and in the Kingdom. In consequence, it would be appropriate to remedy this problem by augmenting the education in the religious regulations that are the fundamental principles of the religion dictated by the Buddha. If this is accomplished, the task undertaken by the Protectorate to protect the Kingdom and the religion will not be in vain.[171]

He argued that monks leaving the Sangha who had been well versed in *Vinaya* studies would become better "private citizens" upon leaving the order since they would better understand how to regulate their behavior, the lessons and "habits of doing good" having been "engraved in their hearts." Further, he proposed that the administration contract with a number of recent graduates from his school to spread the *Vinaya* message, to "send them out into the pagodas of the provincial seats in the interior to teach the *Vinay* there"—in other words, to become *Vinaya* ambassadors or missionaries to the population at large.[172]

Thoṅ's 1918 report is useful in that it lays out the Khmer case for further modernizing the Sālā Pali curriculum. Thoṅ was not uncomfortable with modern scientific methods of studying Buddhist grammar and history, and like Finot, he advocated the inclusion of Sanskrit in the curriculum. But his clear priority, which takes up most of his report, was the spiritual awakening of Khmer monks and more widely, the Khmer populace, to the powerful message of the *Vinaya* so that its "habits of doing good" could be "engraved in their hearts." Like Baudoin, he thought that Khmer monks had been used to having "too much freedom," which he wanted to control, although obviously not in the same manner as the administration. Rather, the knowledge of the *Vinaya* would help them to restrain and control their bodies, thoughts, and speech, and such control would ultimately lead them to spiritual liberation.

There is no indication that Thoṅ ever received administrative support to send students out to the provinces as *Vinaya* "ambassadors"; Baudoin in fact scrawled "abstain from entering into the quarrels that appear in this report," on the bottom of Thoṅ's letter, suggesting his wariness of the modernist-traditionalist battle that had continued to escalate. In 1918 Baudoin also sent his own report on the school's functioning to the governor-general, expressing his view of the results that had been achieved there. He assured the governor-general that he had achieved a "tightened control" over monks as a result of the new school. The report, in fact, features a completely different kind of "control" being realized at the Sālā Pali than the purifying self-restraint Braḥ Mahā Vimaladhamm Thoṅ understood to be attached to *Vinaya* studies:

> The high degree of control our Administration has attained over students in Pali as a result [of sponsoring] the official School of Pali assures us in the future, of the disposition of minds of elite intellectuals in Cambodia and in the pagodas, especially the day when it is decided that the monk dignitaries and abbots must obligatorily be chosen from among those certified by this school.[173]

This control had already been utilized, Baudoin's report continued, in the sense that the director of the school, Braḥ Mahā Vimaladhamm Thoṅ, had intervened to "defuse" the tensions between traditionalist and modernist factions over the school's curriculum. The more conservative curriculum for the school had been adopted in 1915 to ensure that the "opinions of monks and faithful Buddhists" were "not aroused." In Baudoin's assessment, this justified the funds that the protectorate was using to support the school.[174]

Baudoin's report suggests that although in private correspondence Thoṅ was advocating a more modernizing agenda for Buddhist learning, in public he was trying to appease both factions. This approach broke down to a certain extent, however, after about 1920, when the modernist and traditionalist factions again clashed over an issue to which Thoṅ was deeply ideologically committed. Like other modernists, Thoṅ's viewpoints grew out of the larger aim of purification. In connection with his desire to help the Khmer Sangha and populace achieve purification through knowledge of the *Vinaya* and through proper conduct, Thoṅ was also concerned with a different sort of purification: that of language. Khmer intellectual interest in language reform was linked to the notion of purifying texts. The scribal practices of Khmer monks who had scant knowledge of Pali and who were merely copying texts without necessarily possessing the ability to read and analyze them lent themselves to the production and reduplication of errors. Monks such as Thoṅ, Chuon Nath, and Huot Tath who were trying to compile authoritative new editions of texts from a multitude of manuscript sources constantly confronted the problem of scribal errors and inconsistencies.

As the new Sālā Pali began to function in 1915, Thoṅ and several other Khmer intellectuals urged Coedès to ask EFEO to petition for administrative support of work on the first Khmer dictionary.[175] Coedès wrote to Finot that Cambodian scholars had long been asking for a commission to address the problems of the "odiously disfigured Khmer language":[176]

> The Cambodian language, in effect, does not yet possess an official orthography. All those who have had the opportunity to study and read manuscripts . . . know of

> the orthographic fancies indulged in by the scribes, through ignorance or through false science: employment of so-called etymological final consonants, frequent confusion between simple consonants and aspirated consonants. . . . It is time to remedy this state of affairs, which the Cambodians are the first to deplore.[177]

Finot agreed and the administration was willing to underwrite the effort financially. Early French efforts to develop a system of romanization like that of Vietnamese had never materialized,[178] and frustrated by the lack of a coherent, unified way of spelling and transliterating the Khmer language since the advent of the protectorate, French civil servants engaged in mapping and recording the names of villages, towns, and provinces had long been calling for a standardization of the spelling system.[179] A dictionary commission, composed of the "Cambodian literati knowing their language best," who were charged with "fixing once and for all the orthography of their language," was formed by royal ordinance in June 1915.[180] Work on the orthographic reform and dictionary commenced in August 1915, with Coedès as an "honorary member and advisor" to the working group.[181]

From Coedès' description, the work of the commission was a labor of love for those most closely involved, a small group of men that included Thoṅ, Ukñā Suttantaprījā Ind, Minister of War and Minister of Public Instruction Ponn (named as president of the commission),[182] Braḥ Sīlasaṅvar Hak (a monk from Vatt Uṇṇālom who was a long-time compatriot of Thoṅ,[183] apparently a modern Dhamma advocate and later a faculty member at the Sālā Pali),[184] Braḥ Mahārājā Dham-Suas (a Dhammayut monk and abbot of Vatt Braḥ Yoravaṅ), and two elderly palace officials, Ukñā Piphit Eisór Mei and Ukñā Dhammānikar Kong.[185] Chuon Nath eventually joined the group as well. The active members of the commission met every day at the École de Pali for nearly a decade. Their lively discussions and passionate disagreements over the meanings and uses of words, Coedès recalled later, often required a vote in order to reach resolution.

As Sanskrit and Pali scholars, the men on the commission were particularly concerned with purifying the Khmer language in order to show its Sanskrit and Pali roots and to bring it more in line with the Khmer appearing on ancient inscriptions. Ācāry Ind[186] in particular, Coedès commented, although educated in Siam, was an "ardent patriot," and it was at his insistence that the silent final "r" appearing in many Khmer words be maintained. The final "r" was still pronounced in some western dialects and conformed to ancient usage.[187] Likewise, the other reforms they proposed,[188] which featured the usage of three key diacritical marks, were not so much an innovation, Coedès pointed out, "but more . . . a return to an ancient Cambodian tradition abandoned without reason in a recent epoch."[189]

By 1920, however, the commission's work had become caught up in a particularly ugly phase of the struggle between traditionalists and modernists. Conservatives brought some members of the Council of Ministers over to their side by charging that in adopting diacritical reforms—in particular, the new usage of the three diacritical marks—the dictionary commission had overstepped its authority and acted without proper sanction from the king and Council of Ministers. Furthermore, traditionalists charged that these reforms flouted the orthographic renovation established by Sugandhādhipatī Pān in the nineteenth century[190] and thus circumvented Royal Ordinance 71 of 2 October 1918 requiring that the two sects refrain from innovation and observe the traditions established by Samtec Braḥ Sangharāj Diaṅ and Sugandhādhipatī Pān.[191] The "savage opposition" mounted by the traditionalists against the new orthography and the dictionary resulted in the suppression of a spelling primer authored by Thoṅ, Ind, Nath, and Hak for distribution in pagoda schools,[192] as well as the new dictionary they had produced.[193] The Résidence Supérieur, which had been supporting the work of orthographic reform at the recommendation of EFEO scholars without anticipating the fury it would unleash, turned its attention to ensuring that the outraged traditionalist monks and their supporters would not riot in the streets.[194] Baudoin issued a statement that "the usage of the signs advocated by the reformists is strictly forbidden."[195] In May 1926, just as they were about to be printed, the proofs for the original dictionary were literally and dramatically pulled from the presses.[196]

It would "always be regrettable that a simple procedural error had condemned [a project] recommendable for its intrinsic merits,"[197] Finot wrote of the work of the original dictionary commission. As the furor died down, Thoṅ and a number of his compatriots, including Hak, Chuon Nath, Huot Tath, and Uṃ Sūr, were appointed to a second commission in 1926 that was charged with reworking the dictionary and orthography utilizing most of the elements of the more traditional orthographic system.[198] Thoṅ died before the work was completed, and Chuon Nath became its primary author. In spite of the controversy, the dictionary had been crafted primarily by modernist-leaning monks and scholars. Although the original efforts at language purification could not be salvaged, the highly politicized process of the orthographic reform and dictionary production had contributed to the development of an alternative conception of the role of language and writing as part of the newly emerging discourse of cultural identity rather than as a primarily sacred activity.[199]

By 1922, through his collaboration with EFEO scholars, Thoṅ had managed to effect many of the changes in the Sālā Pali curriculum that he had voiced in his 1918 report. Reorganized in 1922 as the Sālā Pali jā khbas', or École Supérieure de Pali, the new curricular changes included Khmer history and archeology, Asian geography, Buddhist doctrinal philosophy, the general history of Buddhism, Sanskrit, and French.[200] After 1922, the traditional monastic choice of texts such as the *Maṅgaladīpanī* and even the *Paṭhamasambodhi* continued to be taught, but the study of *Vinaya* works[201] also grew in importance.[202] By 1928, with the proclamation of another royal ordinance, further curricular innovations emphasizing Sanskrit studies and the teaching of Khmer literature, "profane as well as religious" were introduced.[203]

Braḥ Mahā Vimaladhamm Thoṅ had died the previous year, but his young modernist colleagues Chuon Nath and Huot Tath were professors at the school, with Lvī-Em, another modernist monk, named as his replacement. The school's annual reports from the mid-1920s through the mid-1930s demonstrate continual experimentation with the arrangement of texts and other kinds of studies, such as Buddhist history and archeology, but in general, the modernist emphasis on translating the *Tipiṭaka* and especially the *Vinaya* appears as its central aim. Increasingly, the school's curriculum took on an arrangement reflecting the three sections or "baskets" of the *Tipiṭaka:* after an initial year of grammar, second- and third-year classes focused on the *Suttantapiṭaka, Vinayapiṭaka* studies commenced in the fourth year, *Abhidhammapiṭaka* texts were introduced during the final year.[204] In 1929, for example, fifth-year students began studying the *Abhidhammapiṭaka* as well as the *Pātimokkha* (the *Vinaya* compilation of monastic precepts) and were required to compile and edit portions of texts containing "explications of the *Vinaya.*"[205]

The new discursive methodology that was being implemented at the Sālā Pali was tied to the emergence of print culture in Phnom Penh. As new pedagogical methods superseded the traditional methods of education and memorization that had been based on the use of verse and sung according to a highly complex system of metrification, so were manuscripts being increasingly supplanted by printed texts. As I will suggest below, as a result of policies introduced by Suzanne Karpelès at the National Library, even those manuscripts that were still being maintained and copied were assuming a meaning more equivalent to that of printed books than to devotional, sacred objects. The beginning of the end of manuscript culture that had been signaled by the publication of Huot Tath's *Sāmaṇeravinaya* in 1918 fell into place rapidly after the establishment of the new library in 1921.

PROSELYTIZING MODERN BUDDHISM

Producing Khmer versions of Buddhist texts had been an implicit part of the policy of retaining monks within the protectorate since the 1909 ordinance prohibiting monks to travel to Bangkok for study. Between the resistance of traditionalist monks to print and lack of exertion on the part of the administration, little had been achieved, however, in the task of supplanting Bangkok as the kingdom's primary repository for Buddhist texts. As late as 1914, Braḥ Mahā Vimaladhamm Thoṅ had been forced to return to Bangkok to acquire texts needed for the Sālā Pali.[206] Throughout the decade preceding the establishment of the library, beyond the fear of Siamese influence, French officials were also concerned (at least rhetorically) with establishing Cambodia as a Buddhist center able to rival Burma and Ceylon as well as Siam, and as an effort to boost the prestige of their colonial possession vis-à-vis Britain.[207] With Coedès "lent" to the Vajirañāṇa Library in Bangkok, the publications program of the newly expanded Siamese institution became the model for the Khmer library and its activities. It reflected poorly on the French administration that while Coedès was sending new editions of Thai publications to libraries all over the world from Bangkok,[208] Cambodia of 1918—

where Chuon Nath and Huot Tath were suffering vicious recriminations for attempting to print the *Sāmaṇera-vinaya*—appeared as a backwater colonial possession in respect to Buddhist literary culture. Finot pointed this out to the résident supérieur in 1922, emphasizing the need to raise the standards of indigenous Buddhist scholarly writing, "in order to call attention, in the scholarly world, to the work accomplished in Cambodia by the Administration for the improvement of local clergy and Pali studies."[209]

The establishment of the National Library in 1921[210] was crucial to these efforts. As a repository of texts, it held great symbolic importance for the kingdom in the cultural terms examined in the previous chapter, but its policies also irrevocably ended the traditional practices of manuscript production—in spite of appearances otherwise. Although part of its original mission was to "acquire and conserve manuscripts" as well as to collect printed books, its larger aim was "to publish texts and works in Cambodian and French . . . relating to the history, religions, literature, art, institutions, and customs of ancient and modern Cambodia, as well as to the political, artistic, and religious history of countries adhering to the Southern Buddhist doctrine,"[211] and in particular, to publish the new works being produced by students and professors at the Sālā Pali.[212] Manuscripts became collectible items to be copied and preserved as cultural documents, while new, corrected, printed critical editions of texts contained the authentic *Dhamma-vinay* interpretations.

By the mid-1920s, Karpelès had been sent to Phnom Penh to run the library and spearhead the publication of Buddhist texts. After an inspection tour of monastic libraries throughout the country she wrote of her fear that texts were rapidly disappearing or becoming damaged. Among monks in the countryside, whose command of Pali was limited or nonexistent, Karpelès noted what she saw as an appalling lack of access to vernacular versions of canonical texts. Furthermore, she reports, in many libraries the majority of texts were written in Siamese or in Siamese Pali characters. "Printing the sacred books in Cambodian characters or language is, as you can see, a veritable necessity from a double point of view, first for erasing the last influences of the Siamese, and second, for aiding the culture of rural monks."[213] She began to collect texts from all over the country for the library, an effort that met with wild success and support from the Cambodian population, at least in part because of Karpelès' success at staging spectacles. Aided by the growing public prestige of professors at the Sālā Pali, Karpelès' efforts to promote the library included personal tours of monasteries by monks such as Chuon Nath, sometimes with Karpelès accompanying; journalistic interviews with monks; a "bookmobile" library that traveled to remote areas; cinema screenings; and distribution of tracts and images.[214] In Karpelès' words, enthusiastic villagers often formed "veritable crusades" to collect manuscripts, and organized festivals and processions to present them to the library: "hundreds and hundreds of bonzes, women, young girls, and old people came down the river in junks adorned with the sacred colors or arrived in auto trucks decorated with pennants."[215]

As manuscripts were donated to the library's collection, Karpelès hired monks and lay scribes to produce copies of the manuscripts on palm leaf, probably to satisfy traditionalist monks and gain their support for the library. This way of producing manuscripts undermined rather than preserved the sacred dimension of these texts, however; copies produced by Karpelès' scribes were often hurriedly executed, lacking the meticulousness and aesthetic beauty of earlier texts, more like mass-produced printed books than devotional objects.[216]

In political terms, the collection and production of texts, and particularly the production of a Khmer version of the *Tipiṭaka,* were viewed as prime means of winning over the Sangha.[217] By the end of the 1920s, Karpelès wrote that her most important work was the printing of the Khmer dictionary and a Khmer-Pali version of the scriptures, which she regarded as "the sole means of definitively attaching the Buddhist clergy to the Protectorate."[218] In educational and moral terms, the development of the library's publication program was also a means for developing the Khmer mentality by promoting the work of Sālā Pali students and professors, whom Karpelès viewed as "having lost confidence in themselves, for no one had ever published the manuscripts which they had offered."[219]

The writing and reading habits of educated Khmer Buddhists changed dramatically during the 1920s. In 1922, the curricular revisions introduced at the Pali school added the requirement of an "individual work," which was to consist of a critical edition of a text.[220] This requirement led to a burst of new printed editions of Buddhist texts by the mid- to late 1920s, with young monks coming out of the Pali school trained to conceive of their translations as printed texts. In 1926, the (now-renamed) Royal Library proposed a literature contest, for which the three best essays in the categories of eighteenth- and nineteenth-century Khmer history, Khmer sociology, and a translation of a previously untranslated Pali work would receive a cash award and be published by the library.[221] Two popular Buddhist periodicals were also introduced in 1926 and 1927, *Kambujasuriyā* and *Ganthamālā.* Although both periodicals printed translations of Buddhist texts, *Ganthamālā* was intended primarily as a vehicle for publishing the new critical editions produced at the Sālā Pali.[222] *Kambujasuriyā* had a more diverse mission, and in addition to Buddhist literature and scholarship, it published "national literature" such as collections of Khmer oral folklore.

To better track her constituency, Karpelès had introduced a register at the library and requested that monks and other visitors leave a record of their names and the titles of books and texts they wished to read. From this record, she recounted, "[W]e were able to discover that the Cambodians were avid for learning; that all of them wanted translations of their sacred books printed in Cambodian characters and bound in volumes that could be easily handled."[223] These readers included not just monks but laypeople, who were requesting Pali texts translated into Khmer, particularly the translation of the *Vinaya,* which was the "book in greatest demand."[224] During 1926, the library had a total of 3,782 readers. By the next year, there were 4,371, which Karpelès attributed to the growing confidence of "a large part of the Cambodian population in this institution."[225] By 1930, there were 5,437 annual readers, who borrowed 334 manuscripts and 1,118 printed books and reviews.[226]

The sales of printed books in Cambodia also grew. In 1926, the Royal Library reported sales of several thousand volumes of the *Gihipaṭipatti,* a book written by Chuon Nath on lay Buddhist conduct. In 1927, the *Gihipaṭipatti* was still the biggest seller, but the library had sold more than 5,000 copies, and other volumes were being printed in lots of one thousand to five thousand copies. In 1929 the library sold 12,660 volumes in all; a year later, the publications program was printing and reprinting editions of individual books numbering in the tens of thousands. These books were primarily *Vinaya*-related volumes such as the *Sāmaṇera-vinaya* and the *Gihipaṭipatti,* but the library had also begun to print and distribute "national literature" such as the *Paññāsa-jātaka* and Ind's *Gatilok,* as well as Finot's translated *Le Bouddhisme.*[227] Requests were also coming in from individual villagers to edit and print Buddhist texts. For instance, in his introduction to *Attānusāsnī* (Teachings on the self), a compilation of teachings on self-conduct drawn from Pali texts, the translator and author, Chāp-Pin, explains that the book was written at the instigation of a layman named Dhām and other laypeople from the village of Brae Katāgaṅ in Kandal Province, who asked the Buddhist Institute to print the text for the purpose of "dedicating the fruit of the offerings to all *upāsikā* (laywomen) who are mothers [and] who have died."[228]

When the Buddhist Institute was inaugurated on 12 May 1930 in Phnom Penh, it was an outgrowth of the revitalized Buddhist education and institutions put into place in the previous decades. Its mission was to respond to the needs of the Pali schools, libraries, museums, and other programs that had been established to promote and study Theravāda Buddhism. Its major task was to organize and oversee the work of editing, translating, and producing the Pali-Khmer version of the *Tipiṭaka,* a task that had been set into motion with a new royal ordinance in 1929 that charged the commission with producing both a new palm-leaf and a printed redaction of the entire "84,000 verses" of the *Tipiṭaka.*[229] The dual production of both a palm-leaf manuscript and print version of the text signifies political clout still held by traditionalists in 1929, but the *Tipiṭaka* commission, which involved a large number of Khmer savants in the enormous task of compiling and editing the Pali version of the *Tipiṭaka* as well as translating the edited texts into a side-by-side Khmer version, was led by the inner core of modern Dhamma monks: Lvī-Em, Uṃ-Sūr, Chuon Nath, and Huot Tath.[230]

The project of producing and printing the entire Pali-Khmer *Tipiṭaka* took forty more years to achieve. By the time it was finished in April 1968—quite unbelievably from the standpoint of 1918—Chuon Nath was the supreme patriarch of the Khmer Sangha. He had been appointed to the position in 1948, and following his death in September 1969, Huot Tath assumed the position as Sangha chief. Unsurprisingly, the first volume of the *Tipiṭaka* that was printed, in 1931, was a volume of the *Vinaya.*[231] In a ceremony commemorating the occasion, a young Franco-Khmer woman offered a poem she had composed in French that expressed a decidedly different version of what it meant to be a Buddhist from what one could have found in nineteenth-century Buddhist writings.[232] It integrated being Buddhist, Khmer, ancient, morally pure, spiritual, and modern. "Who are the Khmer?" she asked in her poem:

> Oh Modern Asia,
> Oh Modern Europe.
> This people! Ho! Ho! Which people?
> . . .
> This is the people, son of the people who raised Angkor Vat, the
> Bayon . . .
> And one hundred thousand other temples. . . .
> They are the children of the Angkorian people,
> They are the children of the great Khmer people,
> Oh Europe, Oh Asia,
> Who have risen up to renew the Word of the Buddha. . . .
> . . .
> Oh people with souls, the few Khmer people,
> You who have pulled from the ashes the only Word
> That can free the world
> And dry up the tears of gods, spirits, and men,
> Of demons, beasts, trees, and stones,
> Oh my Khmer people,
> Oh my people with souls,
> Oh my people full of grace . . .
> Continue to rise up in the ecstasy of your faith and your humility;
> Go, my people, walk without fear between Orient and Occident,
> Go with your *sampot* rolled around your loins
> And the Jewel of the Triple Basket that shines upon your heart;
> Spread out, Khmer people, over Europe,
> Spread out, Khmer people, over Asia,
> The Light for which yearn
> . . . gods, men, giants,
> Beasts, rocks and plants;
> Oh universe full of tears,
> This is the Light . . . of Buddhist Peace and Love.[233]

With this view of colonial policy and the development of Buddhist institutions in the early twentieth century, a history of Khmer Buddhism from 1848 to 1930 has emerged here. However, one significant religious discourse relevant to the construction of modern values remains to be examined. The encounters, mimesis, collusions, and other local and translocal currents of ideas and events from which modern Khmer Buddhism emerged included the important interaction between Khmer vernacular renderings of the Theravāda and the cosmopolitan Pali tradition. The ideological and pedagogical innovations introduced by modernists altered and dominated the nature of that interaction, as Khmer Buddhists underwent a shift from a manuscript to a print culture.

5 How Should We Behave?

Modernist Translations of Theravāda Buddhism

"Nowadays," Ukñā Suttantaprījā Ind observed in the *Gatilok,* his primer on moral conduct, "people are not the same as they [once] were." Although they intend to behave in accordance with the Dhamma, more often they end up being "swayed by the ways of the world instead."[1] Thus, it was necessary to give scrutiny to the question of moral conduct: "how should we behave if we want to make ourselves pure?"[2]

Ind's comments prelude my return in this chapter to reading Khmer Buddhist representations of moral development, the bookend to the nineteenth-century ethical literature I examined in chapter 1. Returning to a close reading of Khmer Buddhist vernacular works written from 1918 to the early 1930s makes it possible to see how Khmer ideas about moral development shifted during the course of several decades, and how they inscribed a Buddhist modernism. Moral development, in the literature of the nineteenth century, was dominated by the cosmic biography of the Bodhisatta cycling through rebirths in a quaking, awe-struck world shaped by the purification of successive buddhas. Modernism, which explicitly rejected the literary excesses of nineteenth-century representations of moral landscape, nonetheless refashioned the trope of purification and melded it to a new complex of values surrounding issues of authenticity, rationalism, moral behavior, and a broadened application of Buddhist aims and ideals to laypeople as well as *bhikkhu*s and bodhisattas. The vernacular writings produced in the early twentieth century suggest the outlines of a Khmer Buddhist approach to modernity that combined elements of a critique of contemporary moral degeneration with an "authentic" Buddhist vision of how to live a purified life, even amid the temptations and confusions of the modern world. As in other modernist religious movements of the period in Southeast Asia, religious rationalism was an attempt to recapture the true essence of the original religion—freed from improper rituals and faulty knowledge—rather than a total rupture with the past.

My reading of ethical writings in this chapter allows us to consider one further historical factor in the development of modern Buddhist values in colonial Cambodia. In addition to understanding the rise of modernism in the context of socio-political events, regional influences, and nineteenth-century Khmer Buddhist preoccupations, we need to see modernism also as an aspect of the long ongoing interactions between the vernacular and cosmopolitan literatures of Theravāda Buddhism. A close reading of several modernist ethical texts will allow us to see the content of modern values as well as how the new forms in which they were produced and expressed were shaped by the textual and ethical interactions between new vernacular translations of Buddhism and normative notions of authenticity and authority in the Theravāda tradition. Khmer expressions of modernity were inseparable from this interaction, which helped to give shape to the thought-world of Buddhist monks and Pali scholars within the modernist faction as well as the traditionalists whom they opposed.[3]

For modernists, the awakening to the *Vinaya* in the late nineteenth and early twentieth centuries had at first focused on regulations for monastic behavior and on assuring that monastic behavior was authentic and pure. From *Vinaya* compilations on monastic ritual procedures, their attention turned more generally to the question of how Buddhists, especially Khmer Buddhists in the modern era, should conduct themselves. Their translations and other writings on this subject suggest a system of moral values in which the individual actor is represented in terms of his or her conduct, understood as the actions and interactions performed with body, speech, and thought. Purification was predicated on rational knowledge; implicit in their writings is the assumption that there are clearly discernible grounds for knowing what is true and false and right and wrong, as well as rules for how to conduct one's self. These could be apprehended through proper study and understanding of the *Dhamma-vinay.* For Buddhists who wanted to become pure, the cultivation of awareness, perception, recognition, and understanding —as well as scholastic knowledge in general—was the most important pursuit for achieving purification of the self, which in turn led to purification of the religion and the community of adherents. At the same time, as I have suggested in previous chapters, older traditionalist methods for textual production and study were regarded as corrupt and in need of updating with new modern methods and techniques such as critical translation and print dissemination. The trope of "purification" permeated every aspect of modernism; texts, like understanding, conduct, language, and orthography, had to be made pure.

Writings produced by the modern Dhamma group and Ukñā Suttantaprījā Ind from the second decade of the century to the early 1930s reveal the contours of the modern Buddhism emerging in Cambodia. The new focus on the purified individual, the *sāsana,* and the religious community that appears in these writings is linked to nineteenth-century constructions of exemplary moral figures traversing through a hierarchical moral cosmos. But as I have suggested, in modern understanding, these conceptions were visibly altered—demythologized, less bodhisatta-centric, and more concerned with lay social ethics. They feature the development of new temporally and geographically localized imagery of the individual moral agent, the *sāsana,* and the collective body or community of Buddhists. They also begin to evoke notions of a distinctive Khmer society, culture, and "national religion" that became more pronounced in Khmer thought and literary production after this period.[4]

Modernist monks of the 1920s and 1930s were most interested in studying and disseminating translations of *Tipiṭaka* texts and their commentaries that dealt with codes of conduct and purification of conduct through close practice and understanding of the *Dhamma-vinay*. This emphasis on texts about conduct was integral to their project of delineating authentic, purified values appropriate for modern Buddhists, notably for lay Buddhists as well as clergy. Through the establishment of authoritative translation methods and texts, these values became the basis for the new discipline that spread rapidly in Cambodia during the 1920s and 1930s. Yet the process of vernacular translation involved more than simply the promotion and dissemination of certain texts over others. In addition, it necessitated the development of new textual forms and literary styles, new modes of textual production and translation, the transformation of ideas of textual authority, and finally the translation of the Theravādin religious imagination into locally resonant tropes and values.

I turn first to a discussion of the relationship between textual purification and self-purification in the two most prominent forms of modernist writing from this period: *saṅkhep* (abridgments) and *saṃrāy* (vernacular translations), literary forms that modernists reshaped to fit their new ideologies and translation methods. Second, to suggest the ways in which Khmer writers localized their interpretations of Theravādin values, I turn to a reading of purification and moral agency in Ukñā Suttantaprījā Ind's primer *Gatilok*. Ind coined still another new literary style in the *Gatilok*. He referred to his work as a "*tamrā*" or "manual"[5] for its combination of abridgements and vernacular translations of Pali canonical verses, which he interwove with Buddhist stories, translations of French fables, and Khmer oral folktales. In a marked departure from his own previous literary compositions and from the styles that dominated the nineteenth century, Ind composed this new work almost entirely in prose.

PURIFYING TEXTS, SELF-CONDUCT, AND *SĀSANA*

On 12 May 1930, at the inaugural ceremony of the Buddhist Institute, Braḥ Ñāṇapavaravijjā Lvī-Em preached a sermon titled "Sāsanahetukathā" (Verses on the foundations of the doctrine) to the assembled audience of dignitaries, colonial officials, Buddhist clergy, and laypeople. It highlighted the central modernist values concerning authenticity, rational knowledge, and moral conduct associated with the new doctrine. The sermon also revealed how notions of moral development were being melded into a new view of the ethical intersections between the self and others, or in other words, why and how everyone's individual behavior determined the purity of the collective body of the religious community.

The "authentic doctrine" had been realized by the enlightened Buddha, "who elucidated it," Lvī-Em explained pointedly to the assembled European and Khmer audience, "as a torch for all beings in the world."[6]

> We can take up this torch of *Dharm* and *Vinay* to shine as a light for seeing causes and intentions[7] that are true and not true, actions that are good and evil, rewards and punishments that are just and unjust, and in order for us to discern clearly how to transform and reorient our hearts and minds away from causes and intentions that are not right and away from actions that are evil. Endowed with . . . [these teachings,] we can act in accordance with what is beneficial and good in this world and the next.[8]

How is it possible to recognize the difference between authentic and inauthentic doctrine? Drawing from a variety of scriptural sources, Lvī-Em suggested that "the true and authentic Buddhist *Dhamma-vinay*" could be understood through the means elucidated in detail in the *Dhamma-vinay* itself, in short, by "making an effort to ponder, think, analyze, and reflect on teachings in Pali and to let them penetrate one's heart and mind deeply."[9] Thus, through clear understanding of the authentic *Dhamma-vinay,* Buddhists could purify their conduct and bring it in line with the Buddha's Dhamma; purifying one's own individual conduct simultaneously purified and strengthened the religious community as a whole. "Whether performed by a householder . . . or a *bhikkhu,*" Lvī-Em emphasized, this form of purification represented the "highest kind of homage or worship to the Buddha."[10]

> Offering good conduct *(paṭipatti-pūjā)* is the highest homage, higher than offerings of food, because it is the means for making the Buddhist religion resplendent, the means for ensuring that the purest forms of behavior practiced by the Fully Enlightened Buddha become firmly established and endure for an epoch of five thousand years.[11]

The goal of Buddhists was purification, both for individuals and for the religious collectivity, described in the sermon as the "fourfold *parisāḷ,*" referring to the assembly of all four groups of monastic and lay Buddhists, male and female: *bhikkhu-bhikkhunī-upāsak-upāsikā.* For monks and laypeople alike, purification was to be achieved by bringing one's moral conduct in line with the true teachings of the *Dhamma-vinay.* Purification raised questions of authenticity. To become pure necessitated developing the ability to distinguish between what was authentic and inauthentic *Dhamma-vinay,* the ability to recognize whether others truly knew the *Dhamma-vinay* or whether they did not, the ability to judge which behaviors were in line with the *Dhamma-vinay* and which were not. Implicit in this agenda was the perception that discerning the underlying nature and authenticity of persons, ideas, values, and teachings was not obvious; it required education, awareness, mindfulness, and above all, knowledge of the world attainable only through correct grounding in the *Dhamma-vinay.* Although it required discipline, moral purification could be attained by ordinary people through rational means rather than in the elusive and mythological sense in which it attached to the bodhisattas, *cakkavattin,* and millenarian leaders discussed in chapters 1 and 2.

These modern values, as I have suggested, were closely connected to new modes of translation, learning, and textual production, which I will discuss below. "Sāsanahetukathā" explicitly suggests the centrality of these new methods for cultivating purification through moral conduct. Being knowledgeable about the Dhamma, according to Lvī-Em, required at least five kinds of "respectful practice":

> making an effort to understand the *Dharma . . . ;* making an effort to study Pali and learn it by heart so that one knows it thoroughly . . . ; making an effort to support the remembrance of Pali . . . ; making an effort to ponder, think, analyze, and reflect on teachings in Pali and to let them penetrate one's heart and mind deeply and clearly . . . ; knowing the teachings through explanations and through Pali, and behaving in accordance with them.[12]

These practices led to the kind of true understanding of *Dhamma-vinay* that released its transformative potential in individuals and in the fourfold religious community and thus led "the Religion of the Tathāgata [the Buddha] to become resplendent with a brilliance that outshines even the brilliance of the moon at its brightest, when it is round and full in the middle of the sky."[13]

The new canon that emerged in colonial Cambodia privileged texts that offered prescriptions for purifying one's conduct, imparted advice about the proper and improper ritual procedures and behavior, and clarified false and authentic Dhamma. As I have suggested, a zealous devotion to the *Vinaya* lay at the heart of the modernist textual world. But modernists were also interested in a variety of other literature drawn from the *Tipiṭaka,* as well as in the *Tipiṭaka* commentaries that had been central to monastic education in the nineteenth century, such as the *Maṅgaladīpanī, Samantapāsādikā,* and *Visuddhimagga.* Other prominent nineteenth-century texts such as the *Paññāsa-jātaka, Trai Bhūm, Paṭhamasambodhi,* and *cpāp',* while never disregarded, tended to take on altered significance or were relegated to a more secondary status. Because of their more tangential relationship to the *Tipiṭaka* (they were neither *Tipiṭaka* nor commentaries or subcommentaries on the *Tipiṭaka*), they were not understood to be expressions of authentic *Dhamma-vinay.*[14]

The literary forms, styles, and strategies modernists employed reflected their own ideological aims and the larger shift between manuscript and print textual production that they had helped to effect. Modernists used prose instead of the metered verse that had been popular in nineteenth-century literature. They often rendered their texts as *saṅkhep,* "abbreviated" or extracted texts that distilled the "essence" of a longer *Dhamma-vinay* passage into a single abridged text or compendium. Their translations of *sutta*s were quite different from the older tradition of *saṃrāy* composition in Cambodia. Not only was the choice of texts different, favoring texts other than *jātaka,* but the methods and style of translation were altered as well. Instead of the loose, rambling translations that had been common in the nineteenth century, described previously, the modern *saṃrāy* were produced as "critical editions."[15] The editor of a given text compared different versions of the same *sutta* or *Vinaya* portion and corrected any mistaken Pali words or grammar he discovered in palm-leaf versions. Drawing on the grammatical method of translation described in chapter 3, he produced a vernacular edition of the text containing Pali verses followed by a succinct and grammatically close Khmer translation and commentary.

Texts composed in the brief, extracted *saṅkhep* style were particularly well suited to introducing new concepts and teaching beginners. Huot Tath wrote in the introduction to his controversial 1918 work *Sāmaṇera-vinaya* that the entire *Vinaya* was simply "far too long" for young novices and "for this reason, trying to learn it would cause them to become weary, short-winded and scatter-brained." Thus, he had "extracted the essence . . . to enable them to study it more easily."[16] The distilled nature of this style of writing matched the modernists' concern with purifying texts, language, and rituals; in the *saṅkhep* style, only the most essential elements were presented to the public, exposing them to a redaction of a text purged of the mistakes and commentarial asides found in the old palm-leaf *saṃrāy* and thus enabling them to more clearly understand the message of the *Dhamma-vinay*.

The abbreviated format of the *saṅkhep* was perhaps also a feature of the recent introduction of print technology and print dissemination strategies. The production of sacred texts in Cambodia was, for the first time, being tied to market mechanisms, one of the features of the new production of texts that marked the demise of a devotion-based manuscript culture and the rise of print.[17] Brief volumes were more appropriate to the initial establishment of a new technology and the availability of funding for print. The Royal Library budget for printing was based in part on its previous book sales, which were constrained by the limited number of volumes that could be printed. The production of texts was still motivated in many cases by a desire for making merit, but the funding for these printed merit-making volumes was dependent on donations from individuals and subscriptions raised by temple communities who commissioned particular works to be translated, edited, and printed; the quality and quantity of the print text produced for merit making were thus now dependent on the amount of money that could be generated to underwrite the production and distribution costs. Longer translated works were published first in serialized form rather than as self-contained volumes. The Royal Library's periodical *Kambujasuriyā* provided one venue for serialized works and translations, with lengthy works such as Uṃ-Sūr's 1930 translation of *Milindapañhā* published over the course of more than a dozen issues. Ind's *Gatilok* was serialized over a five-year period, from 1927 to 1931, and subsequently published by the Royal Library in ten volumes, one at a time.

Beyond the exigencies of funding, the literary style of *saṅkhep* and serialized translations reflected and responded to the mood of urgency and transition that marked emerging Buddhist modernism in Phnom Penh.[18] If lengthy narratives about merit and power from the end of the nineteenth century no longer seemed to convey the essence or authentic words of the Buddha, these short, thematically explicit excerpts of *Dhamma-vinay,* painstakingly distilled from a variety of palm-leaf *saṃrāy,*[19] could be more quickly and easily disseminated to a public whose hearts and minds modernists believed to be in urgent need of awakening. The Khmer *sāsana* could not be purified until the authentic teachings were spread among the whole populace, as Braḥ Mahā Vimaladhamm Thoṅ had argued in 1919 with his proposal to send *Vinaya* teachers out into the countryside.[20] While modernist efforts at proselytization were initially hindered by a shortage of monks properly trained in new methods of Pali translation, the texts—as long as they were carefully translated, with accompanying explication—could stand in for teachers. The rapid spread of the modern Dhamma doctrine attests to the success of this translation effort.

The core modern Dhamma proponents—Uṃ-Sūr, Lvī-Em, Chuon Nath, and Huot Tath—were among the most prolific writers and translators in the modernist idioms. All four directed their written work to the emerging new print media. Probably stemming from Thoṅ's influence, their early writings gave attention to issues of monastic ritual performance such as robe styles and ordination procedures. Later, this focus expanded to include considerations of lay ritual participation and moral conduct, which they approached in the same meticulous manner they had applied to monastic codes and rituals. By the early 1920s, they began to enlarge their focus on the mechanics of Buddhist ritual to broader considerations of how to live as a moral person in the modern world, through knowledge of the authentic teachings of the *Dhamma-vinay.*

Beginning in the 1920s, the most prodigious of the translators, Uṃ-Sūr, translated *Milindapañhā* along with portions of commentaries such as *Visuddhimagga, Abhidhammatthasangaha,* and *Dasapāramikathā.*[21] Lvī-Em's *saṅkhep* writings were concentrated on the *Vinaya* and clarifications of ordination procedures for monks and novices.[22] Along with an updated Pali grammar for use at the Sālā Pali, Chuon Nath first translated *Vinaya* works and then moved to producing a number of works directed at clarifying Buddhist rules of conduct and ritual procedures for laypeople.[23] Huot Tath authored a wide variety of works, ranging from a guidebook on the history of various temples at Angkor to translations of Pali *sutta* commissioned by lay Buddhists.[24] Inspired by Louis Finot's earlier comparative work on the *Paññāsa-jātaka,* Uṃ-Sūr and Lvī-Em also began collaborating to compile and edit a critical Khmer edition of the text, a project that took a number of decades to complete.[25]

Like Huot Tath's 1918 work *Sāmaṇeravinaya, Pabbajākhandhaka-saṅkhepa* by Lvī-Em (translated, edited, and printed in the early 1930s at the request of King Monivong) is representative of modernist interests in authenticity and ritual purification that grew out of the original preoccupations of the modern Dhamma movement. Lvī-Em's monastic training had included a novitiate at Vatt Uṇṇālom during the 1890s under Diaṅ's abbotship,[26] and he returned to Vatt Uṇṇālom again later as a young monk to study Pali *Vinaya* commentaries under Braḥ Mahā

Vimaladhamm Thoṅ.[27] *Pabbajākhandhaka-saṅkhepa* is intended to serve as a concise manual for young men seeking ordination as novices. It introduces them to Pali pronunciation and grammar, providing a glossary of key terminology used in the ordination ceremony and clarifying the ritual roles and procedures necessary to correct performance of the ordination ceremony through reference to rituals detailed in the *Vinaya.*

Likewise, *Gihivinaya-saṅkhep* is representative of the modernist effort to make moral purification accessible to laypeople as well as *bhikkhus*. Translated and critically edited by Chuon Nath "from the Pali version of a number of scriptures, including *Maṅgaladīpanī-aṭṭhakathā, Maṅgala-sutta,* and other texts,"[28] it was probably composed during the early 1920s; it appeared in a print version by 1926.[29] The text was written specifically with the aim of providing a reference on Buddhist comportment for traders "so they can take this book with them easily, even during their frequent journeys."[30] It contained lists of right and wrong behavior as well as descriptions and translations of ritual procedures for laypeople. The text detailed, for example, how to seek forgiveness from the Triple Gem of the Buddha, Dhamma, and Sangha by speaking clearly "toward the direction of the face of the Braḥ Buddha image . . . , toward the stūpa, the *cediya* that holds relics of the Buddha . . . , toward the face of an individual who is a *bhikkhu.*"[31] Having begged pardon in this manner, the petitioner "must demonstrate with clearly annunciated speech . . . that he or she has taken refuge as a lay adherent in the *sāsana* of the Lord Buddha, and must profess commitment to continual observance of the precepts."[32]

Chuon Nath's instructions included an insistence that the words spoken by lay ritual participants must follow correct Pali grammatical forms: "If the [petitioner] is a man, he chants *'yohaṃ thā tassa me,'* and if a woman, she chants *'yāhaṃ thā tassā me,'* following the correct Pali gender forms." After meticulously detailing each grammatical case that might be necessary for the ceremony, Chuon Nath concludes, "Once men and women have spoken words committing themselves as those who have taken refuge *(Braḥ trai saraṇa gaman),* a refuge and awakening results, and thus they have *in that moment* achieved the designation of a lay adherent *(upāsak-upāsikā).*"[33] The text emphasizes the modernist insistence that knowledge and understanding are essential to ritual efficacy:

> Whether one has never learned how to chant in Pali or to chant the translation *(saṃrāy)* in one's own language, or whether one knows how to chant both the Pali and the translation accurately, as it has been spoken here, merely chanting the Pali is empty if one does not understand its meaning. This is so because the ritual of asking forgiveness and committing oneself toward gaining faith consists of clear belief and a wisdom involving right views *(sammādiṭṭhi),* for which the measure is true knowing and true and correct understanding.[34]

Similarly, *Trāyapaṇām-saṅkhep,* edited by Chuon Nath and Uṃ-Sūr, is a brief text aimed at monks and laypeople who lacked rudimentary knowledge of

Pali.[35] It was compiled at the request of monks in provincial monasteries to help "villagers who want to study scriptures often," with the aim of "giving them success in obtaining an orientation toward enlightenment *(bodhi-citta).*"[36] The text provides translations of the Pali phrases spoken in the most common rituals of respect and homage performed in monasteries. It begins, for example, with a segment titled (in Pali) "Ratanattayapūjā" and translated into Khmer as "Paying Homage to the Triple Gem."[37] The Pali words to be spoken in the ceremony alternate with the Khmer translation:

> *Imehi dīpadhūpādisakkārehi Buddhaṃ-Dhammaṃ-Sanghaṃ abhipūjayāmi mātāpitājīnaṃ guṇavantā nañca mayhañca dīgharattaṃ attāya hitāya sukhāya.*
>
> This translates as follows: I pay homage to the Buddha/Dhamma/ Sangha who is the Master, with all of the things for offering, candles, incense, and so on, for the purpose of obtaining prosperity, for the purpose of obtaining benefit, for the purpose of obtaining happiness far into the future for all those possessing merit, including my mother and father, and myself.[38]

The text continues in this vein, with ritual phrases for paying homage to the Buddha, Dhamma, and Sangha respectively, including instructions on when and how to prostrate oneself, as well as clarifications regarding common mispronunciations of Pali words. For instance, the authors caution, the word *vijeyyo* (vanquishing) is commonly mispronounced in ritual ceremonies, rendering its meaning unclear. Although "people have become accustomed to pronouncing this word *'vijjayo'* when they chant," Chuon Nath and Uṃ-Sūr write, "close scrutiny reveals that the correct grammatical form is in fact [the gerundive form] *'vijeyyo,'* a variant of *'vijetvā.'*"[39] With the insertion of brief comments such as this, Chuon Nath and Uṃ-Sūr obliquely critique traditionalists for allowing incorrect forms of language to be transmitted.

Trāyapaṇām-saṅkhep concludes with another abbreviated ceremony for homage to the Triple Gem. The vernacular translation and commentary carefully explain not only the Pali phrases but also how merit-making ritual works. The exemplary conduct of monks enriches the soil in which *bodhi-citta* can take root and grow. By accepting homage and alms, monks serve as sites of purification for laypeople, transforming their gifts into benefit:

> *Supaṭipanno bhagavato sāvakasaṅgho*
> *anuttaraṃ puññakkhettaṃ lokassāti . . .*
>
> The translation of *"supaṭipanno bhagavato sāvakasaṅgho"* is "The Sangha consists of the disciples of the Enlightened Lord," and thus their conduct is excellent, meaning that their conduct is in accordance with the Path of the nine higher attainments *(lokuttaradhammā).*[40] *"Anuttaraṃ puññakkhettaṃ lokassā"* means "These [monks] are

unsurpassed merit fields," meaning sites or destinations in which seeds, meaning the merit performed by beings in the world, can grow. Sentient beings are always in need of such fields, which they do not necessarily possess on their own.[41]

Again, the interpretation of the ritual phrases enables the authors to press for a subtle rejection of traditionalism and simultaneous reorientation of Buddhist understanding. Whereas past tradition allowed the ritual words to be spoken without comprehension, in their updated text of the ritual the authors not only provide a literal translation of the Pali ritual phrases to be spoken but also add a clarification that moves the participant toward a fuller understanding of the rite with each act of taking refuge. A final blessing asking for "care from all the gods, through the influence and power of all the buddhas, all parts of the Dhamma, and the entire Sangha"[42] ends the ceremony. These ritual words remind Khmer participants—accustomed to frequent interaction with the spirits or deities of ancestors, the earth, rice, and places—of the proper Buddhist implications and orientation of the ceremony. Care "from all the gods" is mediated through "the influence and power of all the buddhas" and other aspects of the Triple Gem.

A final example of the interwoven ethical themes and stylistic issues in modern Dhamma writing is evident in Huot Tath's translation of the *Siṅgālovāda-sutta.* Compiling a critical edition required different kinds of strategies from those required for abridging *saṅkhep,* since the editor was seeking to present an entire vernacular *Dhamma-vinay* text, "purified" of scribal errors. *Siṅgālovādasutta* was among the first of the *sutta*s to be critically edited; based on Huot Tath's comparison of various manuscript sources, it was translated and printed in Khmer in the first edition of the Buddhist periodical *Ganthamālā* in 1927.[43] The choice of this *sutta* for the inaugural issue of *Ganthamālā* is not surprising given the text's thematic focus on purification through right moral conduct and its delineation of *Vinaya*-like rules for lay conduct. Huot Tath's translation helps us understand the new views of textual authority as well as evidence of the kinds of choices and interpretive strategies that could render an ancient text as a valid site for expressing new, modern values.

The *Siṅgālovādasutta* situates and defines the individual in the context of his or her social relationships. It lists the proper ways in which a good Buddhist layperson should purify and orient him- or herself in terms of six relational directions: toward mother and father, teachers, spouse and children, friends and companions, servants and subordinates, monks and Brahmins.[44] The setting for the preaching of the *sutta* is the Buddha's discovery of a young man named Siṅgāl performing a ceremony of ritual obeisance to the six cardinal directions, according to the last wishes of his dying father. The Buddha admonishes Siṅgāl that he is performing a false ritual and offers him a new, up-to-date interpretation of the ritual based on Buddhist doctrine. The thematic parallels to the modern Dhamma project are all too obvious here. In tone as well as content, the *Siṅgālovādasutta* resonates with modernist investigations of authentic codes of conduct in the

Dhamma-vinay and with their efforts to reverse the degeneration of Buddhist ritual practice inherited from previous generations. After the Buddha inquires about Siṅgāl's actions and hears his explanation, he responds:

> "All sons of householders, the Discipline *(vinay)* of the Noble Disciples is not one of paying homage to the six directions as you are doing."
>
> Siṅgāl respectfully replied, "Master, then how is homage paid to the six directions in the Discipline of the Noble Disciples? Please explain so I will also understand very clearly. . . . "
>
> The Master replied, "All sons of householders should please pay careful attention to this [teaching] and safeguard it in their hearts and minds. Listen and I will explain it to you now."[45]

In his introduction to the *sutta,* Huot Tath recounts an explanatory story taken from Buddhaghosa's fifth-century commentary on the *sutta,* one of Huot Tath's sources for the critical edition.[46] The story explains how it had come about that Siṅgāl's father had given false counsel to his son about whom and how to worship, counsel that the son had obeyed but the Buddha had contradicted. This tension concerning filial piety might well be troubling for a Khmer audience. Huot Tath seems intent on introducing Buddhaghosa's explanation for this problem as quickly as possible, in order to head off any perception of a contradiction within the *sutta* that follows. The *vinay* or regulations for parent-child relationships in the *Siṅgālovādasutta* include *pāpānivārenti* (parents must prevent their children from performing immoral actions), *dāyajjaṃ paṭipajjāmi* (children must resolve to establish a good character in deference to their parents), and *dakkhiṇaṃ anuppadassāmi* (children must resolve that when their parents die, they will make merit for them).[47] If a parent is supposed to look out for his or her child's well-being and a child to respect his or her parents by conforming to their expectations and by carrying out appropriate rituals at their deaths, how could Siṅgāl's father lead him so far astray and how could Siṅgāl, after encountering the Buddha, so readily cast aside his father's religion, even if it was a false doctrine?

As it turns out, the introductory story advises, Siṅgāl's father was not (as it would appear if one read from the Pali text of the *Siṅgālovādasutta* without the aid of the commentary) an unenlightened Brahmin admonishing his son to practice a false doctrine. Rather, the father was a devout Buddhist who had attained the high spiritual level of stream-enterer. The dying father had surmised correctly that when the Buddha was out walking on his morning alms round, he would see the son performing an empty ritual of homage to the six directions and preach a sermon to him on the true meaning of worship, not as obeisance but as proper conduct in regard to one's relationships with others.

Huot Tath's strategy of incorporating the commentary into his introduction puts the contradiction concerning filial piety to rest, shaping a definitive interpretation of the text as the story of a father's wise and compassionate effort to help his son find the proper path to purification. For a Khmer lay audience used to learning about moral conduct through vernacular *cpāp'* sung by parents to children, the conflation of the Buddha's advice with the father's wishes further strengthens the ethical authority of the text. The father's complicity makes the *sutta*'s enumeration of how and how not to behave with respect to others assume the tone of a *cpāp'*, as in *Cpāp' Tūnmān Khluan:*

> My children, listen to your father
> recount another series of guidelines
> for you to learn and imitate precisely,
> to guide your body and your senses.[48]

Likewise, when the Buddha preaches to Siṅgāl that "false friends who are trying to flatter you . . . will only lead you to ruin. Wise people readily recognize from their behaviors that they are not real friends at all, and disassociate from [them],"[49] the advice recalls the *cpāp'* lines

> Do not join together with malevolent people,
> do not associate with thieves;
> they will seize you from behind
> and torture you with blows: see how vile they are![50]

In these contrasting passages we can see evidence of the modernist transformation of ideas of textual authority. The new critical translation draws on the familiar Khmer vernacular imagery of the father advising the child in order to help establish an authoritative textual voice for a modern version of a grammatically translated canonical *sutta.* The older genre of *cpāp'* literature drew on the idea but not precise translations of "precious, Dhamma scriptures" as the source of its moral authority.[51]

Huot Tath writes that he wanted to translate and edit the *Siṅgālovādasutta* because it was a *gihipaṭipatti* and *samaṇapaṭipatti* (a text clarifying how to behave according to the *Dhamma-vinay* for both laypeople and monks): "In my estimation, [the *Siṅgālovādasutta*] is splendidly useful for the wider populace. They would be pleased to learn it if it were translated out of Pali and edited, together with its commentary,[52] into a Khmer version."[53] Huot Tath visually arranges the print text so that the verses spoken by the Buddha are "clearly indicated" for the edification of the wider reading public. His intent in the critical edition is "to give the Pali along with its vernacular translation *(saṃrāy)* . . . in order to ensure correct comprehension." It was important for readers to encounter the *sutta* in this textual format; whether a reader wanted to study and learn both the Pali and the translation, or just the translation alone, the reader needed to know exactly which words were original Pali verses spoken by the Buddha and which were later commentarial additions. "This is the only method for learning the translation properly and with satisfaction," he concluded.[54]

These comments illustrate another dimension of modernist transformations of assumptions about textual authority. In the past, *saṃrāy* were sometimes only loosely connected with the *Tipiṭaka* but were nevertheless regarded as sacred and authoritative by virtue of their mode of production as palm-leaf or mulberry-paper manuscripts. The content of *saṃrāy* had varied widely: some contained both Pali and Khmer, others either Pali or Khmer. By contrast, Huot Tath is highly concerned with the nature of the relationship between the Pali and Khmer words and meanings in the text. In his usage, the term *saṃrāy* no longer refers to a broad category or genre of scriptural texts but to a close translation of a portion of the *Tipiṭaka* produced by someone with Pali knowledge and according to new translation practices.

His comments also suggest new assumptions about how the Pali language is spiritually efficacious: as a vehicle for conveying the spiritually beneficial knowledge of authentic *Dhamma-vinay* rather than in and of itself. Although the modernists championed the learning of Pali, Huot Tath acknowledges here that true understanding might also take place through the medium of vernacular translation, as long as the translation was correctly produced. Huot Tath and his faction had disparaged traditionalists for viewing Pali *gāthā* as authoritative simply because they were words spoken or written in Pali, with understanding of the words as not strictly necessary. He insists here that what makes Pali words meaningful and authoritative is understanding them correctly. Further, through the printed format of indented Pali verses alternating with translation and commentary, even those Buddhists without Pali knowledge could learn to recognize the distinction between what was original *Dhamma-vinay* and what was later interpretation. These interpretations could then be evaluated for their accuracy, for in the final analysis, some interpretations of the *Dhamma-vinay* could be seen to be more "true," some monks more knowledgeable, and some practices more authentic than others.

This emphasis on correct understanding reflects the same imperative about Dhamma knowledge evident in Lvī-Em's sermon, discussed earlier. Correct understanding went beyond merely listening to the Dhamma, which was only the first stage or step to the stage of "making an effort to ponder, think, analyze, and reflect on teachings in Pali and to let them penetrate one's heart and mind deeply."[55] The highest stage of understanding was manifested in conduct, for true understanding required that the teachings had penetrated the heart and mind, causing a transformation that led one's behavior to become pure. Encountering an accurate translation thus enabled those Buddhists who made themselves receptive to the powerful impact of the *Dhamma-vinay* to hear and study it, and as they learned and internalized it, their own effort in combination with the transformative qualities of the words of the would lead to purification.

Huot Tath's translation of the *Siṅgālovādasutta* helps to demonstrate how the notion of the Pali canon as authoritative idea and the modes and strategies of textual production in a local literary culture interact to shape distinctive interpretations. The editing strategies that modernists employed enabled them to emphasize particular ethical values in the texts they translated, values that included, in particular, the need for laypeople as well as monks to purify their conduct according to the teachings of the *Dhamma-vinay* and for all Buddhists to understand and recognize what were the authentic, pure, original, uncorrupted teachings of the Buddha and what were not. These values were expressed in the very forms in which the texts were written and organized,[56] as in the *Siṅgālovādasutta*'s alternation of Pali, translation and commentary to demarcate words spoken by the Buddha.

The modern Dhamma writings surveyed above exemplify the shift away from the production of religious texts for purposes of entertainment, performance, devotion, and merit making toward the edification and reorientation of Buddhists' conduct according to correct understanding of the Buddha's authentic teachings. Their translation techniques are meant to render these teachings accessible and clear and to supply the necessary interpretive grounds for further study and internalization of a path for proper conduct. These texts also illustrate the ways in which new translation strategies and the literary formats in which they were embedded served as vehicles for expressing different and emerging modes of Buddhist thought during this period, formed through interactions between local, vernacular literary imaginings and a cosmopolitan Pali tradition. The Pali *Tipiṭaka* functions, in Steven Collins' words, as "the very idea" of authority by which a local Buddhism defines itself, but with a shifting meaning and content depending on the ways in which it is edited, excerpted, interpreted, and translated.[57] Huot Tath's translation of the canonical *Siṅgālovādasutta,* set in the time of the Buddha, renders it into a recognizable, contemporary idiom by connecting Siṅgāl's actions with what people continue to do:

> Generally, children carry out the instructions their parents have issued from their death beds . . . and so it was that Siṅgāl respected the instructions given by his father and rose at dawn. He wrapped a *sambat'* around himself and with his hair still wet, left from the city of Rājagriḥ and raised his head to *namassa* [pay homage] in all six directions, to the east, to the south, to the north, to the west, to the nadir, to the zenith.[58]

The locus for moral development in Huot Tath's translation is not the exemplary moral figure of the Bodhisatta of nineteenth-century *jātaka,* perfecting virtues in some far-away eon, but the ordinary person who is like Siṅgāl, wrapping himself in a *sambat'* (sarong), the everyday form of Khmer dress. Like Siṅgāl, the ordinary person is involved in a complex web of relationships that require him or her to practice the Buddhist path toward purification while still fulfilling social roles and responsibilities.

Modernist writings from this period also reflect a concern with the localized religious collective. While the concept of Khmer *saṅgam* (society) that developed later in the Khmer language does not yet appear in the Buddhist writings from the second decade of the century to the early 1930s, the writers employ other more Buddhistic phrases that evoke the collective image of Khmer people.[59] These include references to *yoeṅ Khmaer* (we Khmer), to *qanak tām sāsana* (followers of the [Buddhist] doctrine), and to the community or assembly of the four kinds of *parisāḷ* or disciples of the Buddha, consisting of monks, nuns, and men and women lay followers.[60] In these conceptions of collectivity, the actions performed by individuals have moral implications for many others; they determine the purity of the *sāsana* and religious community as a whole.

LOCAL TROPES, LOCAL VALUES

The vernacular-cosmopolitan translation process developed not only in relation to contemporary sociopolitical events and currents of thought such as the introduction of modernist ideas of authenticity and purification but also in the more elusive, dreamlike interactions between local interpreters of Buddhism and the amorphous, moving ideas and images of Theravāda Buddhism that scholars have termed the Pali imaginaire. Collins suggests that the term "imaginaire," drawn from French scholarship, is not easily translated inasmuch as it does not refer to what is "imaginary" in the sense of "unreal," but rather "what is imagined," such as the worlds of texts, which are social facts.[61] He defines the Pali imaginaire as "a mental universe created by and within Pali texts."[62] Similarly in his study of the Zen master Keizan, Bernard Faure understands the imaginaire as "the way beliefs are rendered in images," which in the case of Keizan included a "constellation" of images organized "around poles like awakening, dreams, places, gods and their icons, Chan/Zen masters and their relics"—in other words, images and ideas that constitute a mental universe or system of thought.[63]

To examine these vernacular-cosmopolitan interactions as a factor in the shaping of Khmer Buddhist modernism, I turn to a reading of a portion of Ukñā Suttantaprījā Ind's *Gatilok,* representative of the development and integration of a body of distinctively Khmer literary renderings of the Theravādin imaginaire. Explicitly composed as a *tamrā* (manual) to examine and compare the "ancient" (which might be read here as "authentic") Buddhist ways of behaving with the "modern morality that has arisen,"[64] the *Gatilok* expresses the themes of modernity and moral development at a number of levels. In historically particular ways, it moves between discussions of authentic and inauthentic Theravādin practices among Khmer Buddhists to notions of false and true monks, corrupt and good officials, the "fakery" of particular nineteenth-century millenarian figures in Cambodia, and the degradation of opium addiction. But while the ethics of the text responds to these particular historical issues, the text was also clearly intended as a universal ethical teaching on living the moral life. Its primary focus is on how to recognize whether people are moral and pure or malevolent. This is a tricky business in the modern world, the text suggests. As a result, mature moral agency is not fully achieved except by the person who has cultivated careful moral discernment or *satisampajañña* (mindfulness and discrimination) as the basis for his or her perception, actions, interactions, and relationships with other people.

The ethical reflections on moral development and agency in the text are laid out in narrative form, giving the text's audience insight into the circumstances, characters, and behavior of the moral actors in the *Gatilok.* Living in the world, as the *Gatilok* narratives make clear, involves living with others. Actions bear fruit; their consequences are felt not just by oneself but by many others, most notably one's immediate family members, neighbors, and loved ones. The self of the *Gatilok* is not at all autonomous, but intricately interconnected with those around him or her. As in the *Siṅgālovādasutta,* the self or moral agent is defined by the moral quality of his or her actions and relationships with others. In the analysis of the text, moral identity is part Dhammic and part *lokiya,* "worldly." The parts of a human being that arise (or are born) and die, such as the body and feelings or reactions, are of the "world," which Ind refers to with the Khmer word *lok.* Worldly or "causal" aspects define human beings just as the amount and grade of copper in a gold alloy determines its overall color and appearance.

> All beings are different from each other because Dhamma and *lok* [world] are combined in them differently. . . . [This is] analogous to the way in which textures of gold alloys are varied because the copper element is combined with the gold element in larger or smaller amounts.[65]

Whatever knowledge or truth possessed by the individual never dies because it is "of the category *(jāti)* of Dhamma." Like gold in an alloy, its brilliant pure color shines forth from whatever individual possesses it. A person's unique identity is thus determined by the combination of Dhamma and *lok* that he or she constructs through thought, speech, and actions:

> How do moral people behave? And with regard to those who are said to be "immoral," how should we characterize their behavior?
>
> It has been said that moral people are endowed with three kinds of piety: right body, right speech, and right thoughts. They effortlessly conduct themselves according to the teachings [of the *Dhamma-vinay*]. They have shame and fear concerning wrongdoing, which serves them like a wall or fence surrounding their bodies, preventing what is nonbeneficial from entering in and troubling them. In this manner, they are recognizable as moral persons. People endowed with the three kinds of impiety—wrongdoing with the body, wrongdoing with speech, and wrongdoing with thought—fail to conduct themselves according to the teachings. They lack shame and fear . . . , they spread evil-heartedness and lead others astray with their wrong and malicious behaviors. These people are recognizable in our world as immoral persons.[66]

The world of the *Gatilok* is represented quite differently from the moral cosmos of nineteenth-century religious imagination, which saw it as a reified moral geography (evident in some of the texts discussed in chapter 1). Ind's usage tends to emphasize a social world defined by contemporary behaviors, *gatilok* (worldly ways, or more literally, "ways of behaving in the world"). For Ind, *lok* is everything that is not Dhamma, meaning everything that is causally conditioned, "that arises by the power of the rebirth of aggregates *(khandha)*, . . . all beings on earth, on the surface of the sky and throughout the atmosphere . . . that normally act in the world," all thoughts, words, and actions that come into being.[67] In this causally connected world, the greatest problem for moral agents is the unavoidable interpenetration of the actions or karma of one's self and others, a situation Ind illustrates with a story drawn from Khmer oral folklore.

In the story, a basket weaver climbs a tall sugar-palm tree to cut leaves for weaving baskets. He finds exceedingly good leaves for his purposes, and as he cuts them from the top of the tree, he begins to think about the profits he is certain to reap from the baskets he will weave with these leaves. He thinks that he will have enough profit to buy a hen, and from selling the eggs produced by the hen, he will earn enough to buy pigs, and with the piglets, a cow, and so on, until he has enough profit to buy a rice farm and then plant fruit trees—at which point, he will have earned enough to support a wife. The wife will have a son, and the basket weaver will be wealthy enough to redeem a slave girl to take care of the son, and when the slave rebukes his son too harshly, the basket weaver will kick her.

Caught up in his fantasy at the top of the sugar-palm tree, the basket weaver reaches out with his foot to kick the slave girl, loses his balance, and begins to fall. In the next instant, he is able only to catch onto the end of one of the palm leaves and hold on for dear life.

Hanging from the tree and fearful that he will fall to his death at any moment, he suddenly spots an elephant driver coming toward him through the forest and calls out to the man for help. The elephant driver stops the elephant right under the basket weaver but still can not quite reach him. Standing on the elephant's back to reach up for the basket weaver, the elephant driver moves his feet carelessly on the elephant's back and inadvertently gives him the signal to go. When the elephant takes off, his driver has only enough time to reach up and grab onto the basket weaver's foot.

The two men hang, one clinging to the other's foot, from the leaf of the sugar palm, shouting and blaming each other, both fearful of death. The basket weaver yells to the elephant driver to let go of his foot or they will both fall. The elephant driver refuses, imploring the basket weaver to tighten his hold on the palm leaf. Suddenly, they see four bald men coming toward them with a fishing net. They call out for help, and the four bald men eventually take up their net at each of the four corners and tie it around their necks. The basket weaver and elephant driver jump down—and survive—but the weight of their fall causes the net to tighten, and the four bald men at the corners are thrown together with such force that their heads collide and they all die.[68]

This grimly humorous story reveals Ind's definition of the social world in action, with causes leading to actions leading to results leading to further actions and so on. Like the elephant driver holding onto the foot of the basket weaver grasping a thin sugar-palm leaf with one hand, suspended above the net of the four hapless bald men, this is a world in which one person's careless, ignorant, or malevolent actions produce the conditions in which others must survive. It is also a world in which the individual exists, inescapably, in relationship with and to others; from the moment of birth, the individual exists in a set of relationships that continue even after he or she dies.[69]

Thus, within Ind's text, ethical primacy is placed on the ability to recognize the moral nature of one's own and others' thoughts, words, and deeds through the cultivation of a form of moral discernment known in Pali as *satisampajañña*. *Satisampajañña* can be translated in its compounded sense in terms of *sati* (mindfulness and clarity) and *sampajañña* (discrimination or attention or awareness). Ind defines the Pali term by drawing on a portion of the canonical *Sāmaññaphala-sutta* (Sermon on the fruits of the homeless life):[70]

> People [who possess] *satisampajañña* to analyze the circumstances and occasion . . . do not falter when they are in charge of some activity; whether they are walking, sitting, sleeping, standing, lifting their arms, lifting their feet, urinating or defecating; whether eating food that is soft or tough, when chewing and when swallowing food into the stomach. If you do not have *[satisampajañña]*, if you do not think first, then in all of these actions, you will falter by falling down or getting stuck on thorns, and so on. While eating, you might choke on a fish bone or encounter a hot pepper. Individuals without *[satisampajañña]* are known in everyday language as "careless persons."[71]

Ind's examination of *satisampajañña* continues by weaving together Pali and vernacular stories to explain the concept and to demonstrate its importance for ordinary Khmer.

In the *Sāmaññaphala-sutta, satisampajañña* is explained as one of four kinds of concentration, which is one of the benefits of the homeless life led by the monk. This discussion of *satisampajañña* takes place in the *sutta* when Prince Ajātasattu visits the Buddha in an effort to find relief from the turmoil of his remorse for imprisoning and torturing to death his own father, the righteous King Bimbisāra. The Buddha uses the occasion to preach this *sutta* on the "fruits of the homeless life."

In the *Gatilok,* Ind also draws on a portion of the story about Ajātasattu and King Bimbisāra to explain *satisampajañña.* But for Ind, *satisampajañña* is not explained as one of numerous by-products of world renunciation, but as a necessary moral possession for all people. Here as in other instances, Ind takes religious ideas connected in canonical texts with asceticism and recasts them as values necessary to ordinary people.

Ind's laicization of *satisampajañña* is evident in a passage comparing the responses of three groups of officials who are guards belonging to the retinue of King Bimbisāra. After apprehending Ajātasattu in an attempt to assassinate his father, the guards meet to discuss what should be done next. Two of the groups of guards advocate executing Ajātasattu on the spot, but the captain of the third group argues that under the circumstances—because the assassin is the king's own son—the case should be brought to the king. He prevails, and the king richly rewards the guard because he was "a person possessing *satisampajañña,* knowing how to analyze correctly according to the circumstances and according to the occasion."[72]

Whereas in the canonical *Sāmaññaphala-sutta, satisampajañña* is a moral possession connected with monks who have attained high levels of skill in meditation, in the *Gatilok* it is a moral necessity for anyone who wants to live as a good person in the complex world of social relationships, and even more baldly as a survival skill for the contemporary world, necessary for anyone who does not want to be swindled or deceived at the hands of others. For ordinary people, it is cultivated through life experience and education rather than meditation:

> The knowledge possessed by newborn babies and little children is like very shallow water; *satisampajañña* has not yet arisen to any great extent. Young children can be deceived by adults, who say "Don't cry or the scarecrow will come and bite you" . . . or . . . "Tā Breng[73] will pour rice water on your head." . . . Babies lack *satisampajañña* . . . and are thus ignorant of adults' deceptions.[74]

The problems of day-to-day life are compounded by the fact that "there is a whole category of people who are ignorant because, like babies, they do not possess *satisampajañña.*"[75] The cultivation of *satisampajañña* through education is thus imperative, for without it, the world is full of characters like the basket weaver whose carelessness and lack of discernment leads to absurd and sometimes tragic consequences.

In a more technical Pali canonical sense, as Ind also explains, *satisampajañña* also involves the development of a complex of specific virtues. These are the *sappurisa-dhammā,* the sevenfold "forms of ethical recognition" that enable their possessor to recognize such things as good and evil intentions of others, truth, results of actions, and the nature of the self.[76] Thus, through the development of these virtues, the cultivation of *satisampajañña* leads one to becoming a *sappurisa* (a good or moral person). The larger aim of the *sappurisa* is to become pure,[77] developing the Dhamma aspect of one's identity—which requires a twofold obligation toward others: the absence of spreading harm and injury to others along with "increasing the well-being of others."[78]

For Ind, these more technical ideas drawn from Pali texts are inherently translatable into Khmer terms. Although people are born into differing circumstances, the person with *satisampajañña* is able to discern an appropriate response for the circumstances and occasions, including the ability to perceive the intentions of others. Everyday Khmer life—as reflected in folklore—becomes a medium for expressing the truth of the *Dhamma-vinay.* Conversely, this idea also suggests that ordinary Khmer life can be translated into a universally recognizable idiom: it is a potential medium for achieving purification. This idea is developed in one of the most localized narratives in the text, the "Story of Bhikkhu Sukh from a Phnong Family" (hereafter "Bhikkhu Sukh").

The story is striking in part because it does not appear to have been drawn from oral folklore. It seems likely that it is either a true account of a monk's life, collected by Ind, or an allegory that he composed specifically for the *Gatilok.* The ethical themes of moral development and the relationship between self and others in the story are overlaid with allegorical implications about the "civilizational" capacities of Khmer Buddhism.[79] The protagonist in the story is a "savage" who is rescued and transformed into a literate and "civilized" person through his association with the Triple Gem of the Buddha, Dhamma, and Sangha. In its colonial context, the allegory suggests the capacity of Buddhism for defining and elevating Khmer civilization, an idea also articulated in Lvī-Em's 1930 sermon and Makhali Phal's 1931 poem for the *Vinaya* ceremony (excerpted in chapter 4).[80]

The rich interaction in "Bhikkhu Sukh" between central metaphors of liberation drawn from the Pali imaginaire and the local, vernacular tropes of ethnicity, language, geography, and family and social relationships, as well as the clearly allegorical nature of the story, make it an explicit and useful site for undertaking a historically situated Khmer reading of the Theravāda path to liberation. This story helps to demonstrate how Khmer intellectuals of the period understood contemporary experience through the lens of Buddhist thought and how Buddhist ethical literature served as a medium for working out their new ideas. The text exhibits modern concern with authenticity and purification of conduct. It also offers a critical appraisal of what it takes to live as a Buddhist in this world. While it draws on symbols and imagery that are well established in a variety of Pali texts, it simultaneously offers its own local formulation of normative Buddhist values. For Ind, this formulation involved a critical appraisal of what it meant to live as a Buddhist. He turns his attention, on the one hand, to assumptions about monastic conduct. Rejecting the older literary convention of using the figure of a king or bodhisatta or even the *bhikkhu* for his *sappurisa* (moral person), he turns instead to the lowliest figure he can find to represent the human capacity for transformation and purification on the Buddhist Path: the image of a non-Buddhist, tribal orphan. For Ind, living authentically as a Buddhist was measured by conduct according to the Dhammic teachings, not by one's social role or standing. Just as chanting Pali words with no understanding of their meaning was useless, taking robes as a monk was worthless without purified conduct.

THE IMAGE OF AN ORPHAN

The story begins with a brief preface that explains the circumstances and context in which the story takes place, a situation that Ind regards as highly unjust, highlighting the conditions of the social world, in which human beings live entangled in a web composed of the imperfect and reverberating results of the actions of others. It is also a context of religious and cultural irrationality, which Ind describes with the same sense of incredulity that some French writers applied to their descriptions of Khmer culture (see chapter 4). Ind tells us, by way of preface to the story, that

> the law in the highland region . . . states that if someone knows sorcery and witchcraft for invoking spirits, and if someone else accuses him, the chieftain must . . . seize the accused to come for a deliberation. If at the deliberation it is decided that the accusation is true, then according to law, the entire extended family[81] must be killed. From the smallest newborn baby at a mother's breast, they must all be killed.
>
> Furthermore, if any member in another family threatens either to be a traitor or obstinately refuses to go along with the judgment ordered by the chieftain, according to law, that entire family must be executed and their relatives must become slaves for the military, cutting grass for the horses and elephants. This is sealed for all time. Everyone born into this family will be known as slaves and numbered as a tribute, no matter how many there are. None of them can ever escape to become free citizens. Whosoever is born into this family, even those who are knowledgeable in some area or who possess particular intelligence, cannot claim freedom. They are known in this world as unfortunate beings. The law that is spoken of here is a lasting weight on the part of certain inferior people *(dāp)*.[82] . . . This is the background for the legend Lok Tā Sukh the Phnong.[83]

The notion of enslaved families who cannot escape to become "free citizens," even if they are "knowledgeable," is challenged by the story that follows. Cau Sukh does escape, and he does become knowledgeable. Again, the possibility of Theravāda Buddhism as a means of liberation from oppression and slavery is raised. It is difficult to ascertain whether Ind's intentions with this preface go beyond the strictly spiritual to carry a political or even anticolonial sentiment. In any case, the preface to the story reveals the "inferior" origins of the story's protagonist, Sukh, from the perspective of lowland Khmer, the dominant ethnic group, as a member of an ethnic minority group living in the highlands.

The story continues with a "certain Phnong man" who made his living "in the manner of forest dwellers." As time passed, a group of other highlanders "began to hate this man." They accused him of witchcraft and of causing the deaths of many other villagers. At the trial, the chieftain ordered his men to kill the extended family of the accused.

> Both the husband and wife were killed, along with their entire extended family, with none left alive—except one young boy named Cau Sukh. This boy was about ten or eleven years old. He had been sent to guard the rice in the forest field when he found out that by the chieftain's order, his father and mother, brothers and sisters, aunts and uncles, and grandpa and grandma had all been killed in this way. Terribly afraid, he ran up a tree and hid himself at its top, among branches entangled with creepers, and remained still and quiet. When the chieftain's band had killed the rest of the family, they realized that one child still remained. They went to look for the child in the rice field in order to kill off and utterly eradicate the entire family.[84]

The story tells of the boy's efforts to remain hidden in the tree "tangled with creepers" and his narrow escape from the chieftain's band.

> When night arrived and everything was quiet, the young boy climbed down from the tree and ran away from the garden, cutting straight through the forest to the lower village. He entered the village and pleaded with a certain household of Phnong at the front edge of the village to hide him. The occupants of the house took pity *(āṇit)* on the boy and gave him something to eat and drink, and led him inside their house to hide him. The chieftain's band walked around looking for the boy but failed to find him. When morning came, they came to search for him in the lower village.[85]

Convinced that the boy was somewhere in the village, the chieftain's men searched every house, "in the beginning . . . in the middle . . . and the end of the village."[86] But since the house in which he was hidden was next to the headman's house they neglected to search it thoroughly. The inhabitants of this household urged Cau Sukh to escape:

> "We cannot continue to protect you because our house is right next to our chieftain's. Once it gets quiet, surely he cannot fail to realize you are here. If you want to escape with your life, you have no other option but to go down to the land of the Khmer. Earlier this morning, there was a Khmer merchant's cart returning to their country. If you try to run after that Khmer cart and catch up with it, you can plead with them to take you to Sruk Kraceh." The boy listened and understood. He took leave of the inhabitants of the house and ran after the Khmer cart until he caught up with it in the middle of the road. Utterly exhausted from going after the cart, he could walk no longer so he reached up to grasp the wheel frame under the cart and hung on to it.
>
> The boss of the merchants turned around and saw the young boy hanging under the cart. He got down to ask him in his own language, "Who are you, little child, hanging on to our cart?" The boy then told his story from beginning to end. The merchant boss listened, and having learned it, was filled with a

> horrific grief and pity *(secktī-saṅveg-āṇit).* He said, "Ah—if it's like this, you must come and live with us. We don't have any children. We will take you as our adopted child *(kun dharm).* If anyone tries to harm you, I will protect you. You need not suffer anymore." Having spoken, he let the boy ride in the wagon and drove forward to the lowland until he reached Sruk Kraceh. The merchant boss drove the cart without stopping until he reached his own house. The boy was thus freed from suffering at the hands of his chieftain.
>
> The merchant boss loved Cau Sukh, maintained him as his own son, and diligently taught Cau Sukh how to speak Khmer. Cau Sukh was also diligent and complied with the instruction of the merchant boss. They never had a single quarrel. When some time had passed, the merchant boss sent Cau Sukh to study at the temple and learn how to read and write in Khmer. Cau Sukh studied and recited diligently until he achieved his aim. When he was fifteen, the merchant boss allowed him to be ordained as a novice, at which time he was called Nen Sukh. At the age of twenty-one, his adoptive father *(pita dharm)* had him ordained as a *bhikkhu,* and he was called Lok Bhikkhu Sukh. He remained contented and happy, with the profits from offerings that arise in the *sāsana* of the Lord Buddha.[87]

The story's introduction sets out the conditions of tribal society in terms that also recall the *lok* in Ind's analogy of the gold alloy, described above. Things "of the world" are corrupted and corruptible because, like copper, they contain too much of an "inferior" element and too little of Truth, of Dhamma. The circumstances in which Cau Sukh's innocent family is accused are doubly unjust and absurd because even by the standards of tribal law, the accusation is false; the motivation for the slaying is hatred, not sorcery. Yet in spite of these circumstances, Cau Sukh is able, with the help of others, to fashion a good and beneficial life. He demonstrates that the circumstances and occasions in which human beings must try to act morally are always imperfect, entangled, attached, corrupted. There is no pure moral context in which human beings can perfect themselves, yet even in this reality of social entanglement, it is still possible to achieve moral purification.

Allegorically, the narrative also draws heavily on recognizable metaphors of spiritual development found in a variety of Pali sources. The image of the boy guarding the rice field evokes both the imagery of the fruition of karma and the "guarding" of the sense-doors, a common description applied to *bhikkhus* in Pali texts such as the *Sāmaññaphala-sutta.*[88] Cau Sukh's name is potentially allegorical, referring to *sukha,* "happiness" or "peace," understood as the existential condition opposite to *dukkha,* "suffering." The oddly phrased description of the "beginning . . middle . . . and end" of the lower village, which the chieftain's men search, must refer to the Dhamma or Teaching, which is good or lovely in its beginning, middle, and end[89] and which gives refuge to the young boy Cau Sukh, just as Buddhists take refuge in the Buddha's Dhamma. The spiritual allegory continues with the householders (a Buddhistic reference for laypersons) in the village telling Cau Sukh "if you want to escape with your life, you have no other option but to go down to the land of the Khmer." The Khmer word for "escape" *(ruoc)* used in this passage is fraught with significant religious connotations. It appears in the phrases "to escape from *dukkha*" and "to escape from *kamm*" (karma) and can also mean "released," "liberated," or "finished." The boy runs after the "cart"—an image often used to refer to Buddhism itself—and finds it in the "middle of the path or road," or the Middle Path. He grabs onto the "wheel frame"—as in the imagery of the "wheel of Dhamma," another metaphor for Buddhism.

The boss of the merchants, a common incarnation of the Bodhisatta in *jātaka* stories, speaks to the boy "in his [own] language," like the Buddha himself who always knows how to speak so that others will understand. He "listens to and learns" the boy's story "from beginning to end"—evoking the image of someone listening to this and other Buddhist stories and benefiting from them. With pity, grief, and compassion for the orphan's situation (which stands in for the *dukkha*-filled plight of all unenlightened beings), the merchant boss then offers to release him from suffering and oppression and take him as his "Dhamma child," driving the cart without stopping until he has "freed him from suffering," again an image of someone who once on the Path—often as a result of encountering the Buddha—moves forward, bent on liberation or release from the suffering of *saṃsāra.* The merchant has him ordained as a novice and later as a *bhikkhu,* ritual acts undertaken to produce merit for parents and relatives. While merit making for parents is always important, its urgency is compounded in the context of violent deaths as a means of mitigating the suffering for all concerned, both living and dead. Bhikkhu Sukh "remained contented and happy, with the profits from offerings which arise in the *sāsana* of the Lord Buddha" through which his family's grief could be transformed into spiritual benefit.[90]

The movement in "Bhikkhu Sukh" between the images of homelessness and householder in the narrative suggest that Ind is explicitly contrasting these two types of individuals. The contrast in virtue between the householder and the *bhikkhu* is a common way of exalting the merits of the homeless life in various textual sources that Ind cites in the *Gatilok.* The *Dhammapada,* for example, provides vivid depictions of these two ways of living in the world:

> Just as in a heap of rubbish
> Cast away on a roadside,
> A lotus there could bloom,
> Of sweet fragrance, pleasing the mind,
> So amid the wretched, blinded ordinary folk,[91]
> Among them who have turned to rubbish,
> The disciple of the Fully Awakened One
> Shines surpassingly with wisdom.[92]

In the *Sutta-Nipāta,* another of Ind's textual sources, the *bhikkhu* who wants to be pure must cut himself off completely from the life of the householder. Here, the ordinary person is portrayed as one who from attachment to friends and family members is mired in dissatisfaction and who, because of "sympathizing with friends and companions . . . misses one's goal, being shackled in mind."[93] Most companions, the text states, are like "shining bracelets of gold" which, when "two are on one arm," can be seen "clashing against each other." Only by leaving aside affection toward family members, which are "like a very wide-spreading bamboo tree entangled with others," can one hope to live a pure life:

> Leaving behind son and wife, and father and mother, and wealth and grain, and relatives, and sensual pleasures to the limit, one should wander solitary as a rhinoceros horn. . . . Having discarded the marks of a householder, like a coral tree whose leaves have fallen, having gone out (from the house) wearing the saffron robe, one should wander solitary as a rhinoceros horn.[94]

In "Bhikkhu Sukh," the symbiotic relationship between monk and layperson in the story is far more evident than the detachment. The ascetic ideal of the "rhinoceros horn" appears nearly impossible in the *Gatilok* framework since the communal life of the monks and abbots in the text and their interactions with the world appear to be just as complex and socially attached as those of their lay counterparts. Bhikkhu Sukh, who (unlike other monastic characters in the *Gatilok*) does achieve a level of moral purity and who thrives as a *bhikkhu,*[95] moves toward monkhood as a result of his relationships with others, particularly with his adoptive father. Being cut off from his family and abandoning the world of his own people does not make him a monk. Rather, he becomes a monk through the relationships he cultivates with virtuous laypeople, first with the householders who give him refuge and urge him to escape, and second, with the compassionate merchant boss who raises and educates him.

The overlapping in the narrative between the image of the *bhikkhu* and the image of the orphan is revealing of the ambivalence the text attributes to the idea that one can detach oneself from society. The abandonment of family life idealized in certain Buddhist texts is achieved here by being an orphan, a status that frees one from the bonds of society, but in the worst way.[96] In the Khmer literary context, being an orphan is not only a bad fate; it is a morally precarious one. An 1859 Khmer verse chronicle translated by David Chandler links the imagery of orphanhood with violence, misery, and the fruition of past misdeeds:

> Sometimes people have merit, high status, possessions, more than anyone else, for sure, and on other occasions people are small and low, their lineage and descendants insignificant, like poor orphans altogether. This is . . . *karma;* suffering comes as a result of what we have done; merit and demerit are all mixed up together.[97]

This kind of fate, the poet continues, is "like being in the middle of the sea, with no islands and no shore in sight, with no one to help."[98]

In a variety of other Khmer texts, the image of the orphan is represented as suspect, compromised, or even dangerous to him- or herself and others.[99] "True solitude is being an orphan" reads a line from *Cpāp' Trīneti,* a Khmer religious poem intended to instruct children in proper moral behavior. The image is a strongly negative one, indicative of a way of life that is unbeneficial to others, explicated with illustrations such as "possessing learning, but not teaching others" or "not having children to love you."[100] The *cpāp'* poetry in general highlights the moral relationship between parents and children; parents serve as moral exemplars for their children to emulate and are reminded that "the fruit grows not far from the tree."[101] For children, the strong implication of the *cpāp'* is that those who lack exposure to the moral guidance sung by parents to children through the *cpāp'* lead lives that are morally unrefined and immature. A proper parent-child relationship, then, in the view of these texts, is fundamental to mature moral agency.

In several other well-known folk stories—and these are clearly gendered images of orphans—girls are abandoned in the forest by a parent or parents and assume new morally ambivalent identities in which they are incapable of achieving full agency.[102] Lost and alone in the forest in a defenseless state, these orphaned girls become animalistic. In one story, three young girls abandoned by their mother transmorphize into birds with a cry of *kūn lok,* "child of the world."[103] In another well-known story, the *Rathasena-jātaka,* twelve young orphaned sisters (after various travails and twists of fortune at the hands of an ogress they meet in the forest) are imprisoned in a pit in the ground where eleven of the twelve must eventually resort to eating their own infants.[104] In a somewhat different vein, *Nāṅ Maraṇamātā* tells the story of a young girl whose beloved mother is murdered by her father and his minor wife. The mother, in her various rebirths, takes the form of animal, plant, and spirit to try to help her daughter. Even though the daughter remains a good person who is respectful toward her cruel stepmother, her existence as a *kaṃbrā-mtāy,* a child orphaned of her mother, is fraught with violence and danger. She is eventually murdered by her stepmother and reborn as a bird.[105]

The image of the vulnerable orphan surrounded by and susceptible to harm and violence surfaces in the larger political landscape as well. Chandler points to the use of family-related imagery in the diplomatic correspondence surrounding tensions between states. Cambodia itself was depicted in nineteenth-century chronicles as an "unruly child" in need of a mother and father. The Vietnamese emperor was alleged to have written, "We will be its mother; its father will be Siam."[106] David Wyatt has observed the theme of orphanhood both in temple murals at Vatt Phumin in Nan Province of northern Thailand and in late-nineteenth-century chronicles connected with the fate of the Nan kingdom, a formerly autonomous Thai kingdom that repeatedly lost its protective allegiances with larger kingdoms and patrons. Wyatt suggests that in this case, the orphan trope is employed to develop the "absence of paternal authority and protection" as a theme in the history of the Nan kingdom.[107] In Wyatt's analysis, Khatthana, the main character depicted in the murals, is always seeking a paternal relationship to protect him from "a dangerous world, peopled by many evils." The image of this orphan in the Vatt Phumin murals suggest that "human existence cannot be happy without some sort of patron or protector because [of] the evils and dangers that lurk in the world."[108]

The figure of the orphaned Bhikkhu Sukh is unique as a representation of a *bhikkhu* in Ind's *Gatilok.* Every other monk in the narrative collection is mired in the ways of the world *(gatilok)* instead of reaping spiritual profits from the path of the Dhamma. Several stories feature abbots who become so obsessed with material ambitions such as building a new *vihāra* (monastery building) or choosing a silk robe that they fail to recognize that the supposed patrons for these projects are in reality conning them out of the funds diligently raised by their lay followers to support the ongoing work of their monasteries.[109] In another story, an abbot implicates himself in a vile murder when he finds a corpse propped up against a jackfruit tree in his monastery. Fearful of false accusations against himself, he shaves off the dead man's hair and dresses him as a novice. In the morning, he tells the gathered monks and laypeople that a novice "without relatives or friends" passed through the monastery during the night and died. In truth, the corpse was the lover of a woman who murdered him and then tricked her husband into believing he had inadvertently killed an intruder. Although the abbot eventually surmises the truth about the corpse, he quickly burns it anyway to cover up his own wrongdoing.[110] Several other stories make reference to abbots who engage in sexual misconduct, and one abbot's lover hires a gambler to murder her husband.[111]

The stories of other *bhikkhu* drawn from Pali literary sources also show *bhikkhu* who are corrupt and corrupting of others. Dhaniyathera, a *bhikkhu* who lived at the time of the Buddha, is shown "taking what is not given" in clear violation of the Buddhist precept concerning theft. He misrepresents an edict issued by King Bimbisāra allowing monks to collect wood in the forest in order to requisition lumber from the royal foresters for a new hut. The Buddha himself chides Dhaniya for this action.[112] Kapilabhikkhu, a monk under Kassapa Buddha, is described as "a *bhikkhu* who knew all 84,000 [lines] of the *Braḥ Tripiṭaka* but did not know how to behave in accordance with the Dhamma and the *Vinaya* and . . . twisted the *Braḥ Buddhavacana* to mean something else." His wrongdoing and consequent punishment in Avīci hell (the lowest level of hell) was later explained by Gotama Buddha to fishermen who encountered the former monk Kapila in a rebirth as a beautiful fish with a putrid stench emitting from his mouth.[113] Devadattathera (the Buddha's heretical cousin) emerges as the ultimate symbol of evil within the text, one whose sins were so great that "the entire planet has taken note of this story."[114] Although Devadatta's many efforts to distort the Buddha's Dhamma and to harm the Buddha himself are not narrated in the text, they are examples of the kind of stories that need no telling for Khmer Buddhist audiences. Ind's references to figures such as Dhaniyathera, Kapilabhikkhu, and Devadatta, interwoven with the narratives of more-ordinary *bhikkhu* drawn from vernacular literature, however, seem to suggest that even

Pali textual accounts of the Buddha's time represent monastic life as fraught with the failures of monks to live according to the Dhamma.

Ind's efforts to define the true meaning of Buddhist identity are a reaction to what he sees as a tendency among many Khmer Buddhists to understand monkhood in cultural rather than spiritual terms: "when we see a shaved head and the clothing of a monk, we surmise that he is holy and righteous . . . and we trust and believe in him."[115] The problem with complacency toward the designation of monks, Ind explains—perhaps alluding to the allegations that circulated about "false monks" in early-nineteenth-century Cambodia[116]—is that it enables wicked persons to impersonate monks, easily deceiving and cheating people who assume they are authentic because of their manner of dress. Rather, a "true" monk is apparent in an utterly different way, as "one who strives toward virtue in respect to the four kinds of morality"[117] and who is "endowed with the virtues belonging to the recluse."[118] Then,

> he can be called a "monk" in the *sāsana* of Lord Buddha. But if we take shaved heads and yellow robes as signifiers of monks, the group of *upāsak-upāsikā* (laypeople) young and old, men and women, can have shaved heads too, and they can wear yellow robes as well. Could this group not be called by the name of monk as well?[119]

Although the social roles and responsibilities of monks and laypeople are different—and therefore the exact behaviors, occupations, and mental attitudes that constitute virtue are different for them—the imperative for both groups to purify their conduct is equally forceful. This is not to say that the monastic life as a whole is devalued in the *Gatilok.* For Ind, on the contrary, monasticism is tied to education, which he sees as an essential component of the moral life. Rather, monks who are not living as true monks are as pitiable and blinded as ignorant laypeople, and laypeople have as much need as monks for the cultivation of the *satisampajañña* that enables them to know how to live. Because detachment from society is impossible, the monk, like the layperson, must draw on moral discernment in order to live virtuously in relation to others and improve the purity of self and others at the same time.

One of the most necessary moral attributes for achieving purification, then, is moral discernment or *satisampajañña,* presented in the Bhikkhu Sukh story as the quality that allows the boy Sukh to survive and prosper. First, he recognizes what has happened to his family and understands the intentions of the chieftain's gang toward him. He has the foresight to climb and hide in the tree "tangled with creepers," exactly the same image of an entangled bamboo that is used so derisively in the *Sutta-nipāta* to describe a life lived among others. Then, he is able to escape to the lower village, and by some combination of instinct and perception, to appeal to a compassionate family who will risk their own lives to shelter him. When they ask him to leave, he quickly understands his plight and theirs and runs away, grabbing and hanging on to the right "vehicle," the cart of the merchant, who introduces him to the vehicle of Theravāda Buddhism. Like other morally good protagonists in the *Gatilok,* Sukh exhibits the kind of discernment that causes moral people, possessing *satisampajañña,* to be able to respond to situations of harm in a way that avoids injury to themselves and others. Although Bhikkhu Sukh could not avoid the massacre of his family, he did live in such a way that ended rather than perpetuated the enmity associated with their deaths. What is striking here is the way in which the narrative of an orphan born into a *jāti* with little or no knowledge of the Buddhist *sāsana* is able to transform violence, loss, and disadvantage into wisdom, well-being, and purity. This contrasts with the threads of the Ajātasattu story running through the text, in which the son of a powerful Buddhist king with every advantage manages to transform advantage and benefit into violence and impurity.

Bhikkhu Sukh's story is morally powerful not because he is the only true *bhikkhu* in the *Gatilok* but because, within the worldview of the text, he represents the fundamental ethical problems confronting each and every person. First, all beings born into the world have to live in relationship to others. Although Cau Sukh loses his natal family, he must still learn to construct appropriate and beneficial relationships in order to survive. Second, all individuals living in the world experience *dukkha* and must respond to it as they are able, given the combination of knowledge, abilities, personality, relationships, and other factors that determine their identities as beings. Bhikkhu Sukh is presented as someone who lacks every social advantage in the world that could bring him power or benefit, but he possesses the moral resource of discernment that allows him not only to survive but to achieve spiritual development. As feminist ethicist Katherine Canon has observed in another context, because this "least-advantaged" member of society survives and prospers, it is apparent that others can as well.[120]

Bhikkhu Sukh, however, is not the only moral person of the story. Equally important as a moral figure is the merchant boss who becomes his adoptive father. Confronting the little boy hanging on to his oxcart, he heard his story with "horrific grief and pity"[121]—and then responded compassionately. Etymologically embedded in the Khmer description of the merchant's initial response to the boy's story as *secktī-saṅveg-āṇit* is the Pali word *saṃvega* (anxiety). In this highly allegorical context, this emotion bears religious analysis. *Saṃvega,* in various Pali contexts, refers to the kind of emotional anxiety one feels as a result of the "contemplation of the miseries of this world,"[122] a deep distress based on the recognition of suffering and its causes.[123] One prominent context for *saṃvega* is the contemplation—presumably by monks—of decaying corpses in cemeteries, which leads them to recognize the nature of reality in terms of *anicca* (impermanence).[124] The merchant's response to the orphan's story, then, is the kind of realization that can lead one onto the Path, signifying the merchant's morally advanced and exemplary status. *Saṃvega* seems to be leading the merchant to *mettā-karuṇā* (loving-kindness and compassion).

In contrast to the image conjured up by *saṃvega* of a monk contemplating a corpse, the merchant's realization is represented in relational terms: he takes the orphan as his own child, accepting responsibility for his welfare. This moment of emotional response by the merchant seems to highlight a tension recognizable in many Theravāda Buddhist writings between the values of renunciation and familial responsibility, most notably in the *Vessantara-jātaka* and the Buddha's own biography (discussed in chapter 1). Ind's narrative breaks away from this more traditional template of moral development, instead portraying a moral figure who takes on, rather than giving up, family responsibilities. In the imagery and language of the story, the purity and strength of the *sāsana,* the religion itself, seems to deepen through his care for the suffering of another.

When the passage is read not allegorically but historically, the merchant boss' compassion takes on another kind of heightened significance, since he might have either sold the orphaned boy into slavery or kept him as his servant, both of which would have been seen as acceptable and even appropriate responses. Instead, he adopts him as his own son and then, displaying further generosity, has him educated and eventually sponsors his ordination. The relationship between this adoptive father and son is exemplary of the Buddhist conception of a *kalyāṇa-mitta* friendship, a relationship with a "virtuous friend." This type of friendship represents the best possible kind of social attachment, as it leads one to and keeps one on the Path. Because of the deceptiveness of so many people in the world, *satisampajañña* is particularly important as the moral virtue that enables one to discern who is a virtuous friend and who is not.

The story suggests that just as the world consists of networks of causation exemplified by the basket weaver's daydream and the events that triggered Cau Sukh's escape or "liberation" through grabbing onto the wheel frame of an oxcart, individual purification is inseparable from one's interactions with others. For the individual, purification depends on the ability to live within a complex web of social interactions but not become tainted by the desires and imperfections of others. In Ind's modern, vernacular interpretation, a Buddhist *sappurisa* has the qualities of both the orphaned Cau Sukh and the Khmer merchant: discerning of causes and results, aware of his or her social responsibilities and relationships, compassionate, kind, grateful, and disciplined. Ind's Buddhist modernist reading of this Theravādin ethical category suggests a vision of moral development and progress, located in the translation and understanding of *Dhamma-vinay* into the ordinary lives of Khmer villagers.

CONCLUSION

The imagery of moral persons in the "Story of Bhikkhu Sukh" returns us to the illumination of *Dhamma-vinay* in Lvī-Em's sermon "Sāsanahetukathā" that began my analysis of Buddhist modernist writings. An authentic Buddhist is one with pure moral behavior, which also shapes the nature of the *sāsana* and the religious community as a whole; good moral conduct involves disciplining the body, words (including the articulation of the Buddha's teachings through text and translation), and the heart and mind through a deep understanding of the *Dhamma-vinaya*. These ideas formed the framework of the Buddhist modernism that was in place by 1930 and quickly rose to prominence during the following decade, putting forward a new expression of Buddhist modernity and tradition in Cambodia and supplanting an older orthodoxy connected with manuscript culture.

A curriculum compiled in 1951 for teaching children at the *Dhamma-vinaya* school at Vatt Uṇṇālom—where Chuon Nath and Huot Tath had preached their contentious *Vinaya* sermons thirty-five years earlier—demonstrates how modernist ideas had become absorbed:

> The aim of the Dhamma that is found on the pages of the *Braḥ Suttantapiṭaka* and the *Braḥ Abhidhammapiṭaka* is that one should adopt it as rules of conduct for teaching and guiding one's heart and mind toward purification. The aim of the *Vinaya* is that one takes the rules of conduct found on every page of the *Braḥ Vinayapiṭaka* as rules of conduct for training and disciplining one's body and speech to have an appropriate manner, to have order and discipline, to have modest and seemly conduct.
>
> . . . Buddhism is illustrious, prospers and endures for a long time because the whole community of Buddhists comes together to diligently listen to Dhamma, study Dhamma, support and uphold Dhamma, examine Dhamma, and act in accordance with Dhamma out of respect for it by agreeing to carefully apply it. But when the community of Buddhists does not come together to listen to the Dhamma, to study Dhamma, to support and uphold Dhamma, to examine Dhamma, and to act in accordance with Dhamma, that is when Buddhism will fall into decline, become corrupted, useless, and degenerate.[125]

This brief, clear distillation of modernist values hardly seems to evoke the complexity of the forces and interactions through which it arose: purification and reform movements, millenarianism, arduous travels to Siam, controversies over loofah-gourd rolls in robes, orthography battles, clandestine *Vinaya* study cells, epiphanies caused by grammatical parsing, modern pedagogies, and the introduction of print. Added to these factors, the interactions between a changing cosmopolitan body of ideas, symbols, and notions of authority (the Pali canon) and local interpreters, acting within a colonial context in which Buddhist texts and knowledge were highly politically charged, helped to give rise to the modern Dhamma movement that intertwined modernity with notions of moral purification. During the 1920s and 1930s, modern Dhamma teachings were increasingly incorporated into classes and curricula at the Sālā Pali and pagoda schools and disseminated through the publications of the Royal Library, through funeral volumes and biographies of monks, through Dhamma tours to the provinces undertaken by modernist monks beginning in the early 1930s, by the text "fetes" organized by Karpelès, and through the Buddhist Institute's new traveling "bookmobile."

The 1951 Vatt Uṇṇālom curriculum provided Chuon Nath's answers to common questions about Buddhism. His explication for the meaning of Buddhism incorporated interconnected notions of Khmerness, purification, moral conduct, a historicity situated in a this-worldly temporality, and antiquity. According to the curriculum, "Buddhism" (which in Khmer is expressed as a compound word), was composed of two words, *Buddh* and *sāsana.* Taken together, the phrase referred to the "teachings and discipline, the words of counsel or advice of the Lord Buddha, he who was enlightened and came to know the Truth."[126] The first word in the compound was *Buddh,* which, Chuon Nath explained,

> refers to the name of an extraordinary human being who attained enlightenment through insight into the Dhamma. This is the same Buddha whom we respect and revere today, the Lord who is the Foremost Teacher, who came from the Sakya family, who was born as a *ksatra* in the Middle Country, known today as India. If you think about the number of years between our time to his, it is a span of 2,573 years since the lifetime of this extraordinary person.[127]

The curriculum went on to recount not the cosmic lifetimes of the Bodhisatta of the *jātaka* or Prince Siddhat's duel with Mārā in the *Paṭhamasambodhi,* but the historical life and circumstances of Prince Gotama, who renounced his luxurious life in the palace, took up the life of a wandering ascetic, and went on to discern the true origin of suffering, or *dukkha.*[128]

The second word, *sāsana,* the curriculum continued, referred to teachings, discipline, and advice.[129] In a comparative sense,[130] *sāsana* had certain characteristics:

> Its teachings and discipline are directed at people in the entire world to exhort them to make their behavior right and good and to refrain from wrong actions with body, speech, heart and mind. *Sāsanā* exhorts its followers to lift themselves up from inferiority to self improvement,[131] from ignorance to wisdom, from discontentedness to contentedness, from living in blindness to living in virtue, from living in virtue to becoming Noble,[132] and for those who have not yet achieved compliance with [these teachings], it exhorts them to follow the [teachings] carefully in order to attain these [fruits].[133]

In these passages, *sāsana,* and by extension Khmer Buddhism, is infused with values of purification and moral conduct, rationalism, and a historicist sense of civilizational progress and development. The writings suggest the comparability between Khmer Buddhism and other religions, in terms of the universality of its ethical principles and its historical emergence as a world religion.

Writing still another decade later, in 1961, Huot Tath represented the antiquity of Khmer Buddhism in empirical terms that could be historically proven through the study of Buddhist scriptural texts and inscriptions. The origins of Khmer Buddhism, he wrote in his 1961 history *Braḥbuddh-sāsanā nau Prates Kambujā Saṅkhep*[134] (An abbreviated account of Buddhism in Kampuchea), could be traced nearly to the origins of the Buddhist religion itself. According to Buddhist commentaries such as the *Samantapāsādikā-aṭṭhakathā-vinaya-piṭaka* (a commentary on the *Vinaya*), Huot Tath wrote, right after the Third Buddhist Council in India, "a great *thera* named Mahāmoggaliputtissa arranged to send the *thera*s Soṇatthera and Uttaratthera . . . on a mission to disseminate Buddhism to Suvaṇṇabhūmi, during the realm of the great king named Dhammāsok."[135] Suvaṇṇabhūmi appears to have included all or part of the region now called Southeast Asia, Huot Tath continued. Although every country in Southeast Asia now claimed to have been the location of Suvaṇṇabhūmi, looking closely at scriptural and epigraphical evidence led one to conclude that the establishment of Buddhism among the Khmer coincided with the time frame of this early mission.[136]

Having established the antiquity of Khmer Buddhism, Huot Tath summarized its further development:

> From that period on, Buddhism in Kampuchea became established and never at any point suffered annihilation or disappearance, but merely [periods of] decline alternating with [periods of] growth and prosperity. This was caused by the fact that in certain periods, Buddhism was strongly supported by its adherents, while in other periods, it was only weakly maintained. Throughout its long history, the kings, elites, and populace of Kampuchea have not always followed just one type of Buddhism. At some points, they were Theravādins, at other points Mahāyānists, and at still others, Brahmans. As a result, Buddhism has been subject to continual adaptation, depending on the power and influence of its adherents, which in turn has depended on the particular period of history. Indeed, it is striking how Buddhism in Kampuchea has endured up until the present time. But because its essence was maintained, even when its material means of support was sometimes diminished, it never dwindled away.
>
> At the present time, Buddhism in Kampuchea is in a period of strong growth, progress, and prosperity. Why is this? Because Kampuchea has established itself as an independent country,[137] observing neutrality in political matters, with abundant rights and liberties; because Kampuchea is fortunate in possessing a king . . . at its head who is a protector of Buddhism, and who leads our nation's people to freedom from fear and danger. . . . As the country develops, so does Buddhism—because Buddhism and country are inextricably interconnected; if the country suffers, so does Buddhism; if the country experiences peace and prosperity, so does Buddhism.[138]

This strong identification between Khmerness, Buddhism, and modernity clearly represented in these writings from the 1950s and 1960s, I have suggested, began to emerge in the second decade of the century with the establishment of new Buddhist institutions, new textual and pedagogical practices, and the rise of a modern interpretation of Buddhism.

My chronological narrative of the growth of Khmer Buddhist modernism ends in 1930 with the creation of the Buddhist Institute because it seems to me to mark another shifting point. After 1930, the forces were in place to ensure that modernism would cease to function as a modernism in the sense of an opposing critique, ethos, or movement but increasingly as the dominant religious discourse. The complex nature of the processes and interactions shaping Khmer Buddhist modernism up through 1930 and the creation of the Buddhist Institute are evident through my preceding discussion. Even though there is still more to learn about the particular individuals and ideas involved, it is already apparent that it was more than simply an outgrowth of the colonial presence. Nor was Buddhist modernism a strictly national or nationalist project, although it did provide an intellectual space for the expression of a heightened awareness of Khmer culture, history, language, and literature, as well as for discontents about social organization under colonialism to be voiced.

As in Malaya and the Netherlands East Indies, the nature of religious modernism shifted as other ideologies became more prominent. In Cambodia and elsewhere, religious modernism as a critical discourse was fused to anticolonial nationalism, and among some factions of society, supplanted by secular ideologies.[139] Among Southeast Asian Muslims, the sharp divide between modernists and traditionalists began to fade during the 1920s, when a new generation educated in Dutch-sponsored secular schools came of age; the tensions between Islam and secularism became a more pressing concern to many Muslims than those between traditionalist and modernist camps.[140] In colonial Cambodia, the dynamics between traditionalists and modernists played out somewhat differently. While Buddhism continued to play a central role in imagining nationalism and the modern nation, the religious establishment, led by the modernists who had assumed positions of authority in the Sangha, increasingly suppressed traditionalism.[141]

Although the political and nationalist implications of religious modernism in the Islamic and Theravāda Buddhist worlds of Southeast Asia display some striking parallels, what is also striking—and almost wholly unstudied by scholars of Southeast Asia—are the similar ethical values constructed by colonial Southeast Asian Muslims and Buddhists concerning how to be modern. Debates between modernists and traditionalists in both Islamic and Buddhist contexts centered on how to behave, ritually and ethically, as moral persons in a rapidly modernizing environment. Modernist movements connected with the two religious traditions stressed an ethic of purification and a complex of related values that aided the articulation of new forms of knowledge and new ideas about how to live that were oriented toward modernity. Gayo modernist poetry from highland Sumatra, for example, proselytized about "prayers that are ineffective" because of lack of earnest concentration:

If the heart is roaming,
even though worship has begun.
The mouth is reciting, the heart is figuring all sorts of matters, up and down.

In the middle of worship, thoughts are flying
like a kite no longer held down.
So the heart is long gone:
"there are the hills, the knoll is in view,

there is the field's edge, with every little row . . . "[142]

Comparable ethical ideas in Khmer modernist thought about how to conduct oneself during religious ritual are obvious from the discussion in this chapter. Not only was the crucial importance of rational understanding similarly stressed, but the particular ethical value of attentiveness underscored in this excerpt of Gayo poetry is similar to the ethical priority placed on the cultivation of *satisampajañña* in Ind's work. In both contexts, modernist conceptions of authentic ritual performance demanded rational knowing and correct performance but also the ethical quality of keeping one's mind focused and attentive—rather than flying off "like a kite" or tumbling out of a sugar-palm tree. Closer study of the comparisons and interactions between Southeast Asian Islamic and Buddhist modernist ethics could lead us to recognize regional resonances in the ways that Southeast Asians constructed their distinctive conceptions of modernity.

Setting itself in opposition to traditionalism, Buddhist modernism in Cambodia incorporated currents of thought that had originated with King Ang Duong's efforts to renovate Khmer religion in the 1850s along with notions of purification and conduct inherited from other religious reforms in Siam and Cambodia, from local millenarian movements, and from the discursive and pedagogical collusions between colonial French and Khmer officials and scholars. But although modernists had absorbed older Khmer intellectual assumptions about the moral construction of reality, the nineteenth-century literary preoccupations with merit, power, and the cosmic biography of the Buddha were deemphasized in their writings. In contrast to the older representations of moral development, modern renderings of purification reflected a temporal and spatial shift, locating meaningful Buddhist values in the here and now of the colonial world.

Thinkers such as Chuon Nath, Huot Tath, Uṃ-Sūr, Lvī-Em, and Ind contributed to the articulation of a transformed Buddhism in Cambodia whose values reflected Khmer conceptions of modern ways of being. The result was an array of new translations and compendiums of the Buddhist *Dhamma-vinay* that circulated widely among a population that had become receptive to new forms and articulations of how to behave. They reflected a "demythologized" view of reality characteristic of modern perception elsewhere—but not a "disenchanted" one in the sense of being secular.[143] Associating the purity and health of the *sāsana* and its disciples within the everyday behavior of ordinary Khmer living "right now" in "these present times,"[144] they had begun to construct an understanding of themselves as belonging to an authentic Buddhist moral community defined by their scriptural knowledge, moral development, and purity of conduct. In Buddhist modernism in the 1920s in colonial Cambodia, modernity is perhaps best inscribed not in European terms such as "nation" or the sensation that "all that is solid melts into air,"[145] but by the ethics of moral purification and in the image of an orphan, clinging to the frame of the right vehicle, whose driver can speak to him in his own language.

ARCHIVES AND SPECIAL COLLECTIONS

ABBREVIATIONS AND ACRONYMS

AEFEO	Archives École française d'Extrême-Orient
BEFEO	*Bulletin de l'École française d'Extrême-Orient*
BI	Buddhist Institute
BN	Bibliothèque Nationale
D	*Dīghanikāya*, vols. 1 and 3, edited by T. W. Rhys Davids and J. Estlin Carpenter [1890] 1949.
EFEO	École française d'Extrême-Orient
K.	Khmer
NAC	National Archives of Cambodia
NLC	National Library of Cambodia
P.	Pali
PTS	Pali Text Society
RSC	Fonds Résident Supérieur du Cambodge

ARCHIVES AND LIBRARIES

Archives École française d'Extrême-Orient, Paris
Buddhist Institute Library, Phnom Penh
Cornell University John M. Echols Collection, Ithaca, N.Y.
National Archives of Cambodia, Phnom Penh, Fonds Résident Supérieur du Cambodge
National Library of Cambodia, Phnom Penh
National Museum of Cambodia Library, Phnom Penh
Oriental Manuscript Collection, Bibliothèque Nationale, Paris
Rare Book Collection, Bibliothèque Nationale, Paris
School of Oriental and African Studies Library, London

NOTES

INTRODUCTION

Epigraph: Ind [1921] 1971, vol. 1, 20.

Epigraph: Chuon Nath 1935, 66.

Epigraph: Ibid., 50–51.

1. Tambiah 1976, 211–212.

2. Vajirañāṇavarorasa 1979, 30. The *Kālāma-sutta* was also a favorite text of Khmer modernists.

3. Kurzman 2002, 362.

4. Ibid., 355.

5. Tambiah 1976, 212.

6. Noer 1973, 296–299; Von der Mehden 1993, 2–15; Riddell 2001, 207–230; Marr 1971, 77–248; Tai 1992, 20–31; Bradley 2004, 67–71; Karl 2002, 164–176; McHale 2004, 144, 150, 156–163.

7. Kiernan 1985, 18–23. A transformation had begun to occur earlier, evident in the biographies of a few French-affiliated elites studied by Edwards (1999, 102–140). The Lycée Sisowath became more influential after its reorganization in 1935, and a Khmer-language newspaper, *Nagaravatta,* began circulating in 1936. Edwards also traces the development of sporting associations, scouts, and other secular influences in the 1930s (346–382).

8. Zinoman 2002, 1–30; Rodgers 1995, 3–77; Bradley 2004, 73–81; Tai 1992, 28–59, 120–140; Herbert and Milner 1989, 30–31, 53–55, 82–84, 129–132; Nepote and Khing Hoc Dy 1981; Smyth 2000; Vajirañāṇavarorasa 1979, l–li.

9. K., *saṅkhep.* I follow the transliteration system originally developed by Saveros Pou (Pou 1969, 163–169) and slightly revised by Franklin Huffman (Huffman and Proum 1978, 685). I make two very slight variations in vowel transliterations to more easily accommodate fonts available in the public domain: *y* with a dot above is rendered as *ý; y* with a line above is rendered as *ỳ.*

10. K., P. *sappurisa* or K. *manuss laqa.*

11. K. *citt.* I follow Sid Brown's thoughtful translation of this related word in Thai as "heartmind" (2001, 9).

12. On this topic, see Edwards 1999, 18–20.

13. Ind disrobed in 1897 but remained influential as a writer and Pali scholar (Hansen 2003, 817–818).

14. Hinton 2002, 61–89; Marston 2002a, 48–69, and 1994, 114–115; Chandler 1996, 260–262, 275.

15. Vu Trong Phung 2002.

16. Ibid., 94.

17. Kartodirdjo 1985, 103; Roff 1985, 123–125; Kurzman 2002, 362–363; Vajirañāṇavarorasa 1979, xxxvi–xxxvii; Rodgers 1995, 227–228, 270–272; Bowen 1997, 159–172.

18. Spiro 1970, 168–169, 172–173; Tambiah 1976, 122, and 1984, 298–299,

304–314; Tai 1983 and 1988, 60–164; Bond [1988] 1992, 51, 56, 77; Swearer 1999, 207; McHale 2004, 150, 152, 160–163; Chang 1987, 12–14, 78, 169–170; Malalgoda 1970, 434–439, and 1976, 7–8.

19. Chang 1987, 12–14, 78, 169–170; Malalgoda 1970, 434–439, and 1976, 7–8; Birnbaum 2003, 77.

20. This is Steven Collins' translation (1998, 604).

21. Kartodirdjo 1985, 103–110; Keyes 1977, 283–302; Collins 1998, 346–413; Ishii 1986, 171–187; Tambiah 1976 and 1984, 293–320; Tai 1983; Adas 1979, 34–40, 88–89, 99–102; Sarkisyanz 1965; Herbert 1982; Ileto 1992, 197–244; Shiraishi 1990.

22. McHale 2004, xi, 64–65, 172, and n.d., 1.

23. Hefner 1997, 18; Van der Veer 2001, 14–16.

24. Laffan 2003, 67–73, 106–109, 114–141, 169–170.

25. Chakrabarty 2000, 16.

26. Much of the recent scholarship on this topic rests on and revisits the categories and definitions originally identified by Heinz Bechert (1988), summarized in 1970, 774–778, and 1984, 275–277. See also Gombrich and Obeyesekere 1988, 202–236. Juliane Schober's recent (1995) and forthcoming work on Buddhism and modernity in Burma has redirected scholarly attention to the issue.

27. Kurzman 2002, 4–6.

28. Ibid., 4–27; Hooker 2003, 2–17, 230–235.

29. Hefner 1997, 15; Bowen 1993, 21–30, and 1997, 159–172; Saleh 2001, 3–5, 120–136; Hooker 2003, 47–60, 66–68, 94–98.

30. Hooker 1997, 157–166.

31. Bowen 1993, 58, and 1997, 176; Siegel 2000, 124; Kurzman 2002, 16–17.

32. Johns 1986, 410–412; Bowen 1993, 61–73.

33. Roff 1985, 123–125; Fealy 1996, 9–7; Rodgers 1995, 270.

34. Obeyesekere, 1991, 219–220; Lopez 1995, 7.

35. Duara 1995; Wigen 1995 and 1999, 1186; Chakrabarty 2000 and 2002.

36. Collins 1998, 40–89; Pollock 1998, 7; Van der Veer 2001, 3–13, 55–82; Jory 2002, 893–909; Leve 2002, 844–852.

37. Bizot 1976 and 1992, 25–27.

38. Keyes 1983, 272–273.

39. Ibid., 275–281.

40. Collins 1990, 95–102.

41. Ibid., 102–104.

42. Ibid., 104.

43. Blackburn 1999, 283–284.

44. Hallisey 1995, 33–39.

45. Among many possible examples, see Saddhatissa 1997, 20–23.

46. Harvey 1990, 10–28.

47. Ibid., 23.

48. Ibid.

49. Thongchai 1994, 55.

50. Chakrabarty 2000, 16.

51. David Chandler has pointed to the prevalence, in nineteenth-century Khmer sources, of using past karma as a means for interpreting reality (1996, 78–79).

52. Anderson 1983.

53. Ind [1921] 1971, vol. 1, 8.

54. Ibid., vol. 1, 1, 8; vol. 4, 2, 5; vol. 5, 14.

55. Most notably in passages in vol. 1,1, and vol. 10, 73–74, the introduction and conclusion to the text, when he refers to his reasons for composing the text.

56. Ind [1921] 1971, vol. 1, 1.

57. Ibid., vol. 1, 8.

58. Harvey 1990, 10–38.

59. Obeyesekere 1970, 43–63; Gombrich and Obeyesekere 1988, 7. See Queen and King 1996, 20–21.

60. Blackburn 2001, 41–75, 197–203.

61. Van der Veer 2001, 55–82.

62. Tully 2002, 235.

63. The Dharm-thmī faction later came to be known for a while as the "Dhammakay" (also romanized as "Thammakay"), but I find no references to this moniker in the Khmer sources I surveyed, either in French or Khmer sources from the 1920s and early 1930s or in later biographies of monks. Penny Edwards cites references to the name as early as 1932 in a French-authored report on temple schools by the résident of Kompong Thom and more prominently later, in *Nagaravatta* articles from 1937–1938 (Edwards 1999, 331–332, 338–339).

64. Huot Tath 1993, 11–13; *Jīvaprattisaṅkhep nai Upāsikā So-Suan* [Biography of laywoman So-Suan], 1960, NAC 27, 3; Minister of the Interior K. Chea, "Rapport d'ensemble sur la religion Bouddhique au Cambodge," 28 June 1937 and "Deliberation of the permanent Commission of the Council of Ministers," 2 July 1937, NAC RSC F.942 b.2791 23609. Huot Tath states that Chuon Nath later observed that this terminology was unfortunate, as it gave the erroneous impression that there could be more than one Dhamma (1993, 13).

65. Tambiah 1976.

66. Manuscripts still continued (and continue) to be produced in Cambodia, but the dominance of these practices was curtailed through modernist challenges.

67. Groslier 1921,1–8; Moura 1883, vol. 1, 302; Coedès 1902, 400, and 1924, 15–20, 27; Ginsburg 1989, 8–10.

68. Jacqueline Filliozat, personal communication, November 1996, Paris; Ashley Thompson, personal communication, March 1998, Washington D.C.; Becchetti 1994, 47–62.

69. Coedès 1924, 17.

70. Becchetti 1994, 55; Bizot and von Hinüber 1994, 49–84. This practice is not confined to the Khmer, but is in fact part of a transcultural Theravādin practice of writing.

71. The Buddha is referred to as the Bodhisatta before his enlightenment. Khmer literature uses three terms: Bodhisatta (Pali), Bodhisattva (Sanskrit), Bodhisatt (Khmer).

72. Concern with delineating distinctions between "ways of the world" (also translated as "worldly matters") and "Dhammic matters" was evident in Siam as well, discussed in chapters 3 and 5.

73. I am grateful to John Marston for introducing me to funeral biographies, generally written for the merit-making rituals following a monk's death, and to Kasseka Phon

and Sony Keo, my research assistants during the summer of 2000, who helped me go through boxes of dusty, still unclassified biographies at the NAC. Others of the biographies I surveyed for this book come from the NLC and the libraries at Cornell University and the University of Michigan.

74. In particular, I have benefited from chronicle translations by David Chandler, Milton Osborne, and David Wyatt. I am also indebted to Saveros Pou's analyses and translations of *cpāp'*. These sources and my uses of them are indicated in the notes that follow.

75. These sources are also analyzed and translated in excerpts in Khin Sok 1991, 7–9, and Edwards 1999, 395–407. I am indebted to John Marston for sending me a copy of Huot Tath's memoir.

CHAPTER ONE: DEFENDING THE JEWELED THRONE

1. The date is uncertain, but the theme, versification, and language of the work suggest late-nineteenth-century composition, prior to other dated works by the author, Ukñā Suttantaprījā Ind, including *Nirās Nagar Vatt* and *Gatilok.*

2. Among the entries for "Mārā" in the Buddhist Institute Khmer dictionary (of which the author of this poem was one of the early architects) are "death"; "impediment" or "obstacle," "one who obstructs," and "obstructing or preventing the arise of merit and benefit toward others"; the "name of a *devaputra* (K. 'male deity') who is the enemy of the Lord Buddha." As either abstract qualities or beings, *mārā*s can exist in the plural (Buddhist Institute [BI] [1938] 1967, 883). *Mārā* is also referred to in the poem as an *asura* and a *yakkha,* both designations for types of beings that can be malevolent, but also used metaphorically to refer to malevolence. An *asura* is often understood as a kind of lower-level deity living on Mount Sumeru; as a group, *asura*s are generally antagonistic toward the celestial deities. A *yakkha* or *yakṣa* is a kind of demon or ogre. In Khmer stories, *yakkha* are usually although not universally hostile toward human beings.

3. I.e., the knowledge of awakening.

4. Ind 1934b, 36–38 (stanzas 254–263).

5. On modern usages of the Pali and Khmer word *gati,* see chapter 5 and Hansen 1999, 128–132.

6. Sometimes transliterated as Ly Théan Teng.

7. Lī 1961, 121.

8. Ibid., 147.

9. Jacob 1996, 49; I refer to the Reynolds and Reynolds translation of the Thai text (1982).

10. Guesdon 1906, 92, 94–96, 101–103; Leclère 1899, 5–204. See also Khing 1990, 47, 205; Jacob 1996, 36–41, 49; Coedès 1957, 349–352; Reynolds 1976; McGill 1997, 200–202.

11. Reynolds and Reynolds 1982, 135–172. A version of the story is found in Suṅ S'īv Siddhattho [Braḥ Pāḷāt' Uttamalikhit] 1952 (hereafter Suṅ S'īv 1952), 24–34, which was composed in the 1940s, using older versions (apparently) of the *Visuddhimagga,* the *Cakkavatti-sutta,* and other unspecified sources. See also Thongchai 1994, 20–36; Collins 1998, 357–375, 414–496.

12. P. *kappa.*

13. A complete listing of the divisions of a *kapp* into categories of two, three, four, and six are found in Suṅ S'īv 1952, 17–19.

14. *Adinnādāna, pāṇatipāta, musavāda, pisuṇāvācā, kāmesumicchācāra, pharusavācā, samphappalāpa, abhijjhā, byāpāda, micchādiṭṭhi.* Suṅ S'īv alternates uses of Khmer and Pali in his list of the *dasa akusalakammapatha* and in his narrative; I have given the Pali here. Suṅ S'īv 1952, 40–42. In most cases, I follow Collins' translations of the terms, which appear in different order in Collins 1998, 488 (which he describes as the "normal order" of the list), but in the same order as 1998, 606–609, in his translation of the *Cakkavatti-sīhanāda Sutta.* Suṅ S'īv refers to the *"Cakkavatti-sutta"* from the *Dīghanikāya* (1952, 34, 44) as one of his sources.

15. Suṅ S'īv 1952, 17, 19–24; Reynolds and Reynolds 1982, 305–327.

16. *Varakapp* (splendid *kapp*) with three buddhas, *sāramaṇḍakapp* (superior and eminent *kapp*) with four buddhas, *bhaddakapp* (auspicious, glorious, fortunate *kapp*) with five buddhas. An epoch with no buddha at all is termed a *suññākapp.* Suṅ S'īv 1952, 25–26; Reynolds and Reynolds 1982, 312–313.

17. Reynolds and Reynolds 1982, 317.

18. I.e., in the *gati* or realm of hell-beings, animals, ghosts, humans, *asura*s (a category of lesser, somewhat malevolent deities), or *devā* (celestial beings). Rhys Davids suggests that earlier texts delineate five *gati* (omitting the *asurā*), while later texts differentiate six. Rhys Davids and Stede [1921–1925] 1986, 242–243. See also Feer 1884a and 1884b.

19. Baumann 2002, 55.

20. I follow Ingrid Muan's argument that Khmer "modernity" begins in the nineteenth century (her dating coincides with the declaration of the protectorate) and that "cultural responses to modernization" are what constitute the "modern" (2001, 5–6).

21. Chigas 2000, 136.

22. Guesdon 1906, 101.

23. Khmer scholars of the period, like those gathered around Ang Duong in mid-century and those who studied in Bangkok later on, including Ind, tended to write poetry, manuals on poetic meter, or translations of Pali or Thai texts rather than analytical treatises on literary themes, while French colonial officials and scholars, involved in documenting and displaying Cambodia's cultural difference, inventoried and in some cases translated the texts they encountered.

24. Guesdon 1906, 101–103. Leclère's presentation of Khmer Buddhism gives great prominence to the *Trai Bhūm* in particular, but he refers to the *jātaka* as the most valued, popular, and well-known texts to Khmer monks and lay audiences. See Leclère 1899, 188–189, 193, 213–214, and 1906, 117. The extent to which versions of *jātaka* and the Buddhological biography dominated the Khmer literary imagination is also made evident in Jacob 1996, 36–41, 148–181; Cone and Gombrich 1977, xv.

25. This text (or texts, since it existed in multiple versions) was connected with the *Paññāsa-jātaka* found in Laos, Siam, and Burma, but by the nineteenth century, the texts in all of these regions had developed into distinct versions, and these versions also developed variations. A Khmer prose *saṃrāy* version of the first twenty-five of the Khmer *Paññāsa-jātaka,* drawn from a palm-leaf version of a text that had been previously deposited in the Buddhist Institute library, was edited and published by Braḥ Dhammalikkhit Lvī-Em, Braḥ Uttamamunī Uṃ-Sūr, and Braḥ Ñaṇavīriyā Ḷuṅ, apparently beginning in the early 1940s (Lvī-Em, Braḥ Dhammalikkhit and Braḥ Uttamamunī Uṃ-Sūr, and Braḥ Ñaṇavīriyā Ḷuṅ 1961, 1–12). A Khmer Pali version was edited by Ācāry S'uman at the Sālā Pali in 1942 (BI [1942] 1952). Still other variations of the stories were published separately,

also copied from earlier manuscript texts, such as the 1968 poetic version of the *Rýaṅ Braḥ Sudhanakumār.* The editor of this latter text explains that it was copied from a manuscript found in 1962 at Vatt Nigrodhārām in Kampong Cham province (BI 1968, vi–vii).

26. Guesdon's manuscript gives the title above, but Jacob cites other manuscript titles: *Puññasār Sirsā* and *Sāstrā Puññasār Sirsā* (Jacob 1996, 122).

27. Guesdon 1906, 280–282. Guesdon reproduced the Khmer text of the manuscript. See also Jacob 1996, 167–168; Khing 1990, 166–171.

28. Here, the Khmer text is obscure, suggesting both that they have triangular faces and square faces: "3 *jruṅcaturas.*"

29. Each stanza in the Khmer manuscript is divided into seven strophes, which translates too awkwardly. My translation is literal rather than poetic. Guesdon gives a French translation that differs from mine in some details (Guesdon 1906, 283–285).

30. Reynolds and Reynolds 1982, 135.

31. P. *Nimi.* BI 1960a, 67–101.

32. In notes to his translation of a nineteenth-century manuscript version of the story, Leclère reports that he compared the manuscript he used to a version of the *Trai Bhūm.* He found its descriptions of various levels of hells to be identical to those in the *Trai Bhūm,* while its accounts of the heavens were more highly embellished (1906, 221).

33. Leclère 1906, 120, 221. See also Jacob 1996, 51.

34. K. *pāpakamm.*

35. K. *puññākamm.* BI 1960a, 73 (stanza 143).

36. K. *mān kaṃlāṃṅ mān ṭ'a lāmak.*

37. K. *pāp.*

38. BI 1960a, 74 (stanzas 146–148).

39. K. *puññākamm.*

40. K. *kusalakamm.*

41. K. *mān sīl.*

42. BI 1960a, 90–91 (stanzas 184–185).

43. Leclère 1900, 368–376.

44. Leclère 1916, 46–47.

45. P. Vessantara; K. Vessantar.

46. Leclère 1902, 3.

47. Guesdon 1906, 103. Leclère 1902, 3–4. According to Lī, a version of the *Mahājātak* was composed by King Ang Duong, though the date of composition is uncertain. This version was later redacted and printed by Ñ"am Thaem (a.w. Nhok-Thaem). Jacob discusses this attribution (with further references) in 1996, 116.

48. Leclère 1902, 3–5.

49. P. Jūjaka; K. Jūjak.

50. Cone and Gombrich's translation (1977, 74).

51. The Khmer *Tipiṭaka,* containing Pali and Khmer on alternate pages, was published in its entirety in the 1960s, but many of the editions and translations were produced much earlier, beginning in the 1920s. The printed *Tipiṭaka* was based largely on Khmer palm-leaf manuscripts carried from Bangkok beginning in Ang Duong's reign and throughout the nineteenth and early twentieth centuries and edited and translated under the auspices of the Royal Library and later the Buddhist Institute from the 1920s through 1960s. Many of the *jātaka* texts were edited and printed as separate texts prior to the 1960s.

52. BI 1960b, 166 (stanza 338).

53. This was a nineteenth-century manuscript version translated by Leclère (1902).

54. Leclère gives only the French translation of this text (1902, 62).

55. Leclère 1902, 63. The earthquake appears in other versions of the text as well, one of which I quote later.

56. Leclère 1902, 65. A similar passage appears in the Khmer canonical version of the story. Leclère's manuscript version of the text is similar to the canonical version of the story, but often expands on the canonical verses.

57. Leclère 1902, 66.

58. In other Khmer texts, Jāli and Kanhājina, Krishnajina, or Krasanar. See Leclère 1902, 22nn7, 8.

59. Leclère 1902, 66.

60. Ibid. The *saṃrāy,* a vernacular genre important in the nineteenth and early twentieth centuries generally consisted of a few lines of Pali followed by a Khmer translation that transmitted the ideas of the passage but not necessarily its literal wording. Commentary and canonical verses might be intertwined in the text, not always with clear demarcations, and in some cases, the Khmer translation might be significantly longer than its corresponding Pali passage (Jacob 1996, 50–51).

61. Guesdon 1906, 96–98; Leclère 1906, 147–148. The *Vessantar-jātaksaṃrāy* in particular, because of its popularity, was found (in the 1960s) to exist in numerous versions, containing many variations.

62. BI 1960b, 166 (stanza 338). In this passage I use the standard Khmer translation, part of the corpus of work discussed in note 51.

63. Note that the Khmer word *kittisabd,* "fame" or "good repute," contains the word *sabd,* "sound," "voice," or "word." This type of poetic allusion appears often in Khmer literary writing but is not easily translated.

64. BI 1960b, 188 (stanzas 367–368).

65. Ibid., 210 (stanza 424). I am grateful to David Chandler for pointing out the parallels between this imagery and similar descriptions of King Eng's restoration of the Khmer throne in 1794 in the Cambodian chronicles (Chandler 2000, 118).

66. Jacob 1996, 37, 156–59; Khing 1990, 121; Lī 1961, 118. Lī says the story was composed in 1856; he includes it among a list of well-known literary works of the late Middle Period in Khmer literature.

67. Guesdon suggests that it was a popular story, "particularly in the north of Cambodia" (1906, 813). He gives a French version at 804–813. See also Khing 1990, 121, 193–195; Jacob 1996, 170.

68. The text evidently existed in much older versions, but its history has proved difficult to trace. Swearer suggests it was connected to an older northern Thai biography of the Buddha, probably composed in the fifteenth or sixteenth century (1995, 182n70). Coedès 1967, 215–227; F. Reynolds 1976, 51–3; Guthrie 2001, 10.

69. Leclère 1906, 7–8.

70. Ibid., 9–10.

71. Ibid., 7–10. Diaṅ is variously transliterated as Tieng, Dieṅ, and Teang.

72. Ibid., 30.

73. Ibid.

74. My analysis of the text is indebted to F. Reynolds 1997.

75. Hanks 1962, 1247–1261.
76. P. Siddhattha.
77. Leclère 1906, 31.
78. Ibid., 93–100.
79. Ibid., 81–82.
80. The paint was made from a mixture of water from boiled rice and the black residue from the bottom of the rice pot or sometimes from charcoal. Once it was painted on, it dried and became hard enough to write on.
81. From interview notes, Battambang, 2000 and 2001. I am indebted to assistance from Phon Kaseka in carrying out the 2001 interviews. The poems circulated in a partially oral–partially textual fashion well into the twentieth century; others of Ind's descendants could recite portions of his poetry when I met them in 2000.
82. Ind 1934b, 5–6 (stanzas 1–6).
83. K. *bodhiñāna.*
84. Ind 1934b, 6 (stanza 9).
85. K. cākr-ratan.
86. K. cākr-batr, P. cakkavattin.
87. K. Buddha-cākr.
88. K. mahā-cākr, "great kings."
89. *lokiya.*
90. *Braḥ camanarind rýaṅ raṅsī.*
91. *Cakrī ka' trās'.*
92. I.e., with the connotation of "necessary but impure."
93. *bodi-ñāna.*
94. *asubā.* I take this as P. *asubha,* "impurities," or possibly more specifically, *asubha-kammaṭṭhāna,* "subjects of meditation-impurities," which may refer to meditation exercises on decomposing bodies in a cemetery.
95. Ind 1934b, 11 (stanzas 45–50).
96. Reynolds and Reynolds 1982, 140, 160–170; Collins 1998, 612. It remains difficult to document how well individual *Tipiṭaka* texts such as this latter were known during this period, but I include this text under the general rubric of *Trai Bhūm* cosmology that becomes evident in other texts. A version of this text is later used by Suṅ S'īv in the 1940s (1952, 34, 44).
97. Collins 1998, 612.
98. Ibid., 604.
99. Collins' translation. Ibid.
100. Ibid.
101. Ibid., 373–374.
102. Reynolds and Reynolds 1982, 139.
103. Collins 1998, 612–613.
104. Ind 1934b, 36 (stanza 255).
105. Demons or ogres.
106. A kind of water serpent.
107. A kind of giant, mythical bird.
108. Ind 1934b, 31 (stanza 210).
109. Ibid., 31–32 (stanzas 206–211).

110. P. *puññādhikāra* or K. *puñña-adhikār.*
111. *Braḥ Buddha paṅs damraṅ sakti.*
112. Ind 1934b, 34–35 (stanzas 235–240).
113. *Braḥ camanarind bin munī.*
114. Literally, yāna, "vehicle" or "means of transport."
115. Ind 1934b, 36 (stanzas 244–245).
116. I.e., the three worlds. *Braḥ Aṅg Cam Trai.*
117. *Sīl.*
118. A kind of sea creature that feeds on human blood. Headley 1977, vol. 2, 455.
119. The qualities of a Buddha.
120. *Saraṇa-gamaṇa.*
121. Ind 1934b, 36–38 (stanzas 250–252, 254–264).
122. Guthrie 2001, 7–12.
123. Buddhist Institute [1938] 1967, 883. See note 2 in this chapter.

CHAPTER TWO: BUDDHIST RESPONSES TO SOCIAL CHANGE

1. *Rýaṅ Paḍāṃ Tā Mās* [1908?], BN, 4–5 (hereafter *Mās*). I follow Khin Sok's translation of the last sentence (1991, 106).
2. Collins 1998, 396, 408.
3. Keyes 1977, 283–302.
4. Berman 1982, 6–7, 15–23; Anderson 1983, 22–36; Hobsbawm 1987, 8–10, 50–55; Harvey 1990, 10–30, 201–225, 260–275; Smith 1993, 15–40; Harvey 2003, 23–57, 267–279; Bocock 1996, 150–183; F. Thompson 1996, 396–403; K. Wilson 2000, 157–160.
5. Harvey 1990, 260.
6. *Mās,* 6.
7. Crawfurd [1828] 1967, 447.
8. Chandler 1996, 87. The chronicle was composed in 1859.
9. Ibid., 90.
10. Bowie 1996, 114–126.
11. Crawfurd [1828] 1967, 347. Terwiel notes that heightened military activity by Siam on its borders beginning at the end of the eighteenth century seems to have resulted in a corresponding increase in Siam of the number of *chaloei,* the type of "absolute slaves" captured as prisoners of war who were unable to buy their freedom and whose descendants were also absolute slaves. Rama I instituted a legal change in 1805 that allowed such slaves to redeem themselves by reimbursing their owners for their services (Terwiel 1983, 131–132).
12. Translated from Khin 1991, 239.
13. Pavie 1898a, xx. Pavie does not give a date or location for this encounter, nor detail the events that led to the capture of this village of Khmer prisoners. He describes warfare that he witnessed in Pavie 1995, 68. For other accounts, see Khin 1991, 239, 269; Bowie 1996, 114–126.
14. Chandler 1996, 76–77, 86–92, 102, and 2000, 121.
15. Chandler 2000, 117–136; Crawfurd [1828] 1967, 425.
16. These are Osborne and Wyatt's translations of French translations from the Siamese and Vietnamese (1968, 192).

17. Tauch 1994a, 1–12.

18. Chandler 2000, 123–132; Khin 1991, 78–98; Leclère 1914, 406–429; Crawfurd [1828] 1967, 447.

19. Chandler 2000, 132–36; Osborne and Wyatt 1968, 199–200.

20. Osborne and Wyatt 1968, 200.

21. Ibid., 201.

22. *Dhamma-attha-sāstra-pali.*

23. *Mās,* 5–7.

24. Leclère, using chronicles as his source, describes the religious undertakings of the king, commenting as well on the extent to which his efforts were limited by his lack of financial resources. Leclère states, for instance, that in order to construct new temples in his capital, Udong, Ang Duong had the fort of Phnom Penh demolished and the bricks transported to Udong for the new buildings (1914, 434–440; Chandler 1996, 104–105, 108).

25. Chandler 1996, 96–97, 102–112. I also make this assumption based on the work of French observers dating from the 1870s onward. Aymonier, stationed in Cambodia starting in 1879, records the performance of *phjaṃ piṇḍ,* a ceremony for honoring the dead ([1900] 1984, 46); Leclère observes transference of merit to the dead at the end of the century (1900, 369); Ind lists offerings to the dead as important religious responsibilities in Ind [1921] 1971, vol. 1, 34.

26. *Mās,* 5–9.

27. Jean Moura, a French naval officer who served as representant du protectorat au Cambodge from 1871 to 1876, received permission from King Norodom to read and translate the royal chronicles, which, he states, were normally kept locked away from view. His translation of the chronicles appears in his *Le Royaume du Cambodge.* He explains in his introduction to the volume that he worked in collaboration with a Khmer scholar (unnamed) to produce the translation (1883, vol. 2, 4, 135–136).

28. Mouhot 1989, 202.

29. Garnier 1885, 61.

30. Tauch 1994a, 9–10.

31. Thongchai 1994, 20.

32. Heine-Geldern 1956; Tambiah 1976, 102–131, and 1985, 252–286; Thongchai 1994, 16–18; Schober 1995, 307–325; Chandler 1996, 58–59, 79, 98–99; Wolters 1999, 27–40. This schema is vividly represented in a chronicle description of a ceremony conducted by Ang Duong shortly after his coronation, translated and studied by Chandler, in which he elaborately renames and arranges his nobles in a mandala-like configuration around him (1996, 108–111).

33. Crawfurd [1828] 1967, 425, 447–448; Osborne and Wyatt 1968, 200; Chandler 2000, 113–114.

34. This title was given to kings who abdicated in favor of their heirs or, in some cases, was used to designate highly ranked princes (Khin 1991, 174–175).

35. Khin 1991, 163–236.

36. Ibid., 216–217; Moura 1883, vol. 1, 248–250.

37. Leclère transliterates the name of the ceremony as *"phok tuk Prah Vipheak Sachar."* Maspero tells us that starting in the reign of Sisowath, the ceremony was performed only once each year, on the king's birthday. It continued to be celebrated into the 1960s (personal communication from David Chandler, March 2003). Leclère 1904, 735–

741, and 1916, 220; Moura 1883, vol. 1, 248–256; Khin 1991, 202–206; Porée and Maspero 1938, 152.

38. Moura 1883, vol. 1, 252. As in much of Moura's translation of this chronicle, it is difficult to determine where it is a direct translation and where a paraphrase of the oath. Coedès, however, compares Moura's translation to a version of the oath sworn to Suryavarman I, noting many similarities in content and wording (1913, 16–17).

39. For another example, see the discussion of 1859 and c. 1880 oaths translated and analyzed by Chandler (1996, 25–42).

40. Moura 1883, vol. 1, 252.

41. Guesdon 1906, 91–92, 99.

42. *Kñuṃ* and *bal re* (debt slaves and hereditary slaves). See Pou 1988, 330–331n23.

43. Ibid., 66, 316–317.

44. Khin 1991, 215, 239; Chandler 2000, 105–106.

45. Such realignments are evident, for example, in the 1859 chronicle translated by Chandler (1996, 86–95).

46. Chandler 2000, 109–113; Khin 1991, 239.

47. Collins 1998, 346–413; Keyes 1977, 283–302; Ishii 1986, 171–187; Tambiah 1984, 293–320; Tai 1983; Adas 1979, 34–40, 88–89, 99–102; Sarkisyanz 1965; Herbert 1982; Leclère 1914, 457; Collard 1921, 81–82; Porée and Porée-Maspero 1938, 49–52; Reddi 1970, 33–39; Moura 1883, vol. 2, 159–171.

48. Qým Nuṃ 1974; Khing 1993, 149–150.

49. Edwards (1999, 266) suggests that in the French colonial viewpoint, millenarianism was "dismissed as the workings of fringe elements." It is difficult to document Khmer perceptions of millenarianism during this period, but there must have been a range of viewpoints. Ind's turn-of-the-century poem (discussed later) disparaged a monk claiming the power to grant invulnerability, and his early-twentieth-century work *Gatilok* dismissed millenarian figures of the nineteenth century as ignorant and criminal ([1921] 1971, vol. 1, 77–79).

50. For the non-Khmer speaker unfamiliar with the Huffman transliteration system (found in Huffman and Proum 1978), the pronunciation of this terms is along the lines of "neak mien peun."

51. Holt 1993, 1–17; A. Thompson 2004; Sponberg and Hardacre 1988.

52. Collins 1998, 346–347, 378–383, 395–413.

53. My research on *daṃnāy* texts in Cambodia has been carried out in collaboration with Judy Ledgerwood, for our forthcoming translation, and I am indebted to her many insights on these sources. I am also indebted to discussions with Olivier de Bernon concerning his research on the texts in colonial and contemporary Cambodia.

54. Chandler 1996, 61–75, and 2000, 120.

55. Chandler 1996, 71.

56. Chandler notes an account of floods and epidemics in the royal chronicles, attributed to the year 1818 (1996, 71–72).

57. This is Chandler's translation. The chronicle was composed in the 1850s. Chandler 2000, 121.

58. Tai 1983, 6–7; Chandler 2000, 123–132.

59. Osborne and Wyatt 1968, 199; Chandler 2000, 130–132; Tai 1983, 7.

60. Tai 1983, 7.

61. Carter 1993, 59.
62. Tai 1983, 27–33.
63. Tai's translation. Ibid., 24.
64. Ibid., 20.
65. Ibid., 20–27.
66. Ibid., 40–43.
67. Ibid., 44–59.
68. Ibid., 115–167.
69. Ibid., 44.
70. Borkaṁpor, but I follow the more commonly used transcription used by Chandler and others (2000, 141). The name also appears in some French sources as "Poukambo," "Pokambo," or Pu-Kombo.
71. Leclère 1914, 457–458; Collard 1925, 81–82; Porée and Porée-Maspero 1938, 49–52; Taboulet 1956, 644–646, 649–650; Reddi 1970, 33–39; Moura 1883, vol. 2, 159–171. Moura's history is from the Cambodian Royal Chronicles.
72. Edwards 1999, 265.
73. Osborne 1969, 187.
74. Tai 1983, 25.
75. Moura 1883, vol. 2, 159.
76. Qým Nuṃ, who composed a nationalistic historical novel about Pou Kombo, published in 1974 but written a decade earlier, states in his introduction that he interviewed "many villagers in Kompong Thom and Stung Treng" about Pou Kombo's ethnicity, but heard competing claims that he was Lao, half-Lao and half-Khmer, or "pure Khmer." Qým also heard reports that Pou Kombo was a respected healer with a variety of skills, including predictive powers and mixing and administering traditional medicines (1974, ii–iii). Moura also notes the claim that Pou Kombo had been in Laos for thirty-one years (1883, vol. 2, 155).
77. Leclère 1914, 457n.
78. The dating of the texts is not certain, but based on evidence in the texts, I accept Olivier de Bernon's arguments for situating the translation or composition of the texts in Khmer in the 1860s (1994, 2–3, 92, and 1998, 44). Some current Khmer scholarship on the texts attributes them to much earlier composition, probably the Angkor period (Dhan' Hin 2543, 39–40). The Khmer texts that circulated in the nineteenth century seem to have been translated from Siamese texts that could in turn have been based on much older Khmer texts, so these theories are not necessarily in opposition.
79. Leclère 1906, 1–2; Maspero 1929, 299; Keyes 1977, 295.
80. Yang Sam 1987, 50–53; De Bernon 1994, 86–87, and 1998.
81. One such list of virtues elaborated in Pali *jātaka* texts is the *dasa rājadhammā,* which Collins translates as "Almsgiving, Morality (keeping the Precepts), Liberality, Honesty, Mildness, Religious practice, Non-anger, Nonviolence, Patience, and Non-offensiveness" (Collins 1998, 460–461). Other lists can be found in Reynolds and Reynolds 1982, 151–153, and Leclère 1906, 19–20.
82. Reynolds and Reynolds 1982, 153.
83. Ibid., 153.
84. K. *Dhvoe laṃ iaṅ buṃ ṭoy nūv dharm,* "inclined away" or "not following after the Dhamma."

85. K. *raṃcual.*

86. Khemarapaṇṇākār 1952, 16–17, from a translation in progress with Judy Ledgerwood.

87. De Bernon 1994, 86.

88. Ibid., 45–46, 86–87; Khemarapaṇṇākār 1952, 5–9; Dan' Hin 1999, 74–75. Similar motifs are apparent in the *Anāgatavaṃsa Desanā,* a Sri Lankan sermon based on a much older Pali extracanonical text (Meddagama and Holt 1993, 26–27).

89. Moura 1883, vol. 2, 168.

90. Osborne 1978, 227.

91. Moura 1883, vol. 2, 169.

92. Moura states that the Khmer were to blame for Pou Kombo's death since at night when he was chained, the "foolish imaginations of the Khmer" took over and prompted fearful guards to cut off his head (ibid.). This explanation is improbable, however, as accounts of French executions and display of rebellion leaders with imputed powers of invulnerability appear elsewhere as well. When Tran Van Thanh was killed in battle, for instance, his body was displayed for three days in an effort to discredit the claims of invulnerability surrounding him. Unfortunately for this French strategy, as Tai points out, "the French had not counted on the potency of the idea of reincarnation" (1983, 48).

93. From the historical records available, it is sometimes difficult to know to what extent these other figures and movements put forward an explicitly millenarian vision invoking the arrival of the *dhammik* or the future Buddha (ideas that were not always well understood in French sources); but on the basis of the claims to invulnerability and religious potency they contain, I connect them with the broad rubric of nineteenth-century millenarianism.

94. Or "Assoa." Moura 1883, vol. 2, 151. Ind [1921] 1971, vol. 10, 27; Taboulet 1956, 646–648. He called himself Ang-phim, using the name of a grandson of King Ang-chan who had died in Bangkok.

95. Moura 1883, vol. 2, 151.

96. Leclère 1914, 465–467; Taboulet 1956, 666–667; Osborne 1969, 206–230.

97. Osborne 1969, 189. The urgency of the situation finally receded when Sivotha agreed to withdraw and seek ordination, and Nong's rebellion apparently died down of its own accord. The Cambodian chronicle claims that Sivotha ordained (Moura 1883, vol. 2, 184–185). Osborne gives a somewhat different account of Sivotha's life following the rebellion (1969, 225–227). For another account of the rebellion, see Collard 1925, 82–86.

98. He also claimed to be Ang-phim (see note 94) but was later discredited by rumors challenging the legitimacy of this claim. Leclère, c. 1900, NAC RSC F.65 b.542 5181.

99. Tauch 1994a, 13–22. The epic poem, composed by Ind during his government service under the Thai administration in Battambang, was translated by Hin Sithan, Carol Mortland, and Judy Ledgerwood. According to Tauch (personal communication, July 2000), no intact version of the poem survives. For excerpts in Khmer see Tauch 1994b, 28–37.

100. Keyes 1977, 291–300.

101. Ibid., 298.

102. This is not an exhaustive list of rebellions. For instance, Ind's reference to "evil persons . . . who incite poor people and forest people to raise up as an army" also lists the name of Āchāry Jrāṃ ([1921] 1971, vol. 10, 27), and Leclère refers to an "insurrection"

in Kratie in 1905 involving a former monk named Au-Bach, who distributed *"yant"* (*yantra;* religiously efficacious verses and syllables), protective amulets, and tattoos to an army of three hundred rebels "to render them invulnerable to bullets" (1908, 83–85).

103. Tauch 1994a, 20–21, and Ind [1921] 1971, vol. 10, 27.

104. A. Thompson 2004, 16–18.

105. Tambiah 1976, 179–199; C. Reynolds 1972, 34–62.

106. Chulalongkorn's reforms, as well as those initiated by his father, Mongkut, are well documented in scholarship on their reigns. See especially Wyatt 1969; C. Reynolds 1972; Tambiah 1976, 219–241.

107. Moura 1883, vol. 1, 179.

108. For example, see Collard 1925, 151.

109. It is not entirely clear whether Norodom himself was a co-instigator of this rebellion. Milton Osborne considers the evidence for this possibility inconclusive but compelling (1969, 212–227).

110. Leclère 1914, 465–467.

111. Khin 1991, 235. He transliterates *qanak* as *anak.*

112. Moura 1883, vol. 1, 329; Janneau 1914, 617–632; Aymonier [1900] 1984, 98–102; Taboulet 1956, 638.

113. Moura 1883, vol. 1, 178–180.

114. Collard 1921, 116; Taboulet 1956, 671.

115. Forest 1990, 337–357.

116. See Wyatt's discussion of similar reforms in Siam, introduced before the French promulgation of these measures in 1876 and 1884 in Cambodia (1969, 50–52).

117. This point is raised by Thanet 1998, 174–176.

118. As in the case of slavery, the opium monopoly was concurrently an issue of contention in Siam, where Chulalongkorn publicly condemned the evils of opium use but wrote that he was powerless to stem its use because of the large amount of revenue it provided for the state (Wyatt 1969, 50; McCoy 1991, 100–106).

119. As late as 1877, a French colonial report investigating opium use in Indochina suggests that among the majority of the population employed in agricultural work, the nonmedicinal use of opium was rare, with occasional smoking attributed to certain festivals (unspecified in the report). Report dated 5 October 1877, in Groeneveldt 1890, 52 (appendix 36).

120. For a discussion of the development of the opium franchise in Cambodia, see Descours-Gatin 1992, 21–22, 67–72.

121. Reddi 1970, 43–44; Descours-Gatin 1992, 81. There may also have been aspects of anti-Chinese sentiments in these actions, a response to social turmoil and discontent that emerged in later periods of dissatisfaction. For more on this suggestion, see Osborne 1978, 224n.

122. Groeneveldt 1890, 52 (appendix 36). Forest 1990, 215–216. Aware that most people couldn't afford opium, they initiated their new policy by lowering its price and forbidding the import of Indian hemp (hasheesh, probably what Ind refers to as *gañja*).

123. Descours-Gatin 1992, 223.

124. Chandler 2000, 149.

125. Doumer was governor-general of Indochina between 1897 and 1902 (Descours-Gatin 1992, 181–190).

126. McCoy 1991, 110–111.

127. In 1918, French Indochina had 1,512 opium dens and 3,098 retail shops; by 1930, it had 3,500 licensed opium dens, one for every 1,500 adult men (Descours-Gatin 1992, 209–222; Willoughby 1925, 109; McCoy 1991, 90, 111; League of Nations 1921–1938). Vociferous French writings on opium from Cambodia in the early twentieth century suggest that it was as contentious an issue internally as it was worldwide (Reddi 1970, 62–63; Collard 1925, 269–279; Ind [1921] 1971, vol. 8, 16–17).

128. Harvey 1990, 23.

129. On the Yukanthor affair, see Lamont 1989; Forest 1980, 65–68; Osborne 1969, 243–246. The memorandum, "Mémoire adressé par S.A.R. le Prince Héritier Iukanthor à Monsieur le Président du Conseil des Ministres et à les Membres du Gouvernement de la République Française," is reproduced in Lamont 1989, 228–234.

130. The article, "Deux Civilisations," *Le Figaro* 8 September 1900 is in Lamont 1989, 225–227. Yukanthor's concerns were championed by the French journalist Jean Hess, a critic of French colonialism.

131. Lamont 1989, 227.

132. Ibid., 226.

133. Ibid., 230.

134. Milton Osborne argues that the Khmer protests represent a "traditionalist" rather than "nationalist" stance, since national borders still had little meaning for most Khmer of this time (1969, 227–228).

135. Ibid., 221.

136. Edwards 1999, 120.

137. For details on how this system worked, see Osborne 1978, 218–220.

138. Chandler 2000, 155.

139. Ind [1921] 1971, vol. 2, 19.

140. Ibid., 42.

141. Ibid., 39.

142. K. *bālā.*

143. K. *lokiya.* Literally, "in the world."

144. *"raṅvipāk."* Pou notes the literal translation as "endurer la maturation de ses actes." Pou 1988, 332.

145. Ibid., 68, 323.

146. Ind [1921] 1971, vol. 2, 47–51.

147. Ibid., 14–15.

148. Ibid., vol. 8, 6–11.

149. Ibid., 9–10.

150. Salman 2001, 4–20.

151. Ind [1921] 1971, vol. 4, 50–54.

152. *gatidhamma.*

153. Ind [1921] 1971, vol. 4, 55–56.

154. See Edwards' discussion of Son Diep, a Francophile intellectual who earned numerous *medailles* for his contributions to Khmer intellectual life (1999, 139).

155. This translation is by Edwards (1999, 201). Her discussion includes a more detailed analysis of Ind's emotions at Angkor and more translated excerpts of the poem *Nirās Nagar Vatt.* See also Ind 1934a.

156. Ind [1921] 1971, vol. 5, 70–71.

157. Chandler 1982, 35–49.

CHAPTER THREE: *VINAYA* ILLUMINATIONS

1. Tambiah 1976, 5–6, 162–178, 198–199.

2. Ibid., 211–212.

3. K. *phlūv pratipatti kus trūv.* This phrase could be translated more literally as "paths of conduct according to what is right and wrong." *Kus trūv* carries the connotations of "moral right and wrong," as well as "true and false," "correct and incorrect." Huot Tath 1993, 8.

4. Ibid., 9. The translations included of Huot Tath 1993 are mine, but I am indebted to portions of Penny Edwards' translated version of this memoir in Edwards 1999, 395–407.

5. My analysis draws on my reading of approximately fifty monastic funeral biographies and memoirs of monks born between 1820 and 1910. Most of the biographies were written by close students or ordinands of the deceased monks and draw on the oral accounts and intimate knowledge that monks living in long and close proximity had of each others' lives. Coedès comments that funeral volumes were originated in Siam in 1904 by Chulalongkorn, in part to raise funds for the Vajirañāṇa National Library (1924, 10–11; see also Bee, Brown, and Chitakasem, 1989, 31). The funeral biographies surveyed in this chapter were generally composed in Cambodia in the 1930s or later, printed and distributed on the occasion of merit-making ceremonies in honor of the deceased monk. Most were found either in the NAC or NLC, where they were not yet catalogued when I used the collections (June–August 2000). I am grateful to the directors of both institutions for allowing me to examine unclassified materials.

6. LaCapra 1983, 30.

7. Ibid., 25.

8. On uses of the *Tipiṭaka* in Burma and Siam in this sense, see Tambiah 1976, 83–84, 183–188; on purification and order, see Hinton 2002, 71–77.

9. Moura writes about the secrecy in which the royal chronicles were maintained, suggesting that in his estimation, the kings had purposely let Khmer history be obscured so that the people would not realize the grandeur of their past and accuse the kings of bringing about such a momentous decline of their society (1883, vol. 1, 4–5).

10. Cabaton 1901, 1.

11. Translated by François Bizot from the Institut Bouddhique version of the *Chroniques royales* (1976, 7). The letter is referred to in Meas-Yang 1978, 38; *Dhammayuttipravatti {Dhammayut-nikāya},* "compiled from texts found in the library of Vatt Padumavatīrājavarārām [Vatt Bodum Vaddey]," 1960, NLC 920.71, hereafter *DP.* Khin Sok refers to a delegation sent by Ang Duong to request the return of Pān and a copy of the *Tipiṭak* (1991, 134).

12. Bizot 1992, 25–27.

13. Deliberation du Conseil des Ministres, 3 January 1922, NAC RSC R.91 b.908 10174. See note 82 in this chapter for further description of some of these texts.

14. Edwards 1999, 297.

15. "Karpelès to Finot, 9 Septembre 1927," AEFEO 23 K2, "Bibliothèque du Phnom Penh," no. 495; Finot 1927, 523.

16. Craig Reynolds has pointed out that in the Siamese context during the nine-

teenth century, the term (as it is also used in these sources) generally refers not simply to a monastery, but to a monastery school with students working under the direction of a particular monk-teacher (1972, 196).

17. *Jīvapravatti rapas' Braḥtej Braḥguṇ Jha-Lan nyṅ Sāradharm* [Biography of His Excellency Jha-Lan and the meaning of Dhamma], 1959, NAC 16 b.25, 4.

18. *Jīvapravatti nai Braḥtej Braḥguṇ Candavinay Gaṅ-O* [Biography of His Excellency Candavinay Gaṅ-O], 1954, NAC 16 b.25, 4.

19. The title of a fourth text is unclear. *Braḥ Suvaṇ ṇakesaro Hū-Ḷay nyṅ Pravatti Braḥ Sivījoto Iṅ Ḷuṅ* [Venerable Suvaṇṇakesaro Hū-Ḷāy and the life history of Venerable Sivījoto Iṅ Ḷuṅ], 1955, NLC 920.71, 5; hereafter *HLIL*.

20. *Akkharābhidhānabuddhappvattisankhep*, Ghyn-Ḍuc (Khum chief in Sdyṅ, Sruk Kragar, Bodhisat Province), 1959, NAC 16 b.25, vii.

21. Her gifts included the presentation, on one occasion, of twenty robes. *Jīvapravattisankhep nai upāsikā So-Suan"* [Biography of laywoman So-Suan], Suṅ-Sīv, 1960, NAC 16 b.27, 2–3; hereafter *JSS*.

22. Cabaton 1901, 1. The contents of another collection, amassed by EFEO scholars, is described in Finot? 1902, 387–400. Most of these were inscribed on palm-leaf or accordion-style *(krāṃṅ)* manuscripts; a few of the manuscripts had been composed on modern European-style paper and folded into books, referred to in the inventory as *siavphau* (400).

23. Groslier 1921, 7.

24. Finot to De Lamothe, 16 February 1903, NAC RSC R.91 b.1213 14615.

25. Coedès to Ministre de l'Instruction publique, 15 March 1915; Ministre de Guerre to Résident Supérieur, 20 April 1915; Ministre de l'Instruction publique to Résident Supérieur, 9 June 1915; Coedès to Résident Supérieur, 18 June 1915; *all in* NAC RSC R.91 b.798 9077.

26. Prakash 1999, 18–48; Burris 2001, 7–13, 45–49; Abe 1995, 64–69.

27. This attitude is evidenced, for instance, in a long-running court case in the 1920s documenting the ownership and removal of texts donated to Vatt Braḥ Buddh Nibbāṇ in the 1870s. Deliberation du Conseil des Ministres, 3 January 1922, NAC RSC R.91 b.908 10174.

28. Coedès to Résident Supérieur, 16 December 1912, AEFEO 23 K3, "Ecole de Pali, 09, 18," no. 1031.

29. Coedès 1912, 176.

30. See note 25.

31. Jacqueline Filliozat, personal communication. An undated inventory of the Pali manuscript collection at Vatt Bodhivāl, which may have been conducted as late as 1925, lists 180 Pali manuscripts, including three copies of the *Maṅgaladīpanī* and eighteen *jātaka* manuscripts (the largest group of titles). The inventory shows numerous copies of *Tipiṭaka* texts, commentaries, and subcommentaries, although it is impossible to ascertain from manuscript titles alone exactly what the manuscripts contain. AEFEO 37, "Inventaires," "Vat Po Val."

32. Coedès 1912, 177. Georges Maspero's characterizations of these collections are similar, although he may be relying on Coedès' reports rather than his own knowledge of the collections (1929, 297–307).

33. Coedès 1912, 177. Maspero concurs with this characterization of the importance and prevalence of these texts as "the most widely-known" texts of the period (1929, 298).

34. Pavie 1898a; Guesdon 1906; Maspero 1929, 297–305. According to Maspero, locally composed *jātaka* commonly included vernacular versions of the *Dāsajātaka* [Ten birth stories], *Paññāsa-jātaka* [Fifty birth stories], and the *Satra Rāchā Chāli,* a *jātaka* concerning the life of *Chāli* or *Jāli,* the son of Vessantar (1929, 298).

35. Tambiah 1976, 211; see also 212, 401, 405–406.

36. K. *citt.* See Introduction, note 11.

37. *Jīvapravatti nai Braḥtej Braḥguṇ Mās-Kaṅ* [Biography of His Excellency Venerable Mās-Kaṅ], Maen-Suy Saddhammappaññā Bhikkhu, 1961, NAC 16 b.27, 3, hereafter *JMK.*

38. Now more commonly known as Vatt Po. *JMK,* 3–6. On Vatt Jetabhan during this period, see Tambiah 1976, 205–207.

39. Wyatt 1969, 23–32; Tambiah 1976, 200–229; F. Reynolds 1976, 203–220; Keyes 1989, 39–42; Thongchai 1994, 37–61; Hallisey 1995, 48–49.

40. Tambiah 1976, 200–219, 230–233; C. Reynolds 1972, 63–137; Thongchai 1994, 39–40; Keyes 1989, 49–50; Kamala 1997, 5–7.

41. Tambiah 1976, 208–219; C. Reynolds 1972, 81–112; Griswold 1961, 23; Kamala 1997, 33–34.

42. C. Reynolds 1976, 214–216; Thongchai 1994, 41; Ivarsson 1995, 56–86.

43. Thongchai 1994, 39–40; C. Reynolds 1972, 129–132, 144. The same distinction between "worldly matters" and "religious matters" is evident in Ind's *gatilok* (worldly ways) and *gatidhamm* ("religious matters" or "ways of the Dhamma"), discussed in chapter 5.

44. C. Reynolds 1972, 129–132, and 1976, 216, 218–219. The terminology used in discussions of *Kitchanukit* by some historians comes to seem awkward since scholars of religion have generally regarded the *Trai Bhūm* as one of the primary expressions of Southeast Asian Buddhist ethical thinking (e.g., see Coedès 1957, 349–352). I concur with this perspective as well and do not intend to imply that the cosmological is not ethical.

45. C. Reynolds 1972, 35–62; Tambiah 1976, 179–199.

46. C. Reynolds 1972, 153–154, 235–267; Tambiah 1976, 183–195, 233–241; Keyes 1989, 50–61; Kamala 1997, 40–46; Wyatt 1969.

47. The dates 1824 and 1826 are given in different sources. Khin 1991, 271 (excerpt of a 1912 source) and *DP,* 11. Judging from his date of ordination, he was probably born in 1824 and ordained as a novice at the age of twelve, in 1836.

48. Jacob 1993, 131; Khin 1991, 270, quoting Flauguerges 1914, 182.

49. The *Pāṭimokkha* concerns the 227 precepts observed by monks. It was recited by monks at Uposatha, the holy days observed by Buddhists on the new moon, waxing quarter, full, and waning quarter of the moon days. The *Pāṭimokkha* is generally thought to be recited by Buddhist monks on the full and new moon Uposatha days, but at the end of the century, the Sangha inspection reports from the Siamese provinces suggest that the convention was not uniformly observed (C. Reynolds 1972, 259). Leclère records that the Uposatha days were observed by Khmer monks but that only the most educated monks understood the term; most monks referred to the days with the vernacular designation *thṅai sīl,* meaning "precept day," which suggests that Khmer monks probably recited the *Pāṭimokkha.* Leclère states that the day involved numerous "prayers," but does not specify which ones (1899, 382–383).

50. Jacob 1993, 36–37; Khin 1991, 269–270, quoting Flauguerges 1914, 175–182.

51. *Études Cambodgiennes* 1969, 16.

52. The monastic titles and ranks later shifted in meaning, apparently with the Sangha reorganizations that occurred in 1880 and 1918. One funeral biography refers to the redesignation of ranks in about 1920, which probably followed from the 1918 reforms. *Pravattirūp Braḥ Sab Braḥ Grū Gandhā Ujaysiladharm Braḥ Em-Cāp* [Cremation biography of Braḥ Grū Gandhā Ujaysiladharm Braḥ Em-Cāp], n.d., NLC 920.71, 4, hereafter *PEC.* For a list of more-recent monastic titles, see Chau-Seng 1962, 15–25.

53. Khin 1991, 269–270, quoting Flauguerges 1914, 175–182.

54. *DP,* 11; Khin 1991, 271, quoting from a 1912 source.

55. This appears unusual, as other biographies of monks born in the nineteenth century contained parental information, though these are all of a later origin and generally concern the lives of monks born in 1859 and later. *DP,* 12; Khin 1991 (quoting from 1912 source), 271.

56. Khin 1991 (quoting from 1912 source), 271.

57. Also transliterated as Vatt Boromnivas.

58. The two sources give somewhat different accounts of his studies. Khin 1991 (quoting from 1912 source), 271; *DP,* 13.

59. Mongkut was his *upajjhāy,* the monastic title designating one's primary spiritual teacher and preceptor, a senior monk who had to have been in robes for at least ten years; Sukh was *kammavācā,* a secondary level of preceptor; Koet served as *anussāvanācāry,* another presiding official at the ordination ceremony. (For a description of the ceremony and the functions of these officials, at least as it was celebrated by the beginning of the century in Siam, see Vajirañāṇavarorasa [1913] 1969, 6–8). Headley states that this latter title is the same rank as *grūsūtrchveṅ,* the *grūsūtr* of the left (1977, vol. 2, 1354). *Grūsūtr* is the designation found more commonly in funeral biographies. Craig Reynolds (1972, 6) comments that in nineteenth-century Siam, the relationship between the *upajjhāy* and student was normally one involving "strong bonds." In Cambodia later, the *upajjhāy* also fulfilled an administrative function as chief monk in charge of all ordinations in a *gaṇ,* "dioceses" (Leclère 1899, 392–393).

60. *DP,* 11, 13. A footnote in this source suggests that the sources used included "Burmese and Thai histories written in Thai letters" (10) and the Royal Chronicles of Kampuchea, composed during Norodom's reign (14). Khin, quoting from a 1912 source, gives the date as 1854 (1991, 271). Meas-Yang 1978, 38. The Khmer Dhammayut tradition may well prefer to attribute the founding of the sect to the reign of Ang Duong, considered a period of Buddhist piety and purification rather than the more troubled reign of Norodom. Osborne cites a "continuing oral tradition" of the founding of the sect in Ang Duong's reign (1969, 11). Most non-Khmer sources follow Leclère's attribution of the 1864 date (Leclère 1899, 403). *Études Cambodgiennes* 1969, 30; Forest 1980, 54; Keyes 1994, 48; Kiernan 1985, 3. Chau-Seng (1962, 8) cites 1864 as the date of the incorporation of the Dhammayut into the Khmer Sangha.

61. Vajirañāṇavarorasa [1913] 1969, xiv; *DP,* 13; Khin 1991 (quoting from a 1912 source), 271.

62. Vatt Padum Vatī, but I will follow the more common transcription as Vatt Bodum Vaddey.

63. *DP,* 16.

64. Khin 1991, 271, quoting from a 1912 source.

65. Leclère 1899, 523–524.

66. Khin 1991, 271, quoting from a 1912 source.

67. *DP,* 15.

68. Leclère 1899, 394; Forest 1980, 54–57.

69. "De la surveillance des bonzes au Cambodge," to Gouverneur Général, 2 April 1916, NAC RSC F. 94 b.908 10172; Bezançon 1992, 8–10.

70. *Cpāp', lpaeṅ.*

71. This is Coedès' translation of the term *tamrā* (1924, 28). Jacob (1993, 13) gives the translation as "manual, treatise," while defining *kpuon* as "technical treatise." My sense is that the two terms are used interchangeably in nineteenth- to early-twentieth-century Khmer literary contexts.

72. *Maraṇakathā jā dhammapaṇākār khandisakusal pragen Braḥtej Braḥguṇ Braḥ Mahābrahmamunī Deb-Ū* [Death-verses, being a Dhamma-offering of merit dedicated to His Excellency Braḥ Mahābrahmamunī Deb-Ū], 1960, NAC 16 b.6, 1–2, hereafter *MDU; Jīvapravatti Ukñā Suttantaprījācāry Mī-Nāṅ, Ācāry Vatt Uṇṇālom, Phnom Penh* [Biography of Ukñā Suttantaprījācāry Mī-Nāṅ, Ācāry at Vatt Uṇṇālom, Phnom Penh], 1965, NAC 16 b.28, 4; *Jīvapravatti nai Samtec Braḥ Maṅgaladebācāry Uttamapryksā Chāyā . . . "* [Biography of Samtec Braḥ Maṅgaladebācāry Uttamapryksā Chāyā . . .], 1958, NAC 16 b.25, 2, hereafter *JJ; PEC,* 1–2; *HLIL,* 1, 8. See also Tully 2002, 128.

73. *Therappavattisaṅkhep nyṅ Kantārakathā* [Abbreviated biography of a *thera,* and verses on a "difficult road"], 1961, NAC 16 b.27, vi, hereafter *TSK.*

74. Ibid., vi. The same distinction appears in other sources, probably reflecting the influences of modern Dhamma teachings introduced after 1914, which emphasized this pedagogical issue. See also *MDU,* 3.

75. From the approximately fifty sources I surveyed, this seems to have been a typical pattern. For example, see the accounts in *HLIL,* 8; *JJ,* 2–5.

76. *HLIL,* 2, 8.

77. *JJ,* 5.

78. *DP,* 15.

79. Ibid., 21–22.

80. *MDU,* 4.

81. Ibid., 3.

82. Most of these titles appear in other lists of texts used in monastic education in Cambodia (Deliberation du Conseil des Ministres, 3 January 1922, NAC RSC R.91 b.908 10174). Without reference to the texts, it is impossible to know for certain how closely they are related to the Pali texts that appear under these titles today. We can surmise that the first title refers to a Pali grammar, learned through the long-practiced means of rote memorization. The second two are most likely versions of the vernacular narrative commentaries on the *Dhammapada* and the *Maṅgala-sutta* that appeared widely in Siam and Cambodia during this period (Coedès 1912, 177). Khmer sources also refer to this latter text as *Maṅgalatthadīpanī.* The *Visuddhimagga* was probably a version of the Buddhist commentarial work composed in Sri Lanka in the fifth century CE by Buddhaghosa. *Sāratthasaṅgaha* is most likely a version of a text also known as *Sarasangaha,* noted by von Hinüber as an "encyclopaedic handbook for the use of monks" (von Hinüber 1996, 177; my thanks to Anne Blackburn for this suggestion). Another possibility is that it is a version of a text titled *Vajirasārattha Saṅgaha,* composed in Burma in 1535 (Coedès 1938a, 334). The last title may be a version of *Samantapāsādikā,* a Sri Lankan Pali commentary on

the *Vinaya,* which Craig Reynolds describes as a text used in Mon monasteries and known as *Paṭhamasamantadāsādikā Aṭṭhakathāvinaya* (1972, 179). Blackburn notes the title *Paṭhama Samantapāsādikādi Pañca Vinayaṭṭhakathā* among a list of manuscripts brought from Siam to Sri Lanka in 1756 (2001, 217).

83. C. Reynolds 1972, 178–180. Reynolds notes that Mon monasteries used a more heavily *Vinaya*-oriented curriculum, which influenced Vajirañāṇa in his selection of the new curriculum.

84. *MDU,* 3.

85. Chandler notes that between 1900 and 1930, using corvée labor, the colonial administration constructed nine thousand kilometers of new roads. Rail service between Phnom Penh and Battambang was completed between 1928 and 1932 (2000, 160); Tully 2002, 144.

86. He became head of the Dhammayut order in 1906, supreme patriarch in 1910. Dhammasuddho 1972, 14–20.

87. The sources use *Dhamma-vinay* and *Dharm-vinay* interchangeably. For the case of non-Khmer readers, I have standardized the references as *Dhamma-vinay.*

88. *MDU,* 2–7.

89. *MDU,* 3.

90. In a later "catechism" prepared under Chuon Nath's supervision for use at Vatt Uṇṇālom, *"Dhamma-vinaya"* was defined as the division of the *Tipiṭaka* into two parts, *"Dhamma"* referring to the *Suttantapiṭaka* and *Abhidhammapiṭaka* and *"Vinaya"* to the *Vinayapiṭaka* (Dhan' Vān' 1951, 23).

91. Huot Tath 1993, 8.

92. *MDU,* 10.

93. *DP,* 2–3. The text was published in 1960 but copied from palm-leaf manuscripts composed earlier in the century.

94. Ibid., 3.

95. Ibid., 5.

96. *Iriyāpatha.*

97. Bhūj braḥ ariya maen.

98. *pratipatti.*

99. *DP,* 5.

100. Vajirañāṇavarorasa, 1973, vol. 2, 11–27.

101. Somdet Phra Mahā Samaṇa Chao Krom Phrayā Vajirañāṇavarorasa.

102. Ibid., 19–20.

103. Meas-Yang 1978, 37; C. Reynolds 1972, 63–112.

104. *DP,* 7; Meas-Yang 1978, 38; C. Reynolds 1972, 82–83.

105. C. Reynolds 1972, 64–112.

106. Ibid., 185–186, 192.

107. His biography does not offer an explanation of this method.

108. Craig Reynolds suggests that Mongkut taught beginning students Pali at Vatt Pavaranivesa with reference to the *Maṅgaladīpanī* while more-advanced Pali students worked with additional commentaries (1972, 185n47).

109. Ibid., 6.

110. *JMK,* 3.

111. Ibid., 6.

112. Ibid., 10.

113. Coedès 1924, 34; Tambiah 1976, 211–212.

114. Bee, Brown, and Chitakasem, 1989, 30. The library was founded in 1882, in memory of Mongkut, whose monastic name was Vajirañāṇa. It was later expanded and reopened as the Vajirañāṇa National Library, in 1904 (Coedès 1924, 3–6).

115. Tambiah 1976, 225, 468.

116. C. Reynolds 1972, 134.

117. Jory 2002, 893–896.

118. Wibha 1975, 30–44.

119. Ind [1921] 1971, vol. 1, 16.

120. Ibid.

121. Burris 2001, xvi; Hansen 1999, 16; on the further development of the word *jāti,* see Edwards 1999, 253–255; Thongchai 1994, 134–135. On the growing complexity of this word in Khmer usage, see Tandart 1935, 807–808. This dictionary was originally researched and written at the beginning of the twentieth century by Tandart working together with Ind, and was originally published as Tandart 1910.

122. Ind [1921] 1971, vol. 3, 41.

123. Ibid., 37–39.

124. Ibid., 39–43.

125. Leclère 1899, 403–404. Leclère also states that not all Dhammayut monks wore their robes in the reformed style, since some had been monks before Pān's return to Cambodia. He suggests that Pān did not impose the reforms on all of the monasteries under his control (1899, 402–403).

126. Leclère's observations are often valuable because of his reliance on interviews and conversations with monks (including the two Sangha heads) for his insights.

127. This is a lengthy report on the history and contemporary (1937) state of the Buddhist Sangha in Cambodia. Minister of the Interior K. Chea, 28 June 1937, NAC RSC F.942 b.2791 23609, hereafter Chea, 28 June 1937; "Plainte anonyme," 1909, NAC RSC F.941 b.850 9581. This insight is also gained from my larger survey of monastic biographies.

128. "De la surveillance des bonzes au Cambodge" to Gouverneur Général, 2 April 1916, NAC RSC F. 94 b.908 10172.

129. Minister of the Interior K. Chea, 2 July 1937, NAC RSC F. 942 b.2791 23609, hereafter Chea, 2 July 1937.

130. *Études Cambodgiennes* 1969, 16.

131. Following the traditional administrative pattern, the *gaṇ* were designated as either "right" or "left," with the slightly elevated "right" under the control of Samtec Braḥ Sangharāj Diaṅ, while the "left" was under the control of Samtec Braḥ Sugandhādhipatī Pān (Leclère 1899, 391–392); Forest gives the rank as *upajjhā* (1980, 55); Chea, 28 June 1937. On historically changing usages of the term *gaṇ* in Siam, see C. Reynolds 1972, 10–12.

132. "De la surveillance des bonzes au Cambodge" to Gouverneur Général, 2 April 1916, NAC RSC F. 94 b.908 10172; Chea, 28 June 1937.

133. Chea, 28 June 1937; King Norodom to Council of Ministers, 14 June 1901, NAC RSC F.94 b.850 9562; Leclère 1899, 391–393; Forest 1980, 55.

134. Résident Supérieur to Council of Ministers, 1901; Resident of Kompong Speu to Résident Supérieur, 6 April 1901; Monks in all the pagodas in the province of Kompong

Speu to Samtec Sangharāj Diaṅ, 21 April 1901; Samtec Sangharāj Diaṅ to Résident Supérieur, 22 April 1901; King Norodom to Council of Ministers, 6 June 1901; King Norodom to Council of Ministers, 14 June 1901; *all in* NAC RSC F.94 b.850 9562.

135. Royal Ordinance No. 46 of 25 July 1919; Chea, 28 June 1937; Forest 1980, 147–150.

136. Forest 1980, 54, 56; Leclère 1899, 393.

137. "Plainte anonyme," 1909, NAC RSC F.941 b.850 9581; Chea, 28 June 1937.

138. "Plainte anonyme," 1909, NAC RSC F.941 b.850 9581.

139. Ind [1921] 1971, vol. 8, 63.

140. Ibid., 61–63.

141. Chea, 28 June 1937.

142. Ibid., and 2 July 1937.

143. *JMK,* 10.

144. Ibid., 1.

145. Ibid., 14.

146. Ibid., 14–18. On the Siamese robes controversy, see C. Reynolds 1972, 97–101, 104–105.

147. Huot Tath 1993, 3–31; Minister of the Interior to Résident Supérieur, 7 February 1919, NAC RSC F.94 b.903 10129.

148. Governor of Kompong Siem to Resident of Kompong Cham, 15 January 1919; Minister of the Interior to Résident Supérieur, 7 February 1919; *both in* NAC RSC F.94 b.903 10129.

149. Chea, 28 June 1937.

150. *TSK,* vii.

151. Braḥ Sumaṅgalasīlācāry Dit-Dym, an abbot and *megaṇ* in Siem Reap (1888–1961), studied at the Pali School in Angkor from 1910 to 1913. *Jīvapravatti Braḥ Sumaṅgalasīlācāry Dit-Dym, Megaṇ Vatt Ṭaṃṇāk, Khett Siam Rāp* [Biography of Braḥ Sumaṅgalasīlācāry Dit-Dym, Megaṇ from Vatt Ṭaṃṇāk, Siem Reap Province], 1962(?), NAC 16 b.28, 9–10. Ukñā Suttantaprījācāry Mī-Nāṅ, born in 1889, was among the first group of students admitted to the École de Pali in Phnom Penh, where he studied from 1914 to 1917. A slightly older generation included Braḥ Ū-Cev and Braḥ Bum-Jā, born in 1906 and 1910 respectively. Both of these monks studied with the modernist monk Samtec Braḥ Dhammalikhit Lvī-Em at Vatt Lanka in Phnom Penh as novices, and later were admitted to the École Supérieure de Pali (the name of the École de Pali was changed in 1918). Their biographies make clear that even in the 1920s, the kind of monastic education offered there was still rare and difficult to obtain in Cambodia. *Jīvapravatti Ukñā Suttantaprījācāry Mī-Nāṅ, Ācāry Vatt Uṇṇālom* [Biography of Ukñā Suttantaprījācāry Mī-Nāṅ, Ācāry at Vatt Uṇṇālom], 1965, NAC 16 b.28, 11–15; *Jīvitakathā nyṅ Sinnasīd knuṅ Gambhīr Lokanay* [Biography and extract of the *Lokanay* scripture], 1959, NAC 16, i–iii; *Jīvapravatti Braḥ Dhammavinay Bum-Jā* [Biography of Braḥ Dhammavinay Bum-Jā], Bhikkhu Sya-Sāman, n.d., NAC 16 b.25, 3–5.

152. BI 1970, 1–4.

153. Huot Tath 1993, 3–5.

154. Ibid., 8.

155. French surveillance reports indicate that Uk was a controversial choice within the Sangha because "the majority of dignitaries [within the Sangha]" did not respect him, but

that Sisowath had pushed for his appointment. Gouverneur Générale, "Etat d'esprit des bonzes Mohanikays du Cambodge," 1916, NAC RSC F.94 b.908 10172 (hereafter "Etat d'esprit des bonzes," 1916); Conseil des Ministres, "Au sujet de l'affaire du bonze Chakeyvong Khuon," 18 April 1917, NAC RSC F. 94 b.903 10126. See also Huot Tath 1993, 8.

156. Huot Tath 1993, 8.

157. Ibid., 9.

158. Ibid., 9–11.

159. Blackburn 1999, 283–284.

160. Huot Tath 1927, 7. See also Chuon Nath 1935, 50–51.

161. Huot Tath 1993, 11–13; *JSS*, 3; Chea, 28 June 1937 and 2 July 1937. Huot Tath states that Chuon Nath later observed that this terminology was unfortunate, as it gave the erroneous impression that there could be more than one Dhamma (1993, 13).

162. These phrases could be translated less literally (i.e., "they were delighted by this knowledge"), but I am emphasizing the pathway of "hearts and minds" conveyed in the Khmer as Huot Tath's explanation for the rise of modern Buddhism.

163. *Phlūv pratipatti.* Huot Tath 1993, 14–15.

164. Gouverneur Générale, "Etat d'esprit des bonzes," 1916. The perception of the importance of the *vipassana-dhura* in the traditional Khmer Buddhism of the late nineteenth and early twentieth centuries is noted in Chea, 28 June 1937.

165. A French surveillance report from 1916 refers to "internal anarchy" within the Mahānikāy, especially at Vatt Uṇṇālom. Gouverneur Générale, "Etat d'esprit des bonzes," 1916.

166. Huot Tath 1993, 15–19; Edwards 1999, 397–399. Several other issues concerning modernist interpretations of monastic practice were also at issue.

167. K. *sāstrātrýmtrūv.* Huot Tath 1993, 15.

168. Ibid., 17.

169. Ibid., 18.

170. Ibid.

171. Sisowath, "No. 7 . . . Ordonnance Royale," 2 October 1918, NAC RSC F.942 b.2791 23609.

172. Ibid.

173. Ibid.

174. Huot Tath 1993, 23.

175. Ibid., 23–24.

176. Ibid., 51–53; Nepote and Khing Hoc Dy 1981, 63.

177. See note 49 in this chapter.

178. Huot Tath 1993, 31.

179. Ibid., 8–9.

180. Chea, 28 June 1937 and 2 July 1937.

181. Chea, 28 June 1937.

182. Ibid.

183. Chea 28 June 1937 and 2 July 1937.

CHAPTER FOUR: COLONIAL COLLUSIONS

1. "Note sur l'Institut bouddhique au Cambodge: son organization, son action, des difficultés qu'il rencontre ou suscite," 1934–1937, NAC RSC F.942 b.2791 23609. This

undated report was apparently compiled between 1934 and 1937. Probably written for intelligence purposes, the report lays out the history of the Buddhist institutions, beginning with the establishment of the Pali School in 1914, in order to give the background for current tensions surrounding the influence of the Buddhist Institute.

2. Huot Tath 1993, 13.

3. Hallisey 1995, 33.

4. Ibid., 34–49.

5. Tully 2002, 202.

6. Ibid., 237. Baudoin was not the résident supérieur continuously during this period; Georges Maspero and Hector Létang each served briefly in the post, presumably while Baudoin was occupied elsewhere temporarily, between October 1920 and February 1921 (Tully 1996, 315).

7. Blackburn 2001, 94–95; C. Reynolds 1972, 8. While my attention here is given primarily to the development of modern Buddhism in relation to the *gantha-dhura,* I am not suggesting that other aspects of Buddhist practice are unimportant or unconnected to the scholarly tradition, but rather that they are beyond the scope of this study. Spirit ceremonies, mediumship, traditional healing, ancestor worship, astrology, numerology, and meditation practices merit further historical attention.

8. Forest 1980, 35–45. Spirit practices and other aspects of ritual life (as they developed later in the twentieth century) were documented by the Commission des Moeurs et Coutumes du Cambodge (i.e., [1958] 1985) and examined in the work of Eveline Porée-Maspero (1962), May Ebihara (1968), Ang Choulean (1986), and Alain Forest (1992). Kamala Tiyavanich's (1997) recent study examines the meditation practices and cross-border wanderings of forest monks through northern Thailand, Cambodia, Laos, and Burma at the beginning of the twentieth century, and François Bizot's work (1981, 1992) illumines the kind of Tantric meditation texts and rituals that were likely to have been more widely observed during the nineteenth and early twentieth centuries before the modernist school of Buddhism became prominent. Khin Sok (1982) examines *yant* or *yantra* (religiously efficacious verses and syllables).

9. Governor of Thbanng Khmum (Kompong Cham) to Council of Ministers, 2 February 1907, NAC RSC F.94 b.850 9565.

10. Jory 2002, 910–913; Ishii 1986, 171–185; C. Reynolds 1972, 235–267. By the end of the nineteenth century, Chulalongkorn had already introduced a measure prohibiting monks from the convention of beginning sermons by proclaiming the number of years until the projected demise of the Dhamma predicted in Buddhist texts. The new editions of the *Paṭhamasambodhi* (the Siamese-authored biography of the Buddha discussed in chapter 1) introduced in the 1890s and 1904 also seemed intent upon further disavowing these cosmological predictions (C. Reynolds 1972, 134–136).

11. For example, see a report filed by Leclère c. 1900 on the history of the 1885–1887 rebellion in Kampot, in which he highlights and details claims of invulnerability made in the course of the rebellion. NAC RSC F.65 b.542 5181.

12. M. J. Tripier, Chargé d'Affaires de France au Siam to Gouverneur Générale de l'Indochine, 14 August 1914, NAC RSC F.65 b.898 10063.

13. Ibid.; Tai 1983, 72; Marr 1971, 228–229.

14. "Intelligence furnished by the military authority" to Résident Supérieur, 7 November 1914, NAC RSC F.65 b.898 10063. See also Tully 2002, 148–151.

15. "Intelligence furnished by the military authority" to Résident Supérieur, 7 November 1914, NAC RSC F.65 b.898 10063.

16. Tai 1983, 63–76.

17. Ibid., 64, 66, 70–71.

18. Ibid., 69–70, 73; Marr 1971, 221–223, 230–231.

19. Marr 1971, 143–144.

20. Tully 2002, 160, 165, 171.

21. Tully 2002, 181–182; Balat du Poste de Komchanea (Prey Veng) to Gouverneur de Prey Veng, 5 March 1916, NAC RSC F.941 b.1362 16064.

22. Royal Ordinance no. 21 of 18 March 1916. Ministre de l'Intérieur et du Culte to Gouverneurs, 1916, NAC RSC F.941 b.1362 16064.

23. "De la surveillance des bonzes au Cambodge" to Gouverneur Générale, 2 April 1916, NAC RSC F.94 b.908 10172, hereafter "Surveillance des bonzes," 2 April 1916; Tully 2002, 169, 181. Fears of Cochinchinese monks in Cambodia and Khmer monks in Cochinchina surface even earlier. For instance, in 1909, three Cochinchinese monks who had returned from Bangkok were discovered at Vatt Uṇṇālom and charged with avoiding military conscription in Cochinchina; in 1914, two Khmer monks were arrested for crossing into Cochinchina without passports, and "a large number" of Cochinchinese monks without identity papers were discovered in Battambang, waiting to depart for Bangkok. Samtec Sangharāj Diaṅ to 2eme Bureau, 30 September 1909, NAC RSC F.94 b.850 9581; Dovoine, Chef du 1er Bureau, Administrateur de Longxuyen to Gouverneur de la Cochinchine, 26 February 1914, NAC RSC F.94 b.908 10172; Administrateur des Services Civils to Résident Supérieur, 27 January 1914, NAC RSC F.94 b.908 10172.

24. Chief of Dhammayut Order to all Heads of Dioceses and Pagodas in all provinces of Cambodia, 28 February 1916; Governor of Peareang to Minister of the Interior, 29 February 1916; Minister of the Interior to Résident Supérieur, 22 May 1916; *all in* NAC RSC F.94 b.903 10126. Balat of Kum Chaumea (Prey Veng) to Governor of Prey Veng, 5 March 1916, NAC RSC F.941 b.1362 16064.

25. Chief of Dhammayut Order to all Heads of Dioceses and Pagodas in all provinces of Cambodia, 28 February 1916, NAC RSC F.94 b.903 10126.

26. Chief of Dhammayut Order to Minister of the Interior, 20 February 1916, NAC RSC F.94 b.903 10126.

27. Royal Ordinance no. 21 of 18 March 1916. See note 22.

28. "Surveillance des bonzes," 2 April 1916. See also Yang 1987, 23–24.

29. The custom was followed in Siam as well. C. Reynolds 1972, x.

30. Chea, 28 June 1937 (see note 127 in chapter 3); Leclère 1899, 410–411.

31. Chea, 28 June 1937.

32. *JMK,* 3 (see note 37 in chapter 3); Résident Supérieur to Résidents, 10 November 1915, NAC RSC F.65 b.898 10063; Tully 2002, 181.

33. Résident Battambang to Résident Supérieur, 30 January 1916, NAC RSC F.94 b.908 10173; Tully 2002, 182.

34. Marr 1971, 106, 111–112, 114–119, 149–152.

35. Résident Supérieur to Ministre de France, Bangkok, 7 April 1916, NAC F.94 b.908 10172. These fears also evoke nineteenth-century French cultural perceptions that metaphorically linked germ theory, "contagion," and "immigration," a linkage I will discuss below.

36. My survey of funeral biographies indicates that monks educated in Siam often rose to positions as teachers and dignitaries in Phnom Penh monasteries or as provincial-level abbots and officials.

37. C. Reynolds 1972, 235; Ishii 1986, 69–72.

38. Royal ordinance of 29 October 1907; "Surveillance des bonzes," 2 April 1916.

39. In the first half of 1908, twenty-four monks and novices, all from Phnom Penh, were granted official permission to travel to Bangkok for study; twelve were from Vatt Uṇṇālom, seven from Vatt Sarāvoṅ, and five from Vatt Koh (Samtec Sangharāj Diaṅ to Résident Supérieur, 23 March 1908, 13 April 1908, 21 May 1908, 23 May 1908, 28 May 1908, 28 May 1908, 6 June 1908; Braḥ Saghatīkārabraḥ Tambhīthaer to Résident Supérieur, [illegible] 1908; Braḥ Vinaithaer to Résident Supérieur, 17 June 1908; Braḥ Truv Dhammsārīvuṅs to Résident Supérieur, 2 June 1908; *all in* NAC RSC F.94 b.850 9576). Even if four times this number found their way into Siam, legally and illegally during 1908, this was still a tiny percentage of the total population of approximately 1,500,000 inhabitants, signaling French fears of the prominent influence of this tiny segment of the population. The total population of Cambodia in 1903 was estimated to be 1,190,000. According to 1911 figures, the population had grown to 1,684,000, the majority of whom (1,360,000) were ethnic Khmer (Forest 1980, 182).

40. Royal Ordinance of 18 March 1916. Résident Supérieur to Residents, 10 November 1915, NAC RSC F.65 b.898 10063; "Surveillance des bonzes," 2 April 1916; Gouverneur Générale, "Etat d'esprit des bonzes," 1916 (see note 155 in chapter 3).

41. Novices were required to carry a similar identity card, known as a *saṅghaṭīkā*. Chea, 28 June 1937; "Surveillance des bonzes," 2 April 1916; Forest 1980, 146–147; Tully 2002, 181.

42. "Surveillance des bonzes," 2 April 1916.

43. Ibid.

44. Résident Supérieur to Résidents, Chefs de Circonscription au Cambodge, 10 November 1915, NAC RSC F.65 b.898 10063.

45. Résident Battambang to Résident Supérieur, 30 January 1916, NAC RSC F.94 b.908 10173.

46. Samdach Mongkol Tépéachar and Préa Thom Likhet (Chiefs of the Dhammayut and Mahānikāy orders) to Heads of dioceses . . . , 1916, NAC RSC F.941 b.1362 16064.

47. Similar cases are recounted in Ind [1921] 1971, vol. 1, 67–103; vol. 2, 22–40.

48. Samdach Mongkol Tépéachar and Préa Thom Likhet (Chiefs of the Dhammayut and Mahānikāy orders) to Heads of dioceses . . . , 1916, NAC RSC F.941 b.1362 16064.

49. Louis Finot (?) and M. Sylvain Levi to the Résident Supérieur, 21 December 1922, AEFEO 23 K3, "École de Pali, 1922–29."

50. Kiernan 1985, 7.

51. Chandler 2000, 161; Tai 1983, 84–86.

52. Khy 1975, 316–321; Tai 1983, 84–86; Kiernan 1985, 5–6; Tully 2002, 202–203, 293.

53. Edwards 1999, 318–322.

54. Kiernan 1985, 4–6; Tully 2002, 203.

55. Chief of Dhammayut Order to Minister of the Interior, 20 February 1916, NAC RSC F.94 b.903 10126.

56. Edwards 1999, 319.

57. Tully 2002, 237.

58. Aisenberg 1999, 71–112, 119–123, 131, 175–180.

59. My thanks to Daniel Sherman for pointing me toward this analysis.

60. Gouverneur Générale, "Etat d'esprit des bonzes," 1916; "Surveillance des bonzes," 2 April 1916; Conseil des Ministres, "Au sujet de l'affaire du bonze Chakeyvong Khuon," 18 April 1917, NAC RSC F.94 b.903 10126.

61. "Note sur l'Institut Bouddhique au Cambodge, son organization, son action, des difficultés qu'il rencontre ou suscite," 1934–1937, NAC RSC F.942 b.2791 23609.

62. Tully 2002, 215–228; Osborne 1969, 33–56.

63. Gombrich and Obeyesekere 1988, 202–224; King 1999, 150–152; Queen and King 1996, 20–29; Tambiah 1992, 5–7; Bond [1988] 1992, 45–67; Malalgoda 1976, 191–255, 260–262.

64. Chandler 1991, 6.

65. Moura 1883, vol. 1, 303, 315–316; Leclère 1899, xi–xiii.

66. Collard 1921, 138.

67. Ibid., 30.

68. Moura 1883, vol. 1, 200.

69. Excerpted from a *circulaire* by Albert Sarraut, the governor-general of Indochina, announcing his 1918 native education reforms. Sarraut 1918, 338.

70. Leclère 1899, 195–202.

71. Ibid., 198.

72. Drawn from the *Trai Bhūm.*

73. Ibid., 196–197.

74. Ibid., 199–200.

75. Ibid., 202.

76. Ibid., xiv.

77. Leclère 1899, xi–xiii; Hallisey 1995, 45–46.

78. Bradley 2000, 47–59; Tai 1992, 20–21.

79. Groslier 1918, 547. See also Muan 2001, 18–24.

80. Magnant 1913, 466.

81. Ibid., 464, 466.

82. Conseil de perfectionnement de l'enseignement indigene.

83. The council included Minister of the Palace Thiounn and Minister of War Ponn, whose central roles in Khmer government and society as modern intellectuals are discussed in Edwards 1999, 118–121, 128–129, 135–139.

84. "Notes sur les ecoles de pagodes (1905–1913)," 1905–1913, NAC RSC F.941 b.530 5101, hereafter "Notes sur les ecoles," 1905–1913.

85. In Siam, efforts at expanding the power and reach of the Inspection Bureau in the Department of Education were implemented in 1898. Monastery inspections were added in 1902. Wyatt 1969, 181, 285–286, 303–308.

86. "Notes sur les ecoles," 1905–1913.

87. Ibid.

88. Between 1911 and 1914, under Ernest Outrey, the administration sponsored a contest for the composition of a moral primer, awarding a monetary prize to the winners. Reportedly, more than three hundred monks and other Khmer literati submitted manuscripts. A commission appointed by Outrey to judge the entries awarded the prize to Min-

ister Ponn, and his text was subsequently printed for distribution in schools. Ponn, Ministre de l'Instruction publique, to Résident Supérieur, 5 October 1926, AEFEO 34 II. The title of Ponn's primer is transliterated in documents as *"Thomakreteya,"* probably *"Dhamma-krity,"* meaning "moral actions" or "moral obligations according to the Dhamma." Edwards makes note of an earlier (1905) report that recommended printing *cpāp'* (1999, 279). I have not located any evidence that this plan was ever carried out during this period.

89. "Notes sur les ecoles," 1905–1913.

90. Ibid.

91. Ibid.

92. Ibid.

93. Keyes 1983, 181; Collins 1990, 103, 117; Obeyesekere 1991, 229–234; Strong 1992, xi; Lopez 1995, 2–13; Hallisey 1995, 34–38; King 1999, 100–106, 143–155.

94. C. Rhys Davids [1929] 1989, xviii–xix.

95. Rice 1924, 5.

96. For a fuller discussion of Rhys Davids' attitudes toward *jātaka* texts, see Jory 2002, 899–905.

97. T. Rhys Davids 1925, lxxviii–lxxix.

98. Edwards 1999, 300.

99. Goloubew 1935, 515; Edwards 1999, 184–185.

100. Ibid., 538.

101. Coedès 1935, 511.

102. Goloubew 1935, 516–532, 537.

103. Ibid., 528.

104. Huot Tath 1993, 49–50.

105. Goloubew 1935, 523.

106. Nugent 1996, 6–8; Coedès 1924.

107. Nugent 1996, 8; personal communication from Jacqueline Filliozat, November 1996, Paris.

108. Coedès 1938b, 315.

109. Ibid., 317.

110. Filliozat 1969, 1–2.

111. Baudoin to Gouverneur Générale, 22 January 1925, AEFEO 23 K2, "Bibliothèque Royale du Phnom Penh, 1925–1927."

112. Chandler 2000, 163; Edwards 1999, 303. See also Keyes 1994, 49.

113. Edwards 1999, 301.

114. EFEO correspondence reveals that Coedès himself had to write and ask for her intercession on his behalf to obtain copies of texts that monks were reluctant to let him see (Coedès to Karpelès, 6 October 1934, 20 January 1927, 6 October 1937, AEFEO 23 K2, "Bibliothèque Royale du Phnom Penh, 1934–1943"). Karpelès was also unusual among this group in that she considered herself a Buddhist (David Chandler, personal correspondence, August 2003). Karpelès was not universally admired, however, a point that Edwards has documented (1999, 314–315). Karpelès remained at the Buddhist Institute until 1941, when she was forced to leave, under the Vichy regime, because of her Jewish background. She made her way to the French colony Pondichéry and spent the remainder of her career connected with the ashram of the Hindu yogi Sri Aurobindo (Filliozat 1969, 2–3; Edwards

1999, 300–308). I am grateful for insight into Karpelès' life from Jacqueline Filliozat, who knew her, and from Penny Edwards, who has recently begun work on her biography.

115. Goloubew 1935, 523; Lvī-Em, Uṃ-Sūr, and Ḷuṅ, 1961, vol. 1, 1.

116. Wibha 1975, 30–44; Jory 2002, 891–913. The first collections of oral folk tales in Cambodia were made by Aymonier (1878) and Pavie (1898b and 1903), published in Saigon and Paris respectively. According to Edwards, Thiounn collaborated with Pavie on the 1903 collection. His further work on folklore and a *jātaka* was published in *Kambujasuriyā* in 1927 (1999, 105, 120, 136).

117. Finot, "Observations sur le projet de reorganization de l'École de Pali," 1922(?), AEFEO 23 K3, "École Supérieure de Pali, 1922–1937." This exchange between Thoṅ and Finot about "national literature" is the earliest reference to the term that I found in French; it is used regularly in Royal Library and Sālā Pali correspondence in the 1920s. Chigas traces the earliest published use of the Khmer word *aksar satr,* "literature," to a 1939 novel by Kim Hak, published in *Kambujasuriyā* in 1939 (2000, 138).

118. Lvī-Em, Uṃ-Sūr, and Ḷuṅ, 1961, vol. 1, 1–3.

119. Karpelès, "Assemblée Générale du 22 juillet 1930, Phnom Penh . . . ," AEFEO 23 K2, "Bibliothèque royale du Phnom Penh, 1925–."

120. In Khmer, *Qaṃbībraḥbuddhsāsana* [Concerning Buddhism], [1926] 1964. The original manuscript must have been written in or before 1925. A first Khmer translation appeared in *Kambujasuriyā* in 1926; it was corrected and republished in 1928.

121. Strong 1983, 19–20.

122. Finot [1926] 1964, 88.

123. Finot [1926] 1964.

124. Also transliterated as "Choum-Mau."

125. Karpelès to Finot, 12 September 1925, AEFEO 23 K2, "Bibliothèque Royale du Phnom Penh, 1925–1927"; Finot [1926] 1964, 19.

126. Finot [1926] 1964, 19–21.

127. Karpelès, "Rapport Annuel sur le fonctionnement de la Bibliothèque Royale du 1er Juin 1927 au 1er Juin 1928," AEFEO 23 K2, "Bibliothèque royale du Phnom Penh, 1925–." The same Khmer translation was also published by A. Portail in 1929; the book was translated into Lao and printed in Ventiane in 1932 (Goloubew 1935, 550).

128. Report, Saint-Mlieux, 2eme Bureau, to Résident Supérieur, 5 December 1925, AEFEO 23 K3, "École de Pali"; Louis Finot (?) and Sylvain Levi to Résident Supérieur, 21 December 1922, AEFEO 23 K3, "École de Pali, 1922–1929." Handwritten draft of document titled "Observations sur le projet de reorganisation de l'École de Pali," 1923; Braḥ Mahā Vimaladhamma, "Rapport annuel de l'École Supérieure de Pali à Monsieur l'Administrateur chef du 2eme Bureau de la Résidence Supérieure au Cambodge, Phnom Penh," 27 February 1926; *both in* AEFEO 23 K3, "École de Pali, 1922–1937.

129. Tully 1996, 80–112.

130. Norindr 1996, 17–21, 25–28; Edwards 1999, 141–154, 162–195.

131. Royal Ordinance no. 45 of 13 August 1909.

132. Inspecteur des services civils, Commissaire délégué . . . pour le territoire de Battambang to Résident Supérieur, 26 April 1909, NAC RSC R.57 b.671 7779.

133. Royal Ordinance no. 54, King Sisowath, 13 August 1909, NAC RSC R.57 b.671 7779, hereafter Sisowath, 13 August 1909; Luce 1909, 823–824; royal ordinance of 13 August 1909, AEFEO 23 K3, "École de Pali, 1909–1918."

134. Sisowath, 13 August 1909.

135. Inspecteur des services civils, Commissaire délégué . . . pour le territoire de Battambang to Résident Supérieur, 26 April 1909, NAC RSC R.57 b.671 7779; Directeur de l'École de Pali to Commissaire Délégué du Résident Supérieur à Battambang, 18 August 1910, NAC RSC R.57 b.671 7779.

136. See note 82 in chapter 3.

137. Sisowath, 13 August 1909; Luce 1909, 823–824.

138. C. Reynolds 1972, 192–200; Sisowath, 13 August 1909. A different policy was implemented in 1922 as part of the royal ordinance of 14 February 1922, which reserved administrative posts for clergy graduates of the school; it was revoked in the Sangha reforms of 1928 (Edwards 1999, 297–298, 310).

139. Sisowath, 13 August 1909; Luce 1909, 823–824.

140. Transliterated in correspondence as Préa Buthvong Mey.

141. Prea Pouthavong, Directeur de l'Ensignement à Angkor to Commissaire Délégue à Battambang, 10 February 1910, NAC RSC R.57 b.671 7779.

142. Commissaire Délégué du Résident Supérieur to Président de la Société d'Angkor, 23 May 1910, NAC RSC R.57 b.671 7779.

143. Ordonnance royale no. 29, H. M. Sisowath, 26 June 1911; Résident Supérieur to Commissaire Délégué, Battambang, 21 June 1911; *both in* NAC RSC R.57 b.671 7779. Maigre à Gouverneur Générale, 24 November 1919, AEFEO 23 K3, "École de Pali, 1910, 1922–1929"; Paul Luce à Gouverneur Générale de l'Indochine, 27 January 1911," AEFEO 23 K3, "École de Pali, 1909–1918."

144. George Coedès to Résident Supérieur, 16 December 1912 [found in an addendum to "Director EFEO to Gouverneur Générale, 28 December 1912"], AEFEO 23 K3, "École de Pali, 1909–1918."

145. Ibid.

146. Royal ordinance of 24 November 1914. The name was changed to École Supérieure de Pali in 1922, and in 1955 the school was reorganized again and renamed Preah Suramarit Buddhist Lyceum.

147. Résident Supérieur Outrey to Governor Generale Sarraut, 5 September 1913; Sarraut to Outrey, 22 September 1913; Outrey to Sarraut, 13 October 1913; Sarraut to Outrey, 2 December 1913; Résidence Supérieure to Sarraut, 28 April 1914; *all in* AEFEO 23 K3, "École de Pali, 1909–1918."

148. C. Reynolds 1972, 180; Ishii 1986, 82–88.

149. EFEO 1914, 95.

150. Ibid.

151. Finot 1927, 523.

152. He also translated a version of the *Kālāma-sutta,* which was considered important among modernists during this period for its discussion of inauthentic teachings. Finot 1927, 523; Karpelès to Finot, 9 September 1927, AEFEO 23 K2, "Bibliothèque royale du Phnom Penh, 1925–1927."

153. Karpelès to Finot, 9 September 1927, AEFEO 23 K2, "Bibliothèque royale du Phnom Penh, 1925–1927."

154. Huot Tath, Chuon Nath, and Uṃ-Sūr, [1918] 1928, 1–2.

155. Gouverneur Générale, "Etat d'esprit des bonzes," 1916.

156. Coedès 1915b, 76–77.

157. Ibid., 77.

158. Ibid., 73–74.

159. Ibid.

160. Thoṅ was also consulting with a commission of Khmer scholars appointed in 1921 to advise him. Finot and Sylvain Lévi to Résident Supérieur, 21 December 1922, AEFEO 23 K3, "École de Pali, 1922–1929."

161. Royal Ordinance no. 62, "Réorganisation de l'École de Pali du Cambodge," 13 April 1922, NAC RSC F.942 b.2791 23609; EFEO 1922, 377.

162. EFEO, 1922, 377.

163. Handwritten draft of document titled "Observations sur le projet de reorganisation de l'École de Pali," 1923, AEFEO 23 K3, École de Pali, 1922–1937." This theme is reiterated in other correspondence as well. For instance, see Report, Saint-Mlieux, 2eme Bureau, to Résident Supérieur, 5 December 1925, AEFEO 23 K3, "École de Pali," which suggests that "too many students sitting for the exam have only excellent memories."

164. Finot and Sylvain Lévi to Résident Supérieur, 21 December 1922, AEFEO 23 K3, "École de Pali, 1922–1929."

165. Finot, "Observations sur le projet de reorganisation de l'École de Pali," 1923, AEFEO 23 K3, "École de Pali, 1922–1937."

166. Finot to Baudoin, 1922; Baudoin to Finot, 10 February 1922; Résident Supérieur, "decree," 13 April 1922; 2eme Bureau to Finot, 27 April 1922; *all in* AEFEO 23 K3, "École de Pali, 1922–1929."

167. Huot Tath 1993, 38–39.

168. Baudoin to Finot, 10 February 1922, AEFEO 23 K3, "École de Pali, 1922–1929."

169. He refers to the three *piṭaka* or sections of the *Tipiṭaka.* Braḥ Mahā Vimaladhamma Thoṅ, Directeur de l'École du Pali to Ministre de la Guerre et de l'Instruction publique, 18 February 1919, NAC RSC R.57 b.1428 16473.

170. Ibid.

171. Ibid.

172. Ibid.

173. Résident Supérieur Baudoin, "Rapport au Gouverneur Générale sur le fonctionnement de l'École de Pali pendant l'année 1918," 18 March 1919, NAC RSC R.57 b.1428 16473.

174. Ibid.

175. Coedès, "Note relative à la confection d'un dictionnaire cambodgien," 1915, AEFEO 34 (no folder number), "Dictionnaire cambodgien," hereafter Coedès, "Note," 1915.

176. Coedès relayed that at a recent exam at the Sālā Pali, the "anarchy that reigns in this matter" of orthography had made it difficult to mark exams. Coedès, "Note," 1915; EFEO 1914, 46.

177. Coedès, "Note," 1915.

178. The correspondence indicates that the issue of romanization was raised intermittently until about 1914 and apparently did not reemerge until 1943, when romanization came close to being implemented; see AEFEO 33 F4, "Transcription du cambodgien." See also Monod 1907.

179. See a series of correspondence on this topic beginning in 1912 in AEFEO 33 F4, "Transcription du cambodgien"; Coedès 1938b, 315.

180. "Roume, Gouverneur Générale d'Indochine à Coedès, 28 August 1915," AEFEO 34 II; Coedès, "Note," 1915.

181. Coedès 1938b, 317.

182. Coedès 1933, 561–562; royal ordinance of 15 September 1914, AEFEO 34 II.

183. They traveled to Bangkok together in 1903. Karpelès to Finot, 9 September 1927, AEFEO 23 K2, "Bibliothèque royale du Phnom Penh, 1925–1927."

184. He appears to have disrobed at some point in the 1920s, at least by 1929, when he is designated in Sālā Pali reports as "lay teacher Sīlasaṅvar Hak." Lvī-Em to Delegue du Protectorat, 19 February 1929, AEFEO 23 K3, "École de Pali, 1929–1933"; Coedès 1938b, 317; Kiernan 1985, 3–4.

185. Some of the names are based on Coedès' transliteration. Coedès comments that the latter two officials, who were born during the reign of Ang Duong, possessed a "perfect knowledge" of their language, which predated the French presence in Cambodia (1938b, 316). Kong is probably the same Ukñā Sudhamprījā Kaṅ who later taught *Maṅgaladīpanī* and Cambodian religious history at the Sālā Pali (Lvī-Em to Delegue du Protectorat, 19 February 1929, AFEFO 23 K3, "École de Pali, 1929–1933"). Another participant was Ukñā "Srey Thomea Thireach Ouk," a representative of the Ministry of the Palace, but he does not appear to have been an active participant. The full list also appears in royal ordinance of 15 September 1914, AEFEO 34 II.

186. Ukñā Suttantaprījā Ind was generally referred to by this more humble title used in Battambang and known widely in connection with his poetry rather than with the official title he had been awarded.

187. Coedès 1938b, 316.

188. On the details of the orthographic reforms and consequent controversy, see AEFEO 34 II (files 47 and 67). The EFEO archives contain extensive documentation on this matter, including the details of the orthographic reforms and linguistic analyses of the reforms written by Coedès, which merit further attention than I can give here.

189. Coedès 1938b, 317.

190. Khin Sok records the work of a commission designated by Ang Duong to reform royal vocabulary; the commission included both Samtec Braḥ Sugandhādhipatī Pān and Samtec Braḥ Sangharāj Diaṅ, but the orthographic reform may have come later (1991, 186n73).

191. "Extrait du process-verbal de la 523eme pleniere du Conseil des Ministres," 17 June 1927, AEFEO 34 II, "Dictionnaire cambodgienne."

192. Coedès 1938b, 317; Minister de la Guerre to Finot, 21 November 1921, AEFEO 34 II, "Dictionnaire cambodgienne."

193. Finot to Résident Supérieur, 21 November 1921; Ministre de la Guerre to Finot, 18 January 1922; Finot to Résident Supérieur, 9 February 1924; Résident Supérieur to Sisowath, 21 October 1924; Étudiants de Sugandhādhipatī Pān to Résident Supérieur, 25 December 1925; 2eme Bureau to Résident Supérieur, 3 February 1926; Princess Malika to Résident Supérieur, 27 February 1926; 2eme Bureau to Directeur, Imprimerie du Protectorate, 8 May 1926; Ministre de l'Instruction Publique to Résident Supérieur, 5 October 1926; *all in* AEFEO 34 II, "École Supérieure de Pali." For a summary, see Coedès 1938b, 318–320.

194. Saint-Mlieux, "Rapport à Résident Supérieur," 3 February 1926," AEFEO 34 II (file no. 67).

195. Lomberger, "Circulaire no. 35," 30 April 1926, AEFEO 34 II (file no. 67).

196. Administrative chef du 2eme Bureau to Directeur Imprimerie du Protectorat, Phnom Penh, 6 May 1926, AEFEO 34 II (file no. 67).

197. Finot to Résident Supérieur, 9 February 1924, AEFEO 34 II, "École Supérieure de Pali."

198. Ponn to Résident Supérieur, 13 May 1926, AEFEO 34 II, "École Supérieure de Pali."

199. Coedès 1938b, 320.

200. These were designated in Royal Ordinance no. 57 of 13 April 1922 (EFEO 1922, 377).

201. In 1915, an inventory of texts at the newly established library of the École de Pali indicates the ways in which texts were classified, as belonging to the *Vinaya, Sutta, Abhidhamma,* or miscellaneous. Commentaries such as the *Visuddhimagga* and the *Samantapāsādikā* were categorized as *Vinaya* texts, while the *Maṅgaladīpanī* was a *Suttanta* text and the *Sāratthasaṅgaha* and *Kaccāyana* were classified as miscellaneous (Coedès 1915b, 75–76).

202. "Directeur EFEO à Résident Supérieur, 23 June 1926"; Prah Vimaladham, "Rapport annuel de l'École Supérieure de Pali" to M. l'Administrateur Chef du 2eme Bureau de la Résidence Supérieure au Cambodge, 27 February 1926; Directeur École Supérieure de Pali Em, "Rapport . . . à le Directeur EFEO," 11 January 1928; "Note sur la réorganisation de l'École Supérieure de Pali, Phnom Penh," 11 April 1928; Directeur École Supérieure de Pali (Em), "Rapport annuel sur le fonctionnement de l'École Supérieure de Pali," years 1928, 1929, 1930, 1931, 1932, 1933, 1934, 1935; *all in* AEFEO 23 K3, "École Supérieure de Pali, 1922–1937."

203. Sisowath, royal ordinance no. 62, AEFEO 23 K3.

204. Directeur École Supérieure de Pali Em, "Rapport . . . à le Directeur EFEO," 11 January 1928; "Note sur la réorganisation de l'École Supérieure de Pali, Phnom Penh, 11 avril 1928"; Directeur École Supérieure de Pali (Em), "Rapport annuel sur le fonctionnement de l'École Supérieure de Pali," years 1928, 1929, 1930, 1931, 1932, 1933, 1934, 1935; *all in* AEFEO 23 K3, "École Supérieure de Pali, 1922–1937."

205. Em to le Delegue du Protectorat aupres du Gouvernement Cambodgien, 19 February 1929, AEFEO 23 K3, "École de Pali, 1929–1933."

206. Coedès 1915b, 75.

207. Coedès to Résident Supérieur, 16 December 1912, AEFEO 23 K3, "École de Pali, 1909–1918." A 1918 article in *Revue Indochinoise* also suggests that France had come under attack recently from a Japanese journalist charging that education in Indochina was almost nonexistent (Pasquier 1918, 393–396).

208. Coedès 1924, 11–13.

209. Louis Finot et M. Sylvain Levi to Résident Supérieur, 21 December 1922, AEFEO 23 K3, "École de Pali, 1922–1929."

210. The library was created as the Bibliothèque Nationale in 1921 by the royal ordinance of 15 February 1921 and renamed the Bibliothèque Royale by the royal ordinance of 15 January 1925. It was further reorganized by Royal Ordinance no. 23 of 18 March 1926. S. E. le Samdach Chauféa Véang Thiounn, "Allocution de S.E. le Samdach Chauféa Véang Thiounn, Premier Ministre à la viste de M. le Résident Supérieur Lavit à la Bibliothèque royale à Phnom Penh," 15 October 1929, AEFEO 23 K2, "Bibliothèque royale du Phnom Penh, 1925–"; Chea, 28 June 1937.

211. "Réorganisation de la Bibliothèque royale cambodgienne," *L'Echo du Cambodge* (January 1925), AEFEO 23 K2, "Bibliothèque royale de Phnom Penh, 1925–1943"; Chea, 28 June 1937.

212. Karpelès to Finot, 30 July 1925, AEFEO 23 K2, "Bibliothèque royale du Phnom Penh, 1925–1927."

213. Karpelès, "Extraits du rapport de l'assemblée générale," 9 November 1925," AEFEO 23 K2, "Bibliothèque royale du Phnom Penh, 1925–1927."

214. "Note sur l'Institut bouddhique au Cambodge, son organization, son action, des difficultés qu'il rencontre ou suscite," 1934–1937, NAC RSC F.942 b.2791 23609.

215. Ibid.

216. Jacqueline Filliozat, personal correspondence, November 1996. I am indebted to Jacqueline Filliozat, an expert on Southeast Asian manuscripts, for this analysis of Karpelès' impact on manuscript culture in Cambodia.

217. This view shifted later, when Karpelès, who was described in a surveillance report as a woman "with a rare talent for propaganda," had raised the prominence of the Royal Library to such a high level in the protectorate that administrative authorities had begun to fear the ramifications of her work as well as the influence of the coterie of monks who "always accompanied" her. See the report cited in note 1 of this chapter.

218. Karpelès, "Rapport annuel sur le fonctionnement de la Bibliothèque royale du 1er juin 1927 au 1er juin 1928, 8 janvier 1929," 1929, AEFEO 23 K2, "Bibliothèque royale du Phnom Penh, 1928–1934."

219. Karpelès 1933, 72; "Réorganisation de la Bibliothèque royale cambodgienne," *L'Echo du Cambodge* (January 1925), AEFEO 23 K2, "Documents scientifiques."

220. Louis Finot (?) and M. Sylvain Levi to Résident Supérieur, 21 December 1922, AEFEO 23 K3, "École de Pali, 1922–1929."

221. Saint-Mlieux, Conservateur de la Bibliothèque royale to Résident Supérieur, 7 September 1926, AEFEO 23 K2, "Bibliothèque royale du Phnom Penh, 1925–."

222. Royal ordinance of 8 April 1924, AEFEO 23 K3, "École de Pali, 1922–1929." Volume 1, for instance, consisted of the translation and commentary of *Siṅgālovādāsutta* by Huot Tath (1927, 9–63), discussed in chapter 5.

223. Karpelès 1933, 72.

224. Suzanne Karpelès to Résident Supérieur, 30 July 1925, AEFEO 23 K2, "Bibliothèque royale du Phnom Penh."

225. Karpelès, "Rapport annuel sur le fonctionnement de la Bibliothèque royale du 1er Juin 1927 au 1er Juin 1928," 1928, AEFEO 23 K2, "Bibliothèque royale du Phnom Penh, 1925–1927."

226. Karpelès, "Assemblée du 20 mars 1931," 1931, AEFEO 23 K2, "Bibliothèque royale du Phnom Penh, 1925–."

227. Annual reports from 1926 to 1937, all found in AEFEO 23 K2, "Bibliothèque royale du Phnom Penh, 1925–."

228. Chāp Pin [1932] 1970, i. This custom of making merit through sponsoring the production of printed texts, introduced as a means of merit making and fund raising by the National Library in Bangkok, also became widely popular in Cambodia (John Marston, personal communication, November 2000, Denver). The funeral biographies of monks that I examined also often contained a translation and excerpt of a Pali text.

229. Royal ordinance no. 106, 14 December 1929, NAC RSC F.942 b.2791 23609.

230. Samtec Braḥ Dhammalikhit Lvī-Em (then Braḥ Sirīsammativaṅs), Braḥ Uttamamunī Uṃ-Sūr, Samtec Braḥ Mahāsumedhādipatī Braḥ Sangharāj Chuon Nath (then Braḥ Sāsanasobhaṇ), and Samtec Braḥ Mahāsumedhādipatī Sanghanāyak Huot Tath (then Braḥ Visuddhivaṅs). The leadership also included Braḥ Mahābrahmunī Deb-Ū. Lāṅ Hap Ān 1970, 3–8.

231. The *Vinaya* was the first *piṭaka* produced. Its five sections were translated and published in thirteen volumes between 1929 and 1936. Work on the *Suttanta piṭaka* commenced in 1936 (Krumjaṃnuṃ Prae *Braḥ Traipiṭak* 1940, 16–17).

232. I am grateful to Penny Edwards for sharing her findings on Makhali Phal's Franco-Khmer identity (personal correspondence, April 1999).

233. Makhali 1937, 6–8, 19–24. I am grateful to Jeffrey Merrick for editing my translation of this poem and for rendering it into actual poetry.

CHAPTER FIVE: HOW SHOULD WE BEHAVE?

1. Ind [1921] 1971, vol. 1, 10.

2. Ibid., vol. 1, 20.

3. Collins 1998, 18–19, 58–64.

4. See the Buddhist writings discussed in the concluding portion of this chapter. Edwards 1999, 11–13, 18–20, 383–389.

5. This word might also be translated in this context as "primer."

6. Lvī-Em 1930, 58.

7. K. *hetu.* "Intention" falls short of conveying the full implications of *hetu* here, which refers not just to intentions but more generally to "causes," which give rise to actions *(kamma)* and which bear results or "fruits" *(phala).*

8. Lvī-Em, 1930, 58.

9. Ibid., 67; see also Huot Tath 1958, 58–59.

10. K. *paṭipatti-pūjā,* "offering good conduct." Lvī-Em 1930, 66.

11. I.e., the Dhamma is predicted to endure for only five thousand years, but the observance of *paṭipatti-pūjā* would ensure that the Dhamma endures and is strong (rather than in decline) for the entire five thousand years.

12. Ibid., 67. Similar admonishments are evident in Huot Tath's *Dhammasaṅgaha,* translated and edited for use in a merit-making festival in Kandal Province (Huot Tath 1958, 58–59).

13. Lvī-Em 1930, 67.

14. As I have suggested, from the 1920s on, the *Paññāsājātaka* and *cpāp'* (along with Khmer oral folklore) increasingly took on the status of "national" rather than Dhammic literature; following independence, they were absorbed into secular school curricula as such. In Royal Library reports, these works are assigned to the category "national literature" (see chap. 4, n. 117). A 1966 catalogue of Khmer works published by the Association of Khmer Writers assigns works to the "genres" of Pali, Dhamma, "didactic and diverse," and "mores and customs." Volumes of *Paññāsa-jātaka* and *cpāp'* are assigned to the "didactic and diverse" genre, along with translations of *The Arabian Nights* (Dik 1966, 3–6). While this represents one view of these texts promulgated by modernist intellectuals, I am not trying to argue it is true for all Khmer Buddhists.

15. See chapter 1, n. 60.

16. Huot Tath et al. [1918] 1928, 2.

17. I owe this observation to Angus Lockyer. See also Roy 1995, 30–32.

18. As a point of comparison in modern Shanghai, see Des Forges 2003, 805.

19. Described in Tath's memoir excerpted in chapter 3, n. 158.

20. Braḥ Mahā Vimaladhamm Thoṅ, Directeur de l'École du Pali to Ministre de la Guerre et de l'Instruction publique, 18 February 1919, NAC RSC R.57 b.428 16473.

21. Uṃ-Sūr [1930] 1963, 1930, 1927, 1928.

22. Lvī-Em 1969 (this work was probably commissioned in 1932); Chuon Nath and Lvī-Em 1970 (this work was written prior to 1932, possibly in the early 1920s).

23. Chuon Nath 1935; Chuon Nath and Uṃ-Sūr 1926 and 1935.

24. Huot Tath 1926 [1957], 1926 [1928], 1927, 1935, 1958. (The latter text was apparently translated in the 1930s).

25. Lvī-Em, Uṃ-Sūr, and Ḷuṅ, 1961.

26. Lvī-Em 1950, i.

27. According to a biography of Uṃ-Sūr, Lvī-Em studied under Thoṅ (together with Uṃ-Sūr) at least during the period 1908–1910 (Uṃ-Sūr 1940, xix). In 1915, Thoṅ recruited him as a professor for the newly established Sālā Pali (Lvī-Em 1950, i).

28. Chuon Nath 1935, 35.

29. Chuon Nath and Uṃ-Sūr 1926.

30. Chuon Nath and Uṃ-Sūr 1935, i.

31. Chuon Nath 1935, 37.

32. Ibid.

33. Ibid., 41.

34. Ibid., 50–51.

35. The text was apparently first printed in Phnom Penh by A. Portail in 1926. It was later printed by the Royal Library.

36. Chuon Nath and Uṃ-Sūr 1935, i–ii. "Bodhi-citta" is a complex term to translate since it refers to a multistage awareness of and movement toward enlightenment. Here it signals the turning of one's "heart and mind" toward enlightenment.

37. Ibid., 1. The "Triple Gem" refers to the Buddha, Dhamma, and Sangha.

38. Ibid.

39. Ibid., 29.

40. In more technical terms, the nine *lokuttaradhammā* represent the four paths and their fruitions plus *nibbāṇa.* Nyanatiloka translates the term as "9 supermundane things" (1972, 91).

41. Chuon Nath and Uṃ-Sūr 1935, 29–30.

42. Ibid., 30–31.

43. Huot Tath 1927.

44. The translation refers to *samaṇa-brāhmaṇ,* "monks and Brahmins," but the references in the translation and commentary are to Buddhist *vatt* and merit-making rituals. Ibid., 55–57.

45. Ibid., 12.

46. See chapter 3 for Huot Tath's descriptions of his translation process (Huot Tath 1993, 9–11). The Pali portions of Huot Tath's translation do not appear to follow the Siamese printed translation from the period. Nor does it follow the Burmese printed version. This is evident from Carpenter's 1911 Pali Text Society edition, which makes use of and notes the variations between six different versions of the text, including the king of

Siam's printed edition (Carpenter 1911, 1). From what I can determine, Siamese printed texts appear to have been available only to a limited degree in Cambodia through the 1920s, in the collections of individuals or through exchanges between the Royal Library and the Vajirañāṇa Library (Coedès 1924, 11). Buddhaghosa 1971, 941–959.

47. Ibid., 43–44.

48. Stanza 3 (see other excerpts in chapters 1 and 2). I closely follow Pou's translation to French (Pou 1988, vol. 2, 314–315). See also BI 1974, 95.

49. Huot Tath 1927, 35. The characteristics of such false friends are enumerated on pages 29–35.

50. Stanza 1. Pou 1988, vol. 2, 314–315; BI 1974, 95.

51. Stanza 44 from *Cpāp' Dūnmān Khluan,* Pou 1988, vol. 2, 322; BI 1974, 99.

52. P. *aṭṭhakathā.*

53. Huot Tath 1927, 7.

54. Ibid.

55. Lvī-Em 1930, 67; Huot Tath 1958, 58–59.

56. Blackburn 1999, 281–309; 2001, 130–136, 178–185.

57. Collins 1990, 104.

58. Huot Tath 1927, 11.

59. Tandart 1935, vol. 2, 2125; Chandler 1996, 78, 317.

60. *Bhikkhu-bhikkhunī-upāsak-upāsikā.*

61. Collins 1998, 61.

62. Ibid., 41.

63. Faure 1996, 3, 12.

64. Ind [1921] 1971, vol. 1, 1; vol. 10, 73–74.

65. Ibid., vol.1, 7–8.

66. Ibid., 20–21.

67. Ibid., 2–3.

68. Ibid., vol. 7, 38–44.

69. Bloechl 2000, 3.

70. *D,* vol. 1, 70–71.

71. Ind [1921] 1971, vol. 3, 20–21.

72. Ibid., 20.

73. The name apparently refers to a local village or regional *ganak tā,* "spirit" (Forest 1992, 22–24; Ang Choulean 1986, 201–231; Porée-Maspero 1962, 6–12).

74. Ind [1921] 1971, vol. 3, 27–28.

75. Ibid.

76. Also included among the sevenfold *sappurisa-dhammā* are *mattaññutā* (knowing appropriate ways to make a living), *kalaññutā* (knowing appropriate times or circumstances), and *parisaññutā* (knowing appropriate ceremonial behavior). Compared to commentarial sources, Ind's interpretation of the *sappurisa-dhammā* appears to be reinterpreting the concepts for application to laypersons. Whether Ind himself reinterprets the concept or whether he is drawing on other texts is not clear. Huot Tath gives similar (though more abbreviated) definitions in *Dhammasaṅgaha* (1958, 107–108). In various commentaries, the understanding of *dhammaññu,* for instance, "one who knows the *dhamma,*" is of a person who knows the Pali texts and commentaries. *Atthaññu* is glossed as "one who knows the meaning of that which has been spoken," with an addi-

tional note in the subcommentary that this means understanding not just the words but also the meanings of *sutta-geyya,* a reference to texts. *Attaññu* is interpreted as one who knows one's self, through means of meditation. By contrast, Ind explains *dhammaññutā* as the "condition of one who recognizes causes and results, who recognizes that 'this thing is the cause [that] is the origin of this result. This result is the result that arose from this cause,' and so on." This recognition refers to the perception of the nature of reality, not to the knowledge of texts. *Atthaññutā* in Ind's usage refers to the ability to make moral evaluations of actions, and *attaññutā* to being able to situate oneself morally in relation to others in the social world (Buddhaghosa 2463 (1920), 301; de Silva 1970, 333–334).

77. K. *parisuddh.*

78. Ind [1921] 1971, vol. 1, 20.

79. I use this term, following Collins (1998, 18), who draws on Niccola Tannenbaum's use of the term by Shan villagers as a marker of "civilizational identity" (1995, 10), as well as Hallisey and Reynolds' historical use of the term to refer to Buddhism in its "international" or cosmopolitan phase in which "a monastic elite interacted with imperial elites in urban cultures"(1989, 15).

80. In this sense, the story recalls Partha Chatterjee's analysis of the "inner domain" of spirituality "bearing the 'essential' marks of cultural identity" claimed by anticolonial nationalists (1993, 6).

81. K. *santān,* "family." This term may be used here as a synonym for *juor,* "line," which occurs later in the narrative, referring to the "extended family" of the accused, including siblings (possibly on the paternal side only), parents, and offspring. My thanks to both Sophea Mouth and Vincent Her for help in translating these two words in this context.

82. This description must refer to the sale or trade of ethnic minority members into lowland slavery.

83. Ind employs the ethnonym "Phnong," which in Khmer writings of this period was used as a generic term for highland peoples and carried the pejorative connotation of "savage" or "primitive." In the mid-twentieth century, the term "Khmaer Loe" was introduced to designate highland Khmer. BI [1938] 1967, 784. I am grateful to Thongchai Winichakul and Vincent Her for help with understanding Thai, Lao, and Hmong usages of similar terms. Ind [1921] 1971, vol. 2, 47–51.

84. Ibid., 51–52.

85. Ibid., 53–54.

86. Ibid., 54.

87. Ibid., 55–59.

88. *D,* vol. 1, 63, 70.

89. *D,* vol. 1, 62.

90. My reading of the ritual themes in this narrative is indebted to Charles Keyes.

91. P. *puthujjane.*

92. Carter and Palihawadana 1987, 144–145. In these verses, the commentary emphasizes that "the disciple of the Fully Awakened One" *(sammāsambuddhasāvako)* is "the monk with influxes extinct, though born among ordinary persons . . . shines surpassing the ordinary folk who have 'become blind'" (Carter and Palihawadana 1987, 145).

93. Norman 1994, 4.

94. Ibid., 5–7.

95. It is apparent that Bhikkhu Suk stayed in the monkhood for a long time, perhaps for life, since he is referred to at one point in the text as Lok Tā Suk, indicating advanced status and age.

96. Chandler 1984, 274.

97. Chandler 1996, 85.

98. Ibid., 85–86.

99. Judy Ledgerwood observes this theme as well, in literature as well as in contemporary narratives of diasporic experience (1990, 313–315).

100. Chandler 1984, 274; Pou and Jenner 1981,152. The *cpāp'* were part of Ind's own literary and religious influence, and the thematic and pedagogical interconnections between the *Gatilok* and the *Cpāp' Tūnmān Khluan* in particular are evident.

101. Hansen 1988, 32.

102. The Khmer word *kaṃbrā,* "orphaned," refers not only to having lost both parents but is also used when a child has lost mother *(kaṃbrā-mtāy)* or father *(kaṃbrā-obuk).*

103. Chandler 1982, 55–57.

104. This story, which I have heard in oral forms, is also referred to as "Buddhisaenjātaka" or as "Nāṅ Kaṅrī." These variations are well documented in Jacob 1996, 123, 168–169, and BI 1969, 1–39.

105. The story does not end here, but the versions I have encountered in oral form vary widely. In one oral version I heard from a Khmer woman in Boston in 1986, Nāṅ Maraṇamātā, falsely accused of adultery, turns to gold as she is about to be put to death. Her mother (who has taken the form of a bo tree) drops down a swing to her daughter and the two "flew to heaven . . . and got enlightenment." See also Jacob 1996, 164–165.

106. Chandler 2000, 114–116.

107. Wyatt 1993, 17. I am grateful to Leedom Lefferts for directing me to these historical and political uses of the trope of orphanhood.

108. Wyatt 1993, 17, 33–34.

109. Ind [1921] 1971, vol. 2, 30–41.

110. Ibid., vol. 10, 57–73.

111. Ibid., vol. 1, 46–7; vol. 3, 55–56.

112. Ibid., vol. 3, 21–24.

113. Ibid., vol. 2, 60.

114. Ibid., 61.

115. Ibid., vol. 1, 57.

116. Discussed in chapter 4.

117. This is followed by references to the "*pāṭimokkha-saṃvara-sīla* and the rest" (Ind [1921] 1971, vol. 2, 106). It appears that he is making a reference to the *catu-pārisuddhi-sīla* (four kinds of morality for monks): *pāṭimokkha-saṃvara-sīla* (morality of restraint with respect to the disciplinary code), *indriya-saṃvara-sīla* (morality of restraint with respect to the senses), *ājīva-pārisuddhi-sīla* (morality of the purification of livelihood), and *paccaya-sannissita-sīla* (morality in regard to the four requisites, i.e., of robes, food, dwelling, and medicines).

118. Ind goes on to define and gloss these as "having the virtue of very little desire, meaning having few wants, a kindly disposition, and so forth" (vol. 2, 106). Here, Ind's translation may be a Khmer rendering of the Pali *ariya-vaṃsa.* These are translated by Nyanatiloka as the "noble usages": contentedness with any robe, any food, and any dwelling and delight in meditation and detachment (1972, 2).

119. Ind [1921] 1971, vol. 2, 106–107.

120. Canon 1988, 2–5.

121. K. *secktī-saṅveg-āṇit.* In Khmer, *saṅveg* connotes suddenly feeling an apprehension of evil or a realization of the suffering of others that causes emotional distress or anxiety. *Āṇit* is more easily translated. It means "to have pity on" or "to feel compassion." I translate the noun form of the compound here as "horrific grief and pity" in an effort to convey the compounded emotions and realizations conveyed by the phrase without employing a cumbersome and lengthy translation. The merchant's elevated moral status is seemingly signaled linguistically by the related but different words employed to describe reactions to the orphan's story; the merchant's *secktī-saṅveg-āṇit* is contrasted with the simpler *āṇit* felt by the householders in the lower village.

122. Rhys Davids and Stede [1921–1925] 1986, 658.

123. Coomaraswamy 1977, 179.

124. L. Wilson 1996, 15–17.

125. The curriculum was composed in 1950–1951 and published in 1953. Dhan' Vān' 1953, 22–23, 49–50.

126. Ibid., 14.

127. Ibid., 14–15.

128. Ibid., 15–18.

129. Ibid., 1–3.

130. The curriculum discusses the "different types of *sāsana*" or religions.

131. *attamabhāb.*

132. *kalyānaputhujjan, ariyajan.*

133. Dhan' Vān' 1953, 1–2.

134. Huot Tath [1961] 1970.

135. Ibid., 1.

136. Ibid., 2.

137. *prades.*

138. Huot Tath [1961] 1970, 2–4, 6–7.

139. Kiernan and Chanthou 1982, 114–126; Kiernan 1985, 3–7, 18–33; Yang 1987, 7–47; Edwards 1999, 301–314, 339–345; Harris 1999, 59–65; Chandler 2000, 163–172; Noer 1973, 101–161; Anderson 1983, 116–131; Bradley, 2004, 73–81.

140. Roff 1985, 125–127; Radjab 1995, 271.

141. Recent ethnographic research by John Marston suggests that these tensions have resurfaced with the revival of Cambodia Buddhism 1989 (n.d., 10–30; for the published version, see Marston 2000b).

142. Bowen 1997, 168–169.

143. Chakrabarty 2000, 16, 72.

144. K. *eḷūv neḥ* or *nau smāy neḥ*. See Ind [1921] 1970, vol. 1, 1, 8; vol. 4, 2, 5; vol. 5, 14.

145. Berman quoting Marx (1982, 15); Harvey 1990, 10–11.

SOURCES

Abe, Stanley. 1995. "Inside the Wonder House: Buddhist Art and the West." In *Curators of the Buddha: The Study of Buddhism under Colonialism,* edited by Donald S. Lopez, Jr., pages 63–106. Chicago: University of Chicago Press.

Adas, Michael. 1979. *Prophets of Rebellion.* Chapel Hill: University of North Carolina Press.

Aisenberg, Andrew R. 1999. *Contagion: Disease, Government, and the "Social Question" in Nineteenth-Century France.* Stanford, Calif.: Stanford University Press.

Ang Choulean. 1986. *Les êtres surnaturels dans la religion populaire khmère.* Paris: Cedoreck.

Anderson, Benedict. 1983. *Imagined Communities: Reflections on the Origin and Spread of Nationalism.* Rev. edition. London: Verso.

Aymonier, Etienne. 1878. *Textes Khmers, publies avec une traduction sommaire.* Saigon: E. Aymonier.

———. [1900] 1984. *Notes sur les coutumes et croyances superstitieuses des cambodgiens,* edited by Saveros Pou. Paris: Cedoreck.

———. 1900–1904. *Le Cambodge.* Volumes 1–3. Paris: E. Leroux.

Baumann, Martin. 2002. "Protective Amulets and Awareness Techniques, or How to Make Sense of Buddhism in the West." In *Westward Dharma: Buddhism beyond Asia,* edited by Charles S. Prebish and Martin Baumann, pages 51–65. Berkeley: University of California Press.

Becchetti, Catherine. 1994. "Une ancienne tradition de manuscrits au Cambodge." In *Une ancienne tradition de manuscrits au Cambodge,* edited by François Bizot, pages 47–62. Paris: École française d'Extrême-Orient.

Bechert, Heinz. 1970. "Theravāda Buddhist Sangha: Some General observations on Historical and Political Factors in its Development." *Journal of Asian Studies* 29.4:761–778.

———. 1984. "Buddhist Revival in East and West." In *The World of Buddhism: Buddhist Nuns and Monks in Society and Culture,* edited by Heinz Bechert and Richard Gombrich, pages 273–285. London: Thames and Hudson.

———. 1988. *Buddhismus, Staat und Gesellschaft in den Ländern Theravāda-Buddhismus.* 3 volumes. Göttingen: Seminars für Indologie und Buddhismuskunde der Universität Göttingen.

Bee, P. J., I. Brown, Patricia Herbert, and Manas Chitakasem. 1989. "Thailand." In *Southeast Asia: Languages and Literatures, a Select Guide,* edited by Patricia Herbert and Anthony Miller, pages 23–48. Honolulu: University of Hawai'i Press.

Berman, Marshall. 1982. *All That Is Solid Melts into Air: The Experience of Modernity.* New York: Penguin Books.

Bezançon, Pascale. 1992. "La Rénovation des Écoles de Pagode au Cambodge." Paris: *Cahiers de l'Asie du Sud-Est,* no. 31, 7–30.

Birnbaum, Raoul. 2003. "Master Hongyi Looks Back: A Modern Man Becomes a Monk in Twentieth-Century China." In *Buddhism in the Modern World: Adaptations of an Ancient Tradition,* edited by Steven Heine and Charles S. Prebish, pages 75–124. Oxford: Oxford University Press.

Bizot, François. 1976. *Le figuier à cinq branches.* Volume 130. Paris: École française d'Extrême-Orient.

———. 1981. *Le don de soi-même; recherches sur le bouddhisme Khmer.* Paris: École française d'Extrême-Orient.

———. 1992. *Le chemin de Lanka.* Paris: École française d'Extrême-Orient.

———, and Oskar von Hinüber. 1994. *Itipisoratanamālā: La Guirlande de Joyaux.* Paris: École française d'Extrême-Orient.

Blackburn, Anne. 1999. "Looking for the *Vinaya:* Monastic Discipline in the Practical Canons of the Theravāda." *Journal of the International Associations of Buddhist Studies* 22.2:281–309.

———. 2001. *Buddhist Learning and Textual Practice in Eighteenth-Century Lankan Monastic Culture.* Princeton, N.J.: Princeton University Press.

Bloechl, Jeffrey. 2000. *Liturgy of the Neighbor: Emmanuel Levinas and the Religion of Responsibility.* Pittsburgh, Pa.: Duquesne University Press.

Bocock, Robert. 1996. "The Cultural Formations of Modern Society." In *Modernity: An Introduction to Modern Societies,* edited by Stuart Hall, David Held, Don Hubert, and Kenneth Thompson, pages 150–183. Cambridge: Blackwell.

Bond, George D. [1988] 1992. *The Buddhist Revival in Sri Lanka: Religious Tradition, Reinterpretation, and Response,* reprint edition. Delhi: Motilal Banarsidass Publishers.

Bowen, John. 1993. *Muslims through Discourse: Religion and Ritual in Gayo Society.* Princeton, N.J.: Princeton University Press.

———. 1997. "Modern Intentions: Reshaping Subjectivities in an Indonesian Muslim Society." In *Islam in an Era of Nation-States,* edited by Robert W. Hefner and Patricia Horvatich, pages 158–227. Honolulu: University of Hawai'i Press.

Bowie, Katherine A. 1996. "Slavery in Nineteenth-Century Northern Thailand: Archival Anecdotes and Village Voices." In *State Power and Culture in Thailand,* edited by E. Paul Durrenberger, pages 114–126. New Haven, Conn.: Yale Southeast Asia Studies.

Bradley, Mark. 2000. *Imagining Vietnam and America: The Making of Postcolonial Vietnam, 1919–1950.* Chapel Hill: University of North Carolina Press.

———. 2004. "Becoming *Van Minh:* Civilizational Discourse and Visions of the Self in Twentieth-Century Vietnam." *Journal of World History* 15.1:65–83.

Brown, Sid. 2001. *The Journey of One Buddhist Nun: Even against the Wind.* Albany: State University of New York Press.

Buddhaghosa. 1920. *Sumangalavilāsinī,* edited by Phra Vanaratana Heng. Bangkok: Mahāmuakutarājavidyalayena Press.

———. 1971. *Sumangla-vilasini: Buddhaghosa's Commentary on the Digha-Nikaya,* edited by William Stede, Thomas W. Rhys Davids, and Joseph Estlin Carpenter. Volume 3, 2nd edition. London: Pali Text Society.

Buddhist Institute. [1938] 1967. *Vacanānukram Khmaer.* 5th edition. Phnom Penh: Buddhist Institute.

———. [1942] 1952. *Paññāsa-jātakapālī.* Volume 1, 2nd edition. Phnom Penh: Buddhist Institute.

———. 1960a. "Nemi-jātak." In *Braḥ Traipiṭak Pālī nẏṅ Seckdībrae Khmaer, Suttantapiṭak Khuddhakanikāy Jātak,* vol. 62, pages 67–101. Phnom Penh: Buddhist Institute.

———. 1960b. "Vessantar-jātak." In *Braḥ Traipiṭakpālī nẏṅ Seckdīpraebhāsākhmaer:*

Suttantapiṭak Khuddhakanikāy Jātak, volume 63, pages 94–217. Phnom Penh: Buddhist Institute.

———. 1968. *Ṙyaṅ Braḥ Sudhanakumār.* Phnom Penh: Buddhist Institute.

———. 1969. *Petits ouvrages cambodgiens.* Phnom Penh: Buddhist Institute.

———. 1970. *Biography of Samdech Preah Sanghareach Chuon-Nath, the Chief of Mahanikaya Order.* Phnom Penh: Buddhist Institute.

———. 1974. *Cpāp' Phseṅ-phseṅ.* Phnom Penh: Buddhist Institute.

Burris, John P. 2001. *Exhibiting Religion: Colonialism and Spectacle at International Expositions.* Charlottesville and London: University Press of Virginia.

Cabaton, Antoine. 1901. "Comptes rendus des séances de l'Académie des Inscriptions and Belles-Lettres." In *Rapport sur les littératures Cambodgienne et Chame.* Paris: Alphonse Picard et Fils.

Canon, Katie G. 1988. *Black Womanist Ethics.* Atlanta, Ga.: Scholars Press.

Carpenter, Joseph Estlin, editor. 1911. *Dīgha Nikāya.* Volume 3. London: published for the Pali Text Society by Geoffrey Cumberlege, Oxford University Press.

Carter, John Ross. 1993. *On Understanding Buddhists: Essays on the Theravāda Tradition in Sri Lanka.* Albany: State University of New York Press.

Carter, John Ross, and Mahinda Palihawadana, trans. 1987. *Dhammapada.* Oxford: Oxford University Press.

Chakrabarty, Dipesh. 2000. *Provincializing Europe: Postcolonial Thought and Historical Difference.* Princeton, N.J.: Princeton University Press.

———. 2002. *Habitations of Modernity: Essays in the Wake of Subaltern Studies.* Chicago: University of Chicago Press.

Chandler, David. 1974. "Cambodia before the French: Politics in a Tributary Kingdom, 1794–1848." Ph.D. dissertation, Yale University.

———. 1982. "The Assassination of Résident Bardez (1925): A Premonition of Revolt in Colonial Cambodia." *Journal of the Siam Society* 70:35–49.

———. 1984. "Normative Poems (Chbap) and Pre-Colonial Cambodian Society." *Journal of South East Asian Studies* 15.2:271–279.

———. 1991. *The Tragedy of Cambodian History: Politics, War, and Revolution since 1945.* New Haven, Conn.: Yale University Press.

———. 1996. *Facing the Cambodian Past.* Chiang Mai: Silkworm Books.

———. 2000. *A History of Cambodia.* 3rd edition. Boulder, Colo.: Westview Press.

Chang Hao. 1987. *Chinese Intellectuals in Crisis: Search for Order and Meaning (1890–1911).* Berkeley and Los Angeles: University of California Press.

Chāp Pin, Ācāry Suvaṇṇajoto. [1932] 1970. *Attānusāsanī.* 6th edition. Phnom Penh: Buddhist Institute.

Chatterjee, Partha. 1993. *The Nation and Its Fragments: Colonial and Postcolonial Histories.* Princeton, N.J.: Princeton University Press.

Chau-Seng. 1962. *L'organisation bouddhique au Cambodge.* Phnom Penh: Université Buddhique Preah Sihanouk Raj.

———, Braḥ Suvannajoto Bhikkhu. 1999. *Auvād Paṭimokkha.* Phnom Penh: Buddhist Institute.

Chigas, George. 2000. "The Emergence of Twentieth-Century Cambodian Literary Institutions: The Case of *Kambujasuriyā.*" In *The Canon in Southeast Asian Literatures: Literatures of Cambodia, Indonesia, Laos, Malaysia, the Philippines, Thailand*

and Vietnam, edited by David Smyth, pages 135–146. Richmond, Surrey: Curzon Press.

Chuon Nath, Braḥ Sāsanasobhaṇa. 1935. *Gihivinaya Saṅkhep.* Phnom Penh: Royal Library.

———, Braḥ Grū Saṅghasatthā, and Braḥ Ñāṇapavaravijjā Lvī-Em. 1970. *Braḥ Vinay Paṭimokkh Samvarsīl Saṅkhep nyṅ Khandhaka Vinay Saṅkhep.* 10th edition. Phnom Penh: Buddhist Institute.

———, Braḥ Sāsanasobhaṇa. 1926. *Trayapaṇāma Saṅkhepnyṅ: Gihivinaya Saṅkhep.* Phnom Penh: A. Portail.

———. 1935. *Trayapaṇāma Saṅkhep.* Phnom Penh: Royal Library.

Coedès, George. 1902. "Liste des manuscrits Khmèrs de l'École française d'Extrême-Orient." *Bulletin de l'École française d'Extrême-Orient* 2 (1902): 398–405.

———. 1912. "Chronique." *Bulletin de l'École française d'Extrême-Orient* 12.9:176–188.

———. 1913. "Études cambodgiennes." *Bulletin de l'École française d'Extrême-Orient* 13.2:11–17.

———. 1915a. "Note sur les ouvrages palis composes in pays Thai." *Bulletin de l'École française d'Extrême-Orient* 15.3:39–46.

———. 1915b. "Cambodge." *Bulletin de l'École française d'Extrême-Orient* 15.4:72–77.

———. 1924. *The Vajirañana Library.* Bangkok: Bangkok Times Press.

———. 1933. "Saṃdac Cakrei Pec Pon." *Bulletin de l'École française d'Extrême-Orient* 33.1:561–562.

———. 1935. "In memoriam." *Bulletin de l'École française d'Extrême-Orient* 35.2:507–515.

———. 1938a. "Review of W. A. de Silva, Catalogue of Palm Leaf Manuscripts in the Library of the Colombo Museum, Volume 1." *Bulletin de l'École française d'Extrême-Orient* 38.2:333–334.

———. 1938b. "*Vacanānukrama khmèr.* Dictionnaire cambodgien." *Bulletin de l'École française d'Extrême-Orient* 38.2:314–321.

———. 1957. "The *Traibhumikatha,* Buddhist Cosmology and Treaty on Ethics." *East and West* 7.4 (January): 349–352.

———. 1967. "Une Vie indochinoise du Buddha: *la Paṭhamasambodhi.*" In *Mélanges d'indianisme: à la mémoire de Louis Renou,* volume 28, pages 217–227. Publications de l'Institut de civilisation indienne. Paris: Éditions E. De Boccard.

Collard, Paul. 1921. *Cambodge et Cambodgiens.* Paris: Société d'éditions géographiques, maritimes et colonials.

Collins, Steven. 1990. "On the Very Idea of the Pali Canon." *Journal of the Pali Text Society* 15:89–126.

———. 1998. *Nirvana and Other Buddhist Felicities.* Cambridge: Cambridge University Press.

Commission des Moeurs et Coutumes du Cambodge. [1958] 1985. *Cérémonies privées des Cambodgiens.* Paris: Cedoreck.

Cone, Margaret, and Richard F. Gombrich. 1977. *The Perfect Generosity of Prince Vessantara: A Buddhist Epic.* Oxford: Oxford University Press.

Coomaraswamy, Ananda. 1977. "Saṃvega: Aesthetic Shock." In *Commaraswamy: Selected Papers,* edited by Roger Lipsey. Princeton, N.J.: Princeton University Press.

Crawfurd, John. [1828] 1967. *Journal of an Embassy to the Courts of Siam and Cochin China.* London: Oxford University Press.

De Bernon, Olivier. 1994. "Le *Buddh Daṃnāy:* Note sur un texte apocalyptique khmer." *Bulletin de l'École française d'Extrême-Orient* 81:83–96.

———. 1998. "La prédiction du Bouddha." *Aséanie* 1:43–66.

De Silva, Lily, ed. 1970. *Dīgha-Nikāyaṭṭhakathaṭīkā Līnatthavaṇṇana.* Volume 3. London: Pali Text Society.

Des Forges, Alexander. 2003. "Building Shanghai, One Page at a Time: The Aesthetics of Installment Fiction at the Turn of the Century." *Journal of Asian Studies* 62.3:781–810.

Descours-Gatin, Chantal. 1992. *Quand l'opium finançait la colonisation en Indochine: l'élaboration de la régie générale de l'opium (1860 à 1914).* Paris: Éditions l'Harmattan.

Dhammasuddho Bhikkhu. 1972. *Wat Bovoranives Vihāra.* Bangkok: Siva Phorn.

Dhan' Hin. 1999. "Qaṃbī *Buddh Daṃnāy.*" *Kambujasuriyā* 53.4:34–76.

Dhan' Vān', Braḥ Grū Saṅghasumedh. 1953. *Prasnā Buddhsāsana.* Phnom Penh: Vatt Uṇṇālom.

Dik Keam. 1966. *Catalogue des auteurs khmers et etrangers.* Phnom Penh: Association of Khmer Writers.

Duara, Prasenjit. 1995. *Rescuing History from the Nation: Questioning Narratives of Modern China.* Chicago: University of Chicago Press.

Ebihara, May. 1968. "Svay, a Village in Cambodia." Ph.D. dissertation, Columbia University.

École française d'Extrême-Orient. 1914. "Cambodge." *Bulletin de l'École française d'Extrême-Orient* 14.9:94–96.

———. 1922. "Cambodge." *Bulletin de l'École française d'Extrême-Orient* 22:376–380.

Edwards, Penny. 1999. "Cambodge: The Cultivation of a Nation, 1860–1945." Ph.D. Thesis, Monash University, 1999.

Études Cambodgiennes. 1969. "Le bouddhisme Khmer." *Études Cambodgiennes,* no. 17 (January–March), 15–35.

Faure, Bernard. 1996. *Visions of Power: Imagining Medieval Japanese Buddhism.* Princeton, N.J.: Princeton University Press.

Fealy, Greg. 1996. "Wahab Chasbullah, Traditionalism and the Political Development of Nahdlatul Ulama." In *Nahdlatul Ulama, Traditional Islam and Modernity in Indonesia,* edited by Greg Barton and Greg Fealy, pages 1–41. Clayton, Victoria: Monash Asia Institute.

Feer, L., editor. 1884a. *"Pañcagatidīpana." Journal of the Pali Text Society,* 152–161.

———, translator. 1884b. *"Pañcagatidīpana." Annales du Musée Guimet* 5 (1884): 514–528.

Filliozat, Jean. 1969. "Suzanne Karpelès." *Bulletin de l'École française d'Extrême-Orient,* extrait, 66:1–3.

Finot, Louis. 1902. "Liste des manuscrits khmèrs." *Bulletin de l'École française d'Extrême-Orient* 2:387–400.

———. [1926] 1964. *Qaṃbībraḥbuddhsāsana.* 3rd edition. Translated by Juṃ M"au. Phnom Penh: Buddhist Institute.

———. 1927. "Mahā Vimaladhamma." *Bulletin de l'École française d'Extrême-Orient* 27:523.

Flauguerges, E. 1914. "La mort du chef suprême des bonzes." *Revue Indochinoise* 2 (Février): 175–182.

Forest, Alain. 1980. *Le Cambodge et la colonisation française: histoire d'une colonisation sans heurts (1897–1920).* Paris: Editions L'Harmattan.

———. 1992. *Le culte des genies protecteurs au Cambodge: analyse et traduction d'un corpus de texts sur les neak ta.* Paris: Editions L'Harmattan.

Garnier, Francis. 1885. *Voyage d'exploration en Indo-chine.* Paris: Librairie Hachette.

Ginsburg, Henry. 1989. *Thai Manuscript Painting.* Honolulu: University of Hawai'i Press.

Goloubew, Victor. 1935. "Louis Finot (1864–1935)." *Bulletin de l'École française d'Extrême-Orient* 35.2:515–550.

Gombrich, Richard, and Gananath Obeyesekere. 1988. *Buddhism Transformed: Religious Change in Sri Lanka.* Princeton, N.J.: Princeton University Press.

Griswold, Alexander B. 1961. *King Mongkut of Siam.* New York: The Asia Society.

Groeneveldt, W. P. 1890. *Rapport over het opium-monopolie in Fransch Indo-China.* Batavia: Landsdrukkerij.

Groslier, Georges. 1918. "L'agonie de l'art cambodgien." *Revue indochinoise* 21.6:547–560.

———. 1921. *Recherches sur les Cambodgiens.* Paris: Augustin Challamel.

Guesdon, Joseph. 1906. "La littérature khmère et le Buddhisme." *Anthropos* 1:91–109, 278–295.

———. 1930. *Dictionnaire cambodgien-français.* Paris: Librairie Plon.

Guthrie, Elizabeth. 2001. "Outside the Sima." *Udaya: Journal of Khmer Studies* 2:7–17.

Hallisey, Charles. 1995. "Roads Taken and Not Taken in the Study of Theravāda Buddhism." In *Curators of the Buddha,* edited by Donald S. Lopez, Jr., pages 31–61. Chicago: University of Chicago Press.

———, and Frank E. Reynolds. 1989. "Buddhist Religion, Culture, and Civilization." In *Buddhism and Asian History,* edited by Joseph M. Kitagawa and Mark D. Cummings, pages 3–28. New York: Macmillan.

Hanks, Lucien. 1962. "Merit and Power in the Thai Social Order." *American Anthropologist* 64:1247–1261.

Hansen, Anne. 1988. "Crossing the River: Secularization of Khmer Childbirth Rituals." M.Div. Thesis, Harvard Divinity School.

———. 1999. "Ways of the World: Moral Discernment and Narrative Ethics in a Cambodian Buddhist Text." Ph.D. Dissertation, Harvard University.

———. 2003. "The Image of an Orphan: Cambodian Narrative Sites for Buddhist Ethical Reflection." *Journal of Asian Studies* 62.3:811–834.

Harris, Ian. 1999. "Buddhism *in Extremis:* The Case of Cambodia." In *Buddhism and Politics in Twentieth-century Asia,* edited by Ian Harris, pages 54–78. London: Pinter.

Harvey, David. 1990. *The Condition of Postmodernity.* Cambridge: Blackwell.

———. 2003. *Paris, Capital of Modernity.* New York: Routledge.

Headley, Robert K. 1977. *Cambodian-English Dictionary.* Volumes 1 and 2. Washington, D.C.: Catholic University of America Press.

Hefner, Robert W. 1997. "Islam in an Era of Nation-States: Politics and Religious Renewal in Muslim Southeast Asia." In *Islam in an Era of Nation-States,* edited by Robert W. Hefner and Patricia Horvatich, pages 3–40. Honolulu: University of Hawai'i Press.

Heine-Geldern, Robert. 1956. *Conceptions of State and Kingship in Southeast Asia.* Southeast Asia Program Data Paper, number 18. Ithaca, N.Y.: Cornell University Press.

Herbert, Patricia. 1982. *The Hsaya San Rebellion (1930–1932) Reappraised.* Clayton, Victoria: Monash University Centre of Southeast Asian Studies.

———, and Anthony Milner, editors. 1989. *South-East Asia: Languages and Literatures, a Select Guide.* Honolulu: University of Hawai'i Press.

Hinton, Alexander Laban. 2002. "Purity and Contamination in the Cambodian Genocide." In *Cambodia Emerges from the Past: Eight Essays,* edited by Judy Ledgerwood, pages 60–90. DeKalb, Ill.: Southeast Asia Publications, Center for Southeast Asian Studies, Northern Illinois University.

Hobsbawm, Eric. 1987. *The Age of Empire, 1875–1914.* New York: Vintage Books.

Holt, John. 1993. "Introduction." In *Anāgatavaṃsa Desanā,* translated by Udaya Meddegama and edited by John Holt, pages 1–18. Delhi: Motilal Banarsidass.

Hooker, M. B. 1983. "The Translation of Islam into South-East Asia." In *Islam in South-East Asia,* edited by M. B. Hooker, pages 1–22. Leiden: E. J. Brill.

———. 2003. *Indonesian Islam.* Asian Studies Association of Australia Southeast Asia Publications Series. Honolulu: University of Hawai'i Press and Allen and Unwin.

Huffman, Franklin E., and Ivn Proum. 1978. *English-Khmer Dictionary.* New Haven, Conn., and London: Yale University Press.

Huot Tath, Braḥ Grū Saṃghavijjā. [1926] 1928. *Qambī prāsād khlah nau dī Qangar.* Phnom Penh: Royal Library.

———. [1926] 1957. *Quelques monuments d'Angkor.* Phnom Penh: Buddhist Institute.

———. 1927. *Siṅgālovādasutta (Dīghanikāya* 31). Phnom Penh: Publications of the École Supérieure de Pali, Bibliothèque Royale du Cambodge.

———, Braḥ Visuddhivaṅs. 1935. *Sattaparitta-dvādasaparitta.* Phnom Penh: Royal Library.

———, Braḥ Bodhivaṅs Vajirappañño. 1958. *Dhammasaṅgaha,* 3rd printing. Phnom Penh: Rājabumb Khemaravaddh.

———, Braḥ Mahāsumedhādhipatīsaṅghanāyak. [1961] 1970. *Braḥ Buddhsāsanā nau Prates Kambujā Saṅkhep.* Phnom Penh: Buddhist Institute.

———, Samtec Braḥ Mahāsumedhādhipatī. 1993. *Kalyāṇamitta rabas' khñuṃ.* Phnom Penh: Buddhist Institute.

———, Braḥ Grū Saṃghavijjā; Braḥ Grū Saṃsatthā Chuon Nath; and Braḥ Grū Vimalapaññā Uṃ-Sūr. [1918] 1928. *Sāmaṇeravinaya,* 2nd edition. Phnom Penh: Bibliothèque Royale du Cambodge.

Ileto, Reynaldo. 1992. "Religion and Anti-colonial Movements." In *The Cambridge History of Southeast Asia,* edited by Nicholas Tarling, volume 2, pages 197–248. Cambridge: Cambridge University Press.

Ind, Ukñā Suttantaprījā. [1921?] 1971. *Gatilok.* Volumes 1–10. Phnom Penh: Buddhist Institute.

———. 1934a. "Nirās Nagar Vatt." *Kampbujasuriyā* 6:5–81.

———. 1934b. *"Rȳaṅ Paṭhamasambodhi." Kambujasuriyā* 6.10–12:5–38.

Ishii, Yoneo. 1986. *Sangha, State and Society,* translated by Peter Hawkes. Honolulu: University of Hawai'i Press.

Ivarsson, Soren. 1995. "The Study of the *Traipham Phra Ruang:* Some Considerations." In *Thai Literary Traditions,* edited by Manas Chitakasem, pages 56–86. Bangkok: Chulalongkorn University Press.

Jacob, Judith. 1993. *Cambodian Linguistics, Literature and History: Collected Articles,* edited by David A. Smyth. London: School of Oriental and African Studies, University of London.

———. 1996. *The Traditional Literature of Cambodia: A Preliminary Guide.* Oxford: Oxford University Press.

Janneau, G. 1914. "Le Cambodge d'autrefois." *Revue Indochinoise* 21.6 (June): 617–632.

Johns, A. H. 1986. "Islam in Southeast Asia." In *Encyclopedia of Religion,* edited by Mircea Eliade et al., pages 404–422. New York: Macmillan.

Jory, Patrick. 2002. "Thai and Western Buddhist Scholarship in the Age of Colonialism: King Chulalongkorn Redefines the Jatakas." *Journal of Asian Studies* 61.3 (August): 891–918.

Kamala Tiyavanich. 1997. *Forest Recollections: Wandering Monks in Twentieth-Century Thailand.* Honolulu: University of Hawai'i Press.

Karl, Rebecca. 2002. *Staging the World.* Durham, N.C., and London: Duke University Press.

Karpelès, Suzanne. 1933. "Renascence in Cambodia." *Journal of the American Association of University Women* 26.2 (January): 67–74.

Kartodirdjo, Sartono. 1985. "The Peasants' Revolt of Banten in 1888: The Religious Revival." In *Readings on Islam in Southeast Asia,* edited by Ahmad Ibrahim, Sharon Siddique, and Yasmin Hussain, pages 103–110. Singapore: Institute of Southeast Asian Studies.

Keyes, Charles F. 1977. "Millenialism, Theravāda Buddhism, and Thai Society." *Journal of Asian Studies* 36.2 (February 1977): 283–302.

———. 1983. "Merit-transference in the Kammic Theory of Popular Theravada Buddhism." In *Karma: An Anthropological Inquiry,* edited by Charles F. Keyes and E. Valentine Daniels, pages 261–286. Berkeley: University of California Press.

———. 1989. *Thailand: Buddhist Kingdom as Modern Nation-State.* Bangkok: Editions Duang Kamol [Westview Press].

———. 1994. "Communist Revolution and the Buddhist Past in Cambodia." In *Asian Visions of Authority: Religion and the Modern States of East and Southeast Asia,* edited by Charles F. Keyes, Laurel Kendall, and Helen Hardacre, pages 43–73. Honolulu: University of Hawai'i Press.

Khemarapaṇṇākār, ed. 1952. *Buddh Daṃnāy tām Sāstrā Soḷasanimitt* Phnom Penh: Roṅbumb Khmaer.

Khin Sok. 1982. "Essai d'interpretation de formulas magiques des Cambodgiens." *Asie du Sud-Est et Monde Insulindien* 13.1–4:111–119.

———. 1991. *Le Cambodge entre le Siam et le Viêtnam (de 1775 à 1860).* Paris: École française d'Extrême-Orient.

Khing Hoc Dy. 1990. *Contribution à l'histoire de la littérature khmère: littérature de l'epoque "classique" (XVème–XIXème siècles).* Paris: Éditions l'Harmattan.

———. 1993. *Ecrivains et expressions littéraires du Cambodge au XXème siècle,* volume 2. Paris: Éditions l'Harmattan.

Khy Phanra. 1975. "Les origines du Caodisme au Cambodge (1926–1940)." *Mondes Asiatiques* 3:315–348.

Kiernan, Ben. 1985. *How Pol Pot Came to Power.* London: Verso.

———, and Chanthou Boua. 1982. *Peasants and Politics in Kampuchea, 1942–1981.* London: Zed Press.

King, Richard. 1999. *Orientalism and Religion: Postcolonial Theory, India and "The Mystic East."* London: Routledge.

Krumjaṃnuṃ Prae *Braḥ Traipiṭak.* 1940. *Seckdīatippāy Qaṃpīuppattihetu nai Braḥ Traipiṭak Prai.* Phnom Penh: Buddhist Institute.

Kurzman, Charles, ed. 2002. *Modernist Islam, 1840–1940.* New York: Oxford University Press.

LaCapra, Dominick. 1983. *Rethinking Intellectual History: Texts, Contexts, Language.* Ithaca, N.Y.: Cornell University Press.

Laffan, Michael Francis. 2003. *Islamic Nationhood and Colonial Indonesia: The Umma below the Winds.* London and New York: RoutledgeCurzon.

Lamont, Pierre L. 1989. *L'Affaire Yukanthor: Autopsie d'un scandale colonial.* Paris: Sociéte française d'histoire d'outre-mer.

Lāṅ Hap Ān. 1970. *Uppattihetu nai Braḥ Traipiṭak Prai.* Phnom Penh: Buddhist Institute.

League of Nations. 1921–1938. *League of Nations Report from the Advisory Commission on Traffic in Opium and Other Dangerous Drugs.* Volumes 1–23. Geneva: League of Nations.

Leclère, Adhémard. 1895. *Cambodge: contes et legends.* Paris: Ernest Leroux.

———. 1899. *Le Bouddhisme au Cambodge.* Paris: Ernest Leroux.

———. 1900. "Mémoire sur les fêtes Funéraires et les Incinérations qui ont eu lieu à Phnôm-Penh (Cambodge) du 27 Avril au 25 Mai 1899." *Journal Asiatique* 9.15:368–376.

———. 1902. *Le livre de Vésandār, le roi charitable.* Paris: Ernest Leroux.

———. 1904. "Le *Phok Tuk Pra Vipheak Sachor.*" *Revue Indochinoise,* November, 735–741.

———. 1906. *Les livres sacrés du Cambodge.* Paris: Ernest Leroux.

———. 1908. *Monographie de la Province de Kratie.* Saigon: Imprimerie F. H. Schneider.

———. 1914. *Histoire du Cambodge.* Paris: Librairie Paul Geuthner.

———. 1916. *Cambodge: fêtes civiles et religieuses.* Paris: Imprimerie nationale.

Ledgerwood, Judy. 1990. "Changing Khmer Conceptions of Gender: Women, Stories, and the Social Order." Ph.D. Dissertation, Cornell University.

Leve, Lauren G. 2002. "Subjects, Selves, and the Politics of Personhood in Theravāda Buddhism in Nepal." *Journal of Asian Studies* 61.3:833–860.

Lī Dhām Teṅ. 1961. *Aksarsāstr Khmaer.* Phnom Penh: Seṅ Ṅuon Huot.

———. 1994. "Qnakniban Khmaer dael mān Chmoḥ Lpī." *Kambujasuriyā* 48.1:42–60.

Lopez, Jr., Donald S., ed. 1995. *Curators of the Buddha: The Study of Buddhism under Colonialism.* Chicago: University of Chicago Press.

Luce, Paul (S. M. Sisowath). 1909. "École de pali d'Angkor." *Bulletin École française d'Extrême-Orient* 9:823–827.

Lvī-Em, Braḥ Ñāṇapavaravijjā. 1930. "Sāsana-hetukathā." In *Puṇy Sambodhi Buddhsāsanapaṇḍity,* pages 3–74. Phnom Penh: Bibliothèque Royale du Cambodge.

———, Samtec Braḥ Dhammalikkhit Uttamaprȳksā. 1950. *Vinayavinicchay.* Phnom Penh: Qālapaerabaratai.

———, Samtec Braḥ Dhammalikkhit. 1969. *Pabbajjā Khandhaka Saṅkhep.* 4th edition. Phnom Penh: Buddhist Institute.

———, Braḥ Dhammalikkhit, Braḥ Uttamamunī Uṃ-Sūr, and Braḥ Ñaṇavīriyā Ḷuṅ. 1961. *Paññāsa-jātakasaṃrāy.* 4th edition, volumes 1–5. Phnom Penh: Buddhist Institute.

Mabbett, Ian. 1985. "A Survey of the Background to the Variety of Political Traditions in South-east Asia." In *Patterns of Kingship and Authority in Traditional Asia,* edited by Ian Mabbett, pages 69–84. London: Croom Helm.

———, and David Chandler. 1995. *The Khmers.* Oxford: Blackwell.

Magnant. 1913. "Notes sur les débuts de l'enseignement français au Cambodge (1863–1890)." *Revue Indochinoise* 19.4 (April): 454–469.

Makhali Phāl. 1937. *Chant de Paix.* Phnom Penh: Bibliothèque Royale du Cambodge.

Malalgoda, Kitsiri. 1970. "Millennialism in Relation to Buddhism." *Comparative Studies in Society and History* 12.4 (October): 424–441.

———. 1976. *Buddhism in Sinhalese Society, 1750–1900: A Study of Religious Revival and Change.* Berkeley and Los Angeles: University of California Press.

Marr, David G. 1971. *Vietnamese Anticolonialism, 1885–1925.* Berkeley: University of California Press.

Marston, John Amos. 1994. "Metaphors of the Khmer Rouge." In *Cambodian Culture since 1975: Homeland and Exile,* edited by May M. Ebihara, Carol A. Mortland, and Judy Ledgerwood, pages 105–118. Ithaca, N.Y., and London: Cornell University Press.

———. 2002a. "Democratic Kampuchea and the Idea of Modernity." In *Cambodia Emerges from the Past: Eight Essays,* edited by Judy Ledgerwood, pages 38–59. DeKalb, Ill.: Southeast Asia Publications, Center for Southeast Asian Studies, Northern Illinois University.

———. 2002b. "La reconstrucción del budismo 'antiguo' de Camboya." In *Estudios de Asia y África* 37.2:271–303.

———. n.d. "Reconstructing 'Ancient' Cambodian Buddhism." Manuscript.

Maspero, Georges. 1929. *Un empire colonial français: l'Indochine.* Volume 1. Paris and Brussels: Éditions G. Van Oest.

McCoy, Alfred W. 1991. *The Politics of Heroin: CIA Complicity in the Global Drug Trade.* Brooklyn, N.Y.: Lawrence Hill Books.

McGill, Forrest. 1997. "Painting the 'Great Life.'" In *Sacred Biography in the Buddhist Traditions of South and Southeast Asia,* edited by Juliane Schober, pages 195–217. Honolulu: University of Hawai'i Press.

McHale, Shawn. 2004. *Print and Power: Confucianism, Communism, and Buddhism in the Making of Modern Vietnam.* Honolulu: University of Hawai'i Press.

———. n.d. "Two Transnationalisms? The Buddhist Revival and Popular Devotionalism in Southern Vietnam, 1920–1945." Paper presented at the conference "Transnational Exchange and the Construction of Modern Buddhism," 21 February 2004, Duke University.

Meas-Yang Bhikkhu. 1978. *Le Bouddhisme au Cambodge.* Brussels: Editions Thanh-Long.

Meddagama, Udaya, translator, and John Clifford Holt, editor. 1993. *Anāgatavaṃsa Desanā: The Sermon of the Chronicle-To-Be.* Delhi: Motilal Banarsidass.

Monod, G. H. 1907. "L'orthographe dite 'Quoc-Ngu' appliqué au cambodgien." *Revue Indochinoise* 5.64 (30 August): 1172–1177.

Mouhot, Henri. 1989. *Travels in Siam, Cambodia and Laos, 1858–1860.* Volume 1. Oxford: Oxford University Press.

Moura, Jean. 1883. *Le royaume du Cambodge.* Volumes 1 and 2. Paris: Librairie de la Société Asiatique de l'École des Langues Orientales Vivantes.

Muan, Ingrid. 2001. "Citing Angkor: The 'Cambodian Arts' in the Age of Restoration, 1918–2000." Ph.D. Dissertation, Columbia University.

Nepote, Jacques, and Khing Hoc Dy. 1981. "Literature and Society in Modern Cambodia." In *Essays on Literature and Society in Southeast Asia,* edited by Tham Seong Chee, pages 56–81. Singapore: Singapore University Press.

———, and Michael Tranet. 1983. "Deux sources statistiques relatives à la situation du monarchisme theravāda au Cambodge à la fin du 19th siecle." *Seksa Khmer* 6:40–73.

Noer, Deliar. 1973. *The Modernist Muslim Movement in Indonesia, 1900–1942.* Kuala Lumpur and London: Oxford University Press.

Norindr, Panivong. 1996. *Phantasmatic Indochine: French Colonial Ideology in Architecture, Film, and Literature.* Durham, N.C., and London: Duke University Press.

Norman, K. R., translator. 1994. *The Group of Discourses (Sutta-nipāṭa),* with alternative translations by I. B. Horner and Walpola Rahula. Volume 1. London: Pali Text Society.

Nyanatiloka, Bhikkhu. 1972. *Buddhist Dictionary: Manual of Buddhist Terms and Doctrines.* Edited by Nyanaponika Bhikkhu. 3rd edition, revised. Colombo: Frewin.

Nugent, Ann. 1996. "Asia's French Connection: George Coedès and the Coedès Collection." *National Library of Australia News* 6.4:6–8.

Obeyesekere, Gananath. 1970. "Religious Symbolism and Political Change in Ceylon." *Modern Ceylon Studies* 1.1:43–63.

———. 1991. "Buddhism and Conscience: An Exploratory Essay." *Daedalus* 120.3 (Summer): 219–239.

Osborne, Milton E. 1969. *The French Presence in Cochinchina and Cambodia: Rule and Response (1859–1905).* Ithaca, N.Y.: Cornell University Press.

———. 1978. "Peasant Politics in Cambodia: The 1916 Affair." *Modern Asian Studies* 12.2:217–243.

———, and David Wyatt. 1968. "The Abridged Cambodian Chronicle." *France-Asie* 193.2:189–203.

Pasquier, P. 1918. "L'ensignement supérieur en Indochine." *Revue Indochinoise* 21.4 (June): 393–396.

Pavie, August. 1898a. *Mission Pavie Indo-chine: 1879–1895, études diverses.* Volume 1, *Recherches sur la littérature du Cambodge, du Laos et du Siam.* Paris: Ernest Leroux.

———. 1898b. *Recherches sur la littérature du Cambodge, du Laos et du Siam.* Paris: Ernest Leroux.

———. 1903. *Contes populaires du Cambodge, du Laos et du Siam.* Paris: Ernest Leroux.

———. 1995. *Au Pays des millions d'éléphants et du parasol blanc (à la conquête des coeurs).* Rennes: Terre de Brume Éditions.

Pollock, Sheldon. 1998. "The Cosmopolitan Vernacular." *Journal of Asian Studies* 57.1:6–37.

Porée, Guy, and Éveline Porée-Maspero. 1938. *Moeurs et coutumes des Khmères.* Paris: Payot.

Porée-Maspero, Éveline. 1962. *Étude sur les rites agraires des Cambodgiens.* Volumes 1–3. Paris: Mouton.

Pou Saveros. 1988. *Guirlande de Cpāp'.* Volumes 1 and 2. Paris: Cedoreck.

——— (Lewitz). 1969. "Note sur la transliteration du Cambodgien." *Bulletin de l'École française d'Extrême-Orient* 55:163–169.

——— and Philip Jenner. 1981. "Les *cpap'* ou codes de conduite Khmers." *Bulletin de l'École française d'Extrême-Orient* 70:135–193.

Prakash, Gyan. 1999. *Another Reason: Science and the Imagination of Modern India.* Princeton, N.J.: Princeton University Press.

Queen, Christopher S., and Sally B. King. 1996. *Engaged Buddhism: Buddhist Liberation Movements in Asia.* Albany: State University of New York Press.

Qým Nuṃ. 1974. *Rýaṅ Borkaṃpor.* Phnom Penh: Raksāsiddhi.

Radjab, Muhamad. 1995. "Semasa Kecil di Kampung." In *Telling Lives, Telling History: Autobiography and Historical Imagination in Modern Indonesia,* edited, translated, and with an introduction by Susan Rodgers, pages 149–324. Berkeley: University of California Press.

Reddi, V. M. 1970. *A History of the Cambodian Independence Movement: 1863–1955.* Tirupati: Sri Venkateswara University.

Reynolds, Craig J. 1972. "The Buddhist Monkhood in Nineteenth-Century Thailand." Ph.D. Dissertation, Cornell University.

———. 1976. "Buddhist Cosmography in Thai History, with Special Reference to Nineteenth-Century Culture Change." *Journal of Asian Studies* 35.2 (February): 203–220.

Reynolds, Frank E. 1976. "The Many Lives of the Buddha: A Study of Sacred Biography and Theravāda Tradition." In *The Biographical Process: Studies in the History and Psychology of Religion,* edited by Frank E. Reynolds and Donald Capps, pages 37–61. The Hague: Mouton.

———. 1997. "Rebirth Traditions and the Lineages of Gotama: A Study in Theravāda Buddhology." In *Sacred Biography in the Buddhist Traditions of South and Southeast Asia,* edited by Juliane Schober, pages 19–39. Honolulu: University of Hawai'i Press.

———, and Mani Reynolds, translators. 1982. *The Three Worlds according to King Ruang.* Berkeley: Asian Humanities Press, Motilal Banarsidass.

Rhys Davids, Caroline A. F., translator and editor. [1929] 1989. *Stories of the Buddha; Being Selections from the Jātaka.* New York: Dover Publications.

Rhys Davids, T. W. 1925. *Buddhist Birth Stories.* Revised edition. London: G. Routledge.

———, and J. Estlin Carpenter, editors. [1890] 1949. *Dīgha Nikāya.* Volumes 1 and 3. London: Luzac.

———, and William Stede, editors. [1921–1925] 1986. *The Pali Text Society's Pali-English Dictionary.* London: Pali Text Society.

Rice, Stanley. 1924. *Ancient Indian Fables and Stories: Being a Selection from the Panchatantra.* London: John Murray.

Riddell, Peter G. 2001. *Islam and the Malay-Indonesian World.* Honolulu: University of Hawai'i Press.

Rodgers, Susan. 1995. *Telling Lives, Telling History: Autobiography and Historical Imagination in Modern Indonesia.* Berkeley: University of California Press.

Roff, William. 1985. "*Kaum Muda-Kaum Tua:* Innovation and Reaction amongst the Malays, 1900–1941." In *Readings on Islam in Southeast Asia,* edited by Ahmad Ibrahim, Sharon Siddique, and Yasmin Hussain, pages 123–129. Singapore: Institute of Southeast Asian Studies.

Roy, Tapti. 1995. "Disciplining the Printed Text: Colonial and Nationalist Surveillance of Bengali Literature." In *Texts of Power: Emerging Disciplines in Colonial Bengal,* edited by Partha Chatterjee, pages 30–62. Minneapolis: University of Minnesota Press.

Saddhatissa Hammalawa. 1997. *Buddhist Ethics,* revised edition. Boston: Wisdom Publications.

Saleh, Fauzan. 2001. *Modern Trends in Islamic Theological Discourse in Twentieth-Century Indonesia.* Leiden: E. J. Brill.

Salman, Michael. 2001. *The Embarrassment of Slavery: Controversies over Bondage and Na-*

tionalism in the American Colonial Philippines. Berkeley and Los Angeles: University of California Press.

Sarkisyanz, Emanuel. 1965. *Buddhist Backgrounds of the Burmese Revolution.* The Hague: Martinus Nijhoff.

Sarraut, Albert. 1918. "Le règlement général de l'instruction publique en Indochine." *Revue indochinoise* 21.3:335–356.

Schober, Juliane. 1995. "The Theravāda Buddhist Engagement with Modernity in Southeast Asia: Whither the Social Paradigm of the Galactic Polity?" *Journal of Southeast Asian Studies* 26 (September): 307–325.

———. 2005. "Buddhist Visions of Moral Authority and Civil Society: The Search for the Post-Colonial State in Burma." In *Burma at the Turn of the Twenty-First Century,* edited by Monique Skidmore. Honolulu: University of Hawai'i Press.

———. n.d. (in press). "Buddhism and Modernity in Myanmar." In *Buddhism in World Cultures: Contemporary Perspectives,* edited by Steven Berkwitz. Santa Barbara, Calif.: ABC-Clio.

Shiraishi, Takashi. 1990. *An Age in Motion: Popular Radicalism in Java, 1912–1926.* Ithaca, N.Y., and London: Cornell University Press.

Siegel, James T. 2000. *The Rope of God,* revised edition. Ann Arbor: University of Michigan Press.

Smith, Terry. 1993. *Making the Modern: Industry, Art, and Design in America.* Chicago: University of Chicago Press.

Smyth, David. 2000. "Toward the Canonizing of the Thai Novel." In *The Canon in Southeast Asian Literatures: Literatures of Burma, Cambodia, Indonesia, Laos, Malaysia, the Philippines, Thailand and Vietnam,* edited by David Smyth, pages 172–182. Richmond, Surrey: Curzon.

Spiro, Melford E. 1970. *Buddhism and Society.* New York: Harper and Row.

———. 1982. *Buddhism and Society: A Great Tradition and Its Burmese Vicissitudes.* 2nd, expanded edition. Berkeley and Los Angeles: University of California Press.

Sponberg, Alan, and Helen Hardacre, editors. 1988. *Maitreya, the Future Buddha.* Cambridge: Cambridge University Press.

Strong, John S. 1983. *The Legend of King Aśoka: A Translation of the Aśokāvadāna.* Princeton, N.J.: Princeton University Press.

———. 1992. *The Legend and Cult of Upagupta.* Princeton, N.J.: Princeton University Press.

Suṅ S'īv Siddhattho, Braḥ Pālāt' Uttamalikhit. 1952. *Kappa-kathā.* Phnom Penh: Paṇṇāgār Pio Híat.

Swearer, Donald. 1995. *The Buddhist World of Southeast Asia.* Albany: State University of New York Press.

———. 1999. "Centre and Periphery: Buddhism and Politics in Modern Thailand." In *Buddhism and Politics in Twentieth-Century Asia,* edited by Ian Harris, pages 194–228. New York: Pinter.

Taboulet, Georges. 1956. *La geste française en Indochine: histoire par les texts de la France en Indochine des origins à 1914,* volume 2. Paris: Librairie d'Amérique et d'Orient.

Tai Hue-Tam Ho. 1983. *Millenarianism and Peasant Politics in Vietnam.* Cambridge, Mass.: Harvard University Press.

———. 1988. "Perfect World and Perfect Time: Maitreya in Vietnam." In *Maitreya, the*

Future Buddha, edited by Alan Sponberg and Helen Hardacre, pages 154–170. Cambridge: Cambridge University Press.

———. 1992. *Radicalism and the Origins of the Vietnamese Revolution.* Cambridge, Mass.: Harvard University Press.

Tambiah, Stanley J. 1976. *World Conqueror and World Renouncer.* Cambridge: Cambridge University Press.

———. 1984. *The Buddhist Saints of the Forest and the Cult of Amulets.* Cambridge: Cambridge University Press.

———. 1985. *Culture, Thought, and Social Action.* Cambridge, Mass.: Harvard University Press.

Tandart, S. 1910. *Dictionnaire cambodgien-français.* Hong Kong: Imprimerie Mission Etrangers.

———. 1935. *Dictionnaire cambodgien-français.* Phnom Penh: Albert-Portail.

Tannenbaum, Niccola. 1995. *Who Can Compete against the World? Power-Protection and Buddhism in Shan Worldview.* Ann Arbor, Mich.: Association for Asian Studies.

Tauch Chhuong. 1994a. *Battambang during the Time of the Lord Governor,* translated by Hin Sithan, Carol Mortland, and Judy Ledgerwood. 2nd edition. Phnom Penh: Cedoreck.

———. 1994b. *Pāt'ṭmpaṅ Smay Lok Mcās'.* Phnom Penh: Cedoreck.

Terwiel, B. 1983. "Bondage and Slavery in Early Nineteenth Century Siam." In *Slavery, Bondage and Dependency in Southeast Asia,* edited by Anthony Reid, pages 118–137. New York: St. Martin's Press.

Thanet Aphornsuvan. 1998. "Slavery and Modernity: Freedom in the Making of Modern Siam." In *Asian Freedoms: The Idea of Freedom in East and Southeast Asia,* edited by David Kelly and Anthony Reid, pages 161–186. Cambridge: Cambridge University Press.

Thompson, Ashley. 2000. "Introductory Remarks between the Lines: Writing Histories of Middle Cambodia." In *Other Pasts: Women, Gender and History in Early Modern Southeast Asia,* edited by Barbara Watson Andaya, pages 47–68. Honolulu: University of Hawai'i Press.

———. 2004. "The Future of Cambodia's Past: A Messianic Middle-Period Cambodian Royal Cult." In *History, Buddhism, and New Religious Movements in Cambodia,* edited by John Marston and Elizabeth Guthrie, pages 13–39. Honolulu: University of Hawai'i Press.

Thompson, Kenneth. 1996. "Religion, Values, and Ideology." In *Modernity: An Introduction to Modern Societies,* edited by Stuart Hall, David Held, Don Hubert, and Kenneth Thompson, pages 396–422. Cambridge: Blackwell.

Thongchai Winichakul. 1994. *Siam Mapped.* Honolulu: University of Hawai'i Press.

Tully, John. 1996. *Cambodia under the Tricolour: King Sisowath and the "Mission Civilatrice," 1904–1927.* Clayton, Victoria: Monash Papers on Southeast Asia, no. 37. Monash University.

———. 2002. *France on the Mekong: A History of the Protectorate in Cambodia, 1863–1953.* Lanham, Md.: University Press of America.

Uṃ-Sūr, Braḥ Grū Vimalapaññā. 1927. *Abhidhammatthasangaha.* Phnom Penh: Imprimerie nouvelle A. Portail.

———. 1928. *Dasapāramikathā.* Phnom Penh: Imprimerie du Gouvernement.

———. 1930. *Maraṇanussati Kamatthana.* Phnom Penh: Imprimerie du Gouvernement.

———. [1930] 1963. *Milindapañhā.* Phnom Penh: Buddhist Institute.

———, Braḥ Uttamamunī. 1940. *Qavasānakicca rapas' Braḥ Uttamamunī Uṃ-Sūr Dhammavinayavikkhito.* Phnom Penh: Buddhist Institute.
Vajirañāṇavarorasa, Somdetch Phra Mahā Samaṇa Chao Krom Phrayā. [1913] 1969. *Vinayamukha, The Entrance to the Vinaya,* volume one, translated by Phra Khantipālo and Khun Suchin. Bangkok: Mahāmakuṭarājavidyālaya.
———. 1979. *Autobiography: The Life of Prince-Patriarch Vajirañāṇavarorasa of Siam, 1860–1921,* translated, edited, and with an introduction by Craig J. Reynolds. Athens: Ohio University Press.
Van der Veer, Peter. 2001. *Imperial Encounters: Religion and Modernity in India and Britain.* Princeton, N.J.: Princeton University Press.
Vickery, Michael. 1977. "Cambodia after Angkor: The Chronicular Evidence for the Fourteenth to Sixteenth Centuries." Ph.D. Dissertation, Yale University.
Von der Mehden, Fred R. 1993. *Two Worlds of Islam: Interaction between Southeast Asia and the Middle East.* Gainesville: University of Florida Press.
Von Hinüber, Oskar. 1996. *A Handbook of Pāli Literature.* Berlin and New York: Walter de Gruyter.
Vu Trong Phung. 2002. *Dumb Luck,* translated by Nguyet Nguyet Cam and Peter Zinoman, edited and with an introduction by Peter Zinoman. Ann Arbor: University of Michigan Press.
Walshe, Maurice, translator. 1987. *Thus Have I Heard: The Long Discourses of the Buddha.* London: Wisdom Books.
Wibha Senanan. 1975. *The Genesis of the Novel in Thailand.* Bangkok: Thai Watana Panich.
Wigen, Kären. 1995. *The Making of a Japanese Periphery, 1750–1920.* Berkeley and Los Angeles: University of California Press.
———. 1999. "Culture, Power, and Place: The New Landscapes of East Asian Regionalism." *American Historical Review* 104.4:1183–1201.
Willoughby, Westel Woodbury. 1925. *Opium as an International Problem: The Geneva Conferences.* Baltimore, Md.: John Hopkins University Press.
Wilson, Kathleen. 2000. "Citizenship, Empire, and Modernity in the English Provinces, c. 1720–90." In *Cultures of Empire: Colonizers in Britain and the Empire in the Nineteenth and Twentieth Centuries,* edited by Catherine Hall, pages 157–186. New York: Routledge.
Wilson, Liz. 1996. *Charming Cadavers: Horrific Figurations of the Feminine in Indian Buddhist Hagiographic Literature.* Chicago: University of Chicago Press.
Wolters, O. W. 1999. *History, Culture and Region in Southeast Asian Perspectives.* Revised edition. Studies on Southeast Asia, no. 26. Ithaca, N.Y.: Southeast Asia Program Publications.
Wyatt, David K. 1969. *The Politics of Reform in Thailand: Education in the Reign of King Chulalongkorn.* New Haven, Conn.: Yale University Press.
———. 1993. *Temple Murals as an Historical Source: The Case of Wat Phumin, Nan.* Bangkok: Chulalongkorn University Press.
Yang Sam. 1987. *Khmer Buddhism and Politics, 1954–1984.* Newington, Conn.: Khmer Studies Institute.
Zinoman, Peter. 2002. "Vu Trong Phung's *Dumb Luck* and the Nature of Vietnamese Modernism." In *Dumb Luck,* translated by Nguyet Nguyet Cam and Peter Zinoman, edited and with an introduction by Peter Zinoman, pages 1–30. Ann Arbor: University of Michigan Press.

INDEX

Abhidhamma (*Abhidhamm*, *Abhidhammapiṭaka*), 50, 80–81, 88, 134, 137, 142, 178
Abhidhammatthasangaha, 154
Aisenberg, Andrew, 118
Ajātasattu, Prince, 165–166, 176
alcohol, 70–73. *See also* opium
amulets, 56, 58, 62, 113–114, 118
Ang Chan, Prince, 60
Ang Duong, King, 4, 15, 47, 49–51, 55, 67, 76, 78–80, 86, 132; death of, 51; request for *Tipiṭaka*, 79, 87
Angkor, 75, 120–121, 131–133, 146, 154
anti-French resistance, 58–59, 62, 112
Aśoka, King (Dhammāsok), 129, 180
Attānusāsnī, 145
Aṭṭhikathādhammapada, 89. See also *Dhammapadaṭṭhakathā*
authenticity: of Dhamma, 107, 150–152; of early Buddhism, 124–125, 129, 131; Huot Tath on, 160–161; Ind on, 95–96, 167; in modernist thought, 1–3, 106, 148–152, 154–161, 177; of monastic conduct, 105; Mongkut on, 78–79, 90–92; of texts, 83
authority, textual: to Huot Tath, 103–104; in manuscript culture, 83; in modernist thought, 150, 157, 159–160; and scripturalism, 96; in Theravāda tradition, 149
awakening, as modernist trope, 7, 99, 100, 104–105, 154. *See also* illumination

Bangkok: as Buddhist intellectual center, 84–85; Khmer monks in, 80, 82–90, 92–96, 134; Khmer monks restricted from, 115–116, 132; literary world of, 93–94
baṅsāvatār (chronicle), 79, 129
Bardez, Felix, 76
basket weaver, 164–165, 177
bat (alms bowl), 97–98
Baudoin, François-Marius, 110, 112, 118, 135, 137–139, 141
Bellan, Charles, 123
Bernard Free Library of Rangoon, 82
bhik-dik-sampath (drinking the water of the oath), 52–53
Bimbānibbān, 20
Bimbisāra, King, 165, 174
Bizot, François, 8, 79–81
Blackburn, Anne, 9, 12
bodhi-citta (thought or aim of enlightenment), 3, 156
Bodhisatta (Bodhisattva, the future Buddha): 15, 23–24, 148; in "Bhikkhu Sukh," 171; as exemplary figure, 76, 104, 152; in *Nemirāj*, 25–27; new historicized biography of, 129; in *Paṭhamasambodhi*, 34–35; in *Rẏaṅ Paṭhamasambodhi*, 18–19, 36–43; in *Vessantar-jātak*, 28–33
Bouddhisme au Cambodge, Le (Leclère), 121–122
Bouddhisme, son origine, son evolution, Le (Finot), 129–130, 145
Bowen, John, 181–182
Braḥbuddh-sāsanā nau Prates Kambujā (Huot Tath), 180
Buddh Daṃnāy, 60–61
Buddha Master of Western Peace, 58–60
Buddhabhāsita (words spoken by the Buddha), 103
Buddhavacana (words of the Buddha), 15, 88–89
Buddhist Institute, 5, 107, 109–110, 127, 130–131; inauguration, 145, 150–152
Buddhist studies, 8, 129
Buddh-sāsana (Buddhism), defined by Chuon Nath, 179
Buu Son Ky Huong, 13, 57–60, 113

Cabaton, Antoine, 79
Cakkavatti-sīhanāda-sutta, 38–39

cakkavattin (righteous king), 37–39, 51–56, 152
Cannon, Katherine, 176
canon: as authoritative idea, 160–161; in colonial European scholarship, 124–125; "formal" and "practical," 9; modernist constructions of, 152–153; in nineteenth-century Cambodia, 79–80; scholarly reappraisals of, 8–9; Sinhalese Mahāvihārin, 84
Cao Dai, 6, 113, 117–118
Catholicism, 111
Chakrabarty, Dipesh, 6, 11
Chandler, David, 47, 49, 56, 127, 172–173
Chāp Pin, Ācāry Suvaṇṇajoto, 145
chāyā (record of monastic identity), 115–116, 118–119
cholera epidemic, 57–58
chronicle: in manuscript collections, 79, 81; translated and used as historical sources by Chandler, 47–49, 56–57, 173. See also *baṅsāvatār*
Chulalongkorn (Rama V), King, 2, 64, 83–85, 92, 94; modernization policies of, 85, 112, 116, 119–120, 123
Chuon Nath, Samtec Braḥ Mahāsumedhādhipatī Braḥ Sangharāj, 1, 101–110, 119, 126–127, 135–136, 143, 145, 182; ethical writings, 154–156; *Gihi-vinaya-saṅkhep*, 155; in Hanoi, 129, 137; and orthographic reform, 140–141; *Pāṭimokkha*, 106–107; as supreme patriarch, 145; *Trāyapaṇām-saṅkhep*, 155–156
Cin-Jā, Braḥ, 100
citta (*citt*, heart and mind), 3, 78, 89, 90, 107, 178; hardening of, 104; purification of, 104–105, 179
civilizational development (and degeneration), 95, 120–122, 124, 167, 179
Coedès, George, 82, 110, 117, 125–128, 133–137, 139–140, 142
Collins, Steven, 9, 25, 38, 161–162
Commission on the Production of the *Tipiṭaka*, 108, 127, 131, 145
Communism, 5
community: four-fold religious *parisāḷ* of *bhikkhu-bhikkhunī-upāsak-upāsikā* (monks, nuns, and male and female laypeople), 11; in *Gatilok*, 163, 167, 176; and purification, 77, 149–152, 162, 183; in *Sāsana-hetukathā*, 150–152; in *Trai Bhūm*, 21; in *Vessantar-jātak*, 31
contagion, 112, 118
Convention of 17 June 1884, 65–67
cosmology. *See* hierarchy; *Nemirāj*; *Pañasa-Sīrasā*; *Rȳaṅ Paṭhamasambodhi*; *Trai Bhūm*; *Vessantara-jātaka*
Council on the Improvement of Native Education, 123–124
court, Khmer, 52–54, 65. *See also* hierarchy; Khmer monarchy
cpāp' (didactic poetry), 16, 53, 81, 83, 124, 152, 159, 173
Cpāp' Tūnmān Khluan, 53, 72, 159
Cpāp' Trīneti, 173

Daeb, Yāy, 95–96
daṃnāy (prophesies). *See* prophesies, Buddhist
Damrong, Prince, 85, 126–127
Dāsa-jātak, 88
Dasapāramikathā, 154
Deb-Ū, Braḥ Mahābrahmamunī, 88–89, 92–93, 103
Democratic Kampuchea, 5
demonstrations of 1916, 71, 114
demythologization, 119–120, 149, 182; Chuon Nath, 101–102, 105; in colonial Euopean scholarship, 124–125; Huot Tath, 101–102; Ind, 72; Mongkut, 85
desanā. *See* preaching
Devadattathera, 174
Dhamma (Dharma): defined, 6; in Ind's writing, 11; kings as upholders of, 60–61, 79; in the modern age, 131, 148–149; and social decay, 46, 148; and time, 21–23, 32
Dhammachaksu, 94
Dhammapada, 171
Dhammapadaṭṭhakathā, 101, 132, 134–135
Dhamma-vinaya (*Dhamma-vinay, Dharm-vinay*), 3, 15, 78, 80, 89, 91, 93, 103; authentic understanding of, 106, 151;

Khmer understandings of term, 90; love of, 102; and ordinary Khmer, 177
Dhammayut (Buddhist order): in Cambodia, 87, 96–100; French suspicions of Siamese, 110, 116, 128, 133–134; perceptions of in Cambodia, 97; in Siam, 6, 64, 84–86, 94, 102
dhammik (*dhammika dhammarāja*; righteous ruler), 55–56, 59–63, 118
Dham-Suas, Braḥ Mahārājā, 140
Dhaniyathera, 174
Dharaṇī, Nāṅ, 18, 39–41
Dharm-cās (old or traditional Dhamma). *See* traditionalist
Dharm-thmī (new or modern Dhamma). *See* modern Dhamma
Diaṅ, Samtec Braḥ Sangharāj, 34, 80, 86, 88, 100, 106–107, 121, 131, 134–135, 141, 154; *Jinavaṅs*, 86; *Pāṭimokkha*, 86; *Trai Bhūm*, 86
dictionary, Khmer, 126, 139, 144; commission, 139–141
discipline: and administrative control, 138–139; of *buddhsāsana* (Buddhism), 179; as fields of study, 130, 137, 141; as good moral conduct, 177–178; monastic, 90–92, 97, 99–100, 106–107, 138, 154; new, 109–110, 120
disjuncture (between religious visions and lived experience), 20, 43–44, 45, 54, 57, 63, 76
Doumer, Paul, 68
dukkha (suffering), 57, 73, 179; in "Bhikkhu Sukh," 171, 176
Duong, Braḥ, 80

École française d'Extrême-Orient. *See* EFEO
École Supérieure de Pali, 101. *See also* Sālā Pali
École Supérieur de Pali d'Angkor Vatt, 131–133
education, Buddhist: in Bangkok, 83–87, 89–96; in Cambodia, 87–89, 93; changes in, 78; and Chulalongkorn, 85; French perceptions of, 121–130; French support for, 120; and Mongkut, 83; in the nineteenth century, 20–21; reforms of, 15, 83–84, 123–124, 126, 130–142. *See also* pagoda schools
Edwards, Penny, 75, 127
EFEO (École française d'Extrême-Orient), 81, 110, 120, 125–130, 132–137, 139, 141; promotion of Pali education, 128, 133, 136
ethics, 3–4, 15–16, 149; contrasts between modernist and nineteenth-century literary, 20, 148–150, 152, 156–157, 159, 161, 164, 177, 179; and *Dhammavinay*, 104; Khmer understandings of, 90, 104; for laypeople, 151, 154–161, 165–167; and Pān, 87; and *Vinaya*, 90. See also *Gatilok*; *Siṅgālovāda-sutta*

fables, French, 73–75, 150
Faure, Bernard, 162
Finot, Louis, 110, 125–130, 134, 136–137, 139, 143, 154; *Le Bouddhisme, son origine, son evolution*, 129–130, 145; *Qaṃbībraḥbuddhsāsana*, 129; text collecting, 81
Foucher, Albert, 127
French colonial administration: declaration of Cambodia as a protectorate, 4; intensification of colonial control in Cambodia, 54, 64; perceptions of millenarianism, 64; reforms, 46, 51, 64–68, 98, 120–124; religious policies of, 109, 111–120, 130–137, 139–140, 142
funeral biographies, 15–17, 80–81, 88
funeral rituals, 27

gaṇ (diocese), 98, 132
Gaṅ-O, Braḥ Candavinay, 80–81
galactic polity, 51–54, 64, 85
gambhīr (scripture), 80, 89
gantha-dhura (scholarly tradition), 17, 112
Ganthamālā, 103, 144, 157
gati: as destinations for rebirth, 20; as ways of behaving, 164
Gatilok (Ind; ways of the world), 15, 68, 70–75, 94–96, 148, 150; basket weaver, 164–165; *gati*, 164; individual in, 163, 166, 176; *kalyāṇa-mitta* (virtuous friend), 177; karma, 164, 171–172;

laicization of monastic concepts, 165–166, 172, 175–177; literary form, 150, 167; localization of Theravādin ideas, 167, 170–177; moral agency, 162, 165, 167, 175–176; printing of, 145, 153; purification (*parisuddh*), 148–149, 167, 171–172, 175–176; *saṃvega*, 176–177; *satisampajañña*, 163, 165–166, 175–176; simile of the alloy, 163; social attachment, 163–166, 171–177; true and false monks, 167, 174–176
Gayo poetry, 181–182
genres: of Buddhist literature, 81, 83; of modernist writing, 16, 150; secular and Dhammic (*phlūv lok, phlūv dharm*), 88
geography, 84, 123, 130, 141
Gihipaṭipatti, 107, 145
Gihivinaya, 107
Gihivinaya-saṅkhep, 155
Go, Braḥ, 95
Groslier, Georges, 81
Guesdon, Joseph, 23–24, 28, 30

Hak, Braḥ Sīlasaṅvar, 140–141
Hallisey, Charles, 9, 111, 127. *See also* intercultural mimesis
Harvey, David, 10–11, 46
hells and heavens, 26–27
hierarchy: as ideal of order in upheaval, 43–44; as sociopolitical structure, 51–55, 64, 67, 69; in the three-tiered cosmos, 19–21, 23–32. *See also* galactic polity
history: of Khmer Buddhism, 179–180; as modern scientific discipline, 128, 132, 134, 137–138, 141–142, 144; modernist views of, 131
Hitopadeśa, 94, 128
hunger, 48
Huot Tath, Samtec Braḥ Mahāsumedhādhipatī Saṅghanāyak, 77–79, 100–110, 119, 126–127, 135–136, 182; *Braḥbuddh-sāsanā nau Prates Kambujā*, 180; dictionary commission, 141; ethical writings, 153–154, 157–161; in Hanoi, 129, 137; history of Khmer Buddhism, 179–180; *Kaṭhinakkhandhaka*, 106–107; *Sāmaṇera-vinaya*, 107; *Siṅgālovāda-sutta*; as supreme patriarch, 145
Hū-Ṛāy, Braḥ Suvaṇṇakesaro, 81

Iam, Samtec Braḥ Maṅgaladebācāry, 88–89, 114–115
iddhi (extraordinary powers), 60, 105
illumination, 78; of Deb-Ū, 89–90
imaginaire, 162, 167
immoral persons, 162–163
Ind, Ukñā Suttantaprījā (Āchāry Ind), 1, 4, 11, 16, 32, 35, 46, 62–63, 68, 70–75, 110, 148–150, 182; in Bangkok, 94; "Battle of Ta Kae," 62, 94; "Bhikkhu Sukh," 167–177; influence of Thai reformism on, 94–96; *Nirās Nagar Vatt*, 75; and orthographic reform, 140–141; satire of Dhammayut Pali pronunciation, 98–99. See also *Gatilok*, *Ryaṅ Paṭhamasambodhi*
individual (conceptions of): in *Gatilok*, 163, 165–166, 176; in modernist ethical writings, 149; in *Paṭhamasambodhi*, 35; in *Siṅgālovāda-sutta*; in *Trai Bhūm*, 22–23; in *Vessantar-jātak*, 29, 31–35
intercultural mimesis, 9, 111, 118–119, 126–127, 130–147, 182
intoxication: in *Cpāp' Tūnmān Khluan*, 72; in Ind's writing, 71–73; in Yukanthor's writing, 69–70
inventory (of texts), 82
invulnerability, 56–58, 62, 112–114, 118

Jāli (Jūli), 28–34
jātaka (stories of the Buddha's past lives), 4, 16, 20, 23–34, 76, 80, 82–83, 152; colonial European scholarly views of, 125, 128–129; controversies over interpretation of, 105; reinterpretations of as cultural and national works, 94, 128–129; views of by religious reformers, 85, 92, 94, 101
jāti, in Ind's writing, 94–96, 163, 176
Jha-Lan, Bhikkhu, 80
Jinavaṅs, 86
Joan of Arc, 95–96
Jūjak, 28–30, 32, 105

Juṃ-M"au, 129

Kaccāyana, 132, 135
Kālāma-sutta, 2
kalyāṇa-mitta (virtuous friend), 177
Kambujasuriyā, 17, 103, 129, 144, 153
kamma (karma): defined as actions of mind, speech, and body, 11, 164; imagery, 170–171; and individual identity, 22–23, 25, 34–35, 172; law of, 45; in *Nemirāj*, 26–27; and social order, 53, 63, 69; in *Vessantar-jātak*, 31; wealth, and rank, 53–54
Kaṇhājīnā (Kresna), 28–34
Kapilabhikkhu, 174
kappa (*kapp*, *kalpa*; temporal cycle), 21–22, 59
Karpelès, Suzanne, 125, 127–129, 142–145, 179
Kathathan, Phya, 82
Kaṭhinakkhandhaka, 106–107
Keth, Ukñā Adhipatīsenā, 107
Keyes, Charles, 8–9, 60, 62
Khin Sok, 66
Khmer Rouge, 5
kings, 52–54; contrasted with buddhas, 39–43; Mārā as symbol of, 37–43; in millenarian discourses, 55–56, 59–63; tenfold rules of, 60–61; in *Trai Bhūm*, 21; in Yukanthor's writing, 69–70. See also *cakkavattin*; court, Khmer; *dhammik*; hierarchy; monarchy, Khmer
Kitchanukit, 85, 93
Koet, Chauv Ghun Braḥ Amarābhirakkhit, 87
Kong, Ukñā Dhammānikar, 140
kpuan (technical manuals), 83, 88. See also *tamrā*

LaCapra, Dominick, 78–79
laicization (of monastic concepts), 148–151, 154–156, 159, 165–166, 172, 175–177
language (new perceptions of), 141
Leclère, Adhémard, 25, 27–30, 34–35, 60, 87, 96–97, 111, 121–122; *Le Bouddhisme au Cambodge*, 121–122
Levi, Sylvain, 117, 126
Lī Dhām Teṅ, 20
liberation, 167–168, 171
liberty: in Huot Tath's history of Khmer Buddhism, 180; in Ind's writing, 75; in Yukanthor's writing, 69
literature: Buddhist genres of, 81, 83; current in Bangkok, 84–85, 93–94; French perceptions of Khmer, 23, 121; in nineteenth-century Cambodia, 18–43; in Norodom's library, 81
localization (of Theravādin ideas): by Huot Tath, 148–149, 161–162; by Ind, 167, 170–177
Lokapaññatti, 129
Luce, Paul, 132
Lvī-Em, Samtec Braḥ Dhammalikhit, 107, 110, 128, 136, 145, 182; appointment as director of Sālā Pali, 142; ethical writings, 152, 154, 160, 167, 177; *Pabbajjākhandhaka-saṅkhepa*, 154; *Paññāsa-jātaka*, 154–155; *Sāsanahetukathā*, 150–152

Maddī, 28–33
Mahā-jātaka. See *Vessantara-jātaka*
Mahānikāy (Buddhist order), 4, 82, 91, 93; conflicts within, 99–109; differences from Dhammayut, 96–99; relations with Dhammayut, 96–100. *See also* tensions (between traditionalists and modernists)
Mahāvihāra (Sinhalese Buddhist order), 84
Makhali Phal, 146, 167
Mālai-sutta, 90
maṇḍala, 21
Maṅgaladīpanī (*Maṅgalaṭṭhadīpanī*), 80–81, 89, 101, 132, 134–135, 141, 152, 155; importance of, 82
manuscript: collection at Vatt Bodhivāl, 82; culture, 13–14, 78, 79–83; decline of manuscript culture, 100, 131, 142–144; editing practices, 30–31, 139–140; and modern Dhamma, 78, 82–83, 103; in Nordom's library, 81; protection of, 81–82; recitations of, 35–36; sacred qualities of, 82–83, 103–104, 106. *See also* textual production
Mārā, 18, 37–43
Maraṇamātā, *Nāṅ*, 173

Marchal, Henri, 127
Mās, (Tā, uncle), 45, 47, 49, 55
Mās-Kuṅ, Braḥ: illumination of, 93; journey to Bangkok, 84, 93; and robe controversies, 99–100
McHale, Shawn, 6
meditation, 80, 112
Mei, Ukñā Piphit Eisor, 140
merit: making, 27, 31, 80–81, 83, 117, 153, 156–157, 161, 171; and power, 19, 33–34, 45, 53–54, 182; power, and kingship in *Paṭhamasambodhi* and *Rýaṅ Paṭhamasambodhi*, 34–43; in the *Vessantara-jātak*, 28–31
mettā-karuṇā (loving-kindness and compassion), 176
Metteya (Maitreya), 39, 55–56, 58–59, 118
Mī, Braḥ Buddavaṅ, 133
Milindapañhā, 153
millenarian movements, 6, 13, 54; in Battambang, 62; Buu Son Ky Huong, 57–60; on Khmer-Vietnamese border, 56–60, 62, 113–114, 117–118; on Lao-Siamese border, 60–62; Pou Kombo, 57, 59–62
millenarianism, 4, 55–64; French fears about, 110–116, 118; Ind's critiques of, 63, 162; and modernism, 45–46, 57, 67–68, 76, 118–119, 152
mission civilisatrice, 12, 120
modern Dhamma (*Dharm-thmī*), 5, 13, 16, 76–78, 82–83, 95, 99–110, 118–119, 130, 145, 149, 154, 157, 161; distillation of, 177–178; views of European scholarship, 130
modern: in context of colonial policies, 124, 130; in Ind's terms, 11, 162; institutions, 109–111, 126–127, 130–147; nation, 181
modernism: definitions of, 13, 77; ethos in Cambodia, 95–96; Islamic, 2, 6–7, 13, 181–182; and millenarianism, 45–46, 57; religious, 2, 5, 148, 181; and social criticism, 77, 130, 181. *See also* modern Dhamma
modernity: in Cambodia, 46–47, 120; definitions, 10–11; Southeast Asian debates about, 5–6
Mon monastic interpretations, 84, 91–92
monarchy, Khmer, 51, 55, 64–65; enfeeblement of, 64–68
Mongkut (Rama IV), King, 2, 15, 64, 78, 83–86, 94, 106, 120; Khmer biography of, 90–91
Monivong, King, 118, 154
monks: and civil service posts, 132; colonial restrictions on, 111–112, 114–119, 132, 142; suspicions about political activities, 114; true (and false), 117, 162, 172, 174–176
moral agency. See *Gatilok*
moral decline, 6, 46, 55–64, 67–68, 178; in colonial society, 70–73
moral development: in millenarian discourses, 55; in modernist ethics, 148–149, 162, 167, 176–177, 183; in nineteenth-century literature, 19, 23–29, 32, 34, 45, 177, 182
moral order, 55. *See also* social order
moral persons (*sappurisa*), 163, 166–167, 176–177
Mouhot, Henri, 51, 120
Moura, Jean, 61, 79
Mūlakaccāyana, 80, 89, 92, 100
Müller, Friedrich Max, 124

Nam Thiep (anti-French resistance of), 58, 64
National Library. *See* Royal Library
national literature, 128–129, 137, 144
nationalism, 3, 6, 127, 181
Nemirāj, 25–27, 39
nirās (travel poetry), 83
Nirās Nagar Vatt (Ind), 75, 94
Norodom, King, 55, 59, 61, 64–65, 67; library of, 79, 81
novices. See *sāmaṇer*
nun, Buddhist, 81

Obeyesekere, Gananath, 8, 12
opium, 47, 65–70, 162; as metaphor for moral degeneration, 71–73
Ordinance 71 of 2 October 1918, 100, 106–107, 119, 141
ordination, 50, 86, 102; colonial regulation of, 116–119; modernist concern with,

154–155; Mongkut's concerns about, 90–92; as rite of passage, 115
orphans: in Khmer literature, 172–174, 176–177; in Southeast Asia political imagination, 173–174, 183
orthographic reform, 134, 139–141

Pabbajjākhandhaka-saṅkhepa, 134, 154–155
Pach Chhoeun, 127
pagoda schools, 122–124, 178
Pali, 2; canon in nineteenth-century Cambodia, 79–80; cosmopolitan tradition, 147, 161; examinations, 86–87, 132; importance of correct understanding, 152, 155–157, 159, 161; and Khmer language, 140; literature collection at Vatt Bodhivāl, 82; manuscripts from Siam, 82; methods of learning, 89, 92–93, 96; pronunciation differences between Mahānikāy and Dhammayut, 91–92, 97–99; study in Bangkok, 78, 83. *See also* education, Buddhist; Sālā Pali
Pān, Samtec Braḥ Sugandhādhipatī, 86–88, 96–97, 121, 131; library of, 88; and orthography, 141
Pañasa-Sīrasā, 24–25
Paññāsa-jātaka, 24, 128–129, 145, 152, 154
pāramī (perfections), 24
Parīvāravatth, 80
parisāḷ. *See* community
Pathamasāmant, 89
Paṭhamasambodhi, 20, 34–35, 81, 94, 141, 152, 179; importance of, 82
Pāṭimokkha, 86, 106–107, 142
paṭipatti (behaving in accordance with the Dhamma), 3, 106; *-pūjā*, 151
Phan Boi Chau, 116
Phan Xich Long, 113–114
phū mī bun (those possessing merit), 62. See also *qanak mān puṇy*
phlūv lok, phlūv dharm. *See* genres, secular and Dhammic
Pol, Āchāry, 80
Ponn, Minister of War and Public Instruction, 140–141
Pou Kombo, 57, 59, 61–62, 64
power: of elites dismantled, 66–68; protective, 56, 58, 60; religious, 112. See also *iddhi*; merit; *qanak mān puṇy*
Prāk Ū, Braḥ Nillajoti, 81
preaching (*desanā*), 88
print: in Bangkok, 85, 93–94; controversies about, 82, 106–107, 119; culture, 83, 142; genres, 3; introduction to Southeast Asia, 2–3; serialization, 153–154; strategies in *Siṅgālovādasutta*, 159–161; transition to, 14, 83, 147, 152–154, 160
prophesies, Buddhist, 55–56, 59–62, 64
Protestant Buddhism, 12, 120
purification,14–15; aim of *sappurisa*, 166; in Buu Son Ky Huong, 58; as central value of modernism, 1–3, 77, 118, 131, 148–150, 178; of the collective, 149–152, 161–162; of community, 149, 178; Huot Tath on, 160; Ind on, 166, 170–171, 175–177; of language, 139, 156; Lvī-Em on, 150–152; in millenarian discourses, 58–59; of monastic conduct, 90–92, 102; of moral conduct, 76, 177–178, 183; and problem of social attachment, 165–166, 170–177; reinterpretations of, 83; of religious practice, 95–96, 154–160; and scripturalism, 83; in Southeast Asian religious modernism, 181; and text collecting, 83; through textual study, 107; and *Vinaya*, 77–78, 89–92
purification movement: of King Ang Duong, 4, 13, 15, 47, 50–51, 76; Theravādin, 47, 77–78, 83

Qaṃbībrahbuddhsāsana (Finot), 129
qanak jā (free people), 66
qanak khñuṃ (debt slaves), 66–67
qanak mān puṇy (those possessing merit), 13, 55, 59–63. *See also* millenarian movements
qanak ṅār (nonindentured hereditary slaves), 66–67
qanak tā (spirits), 112
qanak tām sāsana (followers of the doctrine), 162

Qur'an, 2

Rāmakerti, 81
Rāmayāna. See *Rāmakerti*
Rathasena-jātaka, 173
rationalism: as central value of modernism, 1–3, 148; in colonial European scholarship, 124, 130; in Islamic modernism, 7; in Mongkut's thought, 84
rebellion, 55; against French, 113–114; against Norodom, 59; against Siamese, 62; of Sivotha, 65–67, 70; against Vietnamese, 56–57. *See also* anti-French resistance; millenarian movements
recitation (*sūtr*), 88
reform: administrative, 46, 64–65, 98; Buddhist, 4, 7, 15, 76, 78; educational, 120–124; influenced by Mongkut, 84–85, 89–92; Islamic, 2, 4, 7; in Siam, 78, 84–85, 120, 123, 126; sociopolitical, 46, 54, 64–68. *See also* Chulalongkorn; Dhammayut; education, Buddhist; Islamic modernism; modern Dhamma; orthographic reform; purification movement
relics, 83, 87
religion: colonial European scholarly understandings of, 120, 124–125; as *sāsana*, 179
religious building, 51, 80–81, 99, 174
revolts. *See* millenarian movements; rebellion
Reynolds, Craig, 64, 85
Rhys Davids, T. W., 111, 125
robes, monastic (*ticīvaraṃ*), 91; controversies over, 97, 99–100, 106; style in Cambodia, 97–98
Royal Library, 5, 107, 109–110, 127, 129, 131, 142; changing reading habits at, 144–145; founding, 142–143; printing press, 129, 142–146, 153, 178
Russier, Henri, 124
Russo-Japanese War, 116
Ṛyaṅ Jinavaṃs, 33
Ṛyaṅ Paṭhamasambodhi (Ind), 19, 32–33, 35–43, 129
Ṛyaṅ Rājakul, 33

Sālā Pali, 5, 80, 93, 100, 109–110; colonial administrative control, 138–139; curriculum, 130–131, 134–138, 141–142, 154, 178; founding, 133–134; and publishing, 142–143. *See also* École Supérieure de Pali; École Supérieur de Pali d'Angkor Vatt
Salman, Michael, 73
sāmaṇer (*sāmaṇera*; novice), 88–89, 107
Sāmaṇera-vinaya, 135, 142–143, 145, 153–154; and printing controversy, 107
Sāmaññaphala-sutta, 165, 170
Samantapāsādikā, 152, 180
saṃṇāk (monastery; monastery school; lineage), 80
saṃrāy (vernacular translation), 81, 103, 150, 152–153, 155, 157–161
saṃvega, 170, 176–177
Sangha (monastic community): Pali knowledge as criteria for promotion, 133; networks, 84, 116; reorganization, 54, 86–88, 98, 132
saṅkhep (abridgement), 150, 152–153, 157
Sanskrit, 101, 127, 129–130, 134, 137–138, 141; and Khmer language, 140
sappurisa. *See* moral persons
sappurisa-dhammā, defined, 166
Sāratthasaṅgaha, 80, 89, 132
Sāsanahetukathā, 150–152
satisampajañña (mindfulness and discrimination), 163, 165–167, 182; necessary for purification, 175–177
sātrā lpaeṅ (verse novel), 86
science, 85, 110, 124; knowledge of, 120–122
scientific methodologies (in education), 123, 128–130, 134–138, 142
scripturalism, 2, 83–84, 102–103; in modernist practice, 102–103
secret societies, 113–114
Sigālovāda-sutta, 103, 107. See also *Siṅgālovāda-sutta*
sikkhāpada-sīla (precepts), 90, 93
Siṅgālovāda-sutta: Buddhaghosa commentary on, 158; contrast with older form of saṃrāy, 159–160; filial piety in, 157–159; individual in, 157; localization of Theravādin ideas, 161–162; moral purification, 160; and Pali

canon, 160; ritual purification, 157–158; textual authority in, 157, 159–161. See also *Sigālovāda-sutta*
Sisowath, King, 68, 105, 128, 135
Śiva, 95–96
Sivotha, Prince, 62, 65–67, 70
slavery, 45, 47–48, 53–54, 65–68; fable about, 73–75; metaphorical uses of by Ind, 73–75, 168, 177; as possible social origins of Diaṅ and Pān, 86. See also *qanak khñuṃ*; *qanak ṅār*
social attachment: in the *Gatilok*, 165–166, 170–172, 175–177; in *Siṅgālovāda-sutta*, 157, 161
social criticism, 45–46, 55, 57, 64, 68–76; of Ind, 70–76; and modernism, 77, 130; of Yukanthor, 69–70. *See also* millenarian movements
social Darwinism, 7, 124
social order, 47–51; in millenarian discourses, 55–57, 59–61, 63; in nineteenth-century Cambodia, 76; Yukanthor's views of, 69–70
sociopolitical organization (in nineteenth-century Cambodia), 51–54
Soḷas Daṃnāy, 60
Son Ngoc Thanh, 127
So-Suan, nun, 81
Spencer, Herbert, 125
spirits, 157. See also *qanak tā*
Sukh, Bhikkhu, 167–177
Sukh, Chauv Ghun Braḥ Ñāṇarakkhit, 86
Sumedhācāry, Braḥ, 91
Supreme Patriarch of Khmer Sangha, 86–88, 98, 102, 145; contest for in 1914, 135
surveillance: of Khmer monks, 97, 112–117; of Khmer provincial views on war, 113; of Yukanthor, 70, 115
Sutta-nipāta, 171–172, 175
Suttantapiṭaka, 134, 137, 178
Suvaṇṇabhūmi, 180

Tai, Hue-Tam Ho, 57–59, 113
Taksin, King, 85
Tambiah, Stanley, 64, 77, 83
tamrā (technical manuals), 83, 88, 150, 162. See also *kpuan*
taxation, 55, 65–68, 71, 75–76, 114
temporality: and *dukkha*, 57; and modernity, 11, 76, 182; in *Trai Bhūm*, 19–22; in the *Vessantar-jātak*, 30–31
tensions (between traditionalists and modernists), 13–14, 78, 82, 88, 97, 138, 181; about *jātaka* interpretation, 105–106; methods of translation and textual production, 103–105; Ordinance 71, 108–109; orthography, 140–142; Pali school curricula, 134, 136; printed texts, 106–107; robes, 99–100; about *Vinaya* sermons, 101–102
text collecting, 79; by Finot, 81–82; by Karpelès, 142–144; in reign of Ang Duong, 79; at turn of twentieth century, 80–83
textual production, 3, 14, 30–31, 78, 127; by modern Dhamma group, 102–103, 106–108, 131, 149–150, 153–161; at Royal Library, 143–145, 153
Thai Sangha Act of 1902, 119
Thamikarāt (righteous ruler), 60. See also *dhammik*
Thompson, Ashley, 63
Thomson, Charles, 65
Thoṅ, Braḥ Mahā Vimaladhamm, 4, 13, 80, 110, 126–128, 134–142, 154–155
Thongchai Winichakul, 11, 85
Tipiṭaka (*Braḥ Traipiṭak*), 2, 50, 79, 81–84, 86–88, 90, 92; colonial European scholarly views of, 125; first Thai printed version, 94; Khmer printed version, 113, 144–146; in Sālā Pali curriculum, 134, 142; Thai vernacular translation of, 94. *See also* Commission on the Production of the *Tipiṭaka*
traditionalist (as opposed to modernist): commonalities with modernists, 149; decline of influence, 107–108, 119, 131; Islamic, 7; Khmer Buddhist, 13–14, 100, 102–106, 145, 149; modernist critiques of, 156–157, 160
Trai Bhūm, 19; *cakkavattin* and kings in, 37, 61, 76, 129; compared to other ethical texts, 23–27; importance of, 23–24, 51; and *Kitchanukit*, 85, 129; modernist views of, 152; moral development in, 27; notions of individual,

community and cosmos in, 20–23; in textual collections, 80; translated by Diaṅ, 86
Tran Van Thanh, 59, 64
translation: of Arabic, 3, 7; critical edition, 143–145, 153–155, 157, 159; Finot's views of, 136; Khmer manuscript practices of, 78; for Khmer modernists, 3; misperceptions of, 12; modernist methods of, 101–104, 106–107, 152–161; new methods of, 92–93, 96, 106, 143–145, 150; in nineteenth-century manuscripts, 30–31; vernacular, 143, 149, 160. See also *saṃrāy*
Trāyapaṇām-saṅkhep, 155–156
Tully, John, 12, 112, 114, 118
Tyler, E. B., 125

Uk, Samtec Braḥ Dhammalikhit (Tae), 102, 104–107, 119, 135
Uṃ-Sūr, Braḥ Uttamamunī, 101–104, 107, 129, 145, 182; dictionary commission, 141; ethical writings, 154–156; *Milindapañhā*, 153; *Paññāsa-jātaka*, 154; *Trāyapaṇām-saṅkhep*, 155–156
Uposathakatha, 135

Vajirañāṇa Library of Bangkok, 82, 126–127, 142
Vajirañāṇa (varorasa), Prince-Patriarch of Siam, 2, 85, 89, 91, 94, 120, 132
Vajiravudh (Rama V), King, 126
van der Veer, Peter, 12
vatt (monastery), 49; Baṅbas', 80; Bodhi Priks, 101; Bodhivāl, 82, 86; Bodum Vaddey, 51, 87–89; Braḥ Kaev, 82; Braḥ Kaiv Luoṅ, 87; Braḥ Buddh Nibbāṇ, 80; Buṇṇasiriāmātyārām, 89; construction, 51; Jetabhan, 84, 93; Krabuṃbejr, 81; Paramanivās, 86–87; Pavaranives, 89, 92; Phumin, 173; Saket, 86; Sotakorok, 50; Svāy Babae, 88; Ṭaṃrī Sa, 82; Uṇṇālom, 13, 77, 94, 101, 104, 134, 154, 178–179
vernacular religious literature, 88
Vessantar, 28–34
Vessantara-jātaka (*Vessantar-jātak*), 27–34, 80, 83, 105; contrast with modernist ethics, 31, 177; importance of, 28–29; *pāramī* of generosity in, 29; as political history, 32–34; recitation of, 29
Vinaya (*Vinaya-piṭaka*), 50, 77–79, 81, 86, 152; ambassadors, 138, 154; clandestine study groups, 102; controversies about, 100–108; interpretations of monastic rules, 90–91, 97, 104; modernist interpretations, 99–109, 119, 130, 154–155, 178; and purification, 77–78, 83, 87, 89–92; at the Royal Library, 144; in Sālā Pali curricular reforms, 135–139, 141–142; scholarship of Thoṅ, 134–135; sermons of 1914, 101–102, 135, 178
vipassanā (insight, meditation). *See* meditation
Visuddhimagga, 89, 152
Vu Trong Phung, 5

warfare, 45–51, 61, 63
Wyatt, David, 173

Yukanthor, 15, 46, 68–70, 115

zeal, religious, 7, 96, 99, 105–106, 136